THE HIDDEN PLACES OF THE

LANCASHIRE AND CHESHIRE

INCLUDING THE ISLE OF MAN

By David Gerrard

Regional Hidden Places

Cornwall
Devon
Dorset, Hants & Isle of Wight
East Anglia
Lake District & Cumbria
Lancashire & Cheshire
Northumberland & Durham
Peak District and Derbyshire
Yorkshire

National Hidden Places

England
Ireland
Scotland
Wales

Country Living Rural Guides

East Anglia
Heart of England
Ireland
North East of England
North West of England
Scotland
South
South East
Wales
West Country

Other Guides

Off the Motorway
Garden Centres and Nurseries
of Britain

Published by: Travel Publishing Ltd, Airport Business Centre,
10 Thornbury Road, Estover, Plymouth, Devon PL6 7PP

ISBN13   9781904434832

© Travel Publishing Ltd

First published 1990, second edition 1993,
third edition 1995, fourth edition 1998,
fifth edition 2003, sixth edition 2009

Printing by: Latimer Trend, Plymouth

Maps by: ©MAPS IN MINUTES/Collins Bartholomew (2009)

Editor: David Gerrard

Cover Design: Lines and Words, Aldermaston

Cover Photograph: River Ribble at Sawley
© www.picturesofbritain.co.uk

Text Photographs: © www.picturesofbritain.co.uk
and © Bob Brooks, Weston super Mare
www.britainhistoricsites.co.uk

Foreword

This is the 6th edition of the *Hidden Places of Lancashire & Cheshire including the Isle of Man*. The guide has been fully updated and in this respect we would like to thank the Tourist Information Centres in Lancashire, Cheshire and the Isle of Man for helping us update the editorial content. The guide is packed with information on the many interesting places to visit in this north western region of England. In addition, you will find details of places of interest and advertisers of places to stay, eat and drink included under each village, town or city, which are cross referenced to more detailed information contained in a separate, easy-to-use section to the rear of the book. This section is also available as a free supplement from the local Tourist Information Offices.

Lancashire is a county, which has lakes, woods, rolling hills, a sandy coastline and many picturesque towns and villages. **Cheshire** is a county of scenic contrasts. To the east are high moorlands and crags, to the west are the soft red sandstone plains of the Mersey and Dee, whilst to the south may be found a rich, pastoral landscape. Visitors to both counties will certainly find evidence of the significant contributions they have made to England's industrial, political, social and cultural heritage. **The Isle of Man** is blessed with beautiful scenery, sandy beaches, a very interesting heritage and lively seaside resorts. Lancashire, Cheshire and the Isle of Man are definitely worth a visit!

The Hidden Places of Lancashire & Cheshire including the Isle of Man contains a wealth of interesting information on the history, the countryside, the towns and villages and the more established places of interest. But it also promotes the more secluded and little known visitor attractions and places to stay, eat and drink many of which are easy to miss unless you know exactly where you are going.

We include hotels, bed & breakfasts, restaurants, pubs, bars, teashops and cafes as well as historic houses, museums, gardens and many other attractions throughout the area, all of which are comprehensively indexed. Many places are accompanied by an attractive photograph and are easily located by using the map at the beginning of each chapter. We do not award merit marks or rankings but concentrate on describing the more interesting, unusual or unique features of each place with the aim of making the reader's stay in the local area an enjoyable and stimulating experience.

Whether you are travelling around the region on business or for pleasure we do hope that you enjoy reading and using this book. We are always interested in what readers think of places covered (or not covered) in our guides so please do not hesitate to use the reader reaction form provided to give us your considered comments. We also welcome any general comments which will help us improve the guides themselves. Finally if you are planning to visit any other corner of the British Isles we would like to refer you to the list of other *Hidden Places* titles to be found to the rear of the book and to the Travel Publishing website.

Travel Publishing

Did you know that you can also search our website for details of thousands of places to see, stay, eat or drink throughout Britain and Ireland? Our site has become increasingly popular and now receives over **500,000** visits annually. Try it!

website: **www.travelpublishing.co.uk**

Location Map

Chapter 1

Chapter 5

Chapter 3

Chapter 2

Chapter 4

Chapter 6

Chapter 7

Chapter 8

Chapter 9

Chapter 11

Chapter 10

Contents

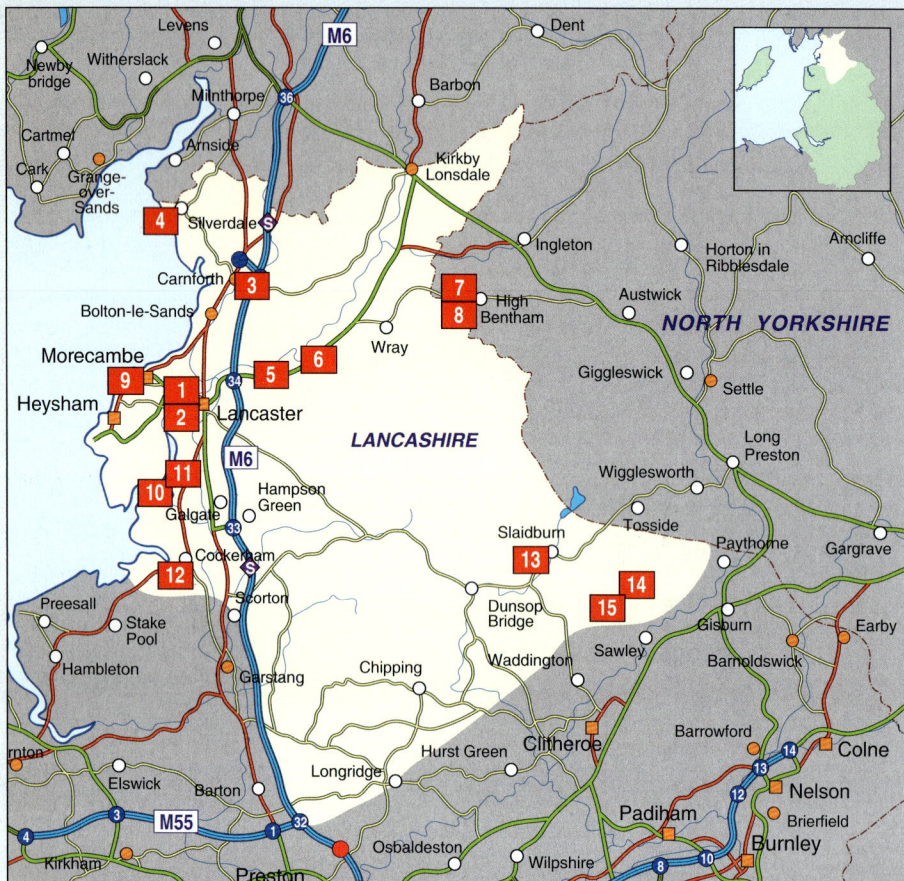

Map labels: Levens, Dent, Newby bridge, Witherslack, Milnthorpe, Barbon, M6, Cartmel, Arnside, Kirkby Lonsdale, Cark, Grange-over-Sands, Silverdale, Ingleton, Horton in Ribblesdale, Arncliffe, Carnforth, High Bentham, Austwick, Bolton-le-Sands, Wray, NORTH YORKSHIRE, Morecambe, Giggleswick, Settle, Heysham, Lancaster, LANCASHIRE, Long Preston, Hampson Green, Wigglesworth, Galgate, Slaidburn, Tosside, Paythorne, Gargrave, Cockerham, Dunsop Bridge, Gisburn, Earby, Scorton, Preesall, Stake Pool, Waddington, Sawley, Barnoldswick, Hambleton, Garstang, Chipping, Barrowford, Colne, Elswick, Hurst Green, Clitheroe, Nelson, Barton, Longridge, Padiham, Brierfield, Kirkham, Osbaldeston, Wilpshire, Burnley, Preston

2

North Lancashire and The Forest of Bowland

As the well-known comedian, Les Dawson, commented in his book on his native county, Lancashire is "many things to many people" with "vast smoky grey blocks of heavy industry" but also a countryside of "lakes and woods and rolling hills". It is also a place of great history: the Wars of the Roses; the old Catholic families and their support of Charles I during the Civil War; the trials of the Pendle Witches; and the innovators that started the Industrial Revolution in the textile industry.

The ancient county town of Lancaster, in the north, is an excellent place to start any journey of discovery. With a variety of museums and a wealth of interesting buildings, the life of Lancastrians through the ages is mapped out for any visitor to explore. Small and compact, it has the added advantage of having been off the general tourist routes which can make its larger, "White Rose" equivalent, somewhat hard going in the height of the season.

To the northeast lies Leck Fell, just south of Kirkby Lonsdale and Cumbria. It is easy for the visitor to mistake this for the Yorkshire Dales as there is a typical craggy limestone gorge along the little valley of Leck Beck, as well as one of the most extensive cave systems in the British Isles. A natural route from Kirkby Lonsdale back to the county town is marked by the River Lune. For those who like walking, the best way to enjoy this wonderful green and hilly area of Lancashire is to follow the Lune Valley Ramble which travels the valley's intimate pastoral setting, through woodland, meadows, and along the riverside itself.

To the west of Lancashire stretches Morecambe Bay, a treacherous expanse where, over the centuries, many walkers have lost their lives in an attempt to make the journey to the Furness Peninsula in Cumbria considerably shorter. Walks across the sands at low tide should only be undertaken with the aid of one of the highly knowledgeable and experienced guides.

Extending across much of the north of the county is the Forest of Bowland, an ancient royal hunting ground that is dotted with small, isolated villages. With no major roads passing through the area, it has remained little changed and, with so many splendid walks and fine countryside, it is also relatively quiet even during the busiest summer weeks.

3

LANCASTER

An architecturally pleasing city, Lancaster is one of the most appealing of English county capitals. Most of the county's administrative offices are now based in Preston so Lancaster enjoys all the prestige of being the capital without the burden of housing the accompanying bureaucrats. The city also takes pride in the fact that the Duke of Lancaster is the only duke in the kingdom who is a woman – no less a personage than HM the Queen

Priory Church, Lancaster

for whom the dukedom is one of many subsidiary titles.

Lancaster's story begins some 2000 years ago when the Romans built a fort on a hill overlooking a sweep of the River Lune, a site now occupied by the unspoiled 15th century **Priory Church of St Mary**. Right up until the Industrial Revolution, Lancashire was one of the poorest counties in England, lacking the wealth to endow glorious cathedrals or magnificent parish churches. St Mary's is a notable exception, the finest medieval church in the county. It stands on the site of Lancashire's first monastery which was closed not, like most others, by Henry VIII, but by Henry V in 1413. Henry was at war with France, the monastery's mother abbey was at Sées in Normandy, so the 'alien priory' in Lancaster had to be dissolved. The present church contains treasures rescued from the closed priory such as the sumptuously carved wooden choir stalls from around 1345.

Each stall is covered by a superb canopy, lavishly carved with around a hundred small heads and faces surrounded by abundant foliage. Also of note are the fragments of Anglo-Saxon crosses and some very fine needlework. The **Priory Tower**, also on the hilltop, was rebuilt in 1759 as a landmark for ships navigating their way into the River Lune. Nearby is one of Lancaster's links with its Roman past – the remains of a bath house which also served soldiers as an inn.

Close by is **Lancaster Castle**, one of the best-preserved Norman fortresses in the country. Dating back to 1200 and with a massive gatehouse flanked by sturdy twin towers, the castle dominates the centre of the city. For centuries, the castle served as a prison, only relinquishing that function as recently as 1996.

At the back of the castle, the **Shire Hall** is still in use as a Crown Court and one of its more macabre attractions is the Drop Room where prisoners were prepared for the gallows. The Court's long history has been blemished by two shocking major miscarriages of justice. The first was in 1612 when the Pendle "witches" (see Chapter 4) were convicted of sorcery and executed; the second in 1975 when the "Birmingham Six" were found guilty of an IRA bombing and spent 15 years in prison before their names were cleared.

A short walk from the castle leads into the largely pedestrianised city centre full of shops, the market, and much besides. The **City Museum** (free) in the Market Place occupies the Old Town Hall, built between 1781-3. As well as the city's art collection and an area of changing exhibitions, there are displays and collections of material illustrating aspects of the city's industrial and social history. Also here is the **Museum of the King's Own Royal Regiment**, a regiment which was based in Lancaster from 1880 onwards.

Lancaster grew up along the

Lancaster Castle, Lancaster

banks of the River Lune which is navigable as far as Skerton Bridge, to the north of the city, so there has always been a strong association between the town and its watery highway. Documents from 1297 make reference to the town's small-scale maritime trade, but it was not until the late 1600s and early 1700s that Lancaster's character as a port fully emerged. The splendid buildings of the 18th century Golden Age were born out of the port wealth, and the layout and appearance of the town was much altered by this building bonanza. Lancaster's importance as a port steadily declined throughout the 1800s so that many buildings

---

1 LANCASTER CASTLE

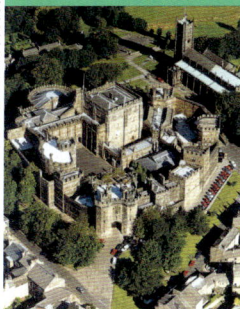

Lancaster

For most of its history the castle has been the centre of law and order for the county, and this magnificent building is still in use as a prison and a crown court.

see page 164

Fire destroyed most of Tudor and Jacobean Lancaster, but one notable survivor is the Judge's Lodging in Church Street, a charming Jacobean house built in the 1620s and now a museum: two museums in fact. There's the Museum of Childhood which includes the Barry Elder Doll collection, and the Gillow and Town House Museum containing many examples of the fine workmanship produced by the famous Lancaster cabinet-makers, Gillows. It was a scion of this family, Richard Gillow who designed the city's Maritime Museum.

2 LANCASTER MARITIME MUSEUM

Lancaster

The Lancaster Maritime Museum was opened in 1985 and occupies the former Custom House of 1764

see page 164

originally intended for maritime purposes were taken over for other uses.

Lancaster enjoyed its era of greatest prosperity during the 18th century when its quays were busy servicing a thriving trade with the West Indies in rum, sugar, cotton – and slaves. The city's rich maritime history is celebrated at St George's Quay which, with its great stone warehouses and superb Custom House, is now an award-winning **Maritime Museum**. Visitors today are given a vivid insight into the life of the mariners and quayside workers with opportunities for knot-tying and the practising of other maritime skills. Every year, over the four days of the Easter weekend, St George's Quay is home to the Lancaster Maritime Festival with a programme that involves boisterous "smugglers", sea songs, and shanties.

Close by is the **Cottage Museum** in a house, built in 1739, that was divided into two dwellings in the 19th century. It is now furnished in the style of an artisan's house of the early to mid-1800s Just around a corner or two, in Sun Street, is the **Music Room**, an exquisite early Georgian building originally designed as a pavilion in the long vanished garden of Oliver Marton. It is notable for some superb decorative plasterwork.

Lancaster's most prominent landmark, visible for miles around, is the extravagant, temple-like **Ashton Memorial** – "the grandest monument in England" according to Nikolaus Pevsner. Erected in

1907 as a memorial to his wife by the local MP and millionaire lino manufacturer Lord Ashton, it stands on the highest point in Lancaster, set within the beautifully landscaped Williamson Park and enjoying sweeping views of the Cumbrian hills and across Morecambe Bay. The building now houses exhibitions and multi-screen presentations about the life and times of Lord Ashton and the Edwardian period.

It was Lord Ashton's father, James Williamson, who created **Williamson Park.** It was his own personal project as a means of providing work for local people during the cotton famine crisis in the textile industry during the American Civil War in the 1860s. Constructed on the site of old quarries, which gives the park its undulating contours, the park was opened in 1896. As well as the magnificent Ashton Memorial there is also a delightful butterfly house in the now restored Edwardian palm house, conservation garden, wildlife pool, a bird enclosure and a small mammal section.

Another place the whole family can enjoy is **Lancaster Leisure Park** on Wyresdale Road. Set in 42 acres of landscaped parkland, the site includes a mini-marina, a Wild West adventure playground, a miniature railway, a rare breeds unit, a children's farmyard, pony rides, a gift shop, a tea garden, and a pottery shop. Also on site are more than 140 antiques shops, the largest antiques centre in North Lancashire.

NORTH OF LANCASTER

HALTON

3 miles NE of Lancaster off the A683

The high mound, **Castle Hill**, which rises above this ancient village on the River Lune was firstly the site of a Roman camp and later a Saxon castle. The village's parish **Church of St Wilfrid** was founded in the 7th century and although nothing survives of that original foundation there are some stone crosses, both inside the building and out, that date from the 9th century. One of them, unusually, bears both pagan and Christian symbols. Roman remains, in the form of a votive altar (where offerings were made before a military operation began), were found on the site in the late 1700s. Around the same time, a labourer tilling his allotment on Halton Moor unearthed more than 1000 coins from the reign of King Cnut (1017-35) together with a gold necklace. This treasure trove is now in the British Museum.

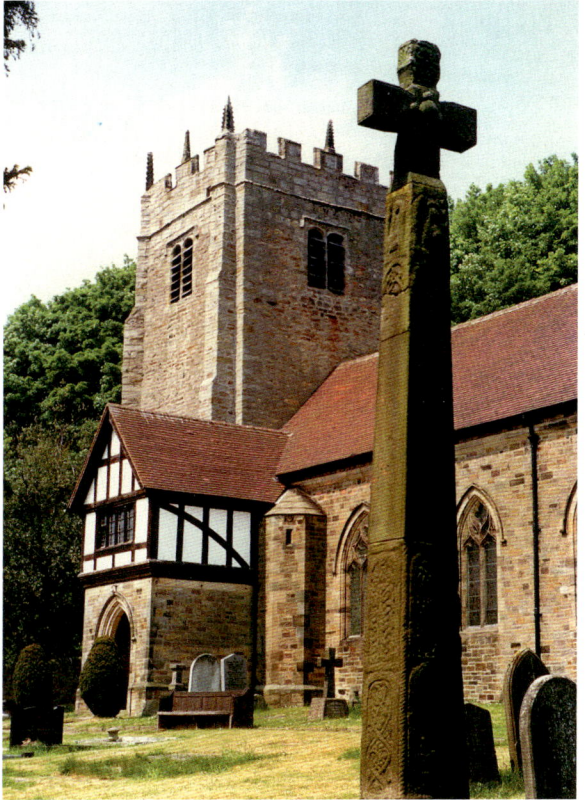

Church of St Winfred, Halton

NETHER KELLET

4 miles N of Lancaster off the B6254

This farming village has a traditional village green which as well as being the central focus of the community also features several old wells and pumps. This is appropriate since the Old Norse word *chellet*, now Kellet, means "a spring". Local brewers of home ale still use the spring water because of its purity and absence of chemicals. Quarrying has taken place here for many centuries and lime burning has been an important local industry. Its remains, in the form of lime kilns, can still be seen around the village and the local pub is named the Lime Burners Arms.

The village also has its own cave, Dunold Mill, through which flows a large stream that dives underground to appear 2 miles further north at Carnforth. During the mid-1800s the cave was occupied by a hermit who lived

3   THE CANAL TURN

Carnforth
The Canal Turn has a perfect setting that compliments the excellent food and great choice of Ales available here.

    see page 164

•

The views from Leighton Hall's extensive grounds, just south of Yealand, are magnificent and take in the nearby Leighton Moss Bird Reserve. N.B. Leighton Hall is currently closed to the public until May 2009, but is open all year round for pre-booked groups of 25 or more.

•

there until his death at the age of 100. His descendants still live in the village.

CARNFORTH

5 miles N of Lancaster on the A6

The town lies around what was once a major crossroads on the A6 but it is, perhaps, its fame as a busy railway junction town whose station was used as the setting for the 1940s film classic *Brief Encounter* - by which most people know Carnforth. Though the station has declined in importance – it is no longer on the main West Coast line – the old engine sheds and sidings are occupied by Steamtown, one of the largest steam railway repair centres in the north of England.

In the film, comic relief was provided by scenes in the Refreshment Room between the affable station attendant (Stanley Holloway) and the starchy refreshment room manageress (Joyce Carey). These scenes were actually shot in Denham Studios but the set was closely modelled on the real Refreshment Room at Carnforth. Sadly, when the station was by-passed by the new West Coast line in the 1970s, the refreshment room became uneconomic. It was closed and allowed to become derelict.

Then, in the 1990s, the **Carnforth Station** and Railway Trust Company was formed to restore the station and its Refreshment Room and also to establish a Visitor Centre with exhibits on the history of both the railway and Carnforth itself. It is now possible to enjoy tea and scones in the setting familiar from the film.

YEALAND

8 miles N of Lancaster off the A6

To the south of the village stands **Leighton Hall** – a splendid early 19th century house which passed through many hands before becoming the property of the famous furniture making family, the Gillows. It is now owned by the Reynolds family, a branch of the Gillows. They take pride in the fact that there are no roped-off areas at Leighton Hall - visitors are invited to sit on the ancient chairs while entertaining and enthusiastic guides reveal the family's history and habits. They are welcome to take their places around the 18th century dining table or even to play a tune on the Concert Steinway piano!

The hall dates from 1800 when it was built out of pale, local sandstone to the Gothic designs of Harrison, a Chester architect. The Leighton Hall estate extends over some 1550 acres and in addition to the landscaped parkland and woodland walks, there's also a very pretty 19th century walled garden. This is the passion of Mrs Suzie Gillow Reynolds who has created a lovely garden which has flowers in abundance, rose covered walls, a fragrant herb patch and an overflowing herbaceous border. It has almost a wild, cottage garden style.

SILVERDALE

8 miles N of Lancaster off the A6

The village lies at the northwesternmost corner of the county and has the Lakeland hills as a backdrop as well as enjoying superb views over Morecambe Bay. The latter half of the 19th century saw Silverdale develop as a quiet seaside resort where those so inclined could take medicinal baths of fresh sea water and stay in one of the many small villas situated along the coast. One frequent visitor was Elizabeth Gaskell who is said to have written some of her books whilst holidaying here.

However, Silverdale's history goes back well beyond the days of a genteel Victorian resort. Its name comes from a Viking family that settled here and which signifies that this was Sigward's or Soevers' valley. Fishing, naturally, was the key provider of local income but in the 18th century a copper smelting works was built here. All, however, that remains of the foundry is the chimney near **Jenny Brown's Point**, said to be named after an old woman who lived here in the 1700s.

Essentially a small residential village, Silverdale is well worth visiting for the network of footpaths from here that pass through the limestone woodlands that are such a joy for the botanist, being rich in wild flowers in spring – primroses, violets, orchids, bird's eye primroses, rockroses, and eglantines abound.

Leighton Moss near Silverdale is a nationally known RSPB bird sanctuary. The reed beds are the most important part of the reserve because they have become a northern stronghold of the rare bearded tit and are also the major British breeding centre for the bittern.

THE LUNE VALLEY

CATON

3 miles NE of Lancaster on the A683

Caton climbs up the hillside from the leafy glades of the Crook o' Lune, subject of one of Turner's paintings, to heather moorlands commanding a panoramic view of Morecambe Bay. A popular commuter town nowadays, in the 1800s Caton was a busy place with no fewer than eight cotton and wood-turning bobbin mills. Just to the south of the village, tucked away among the hills on the northern edges of the Forest of Bowland, is **Littledale**, one of Lancashire's most hidden gems. A walk through the wooded dale alongside Artle Beck to Littledale Hall is well worthwhile and provides a view of Lancashire that is not normally seen.

Widely regarded as one of the most exciting gardens in England, **Gresgarth Hall Garden** is the creation of world-renowned landscape designer and plantswoman, Arabella Lennox-Boyd. Reached through a mature park, the cultivated area of about 12 acres includes lavishly planted terraces leading down to a lake, wild and bog gardens, large herbaceous borders, an extensive

4 THE SILVERDALE HOTEL

Silverdale

A family run hotel with striking gardens, comfortable accommodation and good homecooked food in a pleasant village location.

see page 165

5 RIVER LUNE MILLENIUM PARK

Lancaster

The River Lune Millenium Park stretches some 15 kilometres along the banks of the Lune from Bull Beck near Caton to Salt Ayre in Lancaster.

see page 166

9

HIDDEN PLACES OF LANCASHIRE AND CHESHIRE

6 THE BLACK BULL INN

Brookhouse

A traditional family run village inn, at the heart of the community where customers always come first and can enjoy the finest cuisine

see page 167

walled kitchen garden, the magnolia and rhododendron hillside and a serpentine beech walk. Over a striking Chinese style bridge, crossing the Artle Beck, lies a bluebell wood, the millennium wood and a fine arboretum.

CLAUGHTON

6 miles NE of Lancaster on the A683

The **Old Toll House Garage** on the road into this village (which is pronounced Clafton), is famous for a rather curious reason. In the 1920s the garage owner painted the first white lines on the road at the nearby corner because of the many accidents that had occurred there. After much debate their value was recognised by the government of the day and from then onwards the use of white lines became accepted as a means of road marking, eventually spreading world-wide.

HORNBY

9 miles NE of Lancaster on the A683

Immortalised in paint by J.M.W. Turner, the ruins of **Hornby Castle** (private) were incorporated into a picturesque mock medieval hall in the 19th century. Perched atop a hill, the castle dominates the attractive village of Hornby. Sadly, it isn't open to the public but it's visible for miles around and there's a particularly photogenic view of it from the bridge over the River Wemming at the southern edge of the village.

The situation of this pleasing village, by a bluff overlooking the valley of the River Lune, not only gives Hornby panoramic views of the surrounding countryside but also makes this a strategic position that has been utilised over the centuries. Just to the north of the village is the attractive stone-built **Loyn Bridge**, which takes the road over the River Lune and on to Gressington. Constructed in 1684, it replaced a ford. Beside the bridge is **Castle Stede**, the best example of a Norman motte and bailey castle in Lancashire.

The graceful **Church of St Margaret of Antioch** dates from around 1300 when it was built as a chapel of ease to the parish church at Melling. Its unusual and impressive octagonal tower was ordered by Sir Edward Stanley, Lord Mounteagle, who made a vow before the Battle of Flodden Field in 1513 that if he returned victorious he would

Hornby Castle & River Wenning, Hornby

10

Saxon Crosses, Hornby

7 THE NOSE BAG

Higher Bentham

Old fashioned home cooking at its finest.

see page 166

8 BLACK BULL HOTEL

High Bentham

A tremendous value for money hotel with tastefully decorated rooms and fabulous food; one for all the family.

see page 168

construct the tower in honour of his patron saint, St Margaret.

TUNSTALL
11 miles NE of Lancaster on the A683

The village is famous for its fine 15th century **Church of St John the Baptist**. The Brontë sisters knew it well and it is referred to in *Jane Eyre* as "Brocklebridge church". When the sisters were attending the Clergy Daughters' School at Cowan Bridge they walked the 6 mile round trip to the church each morning. After attending service, they had their mid-day meal in the room above the church porch.

WHITTINGTON
12 miles NE of Lancaster on the B6254

This delightful village in the green and sheltered valley of the River Lune is well worth a visit. It was Wordsworth, in his *Guide to the Lakes*, who recommended that Kendal be approached via the Vale of Lune and it remains a popular place today.

COWAN BRIDGE
13 miles NE of Lancaster on the A65

In 1823, the Rev. William Carus Wilson, vicar of neighbouring Tunstall, opened his Clergy Daughters' School at Cowan Bridge. Amongst his early pupils were four daughters of the Rev Patrick Brontë of Howarth – Maria, Elizabeth, Charlotte and Emily. Charlotte immortalised the school and its austere regime in *Jane Eyre* where it appears as "Lowood". It can still be seen, though it is now part of a row of terraced cottages just north of the bridge on the A65. The school moved to Casterton in 1833.

LECK
13 miles NE of Lancaster off the A65

Over the A65 from Cowan Bridge lies the small village of Leck. To the northeast of this village rises **Green Hill**, surrounded by moorland and the highest point, at 2060 feet, in the county. At just over three feet higher than the top

Morecambe Bay, Morecambe

Morecambe Bay, a vast wide, flat tidal plain situated between Lancashire and Cumbria, is the home of many forms of marine life as well as being a very popular and important habitat for birds. The Rivers Lune, Kent, Keer, Leven, and Crayke create the gulleys, mud and sandbanks that make this not only one of the most important ornithological sites in Europe but also a great source of mussels and shrimps.

of the neighbouring fell, Gragarth, it was only a recent, more accurate survey, that distinguished Green Hill as the higher. This is the most northerly part of Lancashire and from the summit there are superb views of both Cumbria and North Yorkshire, as well, of course, as Lancashire.

WEST OF LANCASTER

MORECAMBE

3 miles NW of Lancaster on the A589

Featuring prominently on the Lancashire coastline, Morecambe has long been one of the most successful and popular seaside resorts in the North, and it can truly be said to enjoy one of the finest views from its promenade of any resort in England – a magnificent sweep of coastline and bay, looking across to the Lakeland mountains.

The largest estuary in Britain, Morecambe Bay is noted not only for its vast expanse of sands and mudflats but also for their treacherous nature. Over the years, many have lost their lives in the Bay's ever-shifting quicksands while attempting to make the apparently straightforward crossing from Morecambe to Grange-over-Sands on the Cumbrian coast. In medieval times, this perilous track formed part of the main west coast route from Scotland to England and at one time the monks of the Furness peninsula acted as guides to those wishing to make their way to Cumbria without taking the long overland route. Today, you can join one of the **Cross Bay Walks** led by the Queen's Guide to the Sands, Cedric Robinson who has been guiding walkers across the Bay since 1963. Cedric is the 25th appointed guide to the sands since the original appointment in 1536.

Modern Morecambe is a relatively recent town that grew up as a direct result of the expansion of the railways to the north Lancashire coast. There were originally three villages, Bare, Poulton, and Torrisholme that were quiet fishing communities. In 1848 all this changed as the railways brought visitors from the textile towns of Lancashire and, especially, Yorkshire to what was jokingly called "Bradford-by-the-Sea". Hotels and boarding houses were built as well as the usual seaside amenities such as parks and promenades and soon the villages were absorbed into one thriving resort.

A lively resort, well-provided with every kind of traditional and modern holiday amusement, Morecambe has always vied with its much larger competitor to the south, Blackpool, in offering varied entertainment for its visitors. During the late 1800s, the town spent lavishly, building two grand piers, an elegant **Winter Garden**, sumptuous theatres and hotels, but the town's attempt to build a tower to rival Blackpool's was not a success. However, Morecambe did manage to introduce its Autumn Illuminations several years before Blackpool caught on to the idea.

Of the many buildings dating from Morecambe's heyday as a holiday destination, one in particular, the recently restored and modernised **Midland Hotel** stands out. Situated on the seafront, at the southern end of the promenade, the hotel, which was built in the early 1930s to designs by Oliver Hill, is concave towards the sea and convex facing inland. The elegant, sweeping balconies of the luxurious rooms remain a superb feature of the hotel. Whilst filming *Brief Encounter* at nearby Carnforth both Celia Johnson and Trevor Howard made their home here along with others working on the film. The Winter Gardens in Morecambe currently arranges tours of the building

Like other resorts, Morecambe has changed with the times and major new attractions include the multi-million pound Bubbles Leisure Park and Superdome, as well as a Wild West Theme Park. **WOMAD**, Morecambe's annual world music festival, attracts

visitors from around the globe. There are also popular seafront illuminations in late summer, together with all the usual lively shops and variety of entertainment associated with a busy seaside resort.

But perhaps the town's most popular attraction is the **Eric Morecambe Statue** near the Stone Jetty. Few can resist the opportunity of posing in suitably one-legged fashion beside sculptor Graham Ibbeson's life-size statue. Lyrics from Eric's best-known song, *Bring Me Sunshine,* are carved into the granite steps leading up to the statue which is surrounded by flower beds and flashing lights that bring this "stage" to life after dark.

HEYSHAM

5 miles W of Lancaster on the A683

Southwards along the coast, Morecambe merges imperceptibly into Heysham, an ancient settlement with a quaint old main street that winds down to the shore. The town is notable for the tiny **St Patrick's Chapel**

9 REGENT COFFEE LOUNGE AND RESTAURANT

Morecambe

A first class coffee house, family run, serving a wide range of hearty meals with a selection of desserts and cakes to die for!

🍴 *see page 169*

St Patrick's Chapel, Heysham

Old Stone- cut Graves, Heysham

been crudely carved by 9th century masons and there is also a rare Viking hog-back gravestone. It is one of the oldest churches in western Europe to have been in continuous use.

Alongside these antiquities is the modern port of Heysham with regular car ferry sailings to the Isle of Man and to Northern Ireland and, of course, the two modern nuclear power stations, Heysham A and Heysham B.

SUNDERLAND

6 miles SW of Lancaster off the A683

which is reckoned to be the oldest religious building in Lancashire. According to tradition, St Patrick himself built the now ruined chapel as a thanks-offering to God after surviving a shipwreck on the rocks below. Historians aren't too sure about the veracity of that legend, but there's no doubting the interest of the chapel graveyard. Hewn out of the rock are six body-shaped coffins with an incised space above them in the shape of a cross. These 8th or 9th century coffins were originally covered by a similarly shaped slab of stone and would have been created as the final resting place for Saxon notables.

The little **Church of St Peter** on the headland below the chapel is equally interesting. It dates back to Saxon and Norman times, with an Anglo-Saxon cross on which the Madonna and other figures have

This is, unbelievably, an old port and seaside resort which flourished until larger-berthed ships, silting channels, and the growth in the mid-1800s of rail-served Morecambe caused it to decline. A little wharf, quiet cottages, some with faded and evocative elegance, and a sandy shore where sea thrift flourishes among the pebbles, are all that remains. The River Lune estuary is now a Site of Special Scientific Interest because of its wildlife value – visitors are likely to see such birds as redshank feeding on the rich supplies of worms, shellfish, and shrimps on the salt marshes, while a variety of wildfowl such as shelduck, widgeon, and mallard, are to be seen in autumn.

A particularly sad story acts as a reminder of Sunderland's time as a port. Sambo was a sea captain's servant at the time of the slave trade into Lancaster. Sambo fell ill of a fever just before the captain was setting off to the West Indies and was left in the care of an innkeeper. Sambo, believing himself abandoned, willed himself to die. Because he was not a baptised Christian, Sambo was not allowed to be buried in consecrated ground. In later years, his death and grave, marked by a simple cross and stone, became a potent local symbol for the anti-slavery cause.

His grave can be still seen, in a field at the west side of Sunderland Point. It can be reached by walking along The Lane from the village foreshore, past Upsteps Cottage, where Sambo died, and turning left at the shore then over a stile on the left which gives access to the simple gravestone. Fresh flowers are usually to be seen here, anonymously placed on the grave.

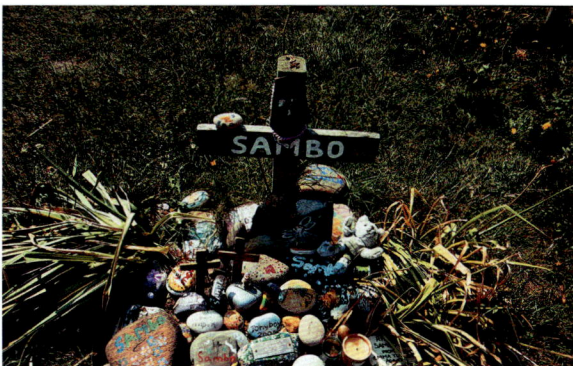

Sambo's Grave, Sunderland

SOUTH OF LANCASTER

GLASSON

4 miles SW of Lancaster on the B5290

A few miles south of Heysham, the river Lune pours into Morecambe Bay. On its south bank is **Glasson Dock**, once an important commercial port for larger boats unable to negotiate the tricky river as far upstream as Lancaster. The dock was built in 1791 and the tiny lighthouse erected at the same time is still in place. The dock could accommodate 25 sea-going ships and traded extensively in slaves, rum, tobacco, sugar, and cotton. Glasson Dock today is a busy, colourful marina, serving both sea-going craft and boats arriving at the western terminus of the

Lancaster Canal. Constructed in 1797, the **Lancaster Canal** is one of the earliest engineering marvels of the Industrial Age. *"The Lanky"*, as it's known, is a favourite with canal travellers since there's not a single lock in the whole of its 41-mile length, thanks to the ingenuity of the canal's designer, John Rennie. He accomplished his engineering tour de force by linking the level stretches with six elegant aqueducts, the most impressive of them being the 5-arched **Lune Aqueduct** near Lancaster which has attracted a stream of admiring visitors ever since it was first opened in 1797.

The canal was supplemented by the arrival of a railway line in 1883. This railway, long dismantled, is now the footpath and cycle-way to Lancaster's St George's Quay.

From Glasson there is a footpath along the coast to Plover Scar, where a lighthouse guards the River Lune estuary, and further along stand the ruins of **Cockersand Abbey**. The abbey was founded in 1190 by the

10 THE LANTERN O'ER LUNE CAFE

Glasson Docks

A welcoming cafe in an enviable location serving a wide range of tasty snacks and wholesome meals at very reasonable prices.

see page 170

15

Glasson Dock, Glasson

THE STORK INN

Conder Green

A traditional English Country Inn with a unique South African influence, offering superb food and drink combined with exceptional customer service.

🍴 🛏 *see page 171*

Premonstratensian Order on the site of a hospital that had been the home of a hermit, Hugh Garth, before becoming a colony for lepers and the infirm. The 13th century Chapter House of the abbey remains since it became a burial chapel for the Dalton family of nearby Thurnham, descendants of Sir Thomas More.

THURNHAM

5 miles S of Lancaster on the A588

Just outside the village and at the end of a sweeping drive stands Thurnham Hall (private) which has been built, over the years, around a 14th century pele tower. For 400 years the Hall was the home of the Dalton family who were responsible for the Elizabethan extensions and the fine Jacobean staircase. Although

the hall has been divided into flats, much of its original character has been retained.

GALGATE

4 miles S of Lancaster on the A6

The village of Galgate was originally located on the banks of the River Conder, which, for about half a mile, forms part of the Lancaster Canal. The village still contains some of its original mills, though they have now been put to other uses. One of them, a silk mill, was reputed to be the oldest working mill in the country, dating back to 1760, closed down in the 1960s. Galgate has a craft centre, a marina for around 100 boats and there's a well maintained pathway that leads from the village through locks to Glasson Dock.

DOLPHINHOLME

6 miles S of Lancaster off the A6

This small village of around 600 souls sits in the foothills of the Pennines at the edge of the Forest of Bowland. Dolphinholme was one of the first villages with a main street lit by gas. This was around 1806 and remains of the old gas holder can still be seen. A single street lamp has survived and is now fuelled by bottle gas.

COCKERHAM

6 miles S of Lancaster on the A588

This sleepy little village lies on the shore of Morecambe Bay

16

between the estuaries of the Lune and the Wyre. Cockerham once boasted a windmill but it was in such an exposed position that a gale in 1802 sent the sails spinning and the friction set fire to the mill. Cockerham Hall, (private) is a fine and rare example of a medieval timber-framed building that dates from the late 1400s. It is now a farmhouse.

EAST OF LANCASTER

QUERNMORE

3 miles E of Lancaster off the A683

Lying at the head of the Conder Valley, this peaceful farming village had a pottery industry as well as slate quarrying in the 1600s. The word "quern" refers to a particularly ancient form of hand-mill that was hewn from the rocks found on the nearby moorside. Corn milling continued here until World War II.

LEE

7 miles SE of Lancaster off the A6

To the northwest of this typical Bowland village soars the highest summit in the forest, **Ward's Stone**. Dotted with outcrops of gritstone boulders, the top of the fell is marked by two triangulation pillars. The panoramic views from this point are magnificent - to the north and east, the Three Peaks of Yorkshire can be seen, whilst the Lakeland fells roll away to the northwest.

FOREST OF BOWLAND

8 miles SE of Lancaster

Designated an Area of Outstanding Natural Beauty in 1964, this extensive scenic area is a veritable paradise for walkers and country lovers, and is dotted with picturesque villages. The Forest of Bowland is rather misleading since the term 'forest' is derived from the Latin 'foris' denoting a royal hunting ground, an unenclosed tract of land, rather than a distinct wooded area. In fact, even this description is not entirely correct. Throughout the 11th century the area was a "chase" – a private rather than a royal hunting ground. Before 1066, the broad acres of Bowland were the personal property of Earl Tostig of Northumbria, a brother of King Harold. Banished from his earldom, Tostig, with the help of the King of Norway, attempted to regain his lands and both he and the Norwegian king were killed at Stamford Bridge, just weeks before the fateful Battle of Hastings.

Following the Norman Conquest, Bowland became part of the Honour of Clitheroe and the vast estates that belonged to the de Lacy family. In time, by marriage, they came into the hands of the Earls of Lancaster and in 1399, when the then Duke of Lancaster ascended the throne as Henry IV, Bowland finally became one of nearly a hundred royal hunting forests.

The remains of a Roman road can be clearly seen traversing the

To the east of the village of Quernmore rises Clougha Pike, on the western edges of the Forest of Bowland, an Area of Outstanding Natural Beauty and one of the few places in the area that is accessible to walkers. Although it is not the highest peak in the forest – it rises to just over 1300 feet – the walk up Clougha Pike is very pleasant and offers splendid views from the summit, not only of the Lakeland Fells but also of Morecambe Bay and, on a clear day, Blackpool Tower.

13 HARK TO BOUNTY

Slaidburn

A traditional old English country inn serving a wide variety of excellent food and choice of real ales.

see page 172

land and many of the village's names in this area date back to the Saxon period. Perhaps the most celebrated of the many routes across Bowland is the minor road from Lancaster to Clitheroe which crosses **Abbeydale Moor** and the **Trough of Bowland** before descending into the lovely Hodder Valley around Dunsop Bridge. This is a popular route in the summer months, with most lay-bys and parking places filled as people pause to take in the breathtaking moorland views.

SLAIDBURN

15 miles SE of Lancaster on the B6478

This pretty village of stone cottages and cobbled pavements lies in the heart of the Forest of Bowland. The village's focal point is the 13th century public house **Hark to Bounty**. The inn was originally named The Dog but one day in 1875 the local Hunt gathered here. A visiting Squire, listening to the hounds giving voice outside, clearly distinguished the tones of his own favourite hound rising above the others. His exclamation of delight, "Hark to Bounty!" was so whole-hearted that the landlord changed the name of his pub on the spot.

The inn also contains an old courtroom with its original oak furnishings. Here from around 1250 the Chief Court of Bowland, or Halmote, was held. The only courtroom between York and Lancaster, it was used by visiting justices from the 1300s onwards, is said to have also been used by

Oliver Cromwell when he was in the area, and continued in use right up until 1937.

From the village, a network of beautiful, little used lanes radiate westwards up into the fell country with some of the best walking that Lancashire has to offer. One walk in particular that provides solitude as well as excellent views of the Bowland landscape leads to the lonely valley of the River Whitendale, northwest of the village.

To the northeast of Slaidburn lies Stocks Reservoir, another popular walker's destination. Beneath its waters lie the remains of 20-odd dwellings that made up the hamlet of Stocks-in-Bolland. They were submerged in 1925 but in very dry summers the remains of the old Chapel bridge can be seen where it crosses the original Hodder river, along with the foundations of houses.

DUNSOP BRIDGE

14 miles SE of Lancaster off the B6478

Often known as the *'Gateway to the Trough of Bowland'* and located in a designated Area of Natural Beauty, Dunsop Bridge is, despite its remote location, the centre of the British Isles. The actual centre point, worked out by the Ordnance Survey, lies near Whitendale Hanging Stones and, to authenticate the claim, the explorer Sir Ranolph Fiennes unveiled a commemorative plaque here. British Telecommunications have also offered the village a unique honour by putting their 100,000th phone box here.

St Hubert's Roman Catholic Church on Lancaster Road has an unusual provenance. It was built by the Towneley family when their racehorse Kettledrum won the 1861 Derby. The family spent a further £1000 on the huge white angel that stands in the graveyard and commemorates Richard Henry Towneley.

WHITEWELL

15 miles SE of Lancaster off the B6478

Little more than a hamlet in the heart of the Forest of Bowland, Whitewell consists of a small church, built in the early 19th century on the site of a medieval chapel, and an inn, built on the site of the old manor house.

Just outside the village, the view looking towards Kitcham Hill provides one of the most scenic panoramic vistas of the Ribble Valley.

NEWTON

15 miles SE of Lancaster on the B6478

Little more than a hamlet, Newton lies on the main route between Clitheroe and Lancaster. In their time, both John Paslew, the last abbot of Whalley, and the Pendle witches passed through on their way to trial in Lancaster. Here also is a **Quaker Meeting House** that was founded in 1767: the associated Quaker school, where the 19th century reformer John Bright was a pupil, has long since gone. Regarded with great suspicion by the Church of England, and by other nonconformists, because of their unorthodox views and their informality, the Quakers sought to settle in out of the way villages. Newton is typical of the places where they built their meeting houses and successfully lived according to their beliefs.

BOLTON-BY-BOWLAND

21 miles SE of Lancaster off the A59

Lying alongside a "bow", or bend, in the River Ribble this tranquil village with its two ancient greens, 13th century stone cross and old stocks, lies on the southern edge of the forest area. Part of the Bolton Hall estate, the village has been protected from insensitive development – the most recent dwelling to be built is already more than a hundred years old.

The 15th century village Church of St Peter & St Paul is home to the famous **Pudsey Tomb** with its engraved figure of Sir Ralph Pudsey in full armour alongside figures of his three wives and their 25 children. In the folds of each lady's gown is inscribed a Roman numeral indicating how many children she bore – respectively six, two and 17.

14 SPRINGHEAD FARM HOLIDAY COTTAGES

Bolton by Bowland

Exceptionally well equipped cottages set amidst beautiful scenery and within easy reach of many places of interest.

see page 174

15 THE COPY NOOK HOTEL

Clitheroe

A charming hostelry offering all the traditional aspects of an English inn, where great beer, good food and enjoyable company will be encountered.

see page 173

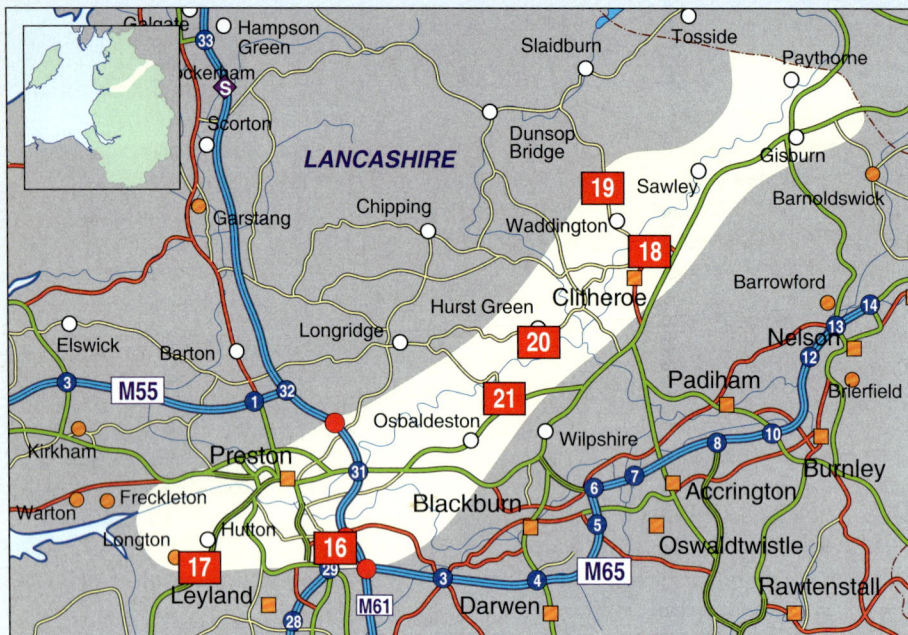

The Ribble Valley

A dramatic contrast of stark fellsides flecked with woolly sheep, and valleys green with woodland and lush pastures grazed by obviously contented sheep. It's not the conventional image of Lancashire as half-Blackpool, half wall-to-wall grimy chimneys. That's because the Ribble Valley is the county's best-kept secret – 150 square miles of peaceful countryside, almost two-thirds of it designated as Areas of Outstanding Natural Beauty.

The best overview of this beautiful area can be enjoyed by walking or driving along **Longridge Fell**. Within the space of a few miles, huge vistas unfold, not just of the Ribble Valley from Pendle Hill to Preston but also of the Fylde Plain, the Loud and Hodder valleys, and the Forest of Bowland. This is captivating countryside so it's no wonder that, according to one of her biographers, the Queen herself has divulged that she would like to retire to this region of rural Lancashire.

Flowing between the Forest of Bowland in the north and the hill country of Pendle in the south, the River Ribble cuts a pleasant and green course along a narrow valley. The **Ribble Way** middle-distance footpath follows the full 70 miles of the river, from its source at Ribblehead in North Yorkshire to the flat, tidal marshes of its estuary west of Preston.

A beautiful, unspoilt yet small area, the Ribble Valley has long been a favourite with the people of Lancashire. Not only is it easily accessible but there are numerous gentle walks in the sheltered valley and a wealth of wildlife is supported by the lush countryside. It is also a place of pretty villages which, even in the 21st century, remain almost unscathed.

The central point of the valley is Clitheroe, a typical ancient Lancashire market town that clusters around one of the smallest Norman castles in the country. The Normans were not the only invaders to build a fortification in the valley: further down stream lies Ribchester and the Roman fort of Bremetannacum. Up-river from Clitheroe lies Sawley and another interesting ruin. The Cistercian monks of Fountains Abbey founded the religious house here in the 13th century and their influence in the area of agriculture can still be seen in the surrounding fields.

The valley is also home to two great houses. The first, Stonyhurst, was originally the home of the Shireburn family and is now the world famous Roman Catholic public school. The second, on the outskirts of Preston, is Salmesbury Hall, a wonderful 14th century house that is now a Mecca for antiques collectors.

Finally, at the mouth of the river is Preston, the county's administrative centre and a town with more to offer than first appearances would suggest. Best known to some as the home of the UK Snooker and World Indoor Bowls Championships, this ancient town also saw one of the key battles of the Civil War and it still continues the tradition of the Guild Celebrations. Dating back to medieval times and occurring once every 20 years, this week-long festival is well worth seeing. Our exploration of the Ribble Valley begins at its estuary near Preston and travels upstream through a fertile and versatile valley to the river's remote source in the bleak Pennine Hills.

PRESTON

The many public buildings of Preston all reflect the prosperity of the town during the Victorian age. This wealth was built upon the textile industry helped by the general location of the town: midway between London and Glasgow, on a major railway route, and with extensive docks. Though the town's prosperity was built on cotton, textiles were not new to Preston as linen had been produced here from as far back as Tudor times.

"Proud Preston" is the largest town in the county and its administrative centre. It's 'Proud' because it was the first town in the county to receive a borough charter, (in 1179), the first borough in which every male over 21 had a vote in parliamentary elections (1798), the first town outside London to light its streets with gas lamps (1816), and in 1958 the Preston bypass was the first stretch of motorway to be built in Britain. Civic pride was fostered even more by Preston's elevation in 2002 to the status of a city, one of only six in the UK so honoured to mark the Queen's Diamond Jubilee. Around the same time, multi-million pound plans were announced to redevelop the City Centre.

During the 19th century, Preston became a 'town of spires' as the evenly-split Protestant and Roman Catholic communities vied to build the most splendid churches. The palm is usually awarded to the Catholic St Walburge's Church whose slender 300ft steeple is the third tallest in England.

In Victorian times, Preston was a major cotton-weaving centre. The mill owners' ruthless exploitation of the cotton workers provoked a major strike in 1854 and the bitter confrontation attracted the attention of Charles Dickens. He had already started to write a novel highlighting the degrading conditions and pitiful wages imposed on industrial workers by outrageously wealthy mill owners.

He came to Preston, staying at the Bull and Royal Hotel in Church Street, and his first-hand observations of the unacceptable face of Victorian capitalism displayed in that conflict were embodied in the grimmest novel he ever wrote, *Hard Times*. Many of Preston's old red-brick mills still stand, although now converted to a variety of imaginative uses.

Lancaster may enjoy the distinction of being the elegant county town, but Preston revels in its macho role as Lancashire's administrative centre – always busy, enterprising, forward-looking but still proud of a historical legacy that stretches back to Roman times. The port activity may have declined but the dockland area, now called Riversway, has become an area of regeneration with a marina catering for pleasure craft, yachts and windsurfers. The complex forms part of the recently opened **Millennium Ribble Link** which forms a 3-mile-long linear waterpark providing opportunities for walking, angling, cycling and boating as well as a sculpture trail.

Also in Riversway is the **Ribble Steam Railway** which boasts a collection of some 40 industrial steam, diesel, petrol and battery locomotives. The oldest dates back to 1894; the most recent to 1968. Visitors can ride in the renovated and hand-painted carriages pulled by restored steam locomotives along a 3-mile return trip alongside the River Ribble.

Though the town has both a Roman and a medieval past,

nothing of this is visible today. However, the lasting legacy of those days is reflected in the famous **Guilds Celebrations** which have been taking place every 20 years since 1500. The Royal Charter establishing the rights to hold a Guild Merchant was granted by Henry II in 1179. These medieval guilds were unions of tradesmen who came together in the pursuit of fair dealing and with the intention of preventing cheats from offering a second rate service. Each guild operated from what amounted to their own weights and measures office, the guild hall. As the guilds grew they also became insurance companies, looking after any member who was taken ill and unable to work. In order to ensure that the high standards within a given trade were maintained the apprentice system was started and any member found to be cheating or offering substandard workmanship was expelled from the guild. The last Guild Celebration took place in 1992 and, already, preparations are under way for the next in 2012.

Preston featured in the *Domesday Book* although at that time it was known as Priest-town. In the 1260s, the Greyfriars settled here and the Catholic traditions of the town continued through the ensuing centuries. At the time of the 1745 Jacobite rebellion, Preston played host to the Catholic Prince Charles Edward, Bonnie Prince Charlie.

Preston was also the place where, in 1768, the single most important machine of the textile industry was invented: Richard Arkwright's water-frame cotton spinning machine. Almost overnight, the cottage industries of spinning and handloom weaving were moved from the workers' homes into factories and the entrepreneurs of Preston were quicker than most to catch on. One gentleman in particular, John Horrocks, saw the potential of combining the spinning and weaving operations under the same roof and so he was able to take raw cotton in and produce the finished article on delivery. His firm became the largest of its kind in the world, further adding to the town's prosperity. Although the great days of the textile industry are long gone in Preston, the cotton workers of the town are remembered in a statue which stands outside the old Corn Exchange.

Perhaps the most impressive building in the town is the **Harris Museum and Art Gallery**. Housed in a magnificent neoclassical building which dominates the Market Square, the museum and art gallery were opened in 1893. With an exterior reminiscent of the British Museum, it houses a fine collection of paintings and watercolours by major 19th century British artists, as well as contemporary paintings, sculptures, decorative art and ceramics. There's also an excellent exhibition telling the story of Preston.

You'll find more art on show at the **Pad Gallery**, a fairly recent

A popular annual event in Preston is the Easter Egg Rolling event held in Avenham Park, one of the city's two splendid Victorian riverside parks: the other is the adjacent Miller Park, noted for its impressive floral displays and an elaborately designed fountain. Both parks are currently undergoing substantial restoration work, a process which will continue until 2011.

16 YE OLDE HOB INN

Bamber Bridge, Preston

A fine hostelry offering a wealth of history, freshly cooked food, well-kept ales and unbeatable hospitality.

see page 174

Located on the northern outskirts of the city is Preston's latest visitor attraction to open; the National Football Museum (free) is Lancashire's only national museum and contains the world's most significant football collections. It includes the official FIFA collection and displays over 1000 items of football memorabilia, photographs, more than 90 minutes of film and a number of lively interactive displays. It is housed in Deepdale Stadium, the home of Preston North End FC which has the oldest football league ground in the world. A founder member of the league, Preston North End also won the first FA Cup in 1890.

addition to the town's cultural life. Its declared mission is to exhibit challenging and innovative works of art and has the work of more than 150 artists and designers on show. The displays include furniture, ceramics, visual art, photography, wood carvings, sculpture, fashion, books, cards and gifts.

The two other major museums in the town are regimental. Housed in the former county court building, and with limited opening times, the **Museum of Lancashire** is guarded by a giant Howitzer gun. It has galleries dedicated to three regiments: the 14th/20th Kings Hussars, the Duke of Lancaster's Own Yeomanry, and the Queen's Lancashire Regiment. There is also an interesting and very informative display on the history of Lancashire, a Victorian school room and a 1940s street.

The Fulwood Barracks, which were built in 1848 of Longridge stone, are home to the **Queen's Lancashire Regiment Museum**. With a rich history that covers many campaigns, the exhibits here are numerous and include the famous silver mounted Maida Tortoise, items connected with General Wolfe, souvenirs from the Crimea War, and artefacts from the Defence of Kimberley, the diamond town in South Africa which the 1st Battalion the Loyals defended without assistance from any other troops.

Preston's 2000-seat Guild Hall was built in 1972 to celebrate that year's Guild. Its interior will be familiar to many snooker and bowls fans since it is the venue for the UK Snooker and the World Indoor Bowls Championships.

Another building, less well-known but still a distinctive landmark is **Preston Prison**. Built in 1789, it replaced the town's first House of Correction. In an interesting move to provide the inmates with work, during the 19th century looms were installed in the prison and the prisoners were paid for their labour. Industrial unrest in the area soon followed and in 1837 it was only the threat of cannon fire which saved the prison from invasion by an angry mob intent on destroying the machines. Although the prison was closed in 1931, it re-opened for military use in 1939, became a civilian prison in 1948 and since 1990 has operated as a Category B local prison.

As might be expected for a town on the banks of a river, there are many bridges but two crossings are particularly worthy of note. **Penwortham Old Bridge** is perhaps the most attractive in Lancashire; slightly hump-backed and built of a mixture of stone. Constructed chiefly of buff gritstone and pink sandstone in 1756, it replaced a bridge that had collapsed. By 1912 traffic had increased to such an extent that its use by motor cars and heavy carts was prohibited. For over 150 years, the bridge was the lowest crossing of the River Ribble.

By contrast the **Ribble Viaduct** is one of the oldest

works of railway engineering in the area and a construction of great elegance and dignity, it was built in 1838 and brought the railway from Wigan to the centre of Preston.

AROUND PRESTON

RIBCHESTER

8 miles NE of Preston on the B5269

Situated on the banks of the River Ribble, the village is famous for its **Roman Fort**, Bremetannacum, on the northern river bank. It was the Roman governor, Gnaeus Julius Agricola, in AD79, who first established a fort here at the junction of the two important roads between Manchester and Carlisle, and York and the west coast. Although little of the fort's walls remain, the granary or storehouse, with its hypocaust (underfloor heating), has been excavated and has revealed some interesting coins, pottery, sculptures, and inscriptions.

Back in the village proper, the discovery of some pre-Norman Conquest crosses in and around **St Wilfrid's Church** would suggest that this 13th century building occupies the site of a Saxon church. The church is named after the first Bishop of Ripon, who in the 7th century took a prominent role in the important Synod of Whitby. A great place for tourists during the summer months, Ribchester not only has these two sights to offer but also several excellent pubs, restaurants and cafés.

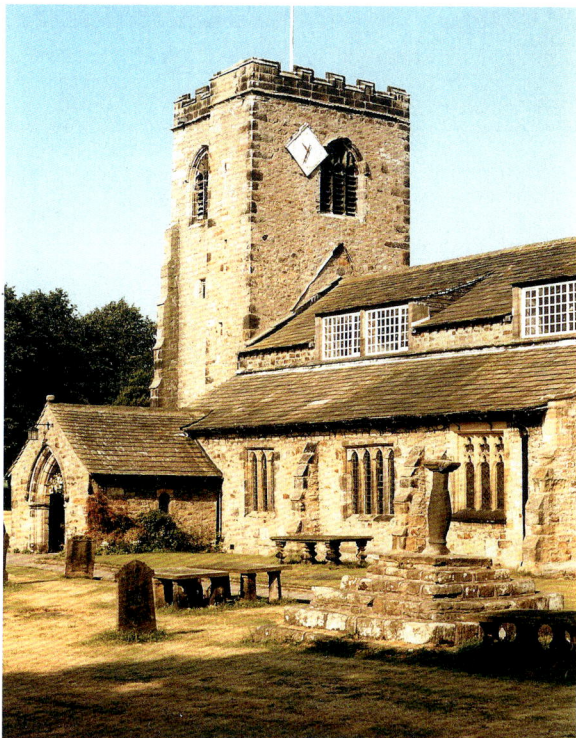

Ribchester Church, Ribchester

SALMESBURY

4 miles E of Preston on the A59

To the east of the village, close to the busy A59, stands **Salmesbury Hall**, built by the Southworth family. The hall seen today, an attractive black and white timbered manor house, is actually the second house they built since their original hall was burned to the ground by Robert the Bruce in the early 1300s. Thinking that the original position, close to a crossing of the River Ribble was too vulnerable to attack, the family built their subsequent home in what was then an isolated location.

•

The Roman Fort's Museum in Ribchester is designed to transport visitors back to the days of the Roman occupation and it offers an excellent insight into those times. Unfortunately, the finest artefact found on the site, an ornate helmet, is not on display here (though they do have a replica) – the original can be seen in the British Museum in London. In July each year, the museum stages a re-enactment of a Roman battle.

•

Salmesbury Hall, Salmesbury

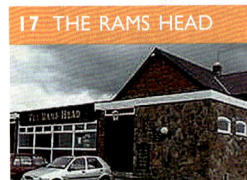

17 THE RAMS HEAD

Longton

A new and exciting
establishment serving
fantastic fish dishes.

see page 174

More peaceful times followed and the hall, surrounded by a moat and with a drawbridge, was a reflection of the family's wealth. A staunchly Catholic family, their 15th century chapel contains a mullioned Gothic window that was rescued from Whalley Abbey after the Dissolution in the 1530s. However, it was the loyalty to their faith that finally saw the demise of the Southworth family. Their continued practice of Catholicism saw Sir John Southworth imprisoned in Manchester in the late 1500s and, by the time of his death a few years later, the family, having kept their faith, had lost their fortune.

The hall was sold to the Braddyll family who, having a house near Ulverston, simply stripped Salmesbury Hall of its assets. Somehow the hall survived but by the 1870s it was in a shocking state of repair. First, Joseph Harrison stepped in and began a successful restoration programme, to the point where he was able to entertain the likes of Charles Dickens. However, the building work took all his money and, facing ruin, Harrison committed suicide. By 1925, the hall was once again in a dilapidated condition and was only saved from demolition by a timber merchant by the efforts of the Salmesbury Hall Trust, a group that is still managing the property today. The hall's unusual history is only equalled by the unconventional manner in which it, quite literally, earns its keep. With no assets left, after being stripped by the Braddylls, the hall is once again full of antiques but these are all for sale. As salerooms go, this has to be one of the most atmospheric.

HIGHER PENWORTHAM

2 miles SW of Preston on the A59

Situated on Penwortham hill and overlooking the River Ribble, **St Mary's Church** has a 14th century chancel and a splendid tower. It stands on the site where the Romans are known to have had a building – probably a fort protecting the river crossing. A charming old bridge of 1755, complete with its cobblestones, still stands but is now only open to pedestrians.

CLITHEROE

Perhaps the most appealing little market town in Lancashire, Clitheroe nestles around its miniature Norman castle. The town has a reputation for high quality specialist shops acclaimed for their individuality, some of which have gained international recognition: establishments such as Cowman's Sausage Shop in Castle Street which offers 58 different varieties of sausage, amongst them Welsh pork & leek, venison and wild boar. Fifty-nine varieties if you count their special Christmas sausage, only available during the festive season and containing exotic ingredients such as port, juniper berries and ground almonds. As with the French, traditional Lancashire meat cuisine wastes no part of the animal. Black Pudding, tripe and onions, chitterlings, lamb's fry and sweetbreads are still popular dishes here although rarely seen in southern England. Interestingly, there's an annual competition between French and Lancashire butchers to see who makes the best Black Pudding.

In King Street there's Byrne's Wine Merchants which stocks more than 1550 different wines and 300 malt whiskies. *Which? Wine Guide* judged the shop to be the best wine merchant in the country. Also well worth visiting is the Platform Gallery, housed in a refurbished railway station of 1870. The Gallery presents a regularly changing programme of visual art exhibitions – paintings and prints, textiles, glassware, ceramics, jewellery, papier maché and baskets, with the majority of the work on show produced by regionally based artists.

Clitheroe is Lancashire's second oldest borough, after Wigan, receiving its first charter in 1147 and since then the town has

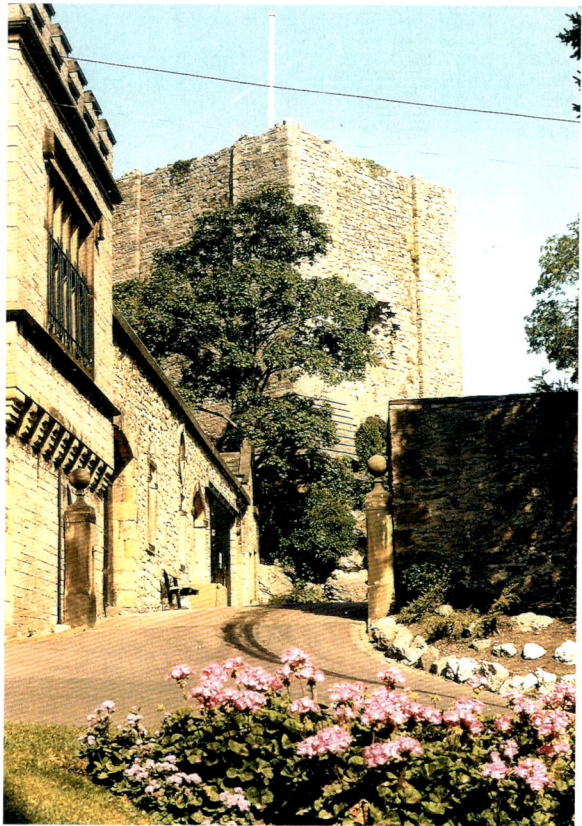

Clitheroe Castle, Clitheroe

served the surrounding villages of the Ribble Valley as their market town. Like Lancaster, it too is dominated by an 800-year-old **Castle** standing on a 100ft high limestone crag high above the town. Today only the Keep remains, the second smallest in England and one of the oldest stone structures in Lancashire. According to local legend, the large hole in the keep's east wall was the work of the Devil who threw a large boulder from the summit of nearby Pendle Hill.

18 THE BLACK HORSE

Pimlico Village

A superbly, friendly Inn with a motto to suit. 'Weary and thin they stagger in, full and stout they stagger out!'

see page 175

Clitheroes narrow, winding streets are full of character and charm and amidst the ancient buildings is the rather incongruous Civic Hall Cinema. Built in 1874 as a public hall, it was converted to a cinema in 1921. It was threatened with closure in 2002 but was rescued by the Lancaster Charitable Foundation. Today this unspoilt monument to the golden days of the silver screen is still lined with plush velvet, has retained its grand piano that was used to accompany the silent films, and presents a regular programme of film and live entertainment.

Just outside the town of Clitheroe can be found Edisford Picnic Area, a popular place for family outings that stands on the site of a battle ground where the Scots fought the Normans. Also near Clitheroe, at Brungerley, are a set of stepping stones across the river that are said to be haunted. Apparently the evil spirit living in the water drags a traveller to his watery death every seven years

Boring historians say it was Oliver Cromwell's troops who inflicted the damage. Modern day visitors can stand within the keep as hidden voices recount the castle's history, complete with appropriate sound effects. Outside, the Castle Grounds feature Lancashire's only Labyrinth and a Rose Garden with metal and limestone sculptures.

More historic voices can be heard at the **North West Sound Archive**, housed in an impressive heritage building on the same site. Its archives contain more than 9000 sound recordings ranging from simple birdsong to conversations with the famous and not so famous. Currently, the Archive and Clitheroe Castle Museum, below, are undergoing major restoration and are scheduled to re-open at Easter 2009.

Standing on another prominent limestone mound, close to the castle, is **Clitheroe Castle Museum**, home to many exhibits and displays reflecting the history and geology of the Ribble Valley area. Archaeological finds illustrate life in the valley from the earliest days and in this section too can be seen the famous Hacking ferryboat now restored to its former glory. Closer to the present day is the re-creation of an Edwardian kitchen, complete with its unique sound system that brings this turn of the century room to life.

As well as the local history displays the museum also has a fine collection relating to the geology of the area. Here, the appearance of the valley is explained in a series of unusual and interesting formats whilst the history of Salthill quarry is also explained. Now a nature reserve and place of special scientific interest, the quarry is famous for the fossils, which have been found here.

A short walk from the Castle Museum stands the parish **Church of St Mary Magdalen** which was founded in the 13th century and rebuilt by the Victorians. At the time of the church's foundation the town already had a school; however, the present Royal Grammar School was not established until 1554. The school's official charter, granted by Mary Tudor but lost for many years, was eventually found in the vaults of a local solicitor's office in 1990.

There are few grand houses in the Ribble Valley open to the public, but **Browsholme Hall**, set in the beautiful Hodder Valley near Clitheroe is open at certain times in the summer. Dating back to the early 1500s, the Hall has been the family home of the Parkers for 600 years and there's a special pleasure in being shown around the house by a member of the family. Notable items on display include some superb oak carved chests, furniture by Gillow, portraits, mementoes of Bonnie Prince Charles, porcelain, arms and armour from the Civil War. The Parkers took their name from the family's hereditary role in medieval times as keepers of the deer park in the royal hunting ground of the Forest of Bowland.

NORTH OF CLITHEROE

WEST BRADFORD

1 mile N of Clitheroe off the B6478

This tucked away village, just south of the Forest of Bowland, was mentioned in the *Domesday Book* and there are records of some villagers paying the first poll tax levied by Richard II in 1379. The old part of the village is set around a green bordering the River Ribble. It's a pleasant spot with a stream running alongside the road through the bottom half of West Bradford and access to the houses bordering the beck is made by crossing a quaint stone bridge.

SAWLEY

4 miles N of Clitheroe off the A59

At the centre of this historic village, easily missed as the main road by-passes it, are the slight remains of **Sawley Abbey**, founded in the 13th century by the Cistercian monks of Fountains Abbey. As well as building their religious house, the monks had great influence over the whole of the surrounding area. Clearing their immediate surroundings, the monks cultivated the land and their ridge and furrow patterns can still be made out in the fields.

Although, during the reigns Edward I and II, the abbots of Sawley were called to the House of Lords, none of the abbots were men of note except, perhaps, William Trafford, the last head of the community. With his colleague and neighbour, the last Abbot of

Abbey Ruins, Sawley

Whalley, Trafford took part in the Pilgrimage of Grace in 1536 and, for his part in the failed uprising, was taken prisoner. Tried for treason at Lancaster in 1537, Trafford, with others like him, was found guilty and executed.

Although little of the abbey remains – much of the stone was cannibalised for village buildings – the site is wonderfully quiet and peaceful.

WORSTON

1 mile NE of Clitheroe off the A59

Hidden away down a lane off the main road, Worston has remained unchanged over the years and can certainly be described as unspoilt. Keen-eyed movie buffs may even recognize the surrounding countryside as one of the locations used during the filming of *Whistle Down the Wind*. Behind the village inn, where the amusing and bizarre ritual of the village's Mock Corporation was revived in 1989, can still be seen the bull ring. Set into a stone, this was where the beast was tethered and baited with

River Ribble, nr Sawley

Whalley Abbey. It was the present Lord Clitheroe's grandfather who paid for the electricity supply cables to be laid underground back in the 1930s and the present squire, Lord Clitheroe of Downham, still refuses to permit the skyline to be spoilt by television aerials, satellite dishes, and even dormer windows. The village phone box has also come under the influence of the family and is not painted a distinctive pillar box red but grey, to tone in with the surroundings.

RIMINGTON

5 miles NE of Clitheroe off the A59

This small hillside village has twice won Lancashire's Best Kept Village competition. Its name means "farmstead on the boundary" and as the Lancashire/Yorkshire boundary has changed over the years the village has been transferred from one county to the other. The most recent transfer was made in 1974 when people who had been Yorkshire born and bred suddenly found themselves Lancastrians.

This pleasant rural village was the home of Francis Duckworth, the famous composer of hymn tunes, including one he named *Rimington*. His parents ran the village post office and shop next door to the Methodist chapel and a plaque on the chapel, now a private house, commemorates him.

GISBURN

7 miles NE of Clitheroe on the A59

Like Rimington, this village was also once in Yorkshire and, as many

specially trained dogs in the belief that the 'sport' tenderized the meat.

DOWNHAM

3 miles NE of Clitheroe off the A59

Some 40-odd villages are sprinkled along the banks of the Ribble Valley, all of them built in the appealing local stone. One of the prettiest is Downham, renowned as a major location for the cinema classic *Whistle Down the Wind*. The village also features prominently in BBC-TV's period drama series *Born & Bred*. Thanks for Downham's unspoilt appearance must go to the Clitheroe family which has owned the whole village since 1558 – the same year in which they acquired locals would like to believe, still is! One of the Ribble Valley's most pleasant and picturesque villages, Gisburn's history is dominated by the Lister family who, from humble beginnings rose to become the Lords of Ribblesdale. Their house, built in the early 1600s in Gisburne Park, is still standing though it is now a private hospital. Over the years, many people were given shelter by the family including, in 1648, Cromwell who is said to have rested at the house whilst on his way to fight at Preston.

PAYTHORNE

10 miles NE of Clitheroe off the A682

The source of the River Ribble lies to the north in Yorkshire, near the famous Three Peaks of Whernside, Ingleborough, and Pen-y-ghent. Paythorne is the first village on its banks on this side of the county boundary. Paythorne also marks the end of the river's journey through the rugged limestone scenery of moorlands and the start of its picturesque course through a lush green valley.

BARNOLDSWICK

10 miles NE of Clitheroe on the B6251

If you approach this former cotton town from the south, off the A56, you may wonder why the road is so straight. The answer is that it was specially constructed in the 1930s to service the new Rolls Royce factory in the town. The B in the names of jet engines such as the RB211 stands for Barnoldswick.

At the western end of the town is **Bancroft Mill Engine**

Museum. The mill was the last weaving shed to be built in Lancashire, in 1922. The mill closed in 1978 but the grand 600hp cross-compound steam engine was preserved and there are regular demonstrations of it in action. The museum also displays tools and documents connected with the weaving industry.

WEST OF CLITHEROE

WADDINGTON

2 miles NW of Clitheroe on the B6478

This is one of the area's best known villages – its attractive Coronation Gardens have appeared on many postcards and even on biscuit tin lids. King Henry VI spent a whole year here in 1464/5, not because he particularly appreciated its charms but because he was hiding at Waddington Hall from the Yorkists who had defeated him at the Battle of Hexham. When his hiding place was discovered he escaped by a secret tunnel that led from the Hall's dining room but he was quickly captured at Brungerley Bridge, down river near Clitheroe, then imprisoned in the Tower of London where he died in 1471.

Waddington has several times won first prize in Lancashire's Best Kept Village competition and it's easy to see why. Waddington Brook splashes the length of the village and 18th century almshouses cluster around the green.

About ten years ago Waddington's villagers enjoyed a certain amount of fame when, for the sake of a television series, they agreed to renounce their TVs for a whole month. This cold turkey treatment proved too much for some and they had to be resuscitated by having their sets returned.

19 MOORCOCK INN HOTEL & RESTAURANT

Waddington

A first-class venue in stunning grounds, catering for all occasions and offering guests spectacular views of the Ribble Valley from their luxurious bedrooms.

see page 177

20 THE EAGLE AND CHILD

Hurst Green

A charming 19th century inn in the heart of the village serving traditional home-cooked food and offering comfortable en-suite accommodation.

see page 176

GREAT MITTON

3 miles SW of Clitheroe on the B6246

Standing opposite the Three Fishes Hotel, which takes its name from the three fishes on the Whalley Abbey coat of arms, is the attractive **All Hallows' Church.** Housing some of the finest relics to be seen in any British church, this is most certainly worth a visit. Built around 1270, little has been done to the building since, although a tower was added in 1438 and the pews are Jacobean. However, it is the Shireburn Chapel that draws most visitors to the church. It was added in 1440 by the Shireburn family of Stonyhurst who claimed to be the direct descendants of the first rector, Ralph the Red of Mytton. The family tombs here are regarded as the best in the county. One of the earliest is the fine alabaster tomb of Sir Richard Shireburn (who died in 1594) and his wife Maude who is dressed in capacious petticoats. The latest is of another Richard who died in 1702 at the age of 9 after eating poisonous berries. Following the fashion of the time the monument displays copious macabre items – a skull, hour glass, sickle, more bones than seem necessary and, emerging from the ground, two skeletal hands.

Confirmation that a settlement existed here before the days of the land ownership by the abbey comes with the name of the village itself. Mitton is derived from the Saxon word 'mythe' which means a farm at the junction of two rivers – perfectly describing the location which is close to where the River Hodder feeds into the River Ribble.

HURST GREEN

5 miles SW of Clitheroe on the B6243

This pretty village of stone-built cottages nestling in the Ribble Valley is best known for its nearby public school. **Stonyhurst College**, the world famous Roman Catholic school, began life as the residence of the local lords of the manor. The present building, begun in around 1523, was the work of Hugh Shireburn although additions were made in 1592 by Sir Richard Shireburn. The core of this imposing building set beside a lake is late-Elizabethan but there have been major additions almost every century, all of them blending remarkably well with their predecessors.

Sir Richard Shireburn was an ambitious man who served the Tudor monarchy well. As well as being the Chief Forester of Bowland he was also one of Henry VIII's commissioners studying the

Dean Brook, Hurst Green

Cromwells Packhorse Bridge, nr Hurst Green

state of the monasteries. He was an eager participant in the suppression of Whalley Abbey. Though the family publicly adopted the new Protestant religion under Elizabeth I, it was with little enthusiasm and in a short time the Shireburn family, like many other Lancashire families, returned to their Catholic faith. It seems strange then that Cromwell, on his way to and from the Battle of Preston, should take shelter at Stonyhurst although rumour has it that the ardent Puritan slept with a pistol at his side and his guards around him.

In 1794, after the house had been left for some considerable time and had fallen into a state of disrepair, the owner, Thomas Weld, offered the property to the Jesuits who had set up an English Catholic School in Flanders. Unwelcome in France following the revolution, the Jesuits gladly accepted and after restoring the original building they extended it during the 19th century. Their finest addition must be the replica of King's College in Cambridge: **St Peter's Church** was built in 1835 and contains many treasures including a 7th century copy of St John's Gospel and a cope of Henry II that was used by Henry VIII at the Field of the Cloth of Gold.

One of the college's most famous sons was Sir Arthur Conan Doyle, the creator of Sherlock Holmes, and JRR Tolkien was a teacher here. Stonyhurst College is occasionally open to the public during the summer holidays and the guided tour takes in Conan

> *Hurst Green itself has become popular with fans of JRR Tolkien since he is believed to have found inspiration here for the 'Middle Earth' featured in his epic* **Lord of the Rings.**

33

The village of Longridge lies at the foot of Longridge Fell from whose 1150ft elevation, especially at Jeffrey Hill or Kemple End, there are superb views northwards over the Loud Valley to Chipping: to the south the land drops away towards the River Ribble.

---

21 ROSE COTTAGE

Clayton Le Dale

A truly picturesque B&B enjoying a rural location, offering outstanding hospitality combined with the most delicious, homecooked breakfast one could wish for!

see page 177

Doyle's desk and Tolkien's classroom where he wrote much of *Lord of the Rings*. The exterior of the College can always be seen from the minor road that runs through its grounds.

Just outside Hurst Green, a lovely old packhorse bridge crosses the Lower Hodder river. It is known as **Cromwell's Bridge** since the Puritan leader rode over it on his way to the Battle of Preston.

STYDD

7 miles SW of Clitheroe off the B6245

Just to the north of Ribchester lies the small hamlet of Stydd. All that remains of the monastery founded here by the Knights Hospitallers of St John of Jerusalem is the Norman **Chapel**, standing alone surrounded by meadows. It contains effigies of some of the knights. A crusading and military order established in 1113, the Knights Hospitallers provided help and assistance to pilgrims travelling to the Holy Land. Their commandery, as their religious houses were called, at Stydd was dissolved by the mid-1300s and, although at one time there were more than 50 of their small monasteries in the country, only 15 survived to the 1530s.

LONGRIDGE

10 miles SW of Clitheroe on the B6243

After Clitheroe, bustling Longridge is the only other town of any size in the area. Like Clitheroe it offers a good selection of independently owned shops along with a range of antique galleries, and is widely

known for its Lancashire Cheese Dairies.

For many years the area around Longridge was an important source of building stone and several of Preston's civic buildings, including the Harris Library and Museum, and the docks at Liverpool were constructed with Longridge stone.

In the 1790s the stone was also used to build a row of 20 terraced cottages in Longridge – numbers 4 to 44 Higher Road, which now have listed building status. They were erected by a group of quarrymen who formed a club into which each member paid a fixed weekly sum. The money was used to pay the cost of materials, £138.3s.6d (£138.17p), for building each cottage. When a cottage was completed, the members drew lots as to who should occupy it. Known as **Club Row**, these mutually funded cottages are the earliest known example of properties built on the principles of a Building Society and have earned themselves an entry in the *Guinness Book of Records*.

GOOSNARGH

12 miles SW of Clitheroe on the B5269

Just to the west of the village stands **Chingle Hall**, a small moated manor house that was built in 1260 by Adam de Singleton. A Catholic family, the Singletons are said to have had a chapel with three priest hides. As well as being the birthplace of St John Wall, one of the last priests to die for his faith, in 1620, it enjoys the reputation of being one of the most haunted houses in Britain. As such, the hall has featured on countless television and radio programmes.

CHIPPING

8 miles W of Clitheroe off the B6243

This picturesque village overlooking the River Loud is now a conservation area and it is also home to a post office, built in 1668, which claims to be Britain's oldest shop. Very much at the heart of the local agricultural communities, the annual village show is one of the best in Lancashire and its very name comes from the old English word for a market place - *chepyn*. In medieval times there were no fewer than five watermills along the banks of Chipping Beck. Later, one of the mills, Tweedies Mill, made ships' portholes which were used on the clipper ships bringing tea back from the east.

There are a number of attractive inns here and one of them, the Sun Inn, is associated with a melancholy tale. The story of Lizzie Dean whose ghost is said to haunt the inn is poignant, sad – and true. In 1835, Lizzie was 18 years old and a serving wench at the inn. She had fallen in love with a local man and a date had been set for their wedding at the church just across the road from the inn. Lizzie lodged at the inn and on the morning of her wedding she heard the church bells ringing. Looking out of her window she saw her intended bridegroom leaving the church with another maiden on his arm.

Humiliated and distraught, Lizzie crept up into the inn's attic and hanged herself. She left a note requesting that she should be buried beneath the path leading to the church porch so that her faithless lover would have to step across her body every Sunday on his way to divine service.

GRIMSARGH

11 miles W of Clitheroe on the B6243

As well as having one of the largest village greens in Lancashire, covering some 12 acres, Grimsargh is also home to **Tun Brook Wood**. Following the line of the brook until it meets the River Ribble, this is one of the largest areas of deciduous woodland in the country.

•

About 3 miles north-east of Chipping, the Bowland Wild Boar Park occupies 65 acres, mainly woodland, set alongside the River Hodder. In addition to wild boar, the Park is also home to longhorn cows, llamas, red deer, goats, lambs and more. There's also a large children's play area and pedal tractors are available for young children. A café has recently been opened serving snacks and wild boar meat is on sale and also features on the café's menu.

•

Fleetwood

Preesall

Stake Pool

Cockerham

Scorton

23 **24**
25 **26**

27

LA

Stalmine

22

Hambleton

Garstang

Chipping

Cleveleys

Thornton

Poulton-le-Fylde

Elswick

Barton

Longridge

Blackpool

28

3

M55

1

32

Osbaldeston

4

29

31

Kirkham

Preston

St Anne's

Freckleton

Lytham St Anne's

Warton

Longton

Hutton

29

3

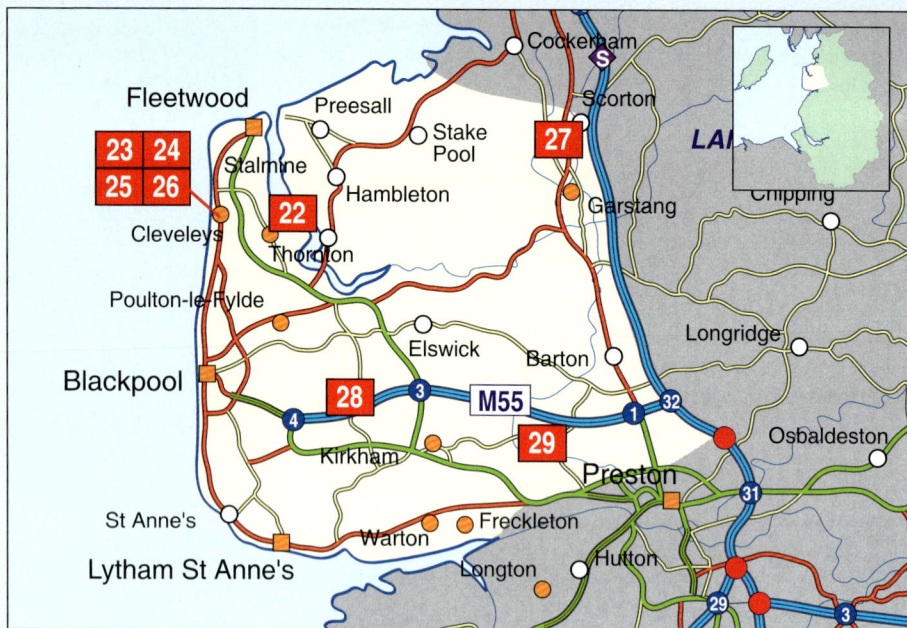

The Fylde

The Fylde derives its name from the Anglo-Saxon word *gefilde* meaning level, green fields, an apt description of this low-lying area that extends from Fleetwood in the north to Lytham St Anne's in the south. It was once known as "Windmill Land" but nowadays windmills are few and far between. A notable exception is the striking example that stands on the waterfront at Lytham. It was built in 1805, worked until 1929 and now houses a small museum.

The coastline of The Fylde is almost completely built up with the brash and boisterous seaside resort of Blackpool as its focus. In its heyday, the town attracted 16 million visitors a year although that has shrunk to less than 9 million and the town is seeking ways of rebranding itself. One of these is a curious co-operative venture with the Victoria & Albert Museum which is currently considering re-housing London's National Theatre Museum in the town.

To the south of Blackpool is the rather more genteel resort of Lytham St Anne's, known world-wide for its outstanding golf course and a regular host of the British Open Championships. Both Lytham and Blackpool developed as a result of the expansion of the railway system in the Victorian age when the former in particular was a popular destination for the mill workers of Lancashire and Yorkshire.

However, The Fylde is also an ancient region that was known to both the Romans and the Saxons. In the north of the region, around the Wyre estuary, the salt marshes have been exploited for more than 2000 years and the process continues at the large ICI plant. Fishing and shipping have also been important sources of revenue here. Fleetwood is still a port though on a much smaller scale than in the past.

BLACKPOOL

Blackpool is as unique to England as Las Vegas is to the United States. Everyone is familiar with Blackpool's brash, warm-hearted attractions but did you know that this single town has more beds available for the 16 million people who used to visit each year than the whole of Portugal has for its visitors?

Today, Blackpool is the largest town in the present county of Lancashire. Little more than a fishing village among the sand dunes of the Fylde coast 150 years ago, Blackpool's huge expansion followed the arrival of the railway. Up until then, travel to and from the village involved considerable discomfort, taking a day from Manchester and two days from York. The great Victorian railway companies put Blackpool well and truly on the map by laying the railway lines right to the coast and building the grand stations – the town had three. The quiet fishing village was quickly transformed into a vibrant resort as day-trippers from the mill towns of Lancashire and Yorkshire took advantage of the cheap excursion rail fares. Local developers enthusiastically began creating new attractions for their visitors. The first pier was constructed in 1863, followed by two more over the next twenty years. A glass-domed Winter Gardens opened in 1875, and ten years later the town's electric tram system began operating, the first in Britain and today the only one. The Pleasure Beach with its permanent fairground rides and amusements arrived in 1890 with the aim of providing "an American-style amusement park where adults could feel like children again".

But the developers' real master-stroke was the construction of the world-famous **Blackpool Tower**. Modelled on the Eiffel Tower and completed in 1894, the Tower stands some 518 feet high, incorporates a Ballroom and Grand Theatre, both of which are decorated in a wonderfully over-the-top rococo style. The **Tower Ballroom** is a much loved institution where tea dances are still a regular feature. It was, for many years from the 1960s to the 1980s, the venue for BBC-TV's enormously popular *Come Dancing* competition. The Tower's centenary celebrations in 1994 were numerous and extravagant and included painting the tower gold.

Also on the 'Golden Mile' of the Promenade is the **Doctor Who Exhibition** with displays celebrating the popular BBC-TV science fiction programme from its beginnings in 1963 to the present day. Nearby, **Louis Tussaud's Waxworks** present the world of celebrities from Hollywood's "A" List to the tabloids' favourites in "Celeb City", as well as more substantial figures.

Blackpool Tower, Blackpool

The introduction of the Blackpool Illuminations helped extend the summer season into autumn, and the late 20th century saw yet more visitor attractions added to the mix. **Pleasure Beach** is an attraction that continues to be extended and improved. However some of its delights are certainly not for the fainthearted. It not only boasts its own railway station, but also the tallest, fastest and, it is claimed, the most thrilling roller-coaster ride in the world. In the summer of 2002 yet another seafront attraction was installed - the world's largest mirror ball. Weighing four and a half tons and 18 feet across, it is made up of 47,000 different pieces.

The **North Pier**, designed by Eugenius Birch, was opened at the beginning of the 1863 season. It soon became the place to promenade and is now a listed building.

Despite its reputation as a brash and lively resort, Blackpool also has its quiet, secluded corners where visitors can escape the hustle of the crowds. There are seven miles of sea front, from the North Shore down as far as Squire's Gate and Lytham, where the pace of life is gentler and the beaches are quieter. **Blackpool Tramways** have provided a most enjoyable way of exploring these less busy sides of the town and its environs for many years. And it should also be remembered that the world's first electric street tram system opened here in 1885. The route was extended along the Lytham road in

Pleasure Beach, Blackpool

1895 and later connected with other routes in nearby Lytham and St Anne's. However, by the 1960s, bus services had put paid to many towns' tram routes, leaving Blackpool's tram system as the only commercial route in the country.

Many of the tramcars date from the 1930s or 1950s and the managing company has a special selection of vintage cars which they run on special occasions. One of these occasions is the now annual **Illuminations** which, following a ceremonial lighting much like that of the Christmas lights in London, is a splendid end to the season. An eagerly awaited free show, running the full length of the promenade, the lights have, over the years, provided many spectacular shows and incorporated many themes.

NORTH OF BLACKPOOL

THORNTON

5 miles N of Blackpool on the B5268

Situated in the west bank of the Wyre estuary, this small town is

•

A couple of miles inland from The Pleasure Beach, Marton Mere bird sanctuary is a 10 acre lake which is the year round home for many geese, swans and ducks, and a temporary resting place for many more. Nearby, Stanley Park is spacious, well-maintained and peaceful.

•

22 THE BEACHVIEW HOTEL

Thornton Cleveleys

A small, personally run, homely hotel located a short stroll from the sea front in Cleveleys and open all year round.

see page 178

39

23 TASTE LICENSED COFFEE HOUSE

Cleverleys

A very popular coffee house offering some tasty treats and a selection of drinks for all the family.

see page 177

24 GRANNY'S COFFEE SHOP & RESTAURANT

Cleveleys

A quaint, homely coffee shop offering good old-fashioned hospitality coupled with hearty wholesome cooking just like granny used to make!

see page 178

25 CAROUSEL LICENSED DINER

Cleveleys

An outstanding eating place renowned throughout the country for it's homemade food and unique ambience.

see page 179

26 BRIARDENE HOTEL

Cleveleys

A highly commended, family run Hotel where first class service is priority and guests can enjoy excellent gourmet cuisine.

see page 180

40

dominated by **Marsh Mill**, which stands over 100 feet high and was constructed in 1794. The grinding of corn ceased here soon after World War I but the building has been restored and it is now a tourist attraction.

At this point the Wyre estuary is wide and provides shelter for shipping, an advantage that was utilised by both the Romans and the Scandinavians. They both took advantage of the salt deposits here and, today, the large ICI plant is still extracting salt.

The **Wyre Estuary Country Park** in Thornton, taking the whole estuary from Fleetwood up river as far as Shard Bridge, is an excellent place from which to discover the area. An initial stop at the Wyreside Ecology Centre, which provides all manner of information about the estuary, is a sensible starting point. From here a number of footpaths take in many of the places along the river as well as leading visitors through important areas of salt marsh, which contain a wide range of plants, insects, and birds.

CLEVELEYS

5 miles N of Blackpool on the A584

This popular seaside resort is less boisterous than its neighbour, Blackpool, to the south and it is altogether more attractive architecturally. This is hardly surprising as the town began to grow after an architectural competition, organised in 1906, in which Sir Edwin Lutyens, the designer of modern Whitehall, London, was involved.

FLEETWOOD

8 miles N of Blackpool on the A587

Cleveleys in turn links up with Fleetwood which until 1836 was just a small fishing village. Local landowner Sir Peter Hesketh-Fleetwood decided to develop the area as a seaside resort and employed the leading architect of the time, Decimus Burton, who had designed London's Regent Street as well as large parts of St Leonards on Sea and Hove.

Prior to the commencement of the building work in 1836, Fleetwood was a small settlement of a few fishermen's cottages. The opening of the railway extension from Preston to Fleetwood was a key element in the town's development and the impressive North Euston Hotel, which opened in 1842, reflects those railway links. Queen Victoria used Fleetwood as she travelled to Scotland for her annual holiday. However, this was all before the railway companies managed to lay a railway over Shap fell in Cumbria in 1847 and thus provide a direct rail link to Scotland. Sir Peter was bankrupted but the town itself continued to flourish as a port and seaside resort.

Fleetwood's museum, overlooking the River Wyre, illustrates the town's links with the fishing industry which suffered greatly from the Icelandic cod wars of the 1970s.

The famous World War I poet, Wilfred Owen, lived in Fleetwood in 1916 when he was 23. He stayed at 111, Bold Street whilst he was in charge of the Gunnery Range in Fleetwood as a Second Lieutenant in the Manchester Regiment. A display about him can be found in the main bar of the North Euston Hotel.

John Lennon also spent his childhood holidays in Fleetwood, returning here on 25 August 1962 when the Beatles played at the Marine Hall.

Upstream from Fleetwood, ICI continues an industry that was well-established in Roman times – extracting salt from the extensive salt marshes lining the river Wyre.

ROSSALL POINT
7 miles N of Blackpool off the A587

Situated at the northern tip of the Fylde coast, this was where the Hesketh-Fleetwood family, the force behind the creation of Fleetwood, had their home. Their impressive mansion is still standing and is now part of Rossall School.

PREESALL
8 miles N of Blackpool on the B5270

The village's original name, Pressoude, as it was written in the *Domesday Book*, is thought to mean a salt farm near the sea and certainly in 1872 rock salt deposits were discovered beneath the village. From then on, for around 30 years, Preesall became a centre for salt mining and in 1883 the Fleetwood Salt Company was established to develop the field. The bulk of the salt was extracted in the form of brine and by the end of 1891 there was a reliable pipeline pumping the salt under the River Wyre to Fleetwood. However, as much of the salt was extracted from underneath the expanding village, subsidence soon became a problem. In 1923 this led to the opening up of a huge pit, known locally as "Bottomless" to the west of the village.

KNOTT END-ON-SEA
8 miles N of Blackpool on the B5270

This small coastal resort on the River Wyre estuary grew into a substantial fishing settlement in the 17th and 18th centuries. It was also a pilot base for the upstream ports of Wardleys and Skippool and later developed into a ferry port. Today its broad flat sands and bracing sea air, along with the decline in the fishing industry, have turned the town into a small, quiet holiday resort much favoured by those who have retired.

Looking out to sea, at low tide, a rocky outcrop can be seen which, some historians have suggested, is the remains of the masonry of a Roman harbour. Whether this is the port that in the 2nd century Ptolemy marked on a map as Portus Setantiorum is certainly in doubt but it is undeniable that such a building existed as the Romans were planning an invasion of Ireland from this stretch of coast.

PILLING
10 miles N of Blackpool off the A588

This quiet scattered village, on the edge of rich, fertile marshland, was for many years linked to the market town of Garstang by a little,

Fleetwood's most famous product is known around the world. In 1865, a local chemist named James Lofthouse created a compound of liquorice, capsicum, eucalyptus and methanol designed to relieve the sore throats and bronchial troubles endured by fishermen at sea. He called the mixture Fisherman's Friend and it was remarkably successful. The only problem was that the bottles in which it was sold frequently shattered in the rough Atlantic seas. So Lofthouse transformed the liquid into a lozenge which is still produced by his descendants and has enormous sales world-wide.

winding, single-track railway known affectionately as the "Pilling Pig" because the train's whistle sounded like a pig having its throat cut. The last passengers were carried in 1930; the last goods train ran in 1950.

Said to be the second largest village in Britain, Pilling boasts no fewer than 5 churches. One of them, **Old St John's** is notable as a "time-warp" church, virtually unchanged since its completion in 1717. Flagged floors, pews and box-pews of unvarnished oak, and a three-decker pulpit have all

survived unscathed thanks to the building of a new church in the village in 1887.

There has been a watermill at Pilling since 1242. The present windmill dates back to 1808 and was built on a raft of brushwood. It is now a private residence.

Another building of interest is The Olde Ship Inn, built in 1782 by George Dickson, a slave trader. Now a listed building, the inn is reputed to be haunted by a lady dressed in Georgian attire wandering around with a pale and worried look on her face.

GARSTANG

12 miles NE of Blackpool on the A6

Garstang is an ancient, picturesque town whose market dates back to the time of Edward II and is still held every Thursday in the central square with its handsome former Town Hall of 1755. A bell is rung at 10am to signify the opening of trading. Another long-standing institution is the Garstang Agricultural Show which was founded in 1809 and is held on the first Saturday in August.

The town has an excellent **Discovery Centre** which deals with a variety of aspects of the region, including the history of the nearby Forest of Bowland and the natural history of the surrounding countryside.

Just to the east of the town, on the top of a grassy knoll, are the remains of **Greenhalgh Castle**, built in 1490 by Thomas Stanley, the first Earl of Derby. Severely damaged during a siege

Butter Cross, Garstang

Greenhalgh Castle, Garstang

27 THE PRIORY SCORTON

Scorton

The Priory Scorton offers supreme facilities, all first class, along with genuine hospitality in a relaxed atmosphere where customers come first and are left wanting for nothing.

see page 181

by Cromwell's troops in 1645-46, the castle was one of the last strongholds in Lancashire to have held out and only surrendered when its Governor died.

Nearby Gubberford Bridge is reputedly haunted. It was during the Civil War siege that a Roundhead soldier named Peter Broughton was standing on the bridge one winter evening when he was approached by a beautiful woman dressed all in white. To his amazement, he recognised the wife who had left him for another man some five years earlier.

She was advancing towards him, smiling and with her arms outstretched, when a Royalist captain, Robert Rowton, burst onto the bridge. In the altercation that followed it emerged that she had bigamously married the captain. Enraged, Rowton stabbed her in the breast and she died within minutes. The two soldiers from opposing sides then joined forces to bury, beside the bridge, the body of the woman they had both known as wife. It was only a death-bed confession by Peter Broughton many years later that brought the deed to light. By then Rowton was dead but the unquiet soul of the White Lady has found no rest and on misty winter evenings she paces silently up and down the bridge.

A little to the north of Garstang, on the B6430, are the remains of a stone-built **Toll House** which probably dates from the 1820s when parts of the turnpike from Garstang to Lancaster were realigned. Although a ruin, the toll house is more than usually interesting as the posts for the toll gates can still be seen on either side of the road. This stretch of road also features some of the finest **Turnpike Milestones** in the county. To the south of Garstang they are round-faced stones with cursive lettering

43

Every Wednesday, a bustling open air market is held in the charming village square of Great Eccleston. However, unlike most markets which have their origins in medieval times, Great Eccleston's first took place in 1974 following a campaign started by the parish council a few years previously. The wide variety of stalls attract visitors from not only the immediate surroundings but also coaches from outside the rural area.

Old Wyre Bridge, Garstang

dating from the 1750s but to the north the stones are triangular, with Roman lettering, and date from the time of the turnpike's realignment in the early 1800s.

HAMBLETON

6 miles NE of Blackpool on the A588

A centre for ship building in medieval times, Hambleton is now a quiet village set around a bend of the River Wyre. A network of narrow lanes radiate from the village and wind through the charming north Fylde countryside.

The village stands on one of the narrowest parts of the river and there was certainly a ford in Roman times, as relics have been found here. However, it is probable that the ford goes back even further, to the Iron Age around 500 BC. On the site of the ford now stands the 325-yard **Shard Bridge**, built in 1864 and still operating as a toll bridge.

EAST OF BLACKPOOL

GREAT ECCLESTON

8 miles NE of Blackpool off the A586

This quiet traditional agricultural community on the banks of the River Wyre was, during the 17th and 18th centuries, known locally as Little London because it was the social centre for the surrounding area. This was probably directly linked to the generous number of public houses and inns in the village at that time.

CHURCHTOWN

12 miles NE of Blackpool on the A586

This delightful village has many buildings of both architectural and historic interest and none more so than the **Church of St Helen** which dates back to the days of the Norman Conquest. Featuring architectural styles from almost every period since the 11th century, this church is well worth exploring. The oldest parts of the building are the circular pillars near the nave which date from around 1200. The roof is the original Tudor structure. Built on the site of a Saxon church, St Helen's is dedicated to the mother of Emperor Constantine and the circular churchyard is typical of the Saxon period.

Known as the "Cathedral of the Fylde", the church has been subjected to flooding by the River Wyre and in 1746 such was the damage caused by the rising waters that the rebuilding of the church looked necessary. However, the builder brought in to survey the scene, suggested that moving the river would be a cheaper option and this method of preserving the church was undertaken. The original course of the river can be seen by taking the footpath from the churchyard in the direction of the new river course.

ST MICHAEL'S ON WYRE

10 miles NE of Blackpool on the A586

The River Wyre at this point is still tidal and for centuries the inhabitants of St Michael's and other villages in the area have suffered the threat of flooding. An old flood bank has been constructed from the village bridge and below, beyond the overgrown banks, are the fertile fields of the flood plain.

Mentioned in the *Domesday Book* as Michelscherche, is it likely that the first church in the village was founded in the 7th century. As well as many memorials to the Butler family, the church also contains a splendid 14th century mural that was only discovered in 1956 when repair work was being undertaken in the sanctuary.

The Butler family, whose home – Rawcliffe Hall – lies a few miles down river, are known to have been in this area for 800 years and their house is built on the site of a Saxon dwelling. Another of the staunchly Catholic Lancashire families, the Butlers finally lost their house and the influence that they had in the area. The house is now part of a private country club.

POULTON-LE-FYLDE

4 miles NE of Blackpool on the A586

This is one of the oldest towns in the ancient area known as Amounderness. The Romans were known to have been in the area and it was probably they who constructed the **Danes Pad**, an ancient trackway. The town developed as a commercial centre for the surrounding agricultural communities and its Market Place remains its focal point. The town's ancient stocks and whipping post have been preserved and can be found in the pedestrianised Market Place.

In 1732, a great fire, started by sparks from the torches of a funeral procession, destroyed most of the thatched cottages that surrounded the market square in those days and a nationwide appeal was launched to help meet the costs of rebuilding the houses -

Fire seems to have played an important role in the life of Poulton-le-Fylde and one ancient custom still observed is Teanlay Night which involves the lighting of bonfires on Hallowe'en. Each bonfire is encircled with white-coloured stones which are then thrown into the flames by the onlookers and left until the next day. The successful retrieval of one's own stone is considered a good omen for future prosperity.

28 THE EAGLE AND CHILD

Weeton

An attractive cosy pub assuring visitors of a genuine welcome serving excellent food and award winning beer.

see page 182

From mid-July to September, a popular attraction is the Singleton Maize Maze where, even on the busiest day, you are likely to lose yourself in the baffling framework of twists and turns.

29 THE SITTING GOOSE

Lower Bartle, nr Preston

A hidden gem with relaxed atmosphere providing superb cuisine and plenty of seating.

see page 183

without thatch.

The present **Church of St Chad** dates from the early 1600s, though the majority of the building is Georgian, and it stands on the site of the original Norman church. Inside there's a splendid Georgian nave from which a magnificent staircase leads to typically Georgian galleries running around three sides. There are several magnificent memorials to the local Fleetwood-Hesketh family.

Strolling around Poulton-le-Fylde now, it is hard to imagine that the town was once a seaport. But, until relatively recently ships sailed up the River Wyre to **Skippool Creek**. Today, the creek is home to the Blackpool and Fleetwood Yacht Club and from here the ocean-going yachts compete in major races around Britain.

The town had a rail link long before Blackpool and it was here that the early holidaymakers alighted from their trains to take a horse and trap the remaining few miles. Fortunately for Poulton, in 1846, the railway reached Blackpool and the town could, once again, return to a more peaceful existence. It is this quiet and charm, as well as sensitive approaches to planning, that have led it to become, in recent years, a much sought after residential area for businessmen now able to travel the M55 to Manchester and Liverpool.

Incidentally, Poulton's "le-Fylde" tag was added to distinguish the town from Poulton-le-Sands – nowadays better known as Morecambe.

SINGLETON

5 miles E of Blackpool on the B5260

Singleton's most famous son is Robert Gillow who lived here in the first half of the 18th century. He left to become an apprentice joiner at Lancaster and later founded the cabinet making business that became Waring & Gillow of Lancaster.

The village Gillow knew was completely demolished in 1853 after it was bought for £70,000 by Alderman Thomas Miller, a cotton manufacturer from Preston. He then rebuilt it as a model village complete with a church, school, public house – *The Millers Arms*, naturally, and an ornate black-and-white shed for the village fire engine, which still stands although it is now an electricity sub-station.

The parish church of this quiet little Fylde village, **St Anne's Church**, was built as part of Miller's model village in 1860. In the sanctuary is a black oak chair which bears the inscription "John Milton, author of Paradise Lost and Paradise Regained 1671" but no-one seems to know where the chair came from and whether the great author did indeed use it.

WOODPLUMPTON

12 miles E of Blackpool off the B5269

This charming little village, centred around its church still has its well-preserved village stocks behind which is a mounting block that is now designated as a historic monument. **St Anne's Church** is also a building of historic note and

46

the keen-eyed will be quick to spot the octagonal cupola shape of tower that is reminiscent of the architecture of Christopher Wren. Completed in 1748, the tower was built to house a new clock which replaced the sundial that for many years adorned the old tower. Bearing the date 1637, this can now be found in the churchyard.

Many small towns and villages in Lancashire have their own tale of witches to tell and Woodplumpton is no exception. In St Anne's churchyard a huge boulder marks the grave of Margaret Hilton, better known in her day as "Meg the Witch". It's said that one day the local squire made a wager with her that she could not turn herself into a hare and outrun their pack of dogs. (This transformation into a hare was apparently a standard feature of any self-respecting witch's repertoire). Meg accepted the bet, stipulating only that one particular black dog should be excluded.

The race duly took place but the squire cheated, letting slip the black dog which managed to nip the hare's back legs just before it vanished into thin air. From that day, Meg suffered from a severe limp – and a nasty temper. Every kind of rural mishap was attributed to her black arts. She was eventually found dead in her cottage, crushed between a water barrel and a well. Her body was buried in the churchyard by torchlight on May 2nd, 1705. But the cadaver kept rising to the surface so a massive boulder was rolled over her grave.

(Similar measures were taken at Samlesbury, to the east of Preston. In the churchyard there's a witch's grave through which iron spikes have been driven to prevent her from returning to plague her neighbours).

KIRKHAM

8 miles SE of Blackpool off the A583

There was a settlement here in Saxon times, and the village is mentioned in the *Domesday Book* as Ciric-ham. Even earlier, the Romans had a fort here though it is now lost under a modern housing estate. Kirkham was first granted a charter to hold a weekly market in 1287 and since then it has been serving the needs of the surrounding farming communities. Some fine Georgian inns and houses reflect the town's importance in stagecoach days and the steep main street features a number of old-fashioned family-run shops. In the cobbled market square, used for markets and fairs since 1296, The Fishstones are still to be seen – flat stone slabs set on stone uprights to form a broken circle which were the counters from which fish was sold.

TREALES

9 miles SE of Blackpool off the A583

Although the M55 runs close by, the village lies in an area of quiet country lanes, small woods, and farms. As well as the tastefully restored cottages, some of which have managed to retain their thatched roofs, this rural village's old windmill has also been converted into a beautiful home.

During World War II the village of Freckleton suffered an appalling tragedy. On a sweltering, thundery day in August 1944 an American Liberator plane took off from nearby Warton aerodrome but because of the adverse weather, the pilot decided to turn back. As the plane descended over Freckleton it clipped some trees and crashed into the village school. Thirty-six children and adults perished. A disaster fund was set up but villagers bitterly disagreed about how it should be spent. It wasn't until 33 years later that the money was used to build the village's Memorial Hall.

Lytham St Anne's has had its fair share of disasters associated with the sea. By far the worst of these occurred in 1886 and it is still Britain's greatest lifeboat disaster. The crew of the St Anne's lifeboat, with the help of the Southport lifeboat, set out to answer a distress signal put up by a German ship, the Mexico. *The sea was so rough that 15 members of the lifeboat crew were lost. The tragedy led to the improvement of lifeboat design. In the Alpine Garden on the Promenade is a monument which pays tribute to the men who lost their lives. The statue features the stone figure of a coxswain looking out to sea with a rope in one hand and a lifebelt in the other.*

FRECKLETON

9 miles SE of Blackpool on the A584

This is the largest village in the Fylde with a population of more than 7000. The name is derived from the Anglo-Saxon *Frecheltun* meaning 'an enclosed area' and this is how it featured in the *Domesday Book*. Situated on the northern banks of the River Ribble, the long straggling village was, until the river was canalised, surrounded by marshland.

CLIFTON AND SALWICK

11 miles SE of Blackpool off the A583

Both Salwick and its neighbour, Clifton, were formed from part of the old Clifton estate. As well as the pleasant walks along the banks of the canal, visitors can also enjoy the delights of The Windmill pub which is, unlike most pubs of that name, housed in a Grade II listed six-storey converted windmill.

LYTHAM ST ANNE'S

4 miles S of Blackpool on the A584

Located on the northern bank of the Ribble Estuary, Lytham St Anne's is based on a much older community, already well established by the time of the Norman Conquest. It has a short pier, a gracious Victorian Promenade, and an attractive grassy expanse called the Beach. Here stands a handsome white-washed windmill, one of very few to have survived from the days when the flat plain of the Fylde was dotted with hundreds of them.

There are actually two towns here: Lytham, which is mentioned in the *Domesday Book*, and St Anne's, which was largely developed in the 1870s as a rather upmarket resort. Before the development of the resort, in the Victorian age, Lytham was an important port on the Ribble estuary and was home to the first fishing company on this stretch of the northwest coast. Shipbuilding also continued here until the 1950s when the last vessel constructed in the shipyards was the Windermere Car Ferry. During the 1940s, parts of the famous Mulberry harbour were constructed in secret here in preparation for the invasion of Normandy in 1944.

The arrival of the railway linking Lytham with Preston prompted a group of Lancashire businessmen to plan the construction of a health resort between the old established port and the rapidly expanding town of Blackpool to the north. There was scarcely a cottage on their chosen site when the work began in 1875 but the growth of the carefully planned town was spectacular. In just 30 years the population increased from 1000 to 17,000 inhabitants.

The **Promenade**, running the full length of the seafront from St Anne's to Lytham was constructed in 1875 and on the landward side there are several fine examples of Victorian and Edwardian seaside villas. Beyond the attractive Promenade Gardens, laid out by a local character, Henry Gregson, is **St Anne's Pier**. Opened in 1885, the elegant pier was built in a mock

Tudor style and up until 1897 fishing smacks and pleasure boats were able to tie up at the end of the jetty. Lytham also had a pier, built in 1865, but during a gale in 1903 two sand barges dragged their anchors and sliced the structure in two. Undeterred, and with the Pavilion still standing at the far end, the pier was rebuilt only to be almost entirely destroyed by fire in 1928.

As well as being an elegant place full of fine Victorian and Edwardian architecture, Lytham St Anne's also contains some reminders of the more distant past. **Lytham Hall**, now privately owned by a large insurance company, started life as a farming cell of Durham cathedral in 1190. After the Reformation, the estate changed hands several times until in 1606 it became the property of Sir Cuthbert Clifton, the first squire of Lytham. The fine Georgian hall standing today was the building that John Carr of York built for Thomas Clifton between 1757 and 1764. The house is open to the public on Bank Holiday afternoons and guided tours are available on some Sunday afternoons. The extensive grounds, once part of the estate, are now **Lytham Hall Country Park**, where visitors can follow several nature trails to discover the birds and wildlife living here which includes three species of woodpecker, the lesser whitethroat, and the hawfinch.

There has been a **Windmill** at Lytham for more than 800 years though the present structure dates from 1805. A well known landmark along the coast, the building has a solid white tower with a cap that looks rather like an upturned boat. In 1929 the wind set the four sails turning the wrong way, ruining the machinery and firing the mill, which has never worked since. Now renovated, the windmill is home to a permanent exhibition on the building's history and on the process of breadmaking. Adjacent to the windmill, and the original home of the Lytham lifeboat, Old Lifeboat House is home to the **Lifeboat Museum**. Both buildings have limited opening times. Two other museums worthy of a visit are the **Lytham Motive Power Museum**, with its large model railway layout and an outdoor display of rolling stock, and the **Toy and Teddy Museum**, housed in the Porrit Victorian building with a varied collection of childhood memorabilia.

No description of Lytham St Anne's is complete without a mention of the **Royal Lytham and St Anne's Golf Course**. The club originated after a meeting held in 1886 when a group of 19 keen golfers sought to furnish themselves with suitable facilities. The course opened in 1898 and it is still considered by many to be one of the finest golf links in the country and is a regular host of the British Open - the next occasion is in July 2012.

For those interested in discovering more about the abundant wildlife of the dune system here, a visit to Lytham St Anne's Nature Reserve is a must. Established in 1968, the reserve is an important scientific site as well as being just a small part of what was once a very extensive sand dune system. As well as the rich plant life, the dunes are home to several rare species of migrating birds including osprey, black redstart, and Lapland buntings.

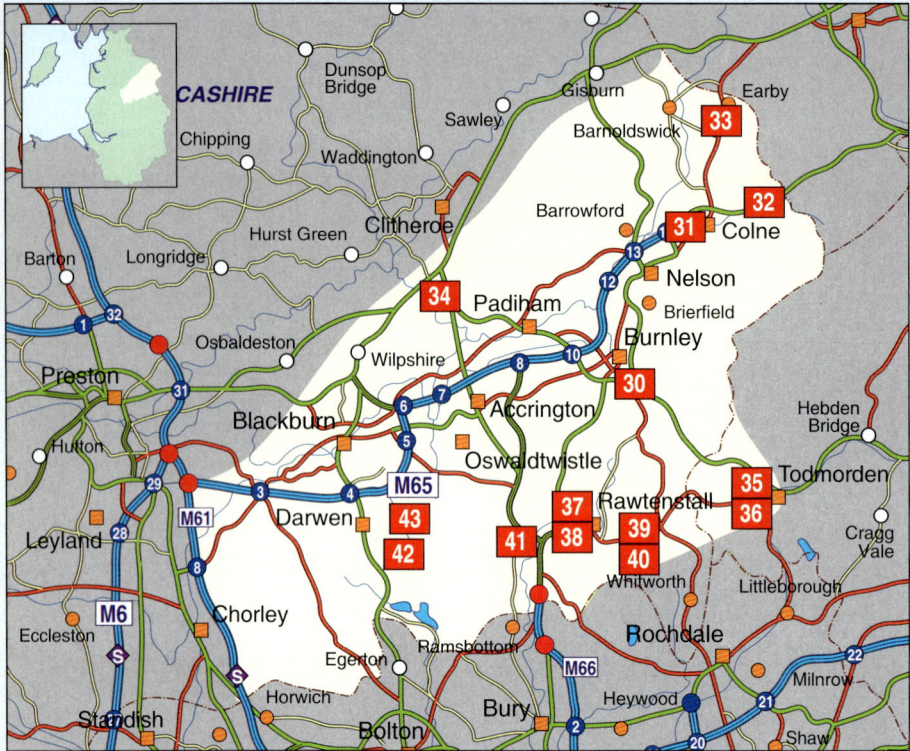

The Forest of Pendell and Rossendale

The Pennine Hills, the *"backbone of England"*, are such a well-known geographical feature that it comes as something of a surprise to find that the name was created as recently as 1750 by a fraudulent professor. Charles Bertram claimed to have discovered a medieval chronicle describing Britain as it was in Roman times. In this non-existent tome, he said, the Romans had named this range of hills 'Alps Penina' because they resembled the Apennine Hills of central Italy. The professor's fake chronicle was soon discredited but his spurious name, the 'Pennines', has been universally adopted.

In the 1720s, Daniel Defoe jogged on horseback through the area and wrote it off as 'a howling wilderness....the English Andes'. A century later the wild, poverty stricken area Defoe had travelled through was throbbing with the sound of churning mill wheels, its sky murky with the smoke of thousands of coal fuelled factories. That sooty, industrial image lingers on despite the fact that this area of Lancashire has re-invented itself in the past few decades. The waste from coalpits has been transformed into smoothly landscaped country parks and energetic local councils are also striving to make the most of the region's natural attractions: swooping hills, stark moorlands and contrasting wooded valleys.

But the area still takes pride in its industrial past, now recognised by its designation as an official Heritage Area. Bacup, for example, as well as being the highest town in Lancashire at 827ft above sea level, is also acknowledged by English Heritage as the best preserved cotton town in Britain. And the Queen Street Mill at Harle Syke near Burnley is the only surviving steam-powered cotton mill in the country. Here, more than 300 deafening Lancashire looms clatter away in the imposing weaving shed where hundreds of metres of cotton cloth are produced weekly. In Burnley itself, the Weavers Triangle is one of the finest examples of a Victorian industrial townscape still in existence.

Southeast Lancashire also possesses some grand buildings from an earlier era. Gawthorpe Hall at Padiham is a Jacobean gem; Towneley Hall, dating back to the 1400s, houses Burnley's excellent Museum & Art Gallery, and Turton Tower, north of Bolton, is a lovely old building which began as a medieval pele.

Despite its industrial history, the southern border of Lancashire boasts some attractive villages. Withnell Fold, 5 miles southwest of Blackburn, is an idyllic model village entirely built by the Parke family in the mid-1800s to house the workforce employed at their paper mill. Rivington, near Chorley, is a captivating small village set around a village green and alongside a huge reservoir beneath whose waters half of the old village lies submerged.

BURNLEY

This cotton town is rich in history as well as being the largest town in this area of East Lancashire. Incorporating some 50 square miles, the town offers visitors a wealth of contrasts, from some of the best preserved industrial landscapes in Britain to the magnificent, untouched moorlands just to the east. First established at the beginning of the 9th century, the town nestles in a basin between the River Calder and the River Brun, from which it takes its name.

With the Industrial Revolution and the building of the Leeds and Liverpool Canal, Burnley not only expanded but grew in stature until, by the end of the 19th century, it was the world's leading producer of cotton cloth. Burnley's fine Victorian **Town Hall** of 1888, is one of many monumental public buildings in the area erected during that period of unparalleled English prosperity.

A walk along the towpath of the canal, through an area known as the **Weavers' Triangle**, is like taking a step back in time. This is an area of spinning mills and weaving sheds; foundries where steam engines and looms were made; canal-side warehouses; domestic buildings, including a unique row of workers' cottages; and a Victorian school house. The Weavers' Triangle Visitors Centre is housed in the former wharf master's house and canal toll office. The centre is open to the public on several afternoons a week during the summer months and on most bank holidays. A short walk from the Visitors' Centre is **Oak Mount Mill** engine house. The splendid old steam engine, originally installed in 1887, has recently been restored and is now operated by electric motor. Opening times are variable.

Even more impressive is the **Queen Street Mill** which is the only surviving steam-powered cotton mill in Britain. A visit here provides a unique insight into Victorian factory life as the 300 deafening looms are powered by the magnificent steam engine, 'Peace'. The mill was recently designated by the government as a

Panopticon Singing Ringing Tree, Burnley

museum with an outstanding collection – one of only 53 in the country to receive the award.

The history of Burnley can also be explored by boat along the Leeds and Liverpool Canal. This famous waterway leaves the Weavers' Triangle via a huge embankment which carries the canal across the town. Known as the 'straight mile', it is in fact less than that but no less exciting and, at 60 feet above the ground, it is one of the most impressive features of the whole canal.

Located on the Todmorden Road on the outskirts of Burnley is the **Towneley Hall Art Gallery and Museum**. The home of the Towneley family since the 1300s, right up until 1902, the present building has parts that date from the 15th century. Its attractions include an impressive art collection, the Whalley Abbey Vestments and a museum of local crafts and industries. Tours of the house are available and take in the kitchens, with their open fires, the servants' hall, a priest's hole and some fascinating family rooms. Towneley Park, which surrounds the Hall, is Burnley's largest park and a popular site for local events and festivals. These include the annual Burnley Balloon Festival weekend in late July and Burnley May Day events. Just behind the hall there's a well-marked woodland trail which has numerous wooden carvings along the way. Subjects include a giant magpie, a crocodile emerging from the water, and a huge cricket. The park also boasts a very popular

children's playground with sandpits and rides galore, and an 18 hole golf course. The grounds also contain a natural history centre, a Museum of Local History and facilities for tennis, bowls and other outdoor pursuits.

Lovers of ghost stories will want to visit the **Rosehill Hotel** which has a resident ghost. She's called Rose and she was an employee at the hotel. In 1860, Rose had an affair with a relative of the hotel proprietor and became pregnant. This was an era when Victorian sexual morality was at its most rigid (and hypocritical). If Rose's illicit pregnancy became known, the hotel's reputation would suffer disastrously. Rose disappeared, completely. The hotel owner said she had been dismissed and left the town but those who knew of her condition suspected murder. Beneath the hotel there were cellars which were later filled with tons of rubble and it's believed that poor Rose was buried there, emerging from time to time when her successors as chambermaids were cleaning the rooms. She has been heard talking to herself about the daily chores to be done but otherwise has never troubled either the maids or the guests.

Overlooking the town, set high on Crown Point, is Burnley's striking **Panopticon**. This is one of a series of landmark sculptures set up by the East Lancashire Regional Park, starting in 2003. Four of these iconic structures, intended as symbols of the

30 TOWNELEY HALL ART GALLERY & MUSEUMS

Burnley

Towneley Hall offers the perfect day out for all the family - a country house, a museum and an art gallery all in one.

see page 180

53

31 THE CROWN HOTEL

Colne

A charming hotel set in the heart of the Yorkshire Dales serving the finest homemade cuisine and offering comfortable accommodation along with weekly entertainment

🍴 🛏 see page 184

32 THE EMMOTT ARMS

Laneshaw Bridge, Colne

A smart village inn, wonderfully welcoming and tastefully decorated, serving top notch food and a good choice of ales.

🍴 see page 185

renaissance of the area, are now in place in Blackburn, Pendle, Rossendale and Burnley. The design selected for Burnley's Panopticon was 'Singing, Ringing Tree' by architects Tonkin Liu. This unique musical sculpture makes the most of the prevailing westerly winds makes an intriguing, tuneful sound, audible only at relatively close range.

NORTH OF BURNLEY

NELSON

3 miles N of Burnley on the A56

Nelson merges with its neighbours Colne and Burnley as they share the same valley running along the length of Colne Water. Nelson is a modern textile town which takes its name from the hotel, The Lord Nelson, that stands by the railway line running along the valley bottom. Although the town itself might have been the product of the Industrial Age, two of its suburbs, Little and Great Marsden, have been here for centuries. Here, above Nelson, is **Marsden Park**,

and once Marsden Hall, the home of the de Walton family until their line died out in 1912. Acquired by the local authority, much of the hall was demolished whilst the parkland was developed.

COLNE

5 miles N of Burnley on the A56

Before the Industrial Revolution turned this area into a valley devoted to the production of cotton cloth, Colne was a small market town specialising in wool. Unfortunately, there are few reminders of the days before industrialisation although **St Batholomew's Church**, founded in 1122, is still here and contains some interesting interior decorations and furnishings. In the centre of the town, next to the War Memorial is another memorial. The statue is of Lawrence Hartley, the bandmaster on the ill-fated *Titanic* who, heroically, stayed at his post with his musicians and played *Nearer my God to Thee* as the liner sank beneath the waves of the icy Atlantic in 1912.

Colne is also the rather unlikely home of the **British in India Museum**, where exhibits covering many aspects of the British rule over the subcontinent, from the 17th century until 1947 can be seen. The collection includes coins, medals, uniforms, model soldiers and a working model of the railway from Kalka to Simla.

Collectors of curiosities will enjoy the unique form of punishment devised for minor malefactors in Colne and

Summer Meadow, Foulridge, nr Colne

preserved in the **Town Museum**. Stocks and pillories enjoyed a long history as a way of humiliating offenders and providing innocent amusement for bystanders. But many of Colne's busy citizens could not spare the time to leave their work and make their way to wherever the stocks were fixed. So a movable cart was constructed, capable of seating three offenders side by side, and the Town Beadle would wheel it around the town so that everyone could join in the fun.

Clam Bridge, Wycoller

WYCOLLER

6 miles NE of Burnley off the B6250

This hamlet lies amidst the moorlands that rise to the east of the textile towns of the Colne valley and extend up to the bleak summits of the Pennines. Now almost deserted, this was once a thriving place as an important centre for the wool trade and as a handloom weavers' settlement but it lost most of its inhabitants to the new factories in the west.

Fortunately, the place has been saved by the creation of **Wycoller Country Park**, surrounding the village, and many of the buildings have been restored. There is also a delightful old hump-backed packhorse bridge crossing a stream and, above the village, a single slab gritstone bridge, **Clam Bridge**, that is thought to date from the Iron Age. Now a ruin, **Wycoller Hall** was the inspiration for Ferndean Manor in Charlotte Brontë's *Jane Eyre*: Wycoller was one of the villages to which the

Wycoller Hall Ruins, Wycoller

Horses grazing, nr Earby

33 THE WHITE LION

Earby

A tranquil place, stooped in history, welcoming locals and visitors alike with a good pint and traditional home-cooked food.

see page 186

sisters walked from their house at Haworth.

A fairly recent addition to the Park's attractions is **The Atom**, Pendle's Panopticon which is one of a unique series of 21st century landmarks set up across East Lancashire as symbols of the renaissance of the area.

The unique, egg-shaped 'Atom' was designed by Peter Meacock with Katarina Novomestska and Architects WCW and was opened by the Mayor of Pendle in September 2006. The bronze-coated structure provides both a striking contemporary viewing point and shelter from which to enjoy the stunning surrounding landscape, and an intriguing and beautiful object which can be viewed from afar.

EARBY

10 miles NE of Burnley on the A56

The town lies almost on the county border with Yorkshire, indeed until 1971 it was part of North Yorkshire. Today, it is home to the **Earby Mines Museum** housed in the old Grammar School building.

It has the largest collection of lead mining tools and equipment used in the Yorkshire Dales on display, including examples of the minerals extracted, a lead crushing mill, and other working models.

PENDLE HILL

5 miles N of Burnley off the A6068

Dominating the landscape here is the great whale-backed mass of Pendle Hill, rising to 1920 feet above sea-level. The hill became notorious in the early 1600s as the location where the **Pendle Witches** supposedly practised their black arts. It has a more uplifting association, though, since it was from the summit of Pendle Hill in 1625 that George Fox saw a vision which inspired him to found the Society of Friends, or Quakers.

Pendle Hill lies at the heart of Lancashire's 'Witch Country', so called because of the events of 1612. On the 18th March of that year, a Halifax pedlar named John Law refused to give some pins to a beggar, Alison Device. She spat out the usual beggar's curse on him. He died almost immediately of a heart attack. The effect of a curse or just a co-incidence? The early 1600s were the years of the great witch-hunts so the authorities had little difficulty in attributing John Law's sudden death to Alison Device's supernatural powers.

Alison was arrested. Under torture, she incriminated eight other 'witches'. All of them were then charged with communing with the Devil and committing a total of sixteen murders. They were tried, found guilty and hanged at Lancaster Castle on August 20th, 1612. All except one: Old Mother Demdike, eighty years old and half-blind, escaped the gallows by dying in gaol. During their trial, the 'Pendle Witches' seem to have taken pride in implicating each other. In effect, they hanged themselves by their fanciful tales of spells, potions, and the coven's naked caperings, fuelling the popular imagination that there really were witches who could affect the lives of other people. The infamous witches were, in the main, old women who dabbled with plants and herbs, knowing which could heal and which, when ingested, would spell certain death.

The Victorian novelist W.H. Ainsworth was inspired to write a colourful melodrama based on the trial, *The Lancashire Witches – A Romance of Pendle Forest*, and although it's doubtful that 'witchcraft' was any more prevalent around Pendle Hill than anywhere else in the country at that time, the legend has proved very durable. Every year now, on the evening of October 31st, Halloween, Pendle Hill is flecked with the dark figures of masked, black-cloaked figures making their way to its summit.

The story of the Pendle Witches is known to everyone with an interest in the occult, but there has always been something of a mystery about why one of them, Alice Nutter, was involved. Unlike the others who were either very poor or even beggars, Alice was a lady of substance. She lived at

View from Barley, Pendle Hill

Roughlee Old Hall, a captivating Elizabethan manor house of 1576 which still stands (but is not open to the public). A recent theory is that she was a Roman Catholic and on her way to a clandestine service when she was caught up with the witches. To avoid betraying her co-religionists she kept silent about her real motives for being on Pendle Hill on the crucial night.

Something of this old, dark tragedy still broods over Pendle and many memories and places which hark back to those grim days remain. Those interested in finding out more about the trials should visit the **Pendle Heritage Centre** at **Barrowford**, to the southeast of the hill. The Centre is housed in a sturdy 17th century farmhouse built by the Bannister family, one of whose descendants was Roger Bannister, the first man to run a mile in less than four minutes.

To the west of Pendle hill's summit rises Apronfull Hill, a Bronze Age burial site, that is said to be the place from which the Devil threw stones at Clitheroe Castle, creating what is known as the Devil's Window.

An old tradition continues at Newchurch – the Annual Rushbearing when dry rushes are scattered on the church floor and in the pews. Originally this was to keep parishioners warm and although the advent of central heating makes it no longer necessary the villagers still process through the village carrying rushes and singing hymns accompanied by a brass band. A Rushbearing Queen is crowned and after a short service in the church everyone repairs to the school for a grand tea.

Historically, witches aside, the hill was one of the many beacon hills throughout the country that, forming a chain, were lit in times of national crisis, such as the sighting of the Spanish Armada.

NEWCHURCH-IN-PENDLE

4 miles N of Burnley off the A6068

This charming Pendle village was named following the consecration of a new church in 1544 by John Bird, Bishop of Chester. Earlier, during the Middle Ages, Newchurch was a cow and deer rearing centre, as well as part of the old hunting forest of Pendle but by the reign of Elizabeth I the area was becoming de-forested and farming was beginning to take over as the primary source of income.

Newchurch did not escape from stories of witchcraft that surrounded the notorious Pendle witches trial in the 17th century, and many ghostly tales and shadowy traditions are said to be associated with the village. You can find many of them explored at **Witches Galore**, a light-hearted look at the world of witches. Outside, two hideous old crones in pointed caps are huddled together, no doubt concocting diabolical spells. Inside, covens of witches on broomsticks fly above the customers; upside-down bats fix them with beady stares. The shop is crammed with a whole host of spooky merchandise, from gruesome gift ideas like model witches, Hallowe'en outfits, posters, pottery, T-shirts, CDs, maps, books, pictures, postcards and much more.

PENDLETON

6 miles NW of Burnley off the A59

Recorded in the *Domesday Book* when the village was part of the vast parish of Whalley, this small settlement of cottages and working farms has retained much of its traditional air – only seven new houses have been built here in the last 100 years. A beck runs through the middle of the village which was designated a Conservation Area in 1968. The discovery of a Bronze Age burial urn in the village in 1969 would indicate that there were settlers here as long ago as 1600BC.

From the village there is a steep road, to the southeast, that climbs up to the **Nick of Pendle** from where there are magnificent views.

PADIHAM

2 miles W of Burnley on the A646

This charming small town of narrow winding lanes and cobbled alleyways still retains characteristics typical of the early days of the Industrial Revolution. However, there was a settlement here long before the Norman Conquest and Padiham was also the market town for the western slopes of Pendle. A market is still held here every Wednesday and Friday.

One of Lancashire's most impressive stately homes is **Gawthorpe Hall** (National Trust) which stands on the bank of the River Calder, surrounded by gardens and woodland. The Shuttleworth family have lived at

Gawthorpe since the early 1400s but the present house is a gracious 17th century mansion, restored and extended in the 1850s by Sir Charles Barry. This was the era of High Victorian extravagance and no expense was spared on the opulent decorations and furnishings. The Hall has many pictures on loan from the National Portrait Gallery which add extra lustre to the already notable collection. Open to the public between Easter and October, the house has beautiful period furnishings, ornately decorated ceilings and the original wood panelled walls. It is also home to the nationally important Kay-Shuttleworth collection of fine needlework and lace.

READ

5 miles W of Burnley on the A671

Read is situated on the banks of the River Calder and it was during a skirmish near **Read Old Bridge** in April 1643 that the Royalist cause in Lancashire was lost.

Read Hall, privately owned and no longer in the hands of the original family, was the home of one of Lancashire's most famous families, the Nowells. It was Roger Nowell, in 1612, who committed the Pendle witches to trial. The Nowells left the hall in 1772 and in 1799 the house was completely rebuilt in the Georgian style seen today.

GREAT HARWOOD

6 miles W of Burnley on the B6535

Before the Industrial Revolution, this was a quiet village of farms and cottages nestling between two streams. Famous for its fine woollen cloth, at the beginning of the 19th century cotton handloom weaving and then, by the 1850s, the introduction of the factory system when the cotton mills took over. Today only one mill remains but at the industry's height the town supported 22 of them. Not surprisingly, Great Harwood's most famous son was very much linked with cotton. In 1850, John Mercer, an industrial chemist, developed the technique of processing cotton to give it a sheen and the technique, mercerisation, is still used today. The free-standing clock tower in the Town Square was erected in 1903 to commemorate Mercer's contribution to the life of his home town.

WHALLEY

7 miles W of Burnley on the B6246

One of Lancashire's most attractive villages, Whalley grew up around a crossing of the River Calder,

Two Stone Crosses, Whalley

Promising an exciting and educational experience, Aquascope situated in Great Harwood is home to 50 different species of fish, reptiles, amphibians, mammals and invertebrates. Popular residents include African pygmy hedgehogs, two black-tipped reef sharks and a Goliath bird-eating tarantula.

34 NUMBER 51

Whalley
A quaint, family run tea room, offering the most mouth watering delights in a pleasant, relaxing atmosphere.

see page 187

Whalley Abbey, Whalley

Whalley's Parish Church is almost a century older than the abbey, its oldest parts dating back to 1206. Built on the site of an even older place of worship, the churchyard is home to three ancient crosses and the church itself contains a set of some of the finest choir stalls anywhere. They were brought here from the abbey after the Dissolution and though they are not elaborate there are some intriguing carvings on the lower portions. Even more intriguing though are the puzzling tombstones in the churchyard, each one inscribed with impossible dates such as April 31st 1752 and February 30th 1839.

between Pendle Hill and the Nab. There are old cottages, Tudor and Georgian houses in the main street, and three out of the four inns at the crossroads date from the 1700s. Soaring above the village is the **Whalley Viaduct**, an impressive 48-arched structure built in 1850 to carry the Blackburn to Clitheroe railway line across the broad valley of the Calder. Rather touchingly, where the viaduct crosses the lane leading to **Whalley Abbey**, the arches have added Gothic details that harmonise with the nearby 14th century gatehouse to the abbey.

The abbey was started in the early 1300s and was the last to be built in Lancashire. The site at Whalley was not the first choice of the Cistercian monks whose work it was. They had already established a religious house at Stanlow, on the banks of the River Mersey, in 1172. That site now lies beneath a huge oil refinery.

Seeking somewhere less harsh and more fertile land, the monks moved to Whalley in 1296 but their attempts to build were hampered as Sawley Abbey felt threatened by the competition for the donations of land and goods expected from the local population. Building finally began in 1310 and by 1400 the imposing and impressive abbey had taken shape. The demise of the abbey came, as it did to all religious houses, under Henry VIII but Whalley's abbot, joining forces with the abbot of Sawley, took part in the Pilgrimage of Grace in an attempt to save their houses. This failed and both abbots were executed.

Now owned and cared for by the Church of England Diocese of Blackburn, Whalley Abbey is one of the best preserved such places in the country. It is set in beautiful grounds and its future is secure since it also acts as a conference centre and offers bed and breakfast accommodation.

RISHTON

7 miles W of Burnley on the A678

Originally a Saxon settlement, the name means the fortified village or dwelling place amid the rushes. During the Middle Ages, the village grew in importance as an early textile centre with the operation of its fulling mill. By the 1600s, Rishton had gained a name for the manufacture of linen cloth and in 1766 it became the first village to weave calico. As the Industrial Revolution advanced, the industry moved from the weavers' homes into newly built mills.

The manor of Rishton, once owned by the Petre family, was part of the larger estate of Clayton-le-Moors and the manor house, **Dunkenhalgh Hall**, is said to have been named after a Scottish raider called Duncan who made his home here. Elizabethan in origin, the hall is now a private hotel.

OSWALDTWISTLE

7 miles W of Burnley on the A679

This typical Lancashire textile town has produced many miles of cotton cloth over the years. The town can justifiably be considered the heart of the industry since it was whilst staying here, at what is now Stanhill Post Office, that James Hargreaves invented his famous 'Spinning Jenny' in 1764. Although he was forced to leave the area after sometimes violent opposition to his machine from local hand spinners, the town's prosperity is largely due to textiles and, in particular, calico printing. However, Oswaldtwistle is a much older settlement than its rows of Victorian terraced houses would suggest as the name means the boundary of the kingdom of Oswald, a 7th century Northumbrian king.

Oswaldtwistle Mills in Collier Street was one of the last working cotton mills in the country. Today, five of its former weaving mills, 88,000 sq ft in all, have been transformed into a unique shopping experience where visitors can buy everything from crafts to clothing, fabrics to furniture, gifts to glassware, and much more. There are more than 80 retail outlets as well as licensed cafes, restaurants and a functioning sweet factory. For younger visitors there's an outdoor play area, sand pit and, in the summer, donkey rides.

ACCRINGTON

5 miles SW of Burnley on the A680

This attractive Victorian market town, as is typical in this area, expanded as a result of the boom in the textile industry of the 18th and 19th centuries. Lancashire has a wealth of indoor markets but Accrington's enjoys the grandest surroundings, housed in the magnificent **Market Hall** built in 1868, the oldest in Lancashire. Accrington is also the place to visit for a real flavour of the old Lancashire: in April it hosts the Lancashire Food Festival, followed in May by the annual Clog Dancing Festival.

The town is also the home of the **Haworth Art Gallery** (free), one of the most appealing galleries in the country – a charming Jacobean-style house built in 1909 and set in beautiful parkland. The gallery owns the largest collection of Art Nouveau Tiffany glass in Europe with no fewer than 130 pieces on display. The collection was presented to the town by Joseph Briggs, an Accrington man who emigrated to New York and worked with Louis Tiffany for nearly 40 years. Briggs joined the studio in 1890 and rose through the company ranks to become the manager of the Mosaic department before finally becoming Tiffany's personal assistant. After the First World War, the fashion for Tiffany glassware waned and during the

Football fans may wish to visit Accrington Stanley FC where they can take a tour of the ground, walk around the stadium, stand on the terraces and buy team memorabilia from the club store.

61

economic depression of the 1920s Briggs was given the sad job of selling off the remainder of the Tiffany stock. Returning to his native Accrington in 1933 with his collection of glass, Briggs gave half to the town and distributed the remainder amongst his family.

Also worth a visit are the elegant glass-roofed Arcade of 1880 and the imposing Town Hall with its Corinthian portico. It was built in 1858 as the Peel Institute in memory of Prime Minister Sir Robert Peel whose family owned several mills in the area and were highly respected employers.

To the west of the town centre, the **Accrington Railway Viaduct** is another magnificent monument to Victorian builders. Erected for the former East Lancashire Railway it sweeps across the River Hyndburn in a graceful curve of 19 arches sixty feet high.

SOUTH OF BURNLEY

GOODSHAW

5 miles S of Burnley on the A682

Just to the north of Crawshawbooth in the small village of Goodshaw and set high above the main road stands **Goodshaw Chapel**, a recently restored Baptist house of worship that dates from 1760.

BACUP

7 miles S of Burnley on the A671

At 827ft the highest town in Lancashire, Bacup was built in the 19th century for the sole purpose of cotton manufacture. It remains one of the best examples of a textile town in England even though the town suffered more than most when the mills began to close. A stroll through the town centre will reveal carefully restored shops and houses, with the grander homes of the mill owners and the elegant civic buildings acting as a reminder of the town's more prosperous times. Also, look out for what is claimed to be the shortest street in the world – Elgin Street off the Market Place which is just 17ft long.

An excellent time to visit the town is during the Easter weekend when the town's famous troop of Morris dancers take to the streets. Known as the **Coconut Dancers**, their costume is unique and involves wearing halved coconut husks strapped to their knees and blackening their faces. The participants maintain that the correct name is 'Moorish' not 'Morris' Dancers, and that the tradition goes back to the times of the Crusades.

RAWTENSTALL

7 miles S of Burnley on the A682

Rawtenstall first developed as a centre of the woollen cloth trade with the work being undertaken by hand workers in their own homes before steam-powered mills were introduced in the early 1800s. The introduction of the cotton industry to the town happened at around the same time. Lower Mill, now a ruin, was opened in 1840 by the Whitehead brothers who were some of the area's first manufacturing pioneers. The **Weaver's Cottage**, purpose-built for a home weaver, is one of the last buildings remaining of its kind and is open to visitors at weekends during the summer.

Also in the town, and housed in a former Victorian mill owner's house called Oakhill, is the **Rossendale Museum**. Naturally, the area's industrial heritage is given a prominent position but collections of the region's natural history, fine art and furniture, and ceramics are on display too.

At one end of the town stands a new railway station which marks the end of a very old railway line – the **East Lancashire Railway**. Opened in 1846 and run commercially until 1980, when the last coal train drew into Rawtenstall, the line is now in the hands of the East Lancashire Railway Preservation Society. Running a passenger service (at weekends with additional summer services), the steam trains offer an enthralling 17 mile round trip along the River Irwell between Rawtenstall and Bury, via Ramsbottom. The railway also operates regular Red Rose Diner trains with Pullman style dining cars offering travellers a gourmet meal and an evening of pure nostalgia.

Rawtenstall itself is noted for having the only remaining temperance bar in Britain – Herbal Health on Bank Street which serves traditional drinks such as sarsaparilla or dandelion & burdock.

At Rawtenstall, you can also join the **Irwell Sculpture Trail**, the largest public art trail in the United Kingdom. New sculptures are appearing all the time and more than 50 regional, national and international artists are being commissioned to produce sculptures with an environmental theme. The Trail follows a well-established 33-mile footpath stretching from Salford Quays through Bury into Rossendale and on up to the Pennine Moors.

HASLINGDEN

7 miles S of Burnley on the A56

The market in this town, which serves much of the Rossendale Valley, dates back to 1676, when the charter was granted by Charles II. Tuesdays and Fridays, market days, still bring the town alive as people flock to the numerous stalls. In Victorian times a familiar figure at the market was Miles Lonsdale, better known as the Haslingden Miser. To avoid spending money on

Churchyard Plague Stone, Haslingden

38 CAFE ARTISAN

Rawtenstall
A contemporary top of the range venue by day and night, offering superb food and drink alongside the best entertainment for miles around.
see page 190

39 THE DUKE OF BUCCLEUGH

Rossendale
A pleasant welcoming inn serving fine food and quality ales. Well worth a visit if you're in the area.
see page 191

40 GLEN VALLEY GUESTHOUSE

Rossendale
A charming guesthouse offering 7 cosy guestrooms and home cooked evening meals if requested. Ideal for small functions.
see page 191

41 HELMSHORE MILLS TEXTILE MUSEUM

Helmshore

An 18th century water powered fulling mill and a Victorian cotton spinning mill, both in working order on one site.

see page 194

food he would gather up discarded fish heads from the fishmonger's and fry them up for an unpalatable, if inexpensive, meal. After his death in 1889 it was discovered that Miles owned stocks and shares worth more than £16,000 - about £1.2m in today's money.

HELMSHORE

8 miles S of Burnley on the B6214

This small town still retains much evidence of the early Lancashire cotton industry. Housed in an old cotton mill, is the Museum of the

Blackburn Cathedral, Blackburn

Lancashire Textile Industry, **Helmshore Mills Textile Museum**. The building dates from 1789 and was one of the first fulling mills to be built in the Rossendale area. It now contains collections that are designated as being of national importance: many are original machines, a number of which are still in working order and demonstrated on a regular basis.

CRAWSHAWBOOTH

5 miles SW of Burnley on the A682

Once an important settlement in the old hunting forest of Rossendale, the village's oldest house, Swinshaw Hall (now privately owned), is said to have played a part in the destruction of the last wild boar in England. The influence of non-conformists can still be seen in the village where a number made their home. The old **Quaker Meeting House** dates from 1716.

BLACKBURN

The largest town in East Lancashire, Blackburn is notable for its modern shopping malls, its celebrated three day market, its modern cathedral, and Thwaites Brewery, one of the biggest independent brewers of real ale in the north of England.

When the textile industry was at its most prosperous, Blackburn was the biggest weaving town in the world. At that time there were one hundred and twenty mills in operation, their multiple chimneys belching out soot and smoke.

Examples of the early machines, including James Hargreaves' Spinning Jenny and his carding machine, invented in 1760, can be seen at the **Lewis Textile Museum**, which is dedicated to the industry.

The town's **Museum and Art Gallery** has amongst its treasures several paintings by Turner, the Hart collection of medieval manuscripts, and the finest collection of Greek and Russian icons in Britain.

Mentioned in the *Domesday Book*, the town was originally an agricultural community before the production of first woollen and then cotton cloth took over. Much of the town seen today was built on the prosperity brought by the cotton trade, a fact symbolized on the dome of **St John's Church** (1789) where there's a weathervane in the shape of a weaving shuttle.

The town's old manor house, Witton House, has long since been demolished but the grounds have been turned into an excellent local amenity. The 480 acres of **Witton Country Park** contain nature trails through woodlands up on to heather covered hill tops. Closer to the town centre, the 60-acre **Corporation Park** is one of the county's most attractive urban parks.

HOGHTON

4 miles W of Blackburn on the A675

A group of hamlets with handloom weavers' cottages, during the 1600s Hoghton was a place where Roman Catholics still practiced their faith in defiance of the law. It was at **Arrowsmith House** that Edmund Arrowsmith said his last mass before being captured and sentenced to death for being a Catholic priest and a Jesuit.

Today, the village is best known as the home of Lancashire's only true baronial residence, **Hoghton Tower**, which dates from 1565. The de Hoghton family have owned the land in this area since the time of the Norman Conquest and the house was built in a style in keeping with their social position and importance. The famous banqueting hall, on the ground floor, is where James I is said to have knighted the Sir Loin of Beef in 1617. The name of the house is today rather misleading since the tower was blown up by Cromwell's troops in 1643 when they overran the Royalist garrison stationed here. Another famous visitor, who caused less disruption, was William Shakespeare who came to perform with William Hoghton's troupe of players. The grounds, too, are well

Houghton Tower, Houghton

Just to the south of the village of Tockholes lies Roddlesworth Nature Trail, a path that follows the line of an old coach drive. Along the trail can be found the ruins of Hollinshead Hall. Built in the 18th century and once very grand, its ruins were tidied up in the early 1990s. Fortunately, its wishing well has withstood the ravages of time and neglect. Located within a building reminiscent of a small Georgian chapel, the well dates back to medieval times when its waters were thought to cure eye complaints.

worth a visit and are as perfectly preserved as the house.

TOCKHOLES

3 miles SW of Blackburn off the A666

This interesting, textile village was once an isolated centre of nonconformism. Standing next to a row of cottages is the **United Reformed Chapel**, founded in 1662, though it has been rebuilt twice, in 1710 and in 1880. The **Parish Church** also has some unusual features. As well as the unique lance-shaped windows, there is an outdoor pulpit dating from the days when the whole congregation could not fit inside the building. Close to the pulpit is the grave of John Osbaldeston, the inventor of the weft fork, a gadget that allowed power looms to weave intricate patterns.

BRINDLE

5 miles SW of Blackburn on the B6256

Brindle is an ancient village with a church, **St James'**, which celebrated its 800 year anniversary in 1990. The church was originally dedicated to St Helen, the patron saint of wells. 'Bryn' is the Old English word for a spring and there are still numerous springs in the village.

WITHNELL FOLD

5 miles SW of Blackburn off the A674

A short walk from Brindle, crossing the Leeds and Liverpool Canal, is the village of Withnell Fold whose name comes from 'withy knool' – a wooded hill. It was developed as a model village

in the 1840s with 35 terraced cottages each with its own garden. The whole village was owned by the Parke family who also owned the cotton mills and paper mill for whose workers the houses were provided. The mills have long since closed but the old mill chimney still towers above the village. Withnell Fold does have a small claim to fame. The paper mill, built in 1844 overlooking the canal, was once the world's biggest exporter of high-quality bank note paper.

DARWEN

3 miles S of Blackburn on the A666

Some visitors to Darwen (pronounced *Darren* locally) may experience a sense of *déjà vu* since the town featured extensively in the BBC series *Hetty Wainthropp Investigates,* starring Patricia Routledge. Dominating the town from the west and situated high on Darwen Moor, is **Darwen Tower**, built to commemorate the Diamond Jubilee of Queen Victoria in 1897. The view from the top of the tower, which is always open, is enhanced by the height of the hill on which it stands (1225 feet) and with the help of the plaques at the top much of the Lancashire landscape, and beyond, can be identified.

A striking landmark, very visible from the tower, and standing in the heart of Darwen is the chimney of the **India Mill**. Constructed out of hand-made bricks, it was built to resemble the

Jubilee Tower, Beacon Hill

Hoddlesden

A traditional English pub serving a fine selection of excellent home cooked dishes and ales in a beautiful secluded location.

see page 192

Hoddlesden

A charming hotel and restaurant set in the most pleasant countryside serving excellent food and drink.

see page 193

campanile in St Mark's Square, Venice. Completed in 1867, it was at that time the tallest and most expensive in the country.

To the west of Darwen lies **Sunnyhurst Wood** and its visitor centre in the valley of a gentle brook that originates on Darwen Moor to the south. Acquired by public subscription in 1902 to commemorate the coronation of Edward VII this area of woodland, covering some 85 acres, is rich in both bird and plant life. The visitor centre, housed in an old keeper's cottage, has an ever changing exhibition and there is also the Olde England Kiosk, built in 1912, which serves all manner of refreshments.

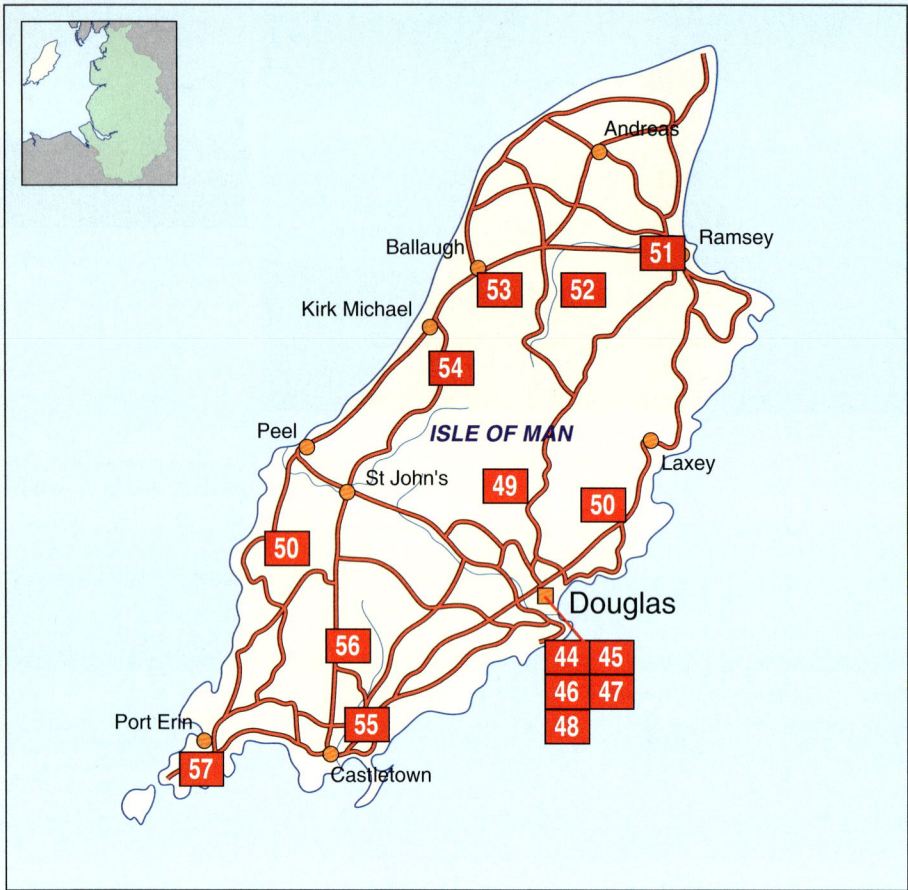

ISLE OF MAN

The Isle of Man

Although only 33 miles long and 13 miles wide, the Isle of Man contains a rich diversity of scenery and heritage and, perhaps best of all, exudes a sense of peacefulness epitomised by the Manx Gaelic saying: *traa-dy-liooar* – "Time enough".

Most British mainlanders are surprised to discover that the island is not part of the United Kingdom but a Crown Protectorate with the Queen as Lord of Mann represented in the island by the Lieutenant Governor. Its Parliament, the Tynwald, dates back more than a thousand years – the oldest continuous parliament in the world. The island issues its own coins and notes with the currency having an equivalent value to that of the UK. Recently issued coins include Harry Potter crowns (2001) and another crown marking the Chinese Year of the Horse, 2002. This island is perhaps best known for its annual TT motorcycle races, its tailless cat, Manx kippers, and as a tax haven for the wealthy. However, there is much more to this beautiful island which, set in the heart of the Irish Sea, is truly a world apart. With around 100 miles of coastline and several resorts, each with its own individual style and character, there is plenty to interest the visitor.

This magical place became an island around 10,000 years ago when the melt water of the Ice Age raised the sea level. Soon afterwards, the first settlers arrived, working and developing the island into the landscape seen today. The distinctive influences of the various cultures who have lived here still remain, leaving a land with a unique and colourful heritage.

Among the first arrivals were the Vikings and evidence of their era, from the early chieftains to the last Norse King, abounds throughout the island. Against the skyline on the seaward side of the road between Ballaugh and Bride are some ancient hilltop Viking burial mounds and, at the ancient castle in Peel, an archaeological dig revealed many hidden Viking treasures which are now on display at the Manx Museum in Douglas.

Despite their reputation for plunder, rape, and pillage, the Vikings also made some positive contributions to life on the island, not least of which was the establishment of the Manx governmental system, known as Tynwald. The Manx name for Tynwald Hill is 'Cronk Keeill Eoin', the hill of St John's Church. Although there is no evidence to confirm the story that it contains earth from all of the 17 parish churches here, it is not unlikely that token portions of soil were added to the mound in accordance with Norse tradition.

The Tynwald ceremony continues today with an annual meeting of the island's governors on Midsummer's Day at the ancient parliament field at St John's, where Manx citizens can also petition parliament. The island's famous three-legged symbol seems to have been adopted in the 13th century as the armorial bearings of the native Kings of the Isle of Man, whose dominion also included the Hebrides. After 1266, when the native dynasty ended and control of the island passed briefly to the Crown of Scotland and then permanently to the Crown of England, the emblem was retained, and among the earliest surviving representations are those on the Manx Sword of State, thought to have been made in 1300. The Three Legs also appeared on Manx coinage from the 17th to the 19th century, and are still seen in everyday use in the form of the official Manx flag.

Why the Three Legs were adopted as the Royal Arms of the Manx Kingdom is unknown. Many heraldic emblems have no meaning and are simply chosen because they are distinctive. This may be the case with the Three Legs, though the emblem as such - something between a cross and a swastika - has a long history reaching far back into pagan times and was originally a symbol of the sun, the seat of power and light.

44 MANX ELECTRIC RAILWAY

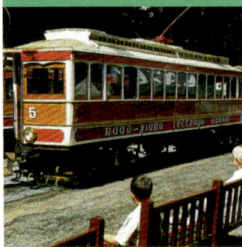

Douglas

From Douglas, the Manx Electric Railway takes you along the east coast to Laxey.

🏛 see page 194

45 TERMINUS TAVERN

Douglas

This is a great property with great character and great food. Definitely one worth visiting.

🍽 see page 195

46 COPPERFIELDS OLDE EDWARDIAN RESTAURANT

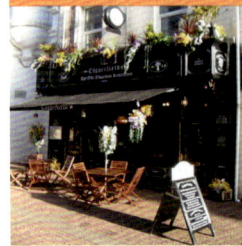

Douglas

This property is a truly splendid experience- a must for all visiting the Isle of Man.

🍽 see page 196

DOUGLAS

The island's capital, Douglas is also a lively resort with a sweeping sandy beach and a two-mile long promenade, the focus of the island's nightlife. There's excellent shopping around Strand Street, a fine park, Noble's Park, on the edge of town with facilities for tennis, bowls, putting, crazy golf and a children's play area. Other attractions include the magnificently restored Victorian Gaiety Theatre, the Manx Superbowl, a casino, the Summerland sport and leisure centre which hosts live entertainment during the summer, a cinema complex and an Aquadrome.

From dawn to dusk, visitors can take a leisurely ride along the wonderful promenade aboard the **Douglas Bay Horse Tramway**, a remarkable and beautiful reminder of a bygone era. It was the brainchild of a civil engineer, Thomas Lightfoot, who retired to the island and, seeing the need for a public transport system along this elegant promenade, designed in 1876 the system still in use today. That the Douglas Tramway has survived into the 21st century is remarkable especially since, in the early 1900s, attempts were made to electrify the line and extend the Manx electric railway along the promenade.

There is a story often told about the horses that pull the trams, which concerns a parrot that lived in a cage at a hotel close to one of the tram's stops. The bird learnt to mimic the sound of the tram's starting bell and used to practise this skill constantly. The tram horses would stop at the pick-up point, the parrot would immediately make the sound of the starting bell and the horses would start off again before the passengers could alight.

Another delightful means of travel is the narrow-gauge Victorian **Steam Railway** that runs between Douglas and Port Erin. Following

Douglas Bay

the line of the cliff tops, the memorable journey also travels through bluebell woods and through steep-sided rocky cuttings. This section of line is all that remains of a railway that once served the whole of the island. Many miles of the old railway network have been developed as footpaths. From Quarterbridge in Douglas **The Heritage Trail** is a 10.5 mile former railway route that cuts across the island to Peel on the west coast. It's a scenic but undemanding trail that passes close to historic Tynwald Hill. Picnic sites and useful information boards are situated along the way.

The Isle of Man's most famous export is probably the Manx cat, notable for having no tail. There are several stories of how the cat lost its tail but one, in particular, is delightful. At the time that Noah was building the Ark there were two Manx cats, complete with tails. Noah sent for all the animals to come to the Ark, two by two, but the Manx cats replied that there was plenty of time and continued to play outside. Finally, when the cats did decide to board the Ark, Noah was just slamming the door and the cats lost their tails. A variation on this tale is that one of the cats reached the Ark safely, the other had its tail chopped off by the closing doors. The tailless cat went on to become the Manx cat and the one who managed to keep its tail became the ever grinning Cheshire cat.

No trip to the island is complete without a visit to the

Manx Electric Railway, Douglas

Manx Museum where the award-winning *Story of Mann* audio-visual presentation uncovers 10,000 years of the island's history. The Manx Museum complex also contains the superb National Art Gallery, the National Library & Archives, as well as exhibits portraying many other aspects of life on the island, including the famous TT races.

One of the Isle of Man's most famous landmarks, the **Tower of Refuge**, looks out over Douglas Bay. Sir William Hilary, founder of the Royal National Lifeboat Institution, lived in a mansion overlooking the bay. In 1830 there was a near disaster when the Royal Mail Steam Packet *St George* was driven on to rocks in high seas, Hilary launched the Douglas lifeboat. Miraculously, all the crew of the *St George* were saved without the loss of one lifeboat man despite the extremely treacherous conditions. It was following this incident that Hilary decided that a form of refuge should be built for shipwrecked mariners to shelter in. Hilary himself laid the foundation

The Manx Electric Railway, completed in 1899, is the longest narrow-gauge vintage line in the British Isles and operates the oldest working tramcars in the world. The 18 mile journey departs from the northern end of Douglas promenade, stops at Laxey, terminus of the Snaefell Mountain Railway, and then continues to Ramsey.

47 THE SEFTON

Douglas

A first class hotel enjoying spectacular views over Douglas Bay, oozing luxury and serving the finest mouth-watering cuisine one could wish for.

see page 197

71

stone in 1832 for the Tower of Refuge which was built on Conister Rock out in the bay.

Perched on a headland overlooking Douglas Bay is a camera obscura known as the **Great Union Camera**. The camera was originally situated on the old iron pier, but when this was demolished in the 1870s the camera was re-sited on Douglas Head. In the camera, the natural daylight is focused on to a white panel through a simple system of lenses and angled mirrors and so provides a living image of the scene outside. At first apparently still, as with a photograph, viewers soon become fascinated as the 'picture' begins to move.

NORTH OF DOUGLAS

PORT GROUDLE

3 miles N of Douglas on the A11

Close to Port Groudle lies **Groudle Glen**, a deep and in places rocky valley with a bubbling stream running through its length. Excellent specimens of beech grow in the upper sections of the glen whilst, lower down, pines and larches are abundant. There is also a small waterwheel in the lower half of the glen. Railway enthusiasts will be delighted to learn that on certain days in the summer the **Groudle Glen Railway** operates. Running on a track just 2ft wide for three-quarters of a mile along the cliffs, the railways lovingly restored carriages are pulled by Sea Lion, the original 1896 steam engine.

LAXEY

5 miles N of Douglas on the A2

Set in a deep, wooded valley, this village is one of interesting contrasts. Following the river up from its mouth at the small tidal harbour leads the walker into **Laxey Glen**, one of the island's 17 National Glens that are preserved and maintained by the Forestry Department of the government.

Great Laxey Wheel, Laxey

Further up the glen is one of the island's most famous sights, the **Great Laxey Wheel** that marks the site of a once thriving mining community. Known as the Lady Isabella Wheel, with a circumference of 228 feet, a diameter of 72 feet, and a top platform some 72 feet off the ground, it is the largest working waterwheel in the world.

It was Robert Casement, an engineer at the mines, who constructed this mechanical wonder and designed it to pump 250 gallons of water a minute from a depth of 200 fathoms. Officially opened in 1854, it was named the Lady Isabella after the wife of the then Lieutenant Governor of the Isle of Man. After considerable repair and reconstruction work, the wheel now operates just as it did when it first opened and it stands as a monument to Victorian engineering as well as the island's industrial heritage.

The largest known megalithic tomb on the island lies in the garden of a private cottage. The Cairn (a conical heap of stones built as a monument or a landmark) grave is made of coloured sandstone and contains three chambers once filled with burials. When excavated only one burial and bowl survived. **King Orry's Grave**, as it is commonly known, tells something of the residents who lived on the Isle of Man during the Neolithic times over 4000 years ago. The site was built by farmers as a memorial to their ancestors. Ceremonies held on

King Orry's Grave, Laxey

the site left traces of hearth and flint.

Situated above Laxey, in a beautiful natural glen, are the magnificent **Ballalheanagh Gardens**. The valley, of steep sides with winding paths and a crystal clear stream running through the bottom, is packed with rhododendrons, shrubs, bulbs, and ferns - in all, more than 10,000 plants.

RAMSEY

12 miles N of Douglas on the A18

The second largest town in the island, Ramsey occupies a scenic location at the foot of North Barrule. This northernmost resort on the island has a busy working harbour, a long stretch of beach and a wide promenade. A popular amenity is **Mooragh Park**, a 40-acre expanse of gardens and recreational facilities with a 12-acre boating lake and lakeside café. During the summer months there's live musical entertainment in the park and around the third week of July each year the park is

51 GOPHERS COFFEE SHOP

Ramsey

A splendid, comfy, little cafe with such a delicious variety of homemade fayre that visitors find themselves returning time and time again!

see page 200

Ramsey is the northern terminus of the Manx Electric Railway, built in 1899. The Manx Electric Railway Museum tells the fascinating story of this world-famous Victorian transport system. From Ramsey the railway follows a scenic route southwards to Douglas, accompanied most of the way by the equally delightful coastal road, the A15/A2.

one of several venues hosting events during Yn Chruinnaght, an inter-Celtic festival of music, dance and literature.

Other major crowd-pullers are the Round the Island Yacht Race, held each summer and starting and finishing in Ramsey, and the Ramsey Motorcycle Sprint, part of the T.T. festival, when bikers show off their skills along Mooragh Promenade.

In the mid-1800s the town assumed the title of "Royal Ramsey" following an unscheduled visit by Queen Victoria and Prince Albert in 1847. The royal yacht anchored in Ramsey Bay following a stormy crossing from Scotland so that the seasick Queen could recover. While Her Majesty recuperated on board, Prince Albert walked to the top of Lhergy Frissel and was much impressed by the view. A few years later the Albert Tower was erected to commemorate the Prince Consort's visit.

Just to the north of the town is the **Grove Rural Life Museum**, housed in a pleasantly proportioned Victorian house. Built as the summer retreat of Duncan Gibb, a wealthy Victorian shipping merchant from Liverpool, and his family, the rooms within the house have all been restored to their Victorian splendour. The outbuildings contain an interesting collection of vehicles and agricultural instruments that were seen on Manx farms in the late 1800s.

For serious walkers, there's the **Millennium Way** which starts about a mile from Parliament Square in Ramsey. Established in

1979 to mark the millennium year of the Tynwald parliament, the 28-mile-long path passes through some magnificent countryside, picturesque towns and villages, before ending at the island's former capital, Castletown.

POINT OF AYRE

18 miles N of Douglas on the A16

This is the northernmost tip of the island and, not surprisingly, there is a lighthouse situated here. The area around the point is known as **The Ayres** and, at the Ayres Visitor Centre, a whole wealth of information can be found about this fascinating part of the island. In the inland heath moorland, a variety of species of birds can be found nesting whilst, on the pebbled beaches, terns can be seen. The offshore sandbanks provide a plentiful supply of food for both the diving gannets and the basking grey seals.

ANDREAS

15 miles N of Ramsey on the A17

Andreas was originally a Viking settlement and the village church contains intricately carved crosses dating back to the days of these early occupants. The church tower's truncated spire dates back to the 1940s when part of it was removed in case it proved to be dangerous to aircraft from the nearby wartime airfields.

SULBY

11 miles N of Douglas on the A3

Located in the heart of the island, Sulby lies on the famous TT course, a circular route on the island's roads that takes in Douglas, Ramsey, Kirk Michael, and St John's. There are several scenic and picturesque walks from the village which take in **Sulby Glen** and **Tholt-y-Will Glen**, both of which are renowned beauty spots. Another route, to the south, crosses over moorland to Sulby reservoir. Bird watchers particularly will enjoy the walks over the higher ground as it provides the opportunity to see hen harriers, kestrels, peregrines and curlews.

BALLAUGH

7 miles W of Ramsey on the A3

Ballaugh also lies on the TT race course and is close to the island's most extensive area of marshland, the perfect habitat for a range of birds, including woodcock and grasshopper warbler, as well as being the largest roost for hen harriers in Western Europe.

Situated on the edge of the Ballaugh Curraghs, **Curraghs Wildlife Park** is home to a wide variety of wetland wildlife that come from all over the world. Curraghs is the Manx word for the wet, boggy, willow woodland that is typical of this part of the island and the site, which was opened in 1965, gives visitors the opportunity to see the animals in their natural environments. This world-renowned wildlife park has been divided into several different habitats, including The Pampas, The Swamp, The Marsh, and the Flooded Forest, and here

endangered animals from around the world, such as Canadian otters, Spider monkeys, Rhea and Muntjac deer, live as they would in the wild.

The Curraghs Wildlife Park also has an enviable breeding record and, as many of the species are becoming rare in the wild, this is a very important aspect of the park's work. Not only have they successfully bred bald ibis, one of the most endangered birds in the world, but tapirs, lechwe antelope and many others also flourish in this environment. Not all the animals and birds are exotic – there are a great number of native species to be seen here too.

Visitors to the park are able to wander around the various habitats, following well laid out paths. There is also an adventure play area for young children and, during the summer, a miniature railway runs around the park. The lakeside café is open during the day for refreshments and, during the main summer season when the park is open until 9pm, barbecues are held here.

KIRK MICHAEL

10 miles N of Douglas on the A3

Close to the village lies **Glen Wyllin**, another of the island's 17 National Glens, and one that certainly deserves exploration. The varied woodland contains elm, ash, sycamore, alder, beech, lime, holm oak and chestnut and in spring the woodland floor is carpeted with bluebell, primrose, wood anemone and wild garlic. Kirk Michael also

52 GINGER HALL HOTEL

Sulby

A lovely property with great Bed and Breakfast situated in a historic part of the Isle of Man.

see page 201

53 THE RAVEN

Ballaugh

Public house, which specialises in traditional Thai cooking. A truly amazing property that's great value for money.

see page 201

54 THE OLD STABLE

Kirk Michael

This is a top-notch accommodation, perfect for family getaways. Also renowned for being great on the Island - a real gem.

see page 202

Recent archaeological excavations have discovered exciting new evidence relating to the long history of Peel Castle. One of the most dramatic finds was the Norse grave of a lady of high social status buried in pagan splendour. The jewellery and effects buried with her can be seen on display, with other excavation finds, at the Manx Museum. The castle is also said to be haunted by the Black Dog, or Mauthe Dhoo. On dark windy nights, it can be heard howling in the castle's dungeons.

lies on a 16 mile footpath that follows the route of an old railway line from Peel to Ramsey. After following the coast, and part of the Raad ny Foillan, the footpath branches off through pastoral countryside before reaching the port of Ramsey on the other side of the island.

WEST OF DOUGLAS

PEEL

12 miles W of Douglas on the A1

Located on the western side of the island, Peel is renowned for its stunning sunsets and the town is generally regarded as best typifying the unique character and atmosphere of the Isle of Man. Traditionally the centre of the Manx fishing industry, including delicious oak-smoked kippers and fresh shellfish, Peel has managed to avoid any large scale developments. Its narrow winding streets exude history and draw the visitor unfailingly down to the busy harbour, sweeping sandy beach, and magnificent castle of local red sandstone.

Peel Castle, one of the Isle of Man's principal historic monuments, occupies the important site of St Patrick's Isle. The imposing curtain wall encircles many ruined buildings, including St Patrick's Church, the 11th century Round Tower and the 13th century Cathedral of St Germans – the cathedral of Sodor and Mann and the very first diocese established in the British Isles, pre-dating even Canterbury. The great curtain wall also encloses the later apartments of the Lords of Mann. In the 11th century the castle became the ruling seat of the Norse Kingdom of Man and the Isles, first united by Godred Crovan – the King Orry of Manx folklore. Today, the castle provides a dramatic backdrop for a variety of plays and musical events during the summer.

Peel Castle, Peel

Connoisseurs of kippers speak highly of the tasty Manx kipper. At **Moore's Traditional Museum** you can watch a kipper curing process that remains unchanged since the late 1700s. Another major museum is **The House of Manannan**, a state of the art heritage attraction which was voted British Isles Museum of the Year in 1998. And for those researching their family history, **The Leece Museum** has an archive of documents and photographs of the town along with a varied display of artefacts connected with the life of a busy fishing port. One final museum, the **Manx Transportation Museum** has displays of various kinds of vehicles that have been used on the island over the years.

Round Tower, Peel

ST JOHN'S

3 miles E of Peel on the A1

Roads from all over the island converge at the village of St John's because this is the site of the ancient **Tynwald Day Ceremony**, held on July 5th which is a public holiday throughout the island. This grand open-air event takes place on Tynwald Hill just north of the village. Here the Tynwald Court – a parliament that can trace its origins to the 9th century – assembles and the new laws of the land are proclaimed in both Manx and English. The serious business over, the rest of the day is devoted to various celebrations and activities culminating in a firework display.

Adjoining Tynwald Hill, the 25 acre **Tynwald Arboretum** was established in 1979 to mark the millennium of the island's parliament.

GLENMAYE

3 miles S of Peel on the A27

A spectacular bridged gorge and waterfall dominate this glen which is one of the most picturesque on the island. Comprising more than 11 acres, its beautiful sheltered woodland includes some relics of the ancient forests that once covered much of the Isle of Man. Another feature of this glen is the **Mona Erin**, one of the many waterwheels which once produced power for the Manx lead mines.

DALBY

4 miles S of Peel on the A27

Just southwest of Dalby village, **Niarbyl Bay** takes its name from the Manx Gaelic, Yn Arbyl, meaning "the tail", so named because of the long reef that curves out from the shoreline. There are stunning views to the north and south, and the grandeur of the south-western coast is seen

50 NIARBYL CAFE

Dalby

This welcoming cafe is surrounded by beautiful scenery and is well worth a visit especially for those who enjoy a coastal walk.

see page 199

77

Niarbyl Bay, Dalby

Calf Sound, the stretch of water between the Calf Of Man and the Isle of Man has seen many ships pass through and it was here that the largest armada of Viking longships ever assembled in the British Isles congregated before setting off to invade Ireland. Centuries later, men from nearby Port St Mary were granted a gallantry medal by Napoleon, thought to be the only such medal he presented to British subjects. They had gone to the rescue of the crew of the St Charles schooner from France which had foundered in the sound.

at its best from this typically Manx setting. The beach here is an ideal place for picnics, relaxing and enjoying the tranquillity of the setting.

PORT ERIN

16 miles S of Peel on the A5

Situated between magnificent headlands, Port Erin's beach is certainly a safe haven. It is also a place of soft sands cleaned daily by the tide with rock pools to one side and a quay to the other. A long promenade above the sheltered sandy beach has a number of cafés and other amenities including bowls, tennis and putting. Nearby is Rowany golf course and there are some superb walks along coastal paths out to Bradda Head. Port Erin is also the terminus for the Steam Railway which runs from here to Douglas.

The town has its own Erin Arts Centre which since 1975 has hosted the annual **Manannan International Festival of Music and the Arts**, now recognized as one the island's most prestigious cultural events. The two week long festival takes place from mid to late June and the eclectic programme ranges through classical music, opera and ballet, jazz and theatre, to films, Indian music and art exhibitions as well as special events for children.

CALF OF MAN

18 miles S of Peel

This small islet of just 616 acres, situated just off the southwestern tip of the island, is now a bird sanctuary owned by the National Trust. The puffins should be grateful – one of the previous owners, the Dukes of Athol, requested that his tenants living on the Calf pickled the nesting puffins!

In 1777, a stone was found on the isle in the garden of Jane's Cottage, though in those days it was called The Mansion. Known as the **Calf Crucifixion Cross**, the stone is believed to date from the 8th century and it is one of the earliest Christian finds in Europe. The cross can be seen in the Manx Museum in Douglas.

In 2002, a new **Visitor Centre** was opened at the southernmost top of the island. The scenic 4 acre site also has a shop, café and car park and provides grand views of Spanish Head, the Calf of Man and the Irish Mountains of Mourne.

CREGNEASH

19 miles S of Peel off the A31

Perched close to the southwestern tip of the island this village is now a living museum, **Cregneash**

Village Folk Museum, which offers a unique experience of Manx traditional life within a 19th century crofting community. The farms here are maintained with horsepower and much of the livestock roam free. Traditional crafts and trades are practised and used in everyday life, keeping the past alive.

Cregneash's isolated position led the village to become one of the last strongholds of the island's ancient skills and customs and all this is beautifully preserved today.

By combining small scale farming with other occupations, a small settlement of Manx men and women have successfully prospered here since the mid 1600s. In the carefully restored buildings, visitors can see the conditions in which they lived and managed to sustain life in this rugged landscape. The centrepiece of Cregneash is without doubt **Harry Kelly's Cottage**. Kelly, who died in 1934, was a renowned Cregneash crofter and a fluent speaker of the Manx language. Opened to the public in 1938, his cottage, still filled with his furniture, is an excellent starting point to any tour of the village. There are various other buildings of interest, including Turner's Shed, a smithy, and the Karran Farm.

The village is also one of the few remaining places where visitors get a chance to view the unusual Manx Loaghtan four-horned sheep, a breed which, thanks to Manx National Heritage and other interest groups, now has a secure future.

BALLASALLA

7 miles SW of Douglas on the A25

In the village of Ballasalla is **Rushen Abbey** – the most substantial medieval religious site in the Isle of Man. This ancient Cistercian monastery now has an interpretive centre that explains the abbey's past importance and illustrates the daily life of the monks.

Monks Bridge, Ballasalla

55 THE WHITESTONE INN

Ballasalla

A comfortable Country Inn serving a variety of hearty, home cooked dishes where customers can relax and enjoy excellent service.

see page 202

56 SILVERDALE GLEN RESTAURANT & TEA ROOMS

Ballasalla

A quaint Tearoom situated in a historic part of the Isle of Man. Popular with locals and visitors, the cream teas are delicious.

see page 204

Rushden Abbey, Ballasalla

A couple of miles along the A5 road towards Douglas, visitors should look out for the **Fairy Bridge**. For centuries, Manx people have taken no chances when it comes to the little people and it is still customary to wish the fairies who live under the bridge a "Good Morning" when crossing.

CASTLETOWN

10 miles SW of Douglas on the A7

The original capital of the island, Castletown is full of character and charm, especially around the harbour area with its narrow streets and small fishing cottages.

Here, in August, is held the **World Tin Bath Championship**, one of the sporting world's more bizarre contests, as well as snake racing and many other aquatic events.

The harbour lies beneath the imposing battlements of the finely preserved **Castle Rushen**, once home to the Kings and Lords of Mann. The present building was mostly constructed between 1340 and 1350 and has recently been restored to provide today's visitors with a vivid impression of what life was like in the fortress many years ago by presenting in authentic detail the sights, sounds and smells of its heyday. Among the various points of interest is a unique one-fingered clock that was presented to the castle by Elizabeth I in 1597 and which still keeps perfect time.

The castle is still used as a courthouse, for the swearing-on of new governors, and for registry office weddings. During the summer months there are regular spectacular displays re-enacting scenes from the castle's history, especially the events of 1651 when Royalists were forced to surrender Castle Rushen to Cromwell's parliamentary troops.

Like Peel Castle, Rushen too is said to be haunted, by a ghost known as the White Lady. Believed to be the ghost of Lady Jane Grey who travelled to the island from Scotland with her family, the spectre has been seen walking the battlements at night and occasionally passing straight through the castle's closed main gate during the day.

Also recently restored to its 19th century state of grace is the **Old House of the Keys**, the seat of the Manx parliament until it removed to Douglas in 1874. In the rather cosy former debating chamber, visitors can vote on various issues which the parliament faced in the past, and some they may face in the future.

Castletown is also home to the island's **Nautical Museum**, where the displays centre around the 1791 armed yacht *Peggy* which sits in a contemporary boathouse. Part of the original building is constructed as a cabin room from the time of the Battle of Trafalgar and there are many other artefacts on display, all with a maritime theme.

A mile or so northeast of Castletown is Ronaldsay, the island's principal airport and close by is the **Aviation Military Museum**. Here, the exhibition rooms have been arranged to represent military, civil, and wartime aviation. There are guns, uniforms, photos, facts, stories, and aircraft parts. A recent addition to the museum tells the story of the Manx Regiment, the 15th Light Anti Aircraft Regiment Royal Artillery, which saw active service during World War II.

The Sugarloaf, nr Port St Mary

PORT ST MARY

13 miles SW of Douglas off the A31

This delightful little working port has both an inner and outer harbour, two piers, and excellent anchorage for visiting yachts. The beach, along a scenic walkway from the harbour, is no more than two miles from the beach at Port Erin but it faces in almost the opposite direction and lies in the most sheltered part of the island.

One of the finest walks on the Isle of Man is the cliff-top route from Port St Mary to Port Erin along the **Raad ny Foillan** - the road of the gull - a long distance footpath that follows the coastline right around the island. From Port St Mary, the first part of the walk takes in **The Chasms**, gigantic vertical rifts that, in some places, descend the full 400 feet of the cliffs.

57 THE SHORE HOTEL

Gansey

A warm, friendly hotel with a stunning location overlooking the sea, where visitors can enjoy well renowned, fresh wholesome food and locally brewed ale.

see page 203

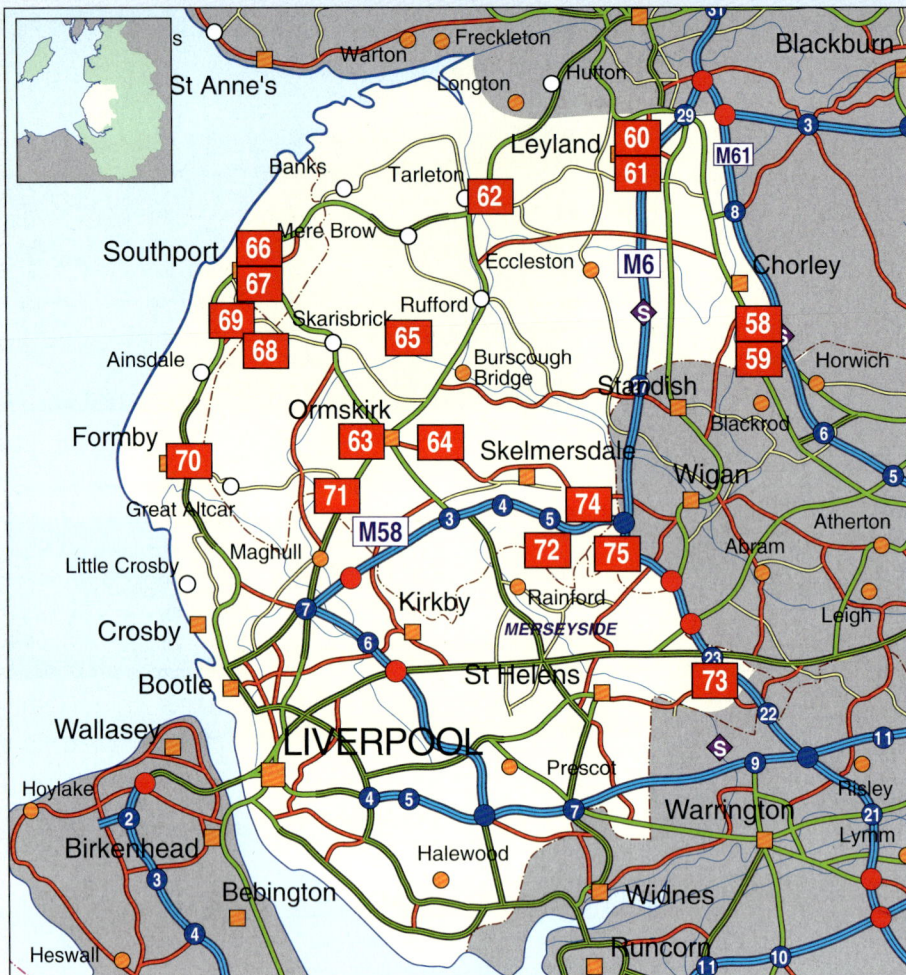

West Lancashire

This area of Lancashire, with its sandy coastline and flat fertile farmland, is home to the elegant Victorian seaside resort of Southport, the ancient market towns of Chorley and Ormskirk, and Wigan, another ancient place with a rich industrial past. Following the reorganisation of the county boundaries in the 1970s and the creation of Merseyside, much of the coast and the south-western area of Lancashire became part of the new county but the individual character and charm of this area has certainly not been lost.

The broad promenades of Southport, its elegant tree-lined streets, and its superb shopping makes it one of the most visited towns in this region. The silting up of the Ribble estuary has created a vast expanse of sand dune and pine forest that is now an important nature reserve.

Behind the coast, the flat lands of the West Lancashire plain were once under water.

Drainage by means of an extensive network of ditches has provided the old towns and quaint villages with rich fertile land that now produces a wealth of produce all year round and roadside farm shops are very much a feature of the area.

Although there are several rivers flowing across the land, the chief waterway, which is hard to miss, is the Leeds to Liverpool Canal. Linking the port of Liverpool with industrial Leeds and the many textile villages and towns in between, this major navigation changed the lives of many of the people living along its length. The section through West Lancashire, passing rural villages, is perhaps one of the more pleasant stretches. There are plenty of charming canalside pubs in the area and walks along the towpath, through the unspoilt countryside, have been popular for many years. There is also, in this section, the wharf at Wigan Pier, now a fascinating living museum that brings the canal to life.

The Civil War brought visitors to Chorley, albeit less welcome ones. Following defeat at the nearby Battle of Preston, Royalist troops were twice engaged in battle here by Cromwell's victorious forces. Though not a happy time for both the Royalists and the town, the skirmishes did place Chorley on the historical map of England.

58 THE VILLAGE KITCHEN

Adlington

Super premises and food, which is recommended far and wide. Most importantly, a extremely hospitable owner.

see page 205

59 THE WHITE HORSE

Adlington

A cosy, family run pub serving great value food and a wide variety of entertainment.

see page 204

CHORLEY

A bustling and friendly place, Chorley is a charming town that is locally famous for its market that dates back to 1498. Today, there are two markets – the covered market and the open, 'flat iron' market. This peculiar and intriguing name stems from the ancient practice of trading by displaying goods on the grounds without the use of stalls.

The town's oldest building is the **Church of St Lawrence** which was completed in 1360 and stands on the site of a Saxon chapel, The church is said to contain the remains of St Lawrence, brought back from Normandy by Sir Richard Standish. Whether they are his relics or not, during the Middle Ages the saint's shrine certainly brought pilgrims to the parish.

Chorley was the birthplace, in 1819, of Henry Tate. The son of a Unitarian minister, Henry was apprenticed in 1832 to the grocery trade in Liverpool and by 1855 he had set up his own business with a chain of six shops. After selling the shops, Henry entered into the world of the competitive sugar trade and founded the world famous business of **Tate and Lyle**. Opening a new sugar refinery equipped with the latest machinery from France, Henry cornered the refining business in Britain and amassed a huge fortune. A great benefactor, Henry gave away vast sums of money to worthy causes , including the London art gallery which now bears his name.

The jewel in Chorley's crown is undoubtedly **Astley Hall**. Built in the late 1500s and set within some beautiful parkland, the hall is a fine example of an Elizabethan mansion. A notable feature is its south wing – "more glass than wall". Inside, the moulded ceilings of the main hall and the drawing room are quite remarkable, as are the painted panels dating from the 1620s and representing a range of heroes that includes Elizabeth I, Philip II of Spain and the Islamic warrior Tamerlane.

Extended in 1666, and again in 1825, this is truly a house of history and the rooms, which reflect the passing of the centuries, contain superb items of furniture from 1600 to the Edwardian period. Whether or not Cromwell stayed at the hall following the Battle of Preston is open to debate but his boots are here on display.

The hall was given to the borough in 1922 by Reginald Tatton and it was he who insisted that the building should incorporate a memorial to those who had died in World War I. As a result, a small room has been devoted to the local men who fought and died for their country. Along with the display of photographs, there is a Book of Remembrance.

NORTH OF CHORLEY

LEYLAND

4 miles NW of Chorley on the B5253

The town is probably best known for its associations with the manufacture of cars and lorries and the **British Commercial Vehicle Museum**, the largest such museum in Europe, is well worth a visit. It stands on the site of the former Leyland South Works, where commercial vehicles were produced for many years. On display are many restored vans, fire engines and lorries along with exhibits ranging from the horse-drawn era, through steam-powered wagons right up to present day vans and lorries. Perhaps the most famous vehicle here is the one used by the Pope and irreverently known as the Popemobile.

Leyland is, however, an ancient settlement and documentary evidence has been found which suggests that the town was a Crown possession in Saxon times, owned by Edward the Confessor. The village cross marks the centre of the old settlement around which the town expanded and it is in this area of Leyland that the older buildings can be seen. Founded in the 11th century, much of the present **St Andrew's Church** dates from 1220 although there was some restoration work undertaken in the 1400s. The Eagle and Child Inn is almost as old, said to date from around 1230, and it served the needs of travellers journeying along the ancient highway which passed through the town.

Whilst not one of the town's oldest buildings, the old Grammar School, parts of which dates from the late 1500s, is hardly modern. Today it is occupied by the town's **Heritage Museum**, a fascinating place that describes, through interesting displays and exhibits, the history of this ancient market town.

TARLETON

8 miles W of Chorley off the A59

This pleasant rural village, now by-passed by the main road to Preston, is home to **St Mary's Church**, one of the finest buildings in Lancashire. Built in 1719, it is constructed from brick except for the cut-stone belfry. No longer the village church, it was replaced in the late 1800s by a larger building but it is still maintained and its churchyard has remained in use.

CROSTON

6 miles W of Chorley on the A581

This historic village in the heart of rural West Lancashire has been a centre for local farmers since it was granted a weekly market charter in 1283. Set beside the banks of the River Yarrow, a tributary of the River Douglas, much of the village, including the 17th century almshouses and the lovely 15th century church, are part of a conservation area. Church Street is a fine example of an 18th century Lancashire street, some of the houses bearing the date 1704; even older is the charming packhorse bridge dated 1682. The strong links with agriculture are still apparent in this area and the open farmland actually extends right into the village centre.

On **Coffee Day** the village turns out with decorated farm horses and carts to take part in a procession led by a band and morris dancers. The name is not

60 THE WAGGON AND HORSES

Leyland

Good honest food and a range of entertainment can be found at this welcoming inn.

see page 206

61 WYNDHAMS TEA ROOM

Leyland

Delightful, welcoming and relaxing, apt words to describe this friendly tea room offering homemade food and a wide choice of drinks.

see page 206

62 PUMPKIN SEED CAFÉ

Tarleton

An inviting café offering a selection of homemade main courses, vegetarian dishes and tempting desserts.

see page 206

derived from the beverage but from
the former "Feoffing Day" when
tenants paid their fees, or rents, to
the squire.

ORMSKIRK

In the days when Liverpool was just
a small fishing village, the main
town in this area was Ormskirk,
founded around AD 840 by a
Viking leader called Orme.
Surrounded by rich agricultural land,
the town has always been an
important market centre with the
locally-grown potatoes, 'Ormskirks',
a firm favourite right across the
north-west. The market is still
flourishing, held every day except
Wednesday and Sunday. In late
Victorian times one of the traders
in Ormskirk market was a certain
Joseph Beecham who did a roaring
trade selling his medicinal 'Little
Liver Pills'. Joseph became a
millionaire through the sales of his
little pills; his son, the conductor Sir
Thomas, went on to become the
most popular and flamboyant figure
of English musical life during the
first half of the 20th century.

The town received its first
market charter from Edward I in
1286 and today the market is still a
key event in the region. The partial
drainage of Martin Mere in the late
1700s to provide more rich, fertile
agricultural land, as well as the
growth of nearby Liverpool,
increased the prosperity of the
town. Ormskirk was also touched
by the Industrial Revolution and,
whilst the traditional farming
activities continued, cotton

spinning and silk weaving also
became important sources of local
income. Today, the town has
reverted to its traditional past.

The **Church of St Peter and
St Paul**, in the centre of the town,
unusually has both a steeple and a
tower. The tower, added in the 16th
century, was constructed to take
the bells of Burscough Priory after
the religious community had been
disbanded by Henry VIII.
However, the oldest feature found
in the church is a stone carving on
the outer face of the chancel's east
wall that was probably the work of
Saxon craftsmen.

NORTH OF ORMSKIRK

BURSCOUGH

2 miles NE of Ormskirk on the A59

Situated on the banks of the Leeds
and Liverpool Canal, the village's
Parish Church was one of the
Million, or Waterloo, Churches
built as a thanks to God after the
final defeat of Napoleon in 1815. A
later addition to the church is the
Memorial Window to those of the
parish who died for their country
during the First World War.

Little remains of **Burscough
Priory**, founded in the early 1100s
by the Black Canons. Receiving
lavish endowments from the local
inhabitants, the priory was at one
time one of the most influential
religious houses in Lancashire.

LATHOM

3 miles NE of Ormskirk off the A5209

The stretch of the famous Leeds

and Liverpool Canal which passes through this village is well worth a visit and it includes the **Top Locks** area, a particularly interesting part of this major canal route.

To the south of the village, in Lathom Park, is Lathom House (private), formerly home of Lord Stanley, Earl of Derby, a Royalist who was executed during the Civil War. Only one wing of the original house remains but within the grounds are the ancient **Chapel of St John the Divine**, consecrated in 1509, and ten adjoining almshouses built for the chapel bedesmen. It's a charming cluster of buildings in an attractive setting and visitors are welcome at the services held in the chapel every Sunday.

RUFFORD

5 miles NE of Ormskirk on the B5246

This attractive village of pretty houses is notable for its church and its beautiful old hall. Built in 1869, the church is a splendid example of the Gothic revival period and its tall spire dominates the skyline.

Rufford Old Hall (National Trust) is an enchanting building. Its medieval part is constructed of richly decorated black-and-white timbering enclosing a glorious Great Hall where angels bearing colourful heraldic shields float from massive hammer-beam trusses. The Hall's 17th century additions are less spectacular but still very attractive and contain displays of historic costumes as well as an interesting local folk museum.

Generally regarded as one of the finest timber-framed halls in the

Old Hall, Rufford

country, Rufford was the ancestral home of the Hesketh family who lived at this site from the 1200s until Baron Hesketh gave the hall to the National Trust in 1936. The superb, intricately carved movable wooden screen, the solid oak chests and the long refectory table, reflect the wealth and position of the hall's former owners.

Later additions to the house were made in the 1660s and again in 1821. Parts of these are now devoted to the **Philip Ashcroft Museum of Rural Life** with its unique collection of items illustrating village life in pre-industrial Lancashire. Another attraction here is the spacious garden alongside the canal.

MAWDESLEY

6 miles NE of Ormskirk off the B5246

A past winner of the Best Kept Village of Lancashire award, Mawdesley lies in rich farming country and was once associated with a thriving basket making industry. The village has a

65 WWT MARTIN MERE

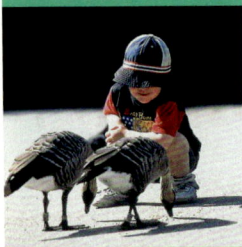

Burscough

WWT Martin Mere is one of nine Wildfowl & Wetlands Centres run by the Wildfowl & Wetlands Trust

see page 208

There is still plenty to see in the small village of Churchtown. The present Meols Hall dates from the 1600s but its appearance today is largely thanks to the work carried out by the late Colonel Roger Fleetwood Hesketh in the 1960s. When the colonel took over the house in the late 1930s, the older and larger part of the hall had been demolished in 1733 and the remaining building was rather nondescript. Taking the gabled bay of the late 17th century, extensions were added to give the house a varied roofline and a three dimensional frontage.

surprising number of old buildings. Mawdesley Hall (private), originally built in the 1500s and altered in the late 1700s, was for many generations the home of the Mawdesley family. At the other end of the village is Lane Ends House, built in 1590, which was occupied by a Catholic family and has a chapel in one of its attics. Other venerable buildings include Ambrose House (1577), Barret House Farm (1695), Back House Farm (1690) and Jay Bank Cottage (1692). By contrast, the oldest of the village's three churches only dates back to 1840.

SCARISBRICK

3 miles N of Ormskirk on the A570

Scarisbrick lies in the heart of rich agricultural land that is intensively cultivated for vegetables, particularly carrots, Brussels sprouts, cabbages, and early potatoes. A feature of this area is the large number of farm shops by the side of the road selling the produce fresh from the fields.

The first **Scarisbrick Hall** was built in the reign of King Stephen but in the mid-1800s the hall was extensively remodelled by the Victorian architect Augustus Welby Pugin for Charles Scarisbrick. In 1945, the hall and surrounding extensive grounds were sold by the last member of the family to live here, Sir Everard Scarisbrick. Today it is an independent boarding school and occasionally open to the public in the summer months. Pugin's flamboyant decoration is well worth seeing if you have the chance.

MERE BROW

7 miles N of Ormskirk on the B5246

Just to the south of the village lies the Wildfowl and Wetlands Trust at **Martin Mere**, more than 350 acres of reclaimed marshland which was established in 1976 as a refuge for thousands of wintering wildfowl. Until Martin Mere was drained in the 1600s to provide rich, fertile farmland, the lake was one of the largest in England. Many devotees of the Arthurian legends believe that the pool into which the dying king's sword Excalibur was thrown, (to be received by a woman's arm *'clothed in white samite, mystic, wonderful'*), was actually Martin Mere.

Today, the stretches of water, mudbanks, and grassland provide homes for many species of birds and, with a network of hides, visitors can observe the birds in their natural habitats. There are also a series of pens near the visitor centre, where many other birds can be seen all year round at closer quarters. The mere is particularly famous for the vast numbers of pink-footed geese that winter here, their number often approaching 20,000. Although winter is a busy time at Martin Mere, a visit in any season is sure to be rewarding. The visitor centre has a shop, café and theatre as well as a wealth of information regarding the birds found here and the work of the Trust.

CHURCHTOWN

7 miles NW of Ormskirk on the A5267

This charming village, now a small

part of Southport, has retained much of its village feel. Considerably predating the seaside resort, Churchtown is, as its name suggests, centred around its church. Since it is dedicated to St Cuthbert, it's possible that whilst fleeing from the Danes, the monks of Lindisfarne rested here with the remains of their famous saint.

It is likely that the village was, for many years, known by the name of North Meols - a chapel of Mele is mentioned in the *Domesday Book*. The name is derived from the Norse word 'melr' meaning sand dune. There was certainly a thriving fishing village here in the early 1100s. In 1224, Robert de Coudrey granted the village the right to hold a market, the likely place for which is the cross standing opposite the church in the heart of the village.

As the settlement lay on a crossroads and at the start of a route over the sands of the Ribble estuary, it was a place of considerable importance. It was also here that the tradition of sea bathing in this area began, when, in 1219 St Cuthbert's Eve was declared a fair day, which later became known as Bathing Sunday.

Meots Hall is the last home of the Hesketh family who at one time had owned most of the coastal area between Southport and Heysham. Originally, the manor had been granted to Robert de Coudrey, coming into the Hesketh family by marriage in the late 1500s. There has been a house on this site since the 13th century. Occasionally open to visitors, the hall has a fine art collection and, in the entrance hall, are three carved chairs that were used in Westminster Abbey during the coronation of Charles II. During World War I, Moels Hall was used as a military hospital.

Originally opened on the site of the old Churchtown Strawberry Gardens in 1874, the **Botanic Gardens** are beautifully maintained and present a superb example of classic Victorian garden design. With magnificent floral displays, a boating lake, wide, twisting paths, and a fernery, little has changed here since the day the gardens were first opened by the Rev Charles Hesketh.

Built in 1938, following the gardens' restoration, the **Botanic Bowling Pavilion** mimics the style of the late Regency architect Decimus Burton. Here too is the Botanic Gardens Museum, with its fine exhibition on local history and its gallery of Victoriana.

SOUTHPORT

8 miles NW of Ormskirk on the A570

The fashion for sea-bathing is usually reckoned to have originated with George III's regular dips at Weymouth in the late 1700s, but at Southport they'd already been doing it for generations. Only once a year though, on St Cuthbert's Eve, the Sunday following August 20th. The holiday became known as 'Bathing Sunday', when folk travelled some distance to throw off their clothes and frolick naked in the sea'. The tradition was associated with the legend, or fact,

Every self-respecting Victorian resort had its Promenade. Southport's is a typical example: flanked by grand hotels on the land side and a series of formal gardens on the other. From the centre of the promenade extends Southport's Pier which, at 1460 yards long was the longest pier in the country until 1897. Following a fire in 1933 it was shortened but it remains the second longest in the country. In its heyday, pleasure steamers were able to depart from the Pier to Barrow in Cumbria, Bangor in Wales, and the Isle of Man. Along the shore line, and opened in the spring of 1998, the new sea wall and Marine Drive is a wonderful modern construction, the length of Southport's sea front, that blends well with the town's Victorian heritage.

66 PIPPINS COFFEE HOUSE

Southport

A friendly, traditional coffee house serving homemade food to suit all tastes, all day.

see page 208

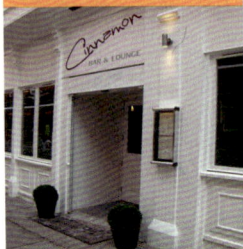

67 CINNAMON BAR & LOUNGE

Southport

An outstanding eating place renowned throughout the country for it's homemade food and unique ambience.

see page 209

that St Cuthbert had once been shipwrecked but had miraculously been able to swim to the shore and safety.

Southport's history as an all-year, rather than a one-day-a-year resort began in 1792 when its first hotel was built. A local man, 'Duke' Sutton, went to the beach, gathered all the driftwood he could find, nailed it together, put in the minimum of furniture, and opened for business.

Within a few years other houses and hotels had sprung up amongst the dunes and by 1802 'Duke'

Sutton felt confident enough to rebuild his makeshift, if environmentally-friendly hotel, in stone. Over-confident as it turned out. The following year he was thrown into Lancaster gaol for debt and later died a pauper.

Southport though continued to thrive and by the 1860s was by far the most popular seaside resort in Lancashire. The town's only problem was that its main attraction, the sea, was getting further and further away as silt from the Ribble estuary clogged the beach. The town council's response was to build the second-longest pier in the country, complete with a miniature railway which is still operating. They also created numerous parks and gardens, and constructed elegant boulevards such as Lord Street. All that activity in Victorian times imbued the town with an appealingly genteel atmosphere which, happily, it still retains.

The town's central, main boulevard, **Lord Street**, is a mile-long broad road that was built along the boundary bordering the lands of the two neighbouring lords of the manor. A superb shopping street today, the exceptionally wide pavements, with gardens along one side and an elegant glass-topped canopy along most of the other side, make this one of the most pleasant places to shop in the country. Many of the town's classical style buildings are found along its length and it has been designated a conservation area.

Off Lord Street, there is one of the town's several covered

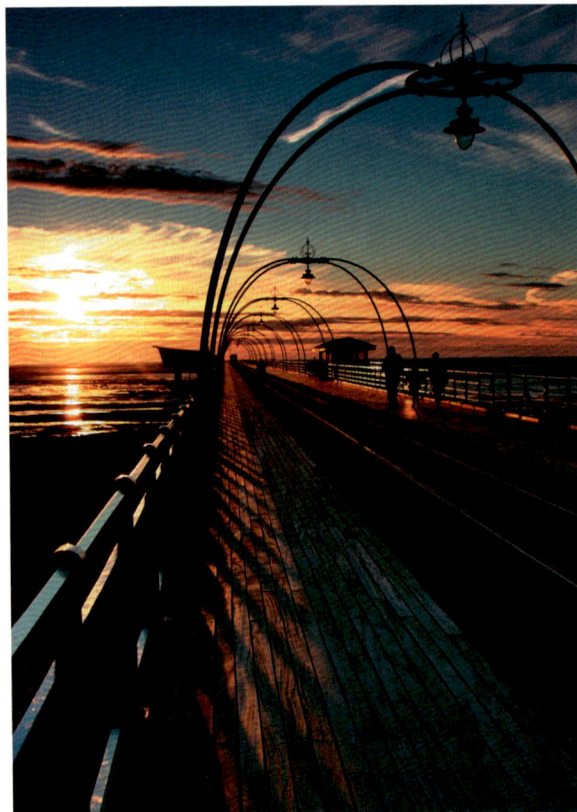

Southport Pier, Southport

arcades – **Wayfarers Arcade**, built in 1898 and a fine example of these popular shopping malls. The modest entrance opens out into a beautiful cast iron and glass conservatory with a first floor gallery and splendid central dome. Originally named the Leyland Arcade after the town's Member of Parliament, it took its present name in 1976 after the arcade's most successful leaseholder.

In a central position along Lord Street stands Southport's rather modest Town Hall. Built in 1852 and of a classical design, its façade includes a beautiful carving in bold relief of the figures of Justice, Mercy, and Truth picked out in white against a Wedgwood blue background. Further along, the Atkinson Central Library was built in 1879 as the premises of the Southport and West Lancashire Bank. The original ceiling of the banking hall can still be seen as can its fireplace. On the first floor is the **Atkinson Art Gallery** which contains collections of British art and Chinese porcelain.

Not all the buildings in Southport are Victorian and the Top Rank Bingo Club opened in 1932. With much of its exterior as it would have appeared when it first opened, it is a wonderful example of the Art Deco style. Lord Street is also home to the town's war memorial, **The Monument**. Opened on Remembrance Day 1923 by the Earl of Derby, this is a large and grand memorial that remains the town's focal point. Its design was the subject of a

competition and the winning entry was submitted by Garyson and Barnish, designers of the famous Royal Liver Building in Liverpool. The central obelisk is flanked by twin colonnades on which the names of the town's more than 1000 dead are inscribed.

As the silting up of the Ribble estuary progressed unchecked the **Marine Lake** was constructed at the northern end of the promenade. At over 86 acres, this man-made lake is the largest in Britain. As well as being an attractive site and a place for the pursuit of all manner of watersports, it is also host to an annual 24-hour yacht race.

SOUTH AND WEST OF ORMSKIRK

HALSALL

4 miles W of Ormskirk on the A5147

Halsall is a charming unspoilt village lying in the heart of fertile West Lancashire and close to the Leeds and Liverpool Canal – the longest canal in Britain with a mainline of 127.25 miles and 92 locks. **St Cuthbert's Church** dates from the mid-1200s and is one of the oldest churches in the diocese of Liverpool. It remains one of the prettiest in the county. The distinctive spire, which was added around 1400, rises from a tower that has octagonal upper stages.

AINSDALE

7 miles W of Ormskirk on the A565

Towards the sea, from the centre of the village, lies what was

68 BRITISH LAWNMOWER MUSEUM

Southport

The British Lawnmower Museum houses a private collection of over 200 pristine exhibits of special interest

🏛 see page 210

69 SATCHMO'S

Birkdale

Fantastic décor and furnishing, fabulous traditional and international cuisine served 6 days a week.

🍴 see page 210

•

Keen gardeners will know Southport for its splendid annual Flower Show, second only to Chelsea, and golfers will be familiar with the name of Royal Birkdale Golf Course, just south of the town centre. Southport has one more sporting association of which it is justly proud. From behind a car show room in the 1970s, Ginger McCain trained Red Rum on the sands of Southport to a record breaking three magnificent wins in the Grand National run at Aintree. A statue of the great horse can be seen in Wayfarers Arcade.

•

70 THE PINEWOODS

Formby

A superb family friendly premise serving fresh, local produce in a homemade fashion, suitable for all tastes.

🍴 *see page 212*

The origins of Formby coastal town lie in the time of the Vikings - the name Formby comes from the Norse Fornebei meaning Forni's town. Between the Norman Conquest and the time of the Dissolution in 1536, there were a succession of landowners here but, by the mid-1500s, the Formby and Blundell families emerged as the chief owners. Formby Hall, built for William Formby in 1523, occupies a site that was first developed in the 1100s. It is now an upmarket hotel, golf resort and spa.

Ainsdale-on-Sea with its old Lido and the more modern Pontin's holiday village. Between here and Formby, further down the coast, the sand dunes form part of the **Ainsdale National Nature Reserve**, one of the most extensive dune systems in the country. It's also one of the few remaining habitats of the endangered natterjack toad which breeds in the shallow pools that form in the sand dunes. As well as supporting the toads, the salt pools are the natural habitat for a variety of dune plants, including dune helleborine, grass of Parnassus and round-leaved wintergreen.

FORMBY

8 miles W of Ormskirk off the A565

Like Ormskirk, Formby has a connection with potatoes. It's said that sailors who had travelled with Sir Walter Raleigh to Virginia brought back potatoes with them and grew them in the fields around what was then a small village. There are still many acres of potato fields being cultivated in the area.

To the west of the town, **Formby Point** and Ainsdale National Nature Reserve form the most extensive dune system in Britain, 450 acres of wood and duneland, one of the last refuges in the country for the quirky natterjack toad, the only species of toad which runs rather than hops.

Today, Formby is perhaps better known as a quiet and desirable residential area and as the home of an important red squirrel

sanctuary at the National Trust's **Freshfield Nature Reserve** and pine forest. Linked with Ainsdale's nature reserve, the two form more than 400 acres of dunes and woodland, as well as shoreline, from which there are magnificent views over the Mersey estuary and, on a clear day, the hills of Wales and of Lakeland are also visible.

GREAT ALTCAR

6 miles SW of Ormskirk on the B5195

Standing on the banks of the River Alt, this old farming village is well-known as the venue for the Liverpool Cup, an annual hare coursing event. In the churchyard of the present church, erected by the Earl of Sefton in 1879, are a pedestal font and a stoup which came from the earlier churches that occupied this site.

SEFTON

8 miles SW of Ormskirk on the B5422

This quiet old village stands at the edge of a rich and fertile plain of farmland that lies just behind the West Lancashire coast. It formed part of the estate of the Earls of Sefton (descendents of the Molyneux family) right up until 1972. The village has a pub, a 16th century corn mill and a delightful church, **St Helen's**, with a 14th century spire. Inside, there's a beautifully restored ceiling with bosses and moulded beams, 16th century screens, well-preserved box pews, two medieval effigies of knights, and an elaborately carved pulpit of 1635. A series of brasses recounts the history of the

Molyneux family from their arrival in Britain with William the Conqueror.

Though this is a small village, its name has also been given to the large metropolitan district of north Merseyside which stretches from Bootle to Southport.

INCE BLUNDELL

8 miles SW of Ormskirk off the A565

The village takes part of its name from the Blundell family who have for centuries exerted much influence on the village and surrounding area. Ince comes from the Celtic word 'Ynes' which means an island within a watery meadow and it would have perfectly described the village's situation before the surrounding land was drained.

LYDIATE

4 miles SW of Ormskirk on the A5147

This is another pleasant old village bordering the flat open farmland created from the West Lancashire mosses. Lydiate itself means an enclosure with a gate to stop cattle roaming and, though the age of the settlement here is uncertain, the now ruined **St Katharine's Chapel** dates from the 1400s. However, the most frequented building in the village is **The Scotch Piper**, a lovely cruck-framed house with a thatched roof that has the reputation of being the oldest pub in Lancashire. The pub was built around an oak tree in the 14th century and known as the Royal Oak until 1745 when an injured highland piper took refuge at the inn. He married the innkeeper's daughter and the pub became known as The Scotch Piper.

AUGHTON

3 miles SW of Ormskirk off the A59

This picturesque village, surrounded by agricultural land, is dominated by the spire of St Michael's Church. An ancient place, it was mentioned in the *Domesday Book* and its register of church rectors goes back to 1246. Much of the building's medieval framework remains though it was restored in 1914.

Close by is Aughton Old Hall (private) which stands on a site that has been occupied since Saxon times. The ruins of a 15th century pele tower are visible in the garden and, as well as having a priest's hole, the house is reputed to have been Cromwell's base whilst he was active in the area.

EAST OF ORMSKIRK

PARBOLD

5 miles E of Ormskirk off the A5209

This is a charming village of pretty stone cottages as well as grand, late-Victorian houses built by wealthy Manchester cotton brokers. The village houses extend up the slopes of **Parbold Hill**, one of the highest points for miles around and from which there are superb views of the West Lancashire plain. At the summit stands a rough hewn monument, erected to commemorate the Reform Act of 1832. Because of its shape it is known locally as Parbold Bottle.

The annual candlelight service at the village Church of the Holy Family in Ince Blundell is an ancient custom that appears to be unique to this country. The people of the parish decorate the graves in the cemetery with flowers and candles before holding a service there. Common in Belgium, this custom was brought to the village at the beginning of the 20th century.

71 STANLEY ARMS

Aughton

A well established property close to the communities church serving a large array of fine foods, with a great hospitable atmosphere and delicious homemade chips.

see page 211

72 CRAWFORD ARMS

Skelmersdale

Home to the Crawford Gut Buster; find out if you can eat a 40oz steak!

see page 213

93

73 THE NEWMARKET

Earlestown

A large welcoming hostelry in the heart of the town with opening hours that complement market days and great food at reasonable prices.

see page 212

74 THE STANLEY

Upholland

The worthy recipient of the Taste of Lancashire Award, 2008 – 09.

see page 215

75 THE HOLT ARMS

Billinge

This family run pub is a real hidden gem, full of character and charm.

see page 214

Ashurst Beacon, another local landmark, was re-erected on Ashurst Hill by Lord Skelmersdale in 1798 when the threat of a French invasion was thought to be imminent.

RIVINGTON

13 miles E of Ormskirk off the A673

One of the county's prettiest villages, Rivington is surrounded by moorland of outstanding natural beauty that forms the western border of the Forest of Rossendale. Overlooking the village and with splendid views over West Lancashire, **Rivington Pike**, at 1191 feet, is one of the area's high spots.

Just to the south of the village lies **Lever Park**, situated on the lower slopes of Rivington Moor, which was made over to the public in 1902 by William Hesketh Lever, who later became Lord Leverhulme. The park comprises an awe-inspiring pot pourri of ornamental, landscaped gardens, tree-lined avenues, ancient cruck-framed barns, a Georgian hall, and a treasure trove of natural history within its 400 acres. The park's moorland setting, elevated position, and adjoining reservoirs provide scenery on a grand scale which leaves a lasting impression.

STANDISH

9 miles E of Ormskirk on the A49

This historic old market town has several reminders of its past and not least of these is the splendid **St Wilfrid's Church** whose size and style reflect the importance of the town in the late 1500s. A look around the interior of the church provides a potted history of the area: there are tombs and memorials to all the local families including the Wrightingtons, Shevingtons, and the Standish family who gave their name to the village.

The Standish family came from Normandy and crossed the channel with William the Conqueror. One of the family members became the Warden of Scarborough Castle and another, Ralph de Standish, was knighted after his part in quelling the Peasants' Revolt. There was even a Standish at Agincourt. However, the most famous member of the family is Miles Standish who sailed to the New World on board the *Mayflower* with the Pilgrim Fathers in 1620. This may seem strange as the Standish family were staunch Catholics. Though there is little left in the way of monuments to the family in this country, their home (put up for sale in 1920 after the last family member died) was demolished and parts transported to America.

WIGAN

10 miles E of Wigan on the A577

The American travel writer, Bill Bryson, visited Wigan in the mid 1990s and wrote "Such is Wigan's perennially poor reputation that I was truly astounded to find it has a handsome and well maintained town centre".

Although to many this town is a product of the industrial age, Wigan is one of the oldest places in Lancashire. As far back as the

1st century AD there was a Celtic Brigantes settlement here that was taken over by the Romans who built a small town called Coccium. Little remains of those far off days but during the construction of a gasworks in the mid-1800s various burial urns were unearthed during the excavation work.

Wigan's development as an industrial town centred around coal mining, which began as early as 1450. By the 19th century, there were more than one thousand pit shafts in operation in the surrounding area, supplying the fuel for Lancashire's expanding textile industry. The Leeds and Liverpool Canal, which runs through the town, was a key means of transporting the coal to the cotton mills of Lancashire and **Wigan Pier**, the major loading bay, remains one of the most substantial and interesting features of the waterway. It was the 1930s novel by George Orwell, *The Road to Wigan Pier*, that really put the old wharf on the map. Recently, the pier was beautifully restored and it is now a key attraction in the area. Visitors can see what locals did on holiday during the traditional Wakes Week break; witness a colliery disaster; sing along in the Palace of Varieties Music Hall, or experience the rigours of a Victorian schoolroom. There's also a superb exhibition, The Way We Were, based on local social history and with costumed actors playing the part of the townsfolk of the 19th century.

As well as having a modern town centre with all the usual amenities, including a theatre and art gallery, Wigan has some fine countryside on its doorstep, some of which can be explored by following the **Douglas Valley Trail** along the banks of the River Douglas. Even the town's coal mining past has interesting links with the natural world: **Pennington Flash** is a large lake formed by mining subsidence that is now a wildlife reserve and a country park. To the north of the town lies **Haigh Hall and Country Park**, one of the first to be designated in England and formed from the estate of the Earls of Crawford. Within its 250 acres of lush and picturesque woodlands are a 15-inch gauge miniature railway; a very well-equipped children's playground; a crazy golf course; a model village and an art and craft centre in the original stables block. There are walks along the towpath of the Leeds to Liverpool canal which bisects the park or around the rose-filled Walled Gardens.

Haigh Hall Country Park, Wigan

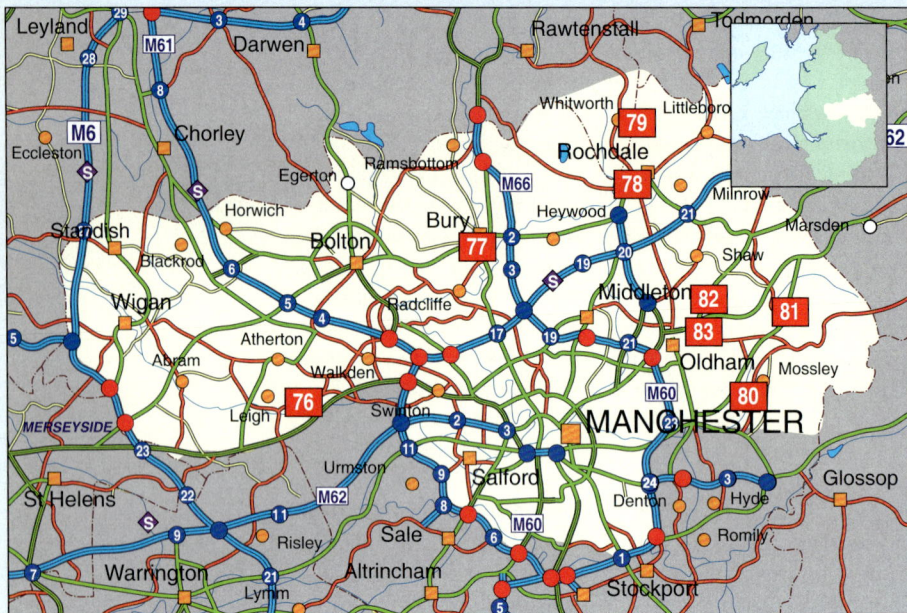

East Lancashire

This area of the county, to the north of Manchester and west of the Pennines, is, perhaps, everyone's idea of Lancashire. A region dominated by cotton, East Lancashire has risen and fallen with the fluctuations in the trade over the years. Before the Industrial Revolution, this was a sparsely populated region of remote hillside farms and cottages that relied chiefly on sheep farming and the wool trade. Many of the settlements date back to before the Norman Conquest and although little may have survived the rapid building of the 19th century there are three surprisingly wonderful ancient houses to be seen here: Smithills Hall and Hall-i'-th'-Wood at Bolton and Turton Tower, just to the north.

However, there is no escaping the textile industry. Lancashire's ideal climate for cotton spinning and weaving – damp so that the yarn does not break – made it the obvious choice for the building of the mills. There are numerous valleys with fast flowing rivers and streams and then the development of the extensive coalfields around Wigan supplied the fuel to feed the power hungry machinery. Finally, there was a plentiful supply of labour as families moved from the hill top sheep farms into the expanding towns and villages to work the looms and turn the wheels of industry.

In a very short time, smoke and soot filled the air and the once clear streams and rivers became lifeless valleys of polluted squalor. There are many illustrations in the region of the harsh working conditions the labourers had to endure and the dirt and filth that covered much of the area. Now that much of this has been cleaned up, the rivers running once again fast, clear, and supporting wildlife, the lasting legacy of those days is the splendid Victorian architecture of which every town has at least one example.

BOLTON

A fairly new major attraction in Bolton is the state-of-the-art Reebok Stadium, home of Bolton Wanderers, one of the world's oldest football clubs. Visitors can take a look behind the scenes at one of Europe's finest stadiums, exploring everything from the players' changing rooms to the bird's eye vantage point of the Press Box.

Synonymous with the Lancashire textile industry, Bolton is also an ancient town that predates its expansion due to cotton by many centuries. First settled during the Bronze Age, by the time of the Civil War, this was a market town supporting the surrounding villages. The town saw one of the bloodiest episodes of the war when in 1644 it was stormed by 3000 Royalist troops led by Prince Rupert of the Rhine. This attack, which later came to be known as the Bolton Massacre, resulted in 1600 residents being killed and 700 taken prisoner.

Later, after the Royalists had been defeated, James Stanley, Earl of Derby, was brought back here by Cromwell's troops In a savage act of revenge for the massacre his army had brought on the town early in the troubles, Stanley was executed and his severed head and body, in separate caskets, were taken back to the family burial place at Ormskirk. Whilst in captivity in the town, Stanley was kept prisoner at Ye Olde Man and Scythe Inn which, dating from 1251, is still standing in Churchgate today and is the town's oldest building.

At its zenith in 1929, Bolton had 216 cotton mills and 26 bleaching and dying works, making it one of the largest and most productive centres of cotton spinning in the world. The centre of the town is a lasting tribute to the wealth and prosperity of that time. The monumental **Town Hall**, opened in 1873, is typical of the classical style of buildings that the Victorian town fathers favoured – tours are available. The hall is still the town's central point and it is now surrounded by the recently refurbished pedestrianised shopping malls, market hall, and the celebrated Octagon Theatre. The town's excellent **Museum, Art Gallery & Aquarium** (free) is one of the largest regional galleries in the northwest with excellent collections of fine and decorative art, including examples of British sculpture and contemporary

Smithills Hall, Bolton

ceramics. There are collections of natural history, geology, and Egyptian antiques here as well as some fine 18th and 19th century English watercolours and some contemporary British paintings and graphics.

Bolton is fortunate in having two particularly fine old mansions, both on the northern edge of the town. **Hall-i'-th'-Wood**, is a delightful part-timbered medieval house dating from 1530 to 1648. A fine example of a wealthy merchant's house, Hall i'th'Wood was saved from dereliction by Lord Leverhulme in 1900 and has been restored and furnished with displays of fine 17th and 18th century furniture along with interesting items of local importance. The hall has a second claim to fame since, for a number of years one of several tenants here was Samuel Crompton, the inventor in 1799 of the spinning mule. Naturally, the hall has a replica of Crompton's mule on display.

Bolton's second grand house, **Smithills Hall**, stands on an easily defended hill on the edge of the moors and was built in the 1300s as a pele, or fortified dwelling. It was extended over the years and this superb Grade I listed building now displays some of the best examples of medieval, Tudor and Victorian Arts & Crafts architecture in the region. The hall was bought by Bolton Corporation in the late 1930s and has been beautifully restored. In addition to the impressive collection of furniture

and artefacts on display, the hall also hosts changing exhibitions throughout the year.

Within the grounds of Smithills Country Park is **Smithills Open Farm** where visitors can feed lambs, stroke calves or ride on donkeys. Staff encourage a hands-on approach and visitors can see and touch a wide variety of traditional farm animals as well as more exotic llamas, peacocks and snakes. There are toy tractors and trailers for the children as well as a bouncy castle and other playground equipment.

Close to Smithills Hall, in Moss Bank Park, is **Animal World & Butterfly House** (free) which provides a safe habitat for a variety of animals and birds ranging from farm animals to chipmunks, from wildfowl and tropical birds. In the tropical atmosphere of the Butterfly House, are free-flying butterflies and moths as well as insects, spiders, reptiles and tropical plants.

AROUND BOLTON

TURTON BOTTOMS

4 miles N of Bolton off the B6391

Turton Tower near Bolton was built both for defensive purposes and as a residence. In 1400, William Orrell erected his sturdy, four-square pele (fortified dwelling) in search of safety during those lawless and dangerous years. Some 200 years later, in more settled times, a lovely, half-timbered Elizabethan mansion was added. Successive owners made further

On the north-western edge of the town is Barrow Bridge Village (free), a small model village built during the Industrial Revolution to house workers at the two 6-storey mills that used to operate here. Small bridges cross a picturesque stream and a flight of 63 steps leads up the hillside to the moors. Barrow Bridge village was the inspiration for Benjamin Disraeli's famous novel Coningsby.

76 MANCHESTER ROAD INN

Astley

A distinguished family run inn with a fine reputation for its excellent food and unbeatable hospitality.

see page 216

Turton Tower, Turton Bottoms

Valley, is well worth visiting. One of the best views of the village and, indeed, the surrounding area can be found from **Peel Tower** which dominates the skyline. Erected in 1852 to commemorate the life of the area's most famous son, Prime Minister Sir Robert Peel, the tower is some 128 feet high. Now restored, the tower itself is occasionally open to the public.

BURY

6 miles E of Bolton on the A58

There was a settlement at Bury in Bronze Age times, but as late as 1770 it was still just a small market town, surrounded by green fields. That was the year a man named Robert Peel established his Ground Calico Printing Works, the first of many mills that would follow. The opening of the works along with the subsequent mills, print and bleach works so dominated this part of the Irwell Valley that not only did they transform the landscape but also heavily polluted the river. At the height of the valley's production it was said that anyone falling into the river would dissolve before they had a chance to drown. Today, thankfully, the valley towns are once again clean and the river clear and fast flowing.

With the family fortune gleaned from those prosperous mills, Robert Peel junior, born in the town in 1788, was able to fund his illustrious career in politics, rising to become Prime Minister in 1841. Famous for the repeal of the Corn Laws, Robert Peel was also at

additions in a charming motley of architectural styles. Quite apart from its enchanting appearance, Turton is well worth visiting to see its display of old weapons and a superb collection of vintage furniture, outstanding amongst which is the sumptuously carved Courtenay Bed of 1593.

RAMSBOTTOM

6 miles NE of Bolton on the A676

One of the stops along the East Lancashire Railway, this picturesque village, overlooking the Irwell

the forefront of the setting up of the modern police force – hence their nickname 'Bobbies'. A statue of Bury's most distinguished son stands in the Market Square and there's an even grander memorial near the village of Holcombe, a few miles to the north.

Another of Bury's famous sons was John Kay, inventor of the Flying Shuttle. Sadly, Kay neglected to patent his invention. He moved to France where he died a pauper and is buried in an unmarked grave. The people of Bury, however, remembered him. In his memory, they created the delightful Kay Gardens in the town centre and erected a splendidly ornate clock-house tower.

This part of town has become known as the "Culture Quarter", since Bury's **Art Gallery & Museum** is also located here. The gallery has a fine collection of paintings, including works by Turner, Constable and Landseer, and the outstanding Thomas Wrighley collection of Victorian oil paintings. Downstairs, visitors can stroll along "Paradise Street", a fascinating re-creation of Bury as it was in the 1950s.

The town has a real treat for those who thrill to the sight, sound and smell of steam locomotives. Bolton Street Station is the southern terminus of the **East Lancashire Railway** which operates regular services along a 9 mile scenic route through the lovely Irwell Valley to Rawtenstall. Bury Transport Museum, just across the road from the station closed in

2003 because of the dangerous state of its roof. A fund-raising project is currently under way to restore the building to how it was in 1848 and provide a worthy setting for the museum's wonderful collection of vintage road and rail vehicles, ranging from a 19th century steam road-roller to a "Stop Me and Buy One" ice-cream vendor's tricycle.

Also currently closed is the **Lancashire Fusiliers Museum** which tells the story of Lancashire's famous regiment from its foundation in 1688 and has an outstanding collection of medals and period uniforms. It is scheduled to re-open in new premises at the Bury Arts and Craft Centre in February 2009. A major shopping centre for the northwest, Bury is also proud of its ancient **Market** which has been operating since 1440. It's now the largest market in the north with more than 370 stalls offering a huge choice of some 50,000 different product lines. Don't leave without purchasing one of Bury's famous black puddings!

WALMERSLEY

2 miles NE of Bolton on the A56

Hidden away in the village of Walmersley, just north of Bury, is **Hark to Dandler**, an attractive pub dating from the mid-1800s that is thought to have originally been a vicarage. During a recent refurbishment a very old child's coffin was found behind the cellar walls. It was full of early 19th century artefacts. Along with the

77 EAST LANCASHIRE RAILWAY

Bury

The East Lancashire Railway offers visitors an opportunity to step back in time to the age of steam and travel along this delightful stretch of track.

see page 215

A short walk from Kay Gardens in Bury, The Met is a lively arts centre which puts on performances to suit all tastes, from theatre and children's shows to rock nights and world music. The Met also organises Bury's Streets Ahead Festival each May, a colourful street carnival which attracts artistes from around the world.

On the outskirts of Bury lies Burrs Country Park which, as well as offering a wide range of activities, also has an interesting industrial trail around this historic mill site.

Running from the southeast corner of Rochdale, the Rochdale Canal is a brave piece of early-19th century civil engineering that traversed the Pennines to link the River Mersey with the Calder and Hebble Navigation. Some 32 miles in length and with 91 locks, it must be one of the toughest canals ever built and, though the towpath can still be walked, the last commercial boat passed through the locks in 1937. The canal was officially abandoned in 1952, but exactly half a century later the entire length has been re-opened to full navigation. Together with the newly restored Huddersfield Narrow Canal it allows a complete circuit of the South Pennine Ring.

78 ROCHDALE PIONEERS MUSEUM

Rochdale

The Rochdale Pioneers Museum is regarded as the home of the world wide co-operative movement.

see page 217

two resident ghosts, this certainly adds an air of mystery to the pub. The name though is more easily explained as it is named after a lead dog of the local hunt.

TOTTINGTON

4 miles N of Bolton on the B6213

Tottington's pub is also named after a dog. The **Hark to Towler**, in the centre of the town, is very much a locals' pub that happily welcomes visitors. Dating back to the 1800s, this imposing red brick pub's unusual name means call - hark - to the lead dog of the hunt - Towler.

An unspoilt farming town on the edge of moorland, Tottington escaped the industrialisation of many of its neighbours due to its, then, isolated position and it is still an attractive place to visit.

ROCHDALE

Lying in a shallow valley formed by the little River Roch, the town is surrounded, to the north and east, by the slopes of the Pennines that are often snow covered in winter. The town, like so many others in Lancashire, expanded with the booming cotton industry and its magnificent Victorian **Town Hall** (1871) rivals that of Manchester in style if not in size.

However, it is not textiles for which Rochdale is most famous but for its role as the birthplace of the Co-operative Movement. In carefully restored Toad Lane, to the north of the town centre, is the world's first Co-op shop, now

the **Rochdale Pioneers Museum**. Today, the Co-op movement represents a staggering 700 million members in 90 countries around the world and the celebration of its 150th anniversary in 1994 focused attention on Rochdale. The story of the Rochdale Pioneers and other aspects of the town's heritage are vividly displayed in the new Arts & Heritage Centre, **Touchstones**. The restored Grade II listed building of 1889 was originally a library but now contains interactive high-tech exhibitions, 4 art galleries, the Tourist Information Centre, a local studies centre, café/bar, bookshop and performance studio.

As well as the Pioneers, Rochdale was home to several other famous sons and daughters, amongst them the 19th century political thinker, John Bright, the celebrated singer Gracie Fields, and Cyril Smith, Rochdale's former Liberal Member of Parliament.

The town's most distinctive church is **St John the Baptist Catholic Church** which has a beautiful dome modelled on the Byzantine Santa Sofya in Istanbul. The church is unique in England because of its huge mosaic of Italian marble depicting the Resurrection of Christ.

NORTH OF ROCHDALE

WHITWORTH

3 miles N of Rochdale on the A671

This pleasant town of cottages and

farms lies on Pennine moorland above Rochdale. Between here and Bacup, a distance of only seven miles, the railway line, climbs more than 500 feet. Not surprisingly, there were many problems during its construction, such as frequent landslides, but once constructed this was a picturesque line with attractive station houses with neat well tended gardens along the route. The line, like so many, fell to the extensive railway cuts of the 1960s.

HEALEY

1 mile N of Rochdale on the A671

Lying in the valley of the River Spodden, this ancient village, now almost engulfed by the outer reaches of Rochdale, is an area rich in wildlife as well as folklore. The oak and birch woodland on the northern river bank is all that remains of a prehistoric forest and, whilst the owners of Healey Hall made some impact, little has changed here for centuries.

LITTLEBOROUGH

4 miles NE of Rochdale on the A58

This small town lies beside the River Roch and on the main route between Lancashire and Yorkshire first laid down by the Romans. Known as the Roman Causey, it was an impressive structure 16 feet 6 inches wide, cambered and with gutters at each side. In the middle of the road is a shallow groove which has been the subject of endless controversy – no-one has yet come up with a satisfactory explanation of its purpose. The road cuts across the bleak Pennine moors by way of **Blackstone Edge** where some of the best preserved parts of the Roman structure can still be seen. At the summit is a medieval cross, the **Aigin Stone**, from which there are spectacular views over Lancashire right to the coast.

Between Rochdale and Littleborough lies Hollingworth Lake, originally built as a supply

Roman Causey Road & Aigin Stone, Littleborough

79 THE RED LION INN

Whitworth
A genuine family run establishment with first class facilities throughout serving award winning cuisine in a relaxed atmosphere.

see page 218

80 HOLLINGWORTH LAKE COUNTRY PARK

Littleborough
Hollingworth Lake provides a surprising haven for wildlife and excitement and entertainment for the young and the not so young.

see page 217

To the south of Littleborough, Hollingworth Lake Water Activity Centre offers sailing, canoeing, windsurfing, rowing and, during the summer months, lake trips on the Lady Alice.

81 THE NAVIGATION INN

Dobcross

A cosy, family run 19th century inn where outstanding cuisine and superb hospitality awaits all who enter.

see page 220

82 THE FARRAR'S ARMS

Grasscroft

This building is oozing with plenty of character and history and serves great homemade food. One to look out for is the golden oldies menu.

see page 219

83 EATS AND TREATS

Lees

A friendly, family run cafe, tastefully decorated, serving great food to eat in or to take away.

see page 220

reservoir for the canal, but for many years a popular area for recreation known colloquially as the 'Weavers' Seaport', as cotton workers unable to afford a trip to the seaside came here. It is now part of the **Hollingworth Lake Country Park** which has a fine visitor centre and a number of pleasant walks around its shores.

SUMMIT

5 miles NE of Rochdale off the A6033

At Summit, the Rochdale to Halifax railway line dives into a tunnel that runs for a mile and a half under the Summit Ridge of the Pennines before emerging in Yorkshire. This extraordinary feat of engineering was completed in 1844, as remarkable in its way as the Roman Causey which follows a similar route on top of the hills.

SOUTH OF ROCHDALE

MILNROW

2 miles S of Rochdale on the A640

It was to this small industrial town in the foothills of the Pennines that John Collier came as the schoolmaster in 1729. Collier is perhaps better known as Tim Bobbin, the first of the Lancashire dialect poets. Collier remained in Milnrow for the rest of his life and, drinking rather more than he should, earned extra money by selling his verse and painting pub signs. The local pub which dates back to the early 1800s is, appropriately, named after him.

SHAW

3 miles SE of Rochdale on the A633

A typical mill town, founded on the wealth of the cotton trade, this was also a market town for the surrounding area. **Jubilee Colliery**, to the northeast of the town centre, closed in 1932 but has been reclaimed as a nature reserve and is now an attractive haven for wildlife in the Beal Valley.

DELPH

7 miles SE of Rochdale on the A6052

Delph's name comes from the old English for quarry, a reference to the bakestone quarries found to the north of the village. Also close by, high on a hill above the village, stands **Castleshaw**, one of a series of forts the Romans built on their military road between Chester and York. The banks and ditches give visitors an excellent indication of the scale of the fort. Many of the items found during recent excavations are on show in the Saddleworth Museum.

DOBCROSS

7 miles SE of Rochdale off the A6052

This attractive Pennine village, once the commercial heart of the district of Saddleworth, retains many of its original weavers' cottages, clothiers and merchants' houses, and little has changed around the village square in the last 200 years. Used as the location for the film *Yanks*, Dobcross is also notable as the birthplace of the giant Platt Brothers Textile Machinery business which was, in the latter part of the 19th century, the largest such machine manufacturing firm in the world.

UPPERMILL

8 miles SE of Rochdale on the A62

Of the 14 villages that make up Saddleworth parish, Uppermill is the most central. It is home to the area's oldest building, **Saddleworth Parish Church** which was originally built in the 1100s by the Stapletons as their family chapel. Extended over the years, it has several interesting features including a gravestone to commemorate the Bill's o'Jack's murders. In 1832, the people of Saddleworth were stunned to learn that the landlord of the Bill's o'Jack's Inn and his son had been bludgeoned to death. Several thousand people turned out for the funeral but the case was never solved. The tombstone relates the whole story.

Almost a century and a half later, the whole country was horrified by the "Moors Murderers", Ian Brady and Myra Hindley, who buried four of their child victims on Saddleworth Moor.

The story of this once isolated area is illustrated at the **Saddleworth Museum**, housed in an old mill building on the banks of the Huddersfield Canal. There is a reconstruction of an 18th century weaver's cottage as well as a collection of textile machinery, a local history gallery and local art exhibitions.

Also in Uppermill is the **Brownhill Visitor Centre**, which

not only has information on the northern section of the Tame Valley but also exhibitions on local wildlife and the area's history.

DIGGLE

8 miles SE of Rochdale off the A62

Part of the **Oldham Way** footpath, a 30 mile scenic walk through the countryside on the edge of the Peak District National Park, crosses the moorland near Diggle. Much of the village itself is a conservation area where the pre-industrial weaving community has been preserved along with some of the traditional skills. However, Diggle Mill, which used to operate the second largest waterwheel in the country, no longer exists.

DENSHAW

5 miles SE of Rochdale on the A640

In the moorland above the village is the source of the River Tame which flows through the Saddleworth area and eventually joins the River Goyt at Stockport. A charming 18th century village, Denshaw's Scandinavian name would suggest that there has been a settlement here for many centuries.

Until 1974, the Saddleworth area was part of the West Riding of Yorkshire and residents of the parish are still eligible to play for the Yorkshire cricket team. Cricket has always been a passion here. One 19th century mill owner built 'Cricketers Row' near Denshaw to house his team and the terrace even includes one for the 12th man.

The Huddersfield Narrow Canal, completed in 1811, is one of three canals that crossed the difficult terrain of the Pennines and linked Lancashire with Yorkshire. The entrance to the Standedge Canal Tunnel, the longest and highest canal tunnel in Britain, is located in Diggle. The last cargo boat passed through the tunnel in 1921 but following a long period of closure, it is now possible to experience an atmospheric guided boat trip into the tunnel which stretches for more than 3¼ miles from Diggle in Lancashire at one side of the Pennines, to Marsden in West Yorkshire at the other. Details of the trips are available from the Visitor Centre.

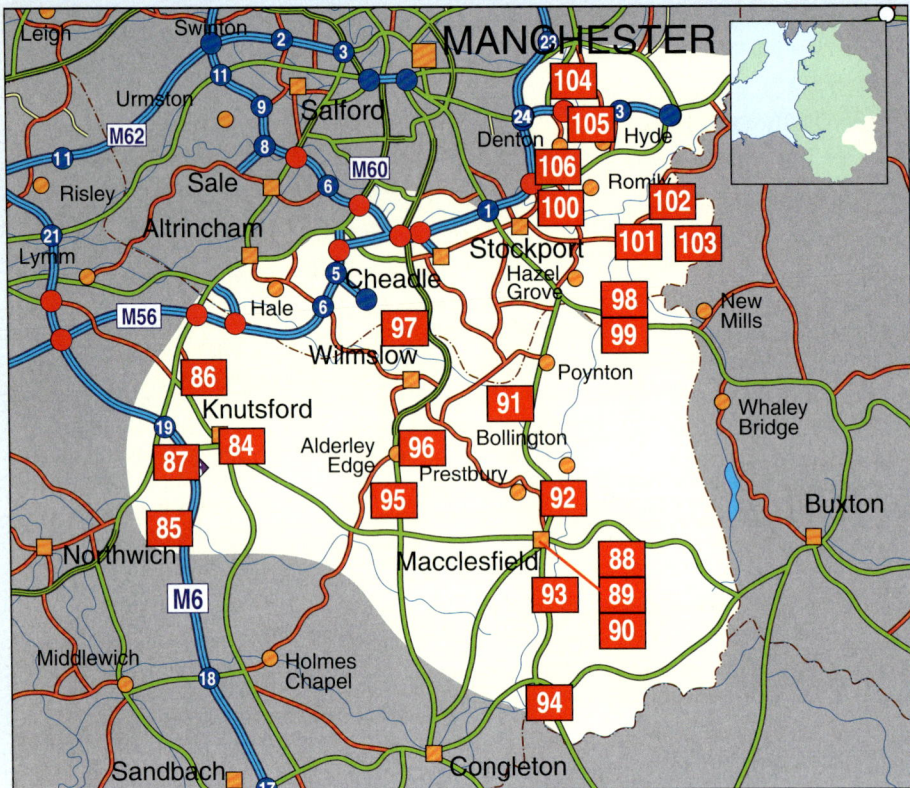

Northeast Cheshire

Although known as part of the Cheshire Plain, this north-eastern area is far from level and contains notable outcrops such as Alderley Edge, 600ft high and the Pennine scenery of The Panhandle, the narrow finger of land pointing up to West Yorkshire

The area is still mainly rural, with just two major settlements. The former silk manufacturing town of Macclesfield, home to the only Silk Museum in the country, is a busy and prosperous place. Knutsford is forever associated with the author Mrs Gaskell who lived here and based the characters in her best-loved novel, *Cranford,* on its inhabitants.

Although comparatively small in area, northeast Cheshire boasts a remarkably rich inventory of historic houses. The noble Georgian mansion of Lyme Hall, familiar as Mr Darcy's residence, Pemberley, in the BBC's 1995 production of *Pride and Prejudice,* has carvings by Grinling Gibbons, tapestries from Mortlake, and a unique collection of English clocks. Tatton Hall, near Knutsford, has a world-class collection of furniture by Gillow of Lancaster, as well as a fine collection of paintings by such Old Masters as Canaletto and Van Dyck. Smaller but equally fascinating are Tabley House near Knutsford, Adlington Hall, home of the Legh family since 1315, and the Elizabethan-style Capesthorne Hall with its magnificent array of turrets, towers, domes and cupolas. Perhaps best of all, because so characteristic of Cheshire, are the lovely 'Black and White' houses such as Gawsworth Hall and Bramhall Hall. Add to the list of attractions a number of picturesque villages - Prestbury, Styal and Lower Peover, for example, and it's clear that northeast Cheshire repays a leisurely exploration.

An unusual exhibition and well worth visiting is the Penny Farthing Museum, located in the Courtyard Coffee House off King Street. These bizarre machines were in fashion for barely twenty years before the last model was manufactured in 1892. The collection includes a replica of the famous "Starley Giant" with a front wheel 7ft in diameter and a sign outside the coffee house promises a free tea to anyone arriving on a penny-farthing.

KNUTSFORD

Knutsford and its people were the heroes of one of the most durable of Victorian novels, Elizabeth Gaskell's *Cranford* which recently received an acclaimed BBC-TV adaptation. Mrs Gaskell's gently humorous, sympathetic but sharply-observed portrait of the little Cheshire town and the foibles and pre-occupations of its citizens, was first published in 1853 and is still delighting readers today. Elizabeth was scarcely a month old when she came to Knutsford. Her mother had died shortly after her birth: her father sent her here to be brought up by an aunt who lived in a road which has now been re-named Gaskell Avenue. The motherless child grew up to be both strikingly beautiful and exceptionally intelligent. Early on she evinced a lively interest in the town's characters and its history. (She was intrigued, for example, to find that in the house next door to her aunt's had once lived a notorious highwayman, Edward Higgins, hanged for his crimes in 1767. She wrote a story about him). Marriage to William Gaskell, a Unitarian pastor in Manchester, took her away from Knutsford, although she returned often and for long periods, and after her death in 1865 was buried in the grounds of the Unitarian Chapel here.

The Knutsford that Elizabeth Gaskell knew so well and wrote about so vividly has expanded a great deal since those days of course, but in its compact centre, now designated an "outstanding area of conservation", the narrow streets and cobbled alleys still evoke the intimacy of a small Victorian town. Two parallel roads, Toft Street and King Street, form a rectangle surrounding the old town. But Mrs Gaskell would surely be astonished by the building erected in King Street to her memory by Mr Richard Harding Watt in 1907. A gifted entrepreneur, Mr Watt had made a huge fortune in Manchester as a glove manufacturer, but what really aroused his enthusiasm was the flamboyant architecture he had seen during his travels through Spain, southern Italy and the Near East.

On his return, he spent lavishly on trying to transform Knutsford in Cheshire into Knutsford-on-the-Mediterranean. At the north end of the town, he built a laundry complete with Byzantine domes and a minaret. A vaguely Ottoman style of architecture welcomed serious-minded artisans to his Ruskin Reading Rooms. In Legh Road, he erected a series of villas whose south-facing frontages are clearly in need of a really hot sun. And in King Street, as homage to the town's most famous resident, Richard Watt spent thousands of Victorian pounds on the Gaskell Memorial Tower. This tall, blank-walled building seems a rather incongruous tribute to the author who was herself so open and so down-to-earth.

But it is eccentrics like Richard Watt who make English

architecture as interesting as it is. He was so proud of his contribution to the town's new buildings that, travelling on his coach to the railway station, he would rise to his feet and raise his hat to salute them. As he did so, one day in 1913, his horse suddenly shied, the carriage overturned, and Richard Watt was thrown out and killed. What other changes he might have made to this grand old town, had he lived, we can only imagine.

Close by, in Tatton Street, is the **Knutsford Heritage Centre**. Knutsford is a town with a long history – Edward I granted the town a Charter in 1262, (on August 3rd of that year, to be precise); at the same time, the local landowner, William de Tabley, was given a money-making licence to control the market. The Heritage Centre is housed in a restored 17th century timber-framed building which in Victorian times was a smithy. During the restoration, the old forge and bellows were found in a remarkable state of preservation. The wrought iron gate in front of the centre was specially created for the Centre and depicts dancing girls taking part in Knutsford's famous Royal May Day celebrations – Royal because in 1887 the Prince and Princess of Wales honoured the festivities with their presence. Every May Day the town centre streets are closed to all traffic except for the May Queen's procession in which colourful characters such as "Jack in Green", "Highwayman Higgins", "Lord

Chamberlain", Morris and Maypole dancers, and many others take part. One curious tradition whose origins are unknown is the practice of covering the streets and pavements with ordinary sand and then, using white sand, creating elaborate patterns on top.

AROUND KNUTSFORD

Sweeping up to the very edge of Knutsford are the grounds of **Tatton Park**, 2000 acres of exquisite parkland landscaped in

85 THE GOLDEN PHEASANT

Plumley

A major refurbishment and new menu has given this pub a whole new lease of life

see page 220

Tatton Hall, nr Knutsford

86 TATTON PARK

Knutsford

Magnificent estate with mansion, grand garden, deer park, farm and Tudor Old Hall

see page 222

87 TABLEY HOUSE

Knutsford

Tabley House was designed by John Carr of York for Sir Peter Byrne Leicester and completed in 1767.

see page 222

the 18th century by the celebrated Humphrey Repton. This lovely park, where herds of red and fallow deer roam at will, provides a worthy setting for the noble Georgian mansion designed by the equally celebrated architect Samuel Wyatt. The combination of the two men's talents created a house and park that have become one of the National Trust's most visited attractions. Tatton's opulent staterooms, containing paintings by artists such as Canaletto and Van Dyck along with superb collections of porcelain and furniture, provided the television series *Brideshead Revisited* with a sumptuous setting for Marchmain House.

More than 200 elegant pieces of furniture were commissioned from the celebrated cabinet-makers, Gillow of Lancaster. Particularly fine are the superb bookcases in the Library, constructed to house the Egerton family's collection of more than 8000 books. By contrast, the stark servants' rooms and cellars give a vivid idea of what life below stairs was really like. The Egerton family built Tatton Park to replace the much earlier **Tudor Old Hall** which nestles in a wood in the deer park and dates back to around 1520. Here, visitors are given a guided tour through time from the late Middle Ages up to the 1950s. Flickering light from candles reveals the ancient timber roof of the Great Hall, supported by ornate quatrefoils, while underfoot, the floor is strewn with rushes, providing a warm place for

the medieval Lord of the Manor and his servants to sleep. There's much more: Home Farm is a working farm, but working now as it did in the 1930s, complete with vintage machinery. Traditional crafts, (including pottery), stables and many farm animals provide a complete picture of rural life some sixty years ago. Tatton's famous gardens include a Victorian maze, an orangery and fernery, a serene Japanese garden, American redwoods, and a splendid Italian terraced garden. There's also a busy programme of educational activities for children, an adventure playground, shops, and a restaurant. You can even get married in the sumptuous mansion and hold your reception either in the house itself, in the recently refurbished Tenants Hall which can cater for parties of up to 430, or in a marquee in the magnificent grounds. With so much on offer no wonder Tatton Park has been described as the most complete historic estate in the country.

Just to the west of Knutsford, on the A5033, is **Tabley House**, home of the Leicester family from 1272 to 1975. Mrs Gaskell often came to picnic in the grounds of the last of their houses, a stately Georgian mansion designed by John Carr for the first Lord de Tabley in 1761. This Lord de Tabley loved paintings and it was his son's passion for art, and his hunger for others to share it, which led to the creation of London's National Gallery. His personal collection of English pictures, on display in Tabley House, includes works by Turner (who painted the house several times), Lely, Reynolds, Opie and Martin Danby, along with furniture by Chippendale, and fascinating family memorabilia spanning three centuries. The 17th century chapel next to the house looks perfectly in place but it was originally built on an island in Tabley Mere and only moved to its present site in 1927.

MERE

3 miles NW of Knutsford on the A50/A556

One of the **Kilton Inn's** more notorious guests, back in the 1700s, was Dick Turpin. The intrepid highwayman made this historic old inn the base from which he plundered travellers along the Knutsford to Warrington road (now the comparatively safe A50). After one such robbery (and murder) Turpin, on his famous horse Black Bess, "galloped to the Kilton and, altering the clock, strolled on to the bowling green and proved an alibi by the short time he took to cover the four miles".

MOBBERLEY

2 miles E of Knutsford on the B5085

Mobberley village is scattered along the B5085, with its notable church set slightly apart. The main glory here is the spectacular woodwork inside: massive roof beams with striking winged figures and one of the finest rood screens in the country, dated 1500. The screen is covered with a rich tracery of leaves and fruit, coats-of-arms, and

religious symbols. Two generations of the Mallory family held the rectorship here, one of them for 53 years. He is commemorated in the east window. Another window honours his grandson, George Mallory, the mountaineer who perished while making his third attempt to climb Mount Everest in 1924.

At the Whitsun Bank Holiday each year steam traction enthusiasts from all across the country descend on the village for the **Mobberley Steam Party** hosted by the Bull's Head Inn.

LOWER PEOVER

4 miles S of Knutsford on the B5081

The village of Lower Peover (pronounced Peever) is effectively made up of two hamlets. One is grouped around the village green on the B5081, the other is at the end of a cobbled lane. It's a picturesque little group. There's a charming old coaching inn, The Bells of Peover, which numbers amongst its former customers Generals Patton and Eisenhower during World War II. The American flag still flies here alongside the Union Jack. Nearby are a handsome village school founded in 1710, and a lovely black and white timbered church, more than 700 years old. St Oswald's is notable as one of the few timber-framed churches in the country still standing. Inside, there is a wealth of carved wood – pews and screens, pulpit and lectern, and a massive medieval chest made from a single log of bog oak. At one

In Tabley, at the Old School, is the Tabley Cuckoo Clock Collection. Brothers Roman and Maz Piekarski are well-known horologists and clock restorers and over the last 25 years they have sought out and renovated some of the rarest and most notable examples of this 300-year-old craft. Amongst them are some mid-19th century cuckoo clocks which incorporated complex musical movements to reproduce popular tunes of the day. Also on display are five fairground organs, 12 trumpeter clocks and tools, all from the Black Forest.

St Oswald's Church, Lower Peover

There's a memorial to him in the church nearby, but many many more to the Mainwaring family whose fine monuments crowd beside each other in both the north and south chapels. (Please note that opening hours at the Hall are restricted).

MACCLESFIELD

Nestling below the hills of the High Peak, Macclesfield was once an important silk manufacturing town. Charles Roe built the first silk mill here, beside the River Bollin, in 1743 and for more than a century and a half, Macclesfield was known as *the* silk town. It's appropriate then that Macclesfield can boast the country's only **Silk Museum** where visitors are given a lively introduction to all aspects of the silk industry, from cocoon to loom. The museum has an award-winning audio-visual presentation, there are fascinating exhibitions on the Silk Road across Asia, on silk cultivation, fashion and other uses of silk. A shop dedicated to silk offers a range of attractive and unusual gifts – scarves, ties, silk cards and woven pictures along with inexpensive gifts for children.

The silk theme continues at nearby **Paradise Mill**. Built in the 1820s, it is now a working museum demonstrating silk weaving on 26 jacquard hand looms. Exhibitions and restored workshops and living rooms capture the working conditions and lives of mill workers in the

88 PARADISE MILL MUSEUM

Macclesfield

Paradise Mill Museum was a working silk mill until 1981.

see page 224

time, local girls who wished to marry a farmer were required to raise its lid with one hand to demonstrate they had the strength to cope with farm life.

About 3 miles east of Lower Peover is **Peover Hall**, very much hidden away at the end of a winding country road but well worth tracking down. During World War II, General George Patton lived for a while at the Hall which was conveniently close to his then headquarters at Knutsford.

1930s. It is also possible to buy locally-made silk products here. The Silk Museum is housed in what used to be the Macclesfield Sunday School, erected in 1813. The school finally closed in 1970 and the Silk Museum now shares this rather grand building with the town's **Heritage Centre** which has some interesting displays on Macclesfield's rich and exciting past, (the town was occupied for five days by Scottish troops during the Jacobite Rebellion of 1745, for example), and on the Sunday School itself.

In pre-Saxon times, Macclesfield was known as "Hameston" – the homestead on the rock, and on that rock is set the church founded by King Edward I and Queen Eleanor. From the modern town, a walk to the church involves climbing a gruelling flight of 108 steps. **St Michael and All Angels** was extended in the 1890s but its 14th century core remains, notably the Legh Chapel built in 1422 to receive the body of Piers Legh who had fought at Agincourt and died at the Siege of Meaux. Another chapel contains the famous Legh Pardon brass, which recalls the medieval practice of selling pardons for sins past, and even for those not yet committed. The inscription on the brass records that, in return for saying five Paternosters and five Aves, the Legh family received a pardon for 26,000 years and 26 days.

One of the Macclesfield area's most famous sons is Charles Frederick Tunnicliffe, the celebrated bird and wild-life artist, who was born at the nearby village of Langley in 1901. He studied at the Macclesfield School of Art and first came to public attention with his illustrations for Henry Williamson's *Tarka the Otter* in 1927. A collection of Tunnicliffe's striking paintings can be seen at the **West Park Museum** on the northwest edge of the town. This purpose-built museum, founded in 1898 by the Brocklehurst family, also includes exhibits of ancient Egyptian artefacts, fine and decorative arts.

Much less well-known than Tunnicliffe is William Buckley who was born in Macclesfield around 1780 and later became a soldier. He took part in a mutiny at Gibraltar against the Rock's commanding officer, the Duke of York, father-to-be of Queen Victoria. The mutiny failed and Buckley was transported to Australia. There he escaped into the outback and became the leader of an aboriginal tribe who took

89 MULBERRY TREE

Macclesfield

Situated in the ideal position for visitors to the excellent and award winning Silk museum.

see page 223

90 WEST PARK MUSEUM

Macclesfield

West Park Museum was donated by Marianne Brocklehurst and her brother, Peter Pownall Brocklehurst "for the education, refinement and pleasure of the people for all time to come."

see page 224

Trinity Stones, Macclesfield

91 ADLINGTON HALL

Adlington

Adlington Hall, the home of the Leghs of Adlington from 1315 to the present day, was built on the site of a hunting lodge which stood in the Forest of Macclesfield in 1040.

 see page 225

this giant of a man, some 6 feet 6 inches tall, as the reincarnation of a dead chief. For 32 years Buckley never saw a white man or heard a word of English. When the explorer John Bateman, on his way to found what is now Melbourne, discovered him, Buckley had virtually forgotten his mother tongue. He was pardoned, given a pension and died at Hobart at the age of 76.

AROUND MACCLESFIELD

PRESTBURY

3 miles N of Macclesfield via the A523/A538

A regular winner of the Best Kept Village title, Prestbury is a charming village where a tree-lined High Street runs down to a bridge over the River Bollin, ancient stocks stand against the church wall, old coaching inns and black and white buildings mingle with the mellow red brick work of later Georgian houses. The Church of St Peter, dating from the 13th

Old Priests House, Prestbury

century, still maintains a tradition which began in 1577. Every autumn and winter evening at 8pm a curfew bell is rung, with the number of chimes corresponding to the date of the month. Close by is a building known as the **Norman Chapel** with a striking frontage carved with the characteristic Norman zig-zags and beaked heads. Even older are the carved fragments of an 8th century Saxon cross preserved under glass in the graveyard. Opposite the church is a remarkable magpie timber-framed house which is now a bank but used to be the Vicarage. During the Commonwealth period, the rightful incumbent was debarred from preaching in the church by the Puritans. Undaunted, the priest addressed his parishioners from the tiny balcony of his Vicarage.

ADLINGTON

4 miles N of Macclesfield off the A523

Adlington boasts a fine old house, **Adlington Hall**, which has been the home of the Legh family since 1315 and is now one of the county's most popular attractions. Quadrangular in shape, this magnificent manor house has two distinctive styles of architecture: black and white half-timbered buildings on two sides, later Georgian additions in warm red brick on the others. There is much to see as you tour the hall, with beautifully polished wooden floors and lovely antique furnishings enhancing the air of elegance and grandeur. The Great Hall is a

114

Adlington Hall, Adlington

92 THE RISING SUN INN

Rainow

A charming old coaching inn offering homemade food and real ales in a friendly environment.

see page 226

breathtaking sight, a vast room of lofty proportions that set off perfectly the exquisitely painted walls. The beautifully preserved 17th century organ here has responded to the touch of many maestros, none more illustrious than George Frederick Handel who visited the Hall in the 1740s.

It wasn't long after Handel's visit to Cheshire that the county was gripped by a mania for building canals, a passion that has left Cheshire with a uniquely complex network of these environmentally friendly waterways.

BOLLINGTON

4 miles NE of Macclesfield on the B5091

In its 19th century heyday, there were 13 cotton mills working away at Bollington, a little town perched on the foothills of the High Peak. Two of the largest mills, the Clarence and the Adelphi, still stand, although now adapted to other purposes. The Victorian shops and

cottages around Water Street and the High Street recall those busy days. A striking feature of the town is the splendid 20-arched viaduct which once carried the railway over the River Dean. It is now part of the **Middlewood Way** a ten mile, traffic-free country trail which follows a scenic route from Macclesfield to Marple. The Way is

White Nancy, Bollington

Just as remarkable as the viaduct in Bollington, although in a different way, is White Nancy. This sugar-loaf shaped, whitewashed round tower stands on Kerridge Hill, more than 900ft above sea level. It was erected in 1817 to commemorate the Battle of Waterloo and from it there are sweeping views in all directions..

93 THE OLD KINGS HEAD

Gurnett

Beautiful property set in a beautiful location. Come here to experience a new and inviting atmosphere and enjoy the great food that is on offer.

see page 226

94 THE HARRINGTON ARMS

Bosley

A charming country inn extending a warm welcome to all guests and serving delicious homecooked food and real ale.

see page 226

open to walkers, cyclists and horse riders and, during the season, cycles are available for hire, complete with child seats if required.

SUTTON

2 miles S of Macclesfield on minor road off the A523

This small village, close to the Macclesfield Canal, is honoured by scholars as the birthplace of Raphael Holinshed whose famous *Chronicles of England, Scotland & Ireland* (1577) provided the source material for no fewer than 14 of Shakespeare's plays. As well as drawing heavily on the facts in the Chronicles, the Immortal Bard wasn't above plagiarising some of Holinshed's happier turns of phrase.

BOSLEY

6 miles S of Macclesfield on the A523

To the east of Bosley town centre runs the **Macclesfield Canal**, one of the highest waterways in England, running for much of its length at more than 500 feet above sea level. Thomas Telford was the surveyor of the 26-mile long route, opened in 1831, which links the Trent & Mersey and the Peak Forest canals. Between Macclesfield and Congleton, the canal descends over a hundred feet in a spectacular series of 12 locks at Bosley, before crossing the River Dane via Telford's handsome iron viaduct. Other unusual features of this superbly engineered canal are the two "roving bridges" south of Congleton. These swing from one bank to the other where the towpath changes sides and so

enabled horses to cross over without having to unhitch the tow-rope.

GAWSWORTH

3 miles SW of Macclesfield off the A536

Gawsworth Hall is a captivating sight with its dazzling black and white half-timbered walls and lofty three-decker Tudor windows. The Hall was built in 1480 by the Fitton family, one of whose descendants, the celebrated beauty, Mary Fitton is believed to be the "Dark Lady" of Shakespeare's sonnets. The Bard would no doubt approve of Gawsworth's famous open-air theatre where performances range from his own plays to Gilbert and Sullivan operas with the Hall serving as a lovely backdrop. Surrounded by a huge park, Gawsworth, to quote its owner Timothy Richards, "is the epitome of a lived-in historic house". Every room that visitors see (which is virtually every room in the house) is in daily use by him and his family. And what wonderful rooms they are. Myriad windows bathe the rooms in light, the low ceilings and modest dimensions radiate calm, and even the richly-carved main staircase is conceived on a human scale. The beautifully sited church, and the lake nearby, add still more to the appeal of this magical place. The Hall is open every afternoon during the season, at other times by appointment.

CAPESTHORNE HALL

5 miles W of Macclesfield off the A34

The home of the Bromley-

Davenport family for generations, **Capesthorne Hall** dates back to 1730 but, following a fire in 1861, was remodelled and extended by the celebrated architects Blore and Salvin. The present building presents a magnificent medley of Elizabethan style turrets and towers, domes and cupolas while inside the house there is a wealth of portraits and artefacts collected by family members during the course of their Grand Tours. In medieval times the head of the Bromley-Davenport family held the post of Chief Forester of Macclesfield Forest which gave him authority to mete out summary justice to anyone who transgressed the savage forestry laws. As a reminder of their power, the family crest includes the severed head of a felon. One of these crests, on the main staircase built in the 1860s, was commissioned by the staunchly Conservative Bromley-Davenport of the day and the felon's head is instantly recognisable as the Liberal leader of the day, W.E. Gladstone.

NETHER ALDERLEY
6 miles NW of Macclesfield on the A34

The village of Nether Alderley lies on the A34 and here you will find **Nether Alderley Mill**, a delightful 15th century watermill that has been restored by the National Trust. The red sandstone walls are almost hidden under the huge sweep of its stone tiled roof. Inside is the original Elizabethan woodwork and Victorian mill machinery which is still in working order, with two tandem overshot

wheels powering the mill. Opening times are restricted.

ALDERLEY EDGE
6 miles NW of Macclesfield on the A34

Alderley Edge takes its name from the long, wooded escarpment, nearly two miles long, that rises 600ft above sea level and culminates in sandy crags overlooking the Cheshire Plain. In Victorian times, this spectacular area was the private preserve of the Stanley family and it was only under great pressure that they grudgingly allowed the "Cottentots" of Manchester access on occasional summer weekends. It was the Stanley daughters who took great umbrage when the Wizard Inn hung up a new sign. They demanded its removal. The Merlin-like figure depicted could, they claimed, be taken as a representation of their father, Lord Stanley, at that time a virtual recluse and more than a little eccentric. Nowadays, however, walkers can roam freely

95 NETHER ALDERLEY MILL

Nether Alderley
One of only four virtually complete corn mills in Cheshire.

🏛 *see page 228*

If you have time whilst visiting Nether Alderley, visit the 14th century Church of St Mary which is almost a private mausoleum for the Alderley branch of the Stanley family: monuments to dead Stanleys are everywhere. Living members of the family were provided with an unusual richly carved pew, set up on the wall like an opera box and reached by a flight of steps outside.

16th Century Corn Mill, Nether Alderly

96 NO. 15 WINE BAR

Alderley Edge

Come to this stunning property for great food and drink. Perfect for a glass of wine after work or for an evening out.

see page 227

97 QUARRY BANK MILL & STYAL ESTATE

Styal

One of Britain's greatest industrial heritage sites, including complete working cotton mill

see page 228

along the many footpaths through the woods, one of which will take them to **Hare Hill Gardens**, a little-known National Trust property. These Victorian gardens include fine woodland, a walled garden themed in blue, white and yellow flowers, and huge banks of rhododendrons. There is access by way of gravel paths for the less able.

WILMSLOW

9 miles NW of Macclesfield off the A34

The oldest building in Wilmslow is **St Bartholomew's Church**, built between 1517 and 1537, and notable for its magnificent ceiling, some striking effigies, and for the fact that Prime Minister-to-be W.E. Gladstone worshipped here as a boy. A hamlet in medieval times, Wilmslow mushroomed as a mill town in the 18th and 19th centuries, and is now a busy commuter town offering a good choice of inns, hotels and restaurants.

STYAL

1 mile N of Wilmslow, on a minor road off the B5166

Cared for by the National Trust, **Styal Country Park** is set in 250 acres of the beautifully wooded valley of the River Bollin and offers many woodland and riverside walks. The Park is open to the public from dawn to dusk throughout the year and is a wonderful place for picnics. Standing within the Park is **Quarry Bank Mill**, a grand old building erected in 1784 and one of the first

generation of cotton mills. It was powered by a huge iron waterwheel fed by the River Bollin. Visitors follow the history of the mill through various galleries and displays within the museum, including weaving and spinning demonstrations, and can experience for themselves, with the help of guides dressed in period costume, what life was like for the hundred girls and boys who once lived in the Apprentice House.

Also within the park is the delightful **Styal Village** which was established by the mill's original owner, Samuel Greg, a philanthropist and pioneer of the factory system. He took children from the slums of Manchester to work in his mill, and in return for their labour provided them with food, clothing, housing, education and a place of worship.

ALTRINCHAM

7 miles NW of Wilmslow on the A560

The writer Thomas de Quincey visited Altrincham in the early 1800s and thought its bustling market "the gayest scene he ever saw". The market is still very active although the old houses that de Quincey also noted have sadly gone. A modern bustling town, Altrincham nevertheless has a long history with a charter granted in 1290 and clear evidence that there was a settlement beside the River Bollin some 6000 years ago. Even older than that is the prehistoric body preserved in peat discovered on Lindow Common nearby. From Victorian times, Altrincham has been a favoured retreat for Manchester businessmen and the town is well-supplied with inns and restaurants.

CHEADLE HULME

7 miles NE of Wilmslow off the A34

Developed in Victorian times as a commuter town for better-off workers in Manchester, Cheadle Hulme is a busy place with a fine park on its eastern edge in which stands one of the grandest old "magpie" houses in Cheshire, **Bramall Hall**. This eye-catching, rambling perfection of black and white timbered buildings overlooks some 62 acres of exquisitely landscaped woods, lakes and formal gardens. The oldest parts of the Hall date from the 1300s: for five of the next six centuries it was owned by the same family, the Davenports. Over the years, the Davenport family continually altered and extended the originally quite modest manor house. But whenever they added a new Banqueting Hall, "Withdrawing Room", or even a Chapel, they took pains to ensure that its design harmonised happily with its more ancient neighbours. Along with Little Moreton Hall and Gawsworth Hall, Bramall represents the fullest flowering of a lovely architectural style whose most distinctive examples are all to be found in Cheshire.

DISLEY

8 miles SE of Stockport on the A6

The small town of Disley lies close to the Macclesfield Canal and little

more than half a mile from **Lyme Park Country Park**. At the heart of the 1400 acre park where red and fallow deer roam freely stands Lyme Park (National Trust), home of the Legh family for more than 600 years. The elegant Palladian exterior of this great house encloses a superb Elizabethan mansion. Amongst the many treasures on show are carvings by Grinling Gibbons, tapestries from Mortlake, and a unique collection of English clocks. The house featured many times in the BBC's 1995 production of *Pride and Prejudice* when it represented the exterior of Pemberley, the home of Elizabeth Bennett's curmudgeonly lover, Mr Darcy. The "Pemberley Trail" guides visitors to the bridge from which Elizabeth (Jennifer Ehle) first sees the imposing building; on through the courtyard and garden to the pool in which Mr Darcy (Colin Firth) takes a sexy dip – a scene which was definitely not part of Jane Austen's original novel. Don't expect the interior of Lyme Park to match the rooms shown in the series – all the "Pemberley" interiors were filmed at Sudbury Hall in Derbyshire.

THE PANHANDLE

The narrow finger of land pointing up to West Yorkshire was chopped off from Cheshire in the 1974 Local Government redrawing of boundaries, but some 35 years later most of its population still consider themselves Cheshire folk.

98 BLUEBERRIES

High Lane

Charming sandwich and coffee shop offering a relaxed atmosphere and an endless list of fillings for your sandwich

🍴 *see page 228*

99 THE RED LION INN

High Lane

Superb Robinsons Brewery pub offering fine food, real ales and 6 well furnished letting rooms.

🍴 🛏 *see page 229*

100 THE DUKE OF YORK

Romiley

The pub's unique Mediterranean inspired restaurant is instrumental in this establishment's popularity.

🍴 *see page 230*

101 RING O' BELLS

Marple

A popular venue with boaters, walkers and locals, offering freshly made food, Real Ales and a wealth of history.

🍴 see page 231

102 THE HARE & HOUNDS

Marple Bridge

This superb country pub is a mecca for walkers, the food providing very good motivation!

🍴 see page 232

103 THE ODDFELLOWS ARMS

Mellor

This three storey restaurant offers fine dining in smart, modern surroundings at pub prices.

🍴 see page 232

At its northern end lie Longdendale and Featherbed Moss, Pennine scenery quite unlike anywhere else in the county. Visitors to Cheshire tend to overlook this orphaned quarter: we strongly recommend that you seek it out.

MARPLE

4 miles SE of Stockport on the A626

Marple's most famous son is probably the poet and novelist Christopher Isherwood who was born at Marple Hall in 1904 and could have inherited it from his grandfather had he so wished. Instead, the author of *Mr Norris Changes Trains* and *Sally Bowles* (the source material for the musical *Cabaret*) renounced the life of a country squire for the more sybaritic attractions of California. But Marple made a great impression on him as is evident from his book *Kathleen and Frank*, based on the letters and diaries of his parents. Isherwood revels in the wildness of the Goyt Valley, not just its scenery but also its weather. This is the wettest part of Cheshire – "it never really dries out" says Isherwood – and winters are often punctuated with ferocious storms.

Marple is also famous for its

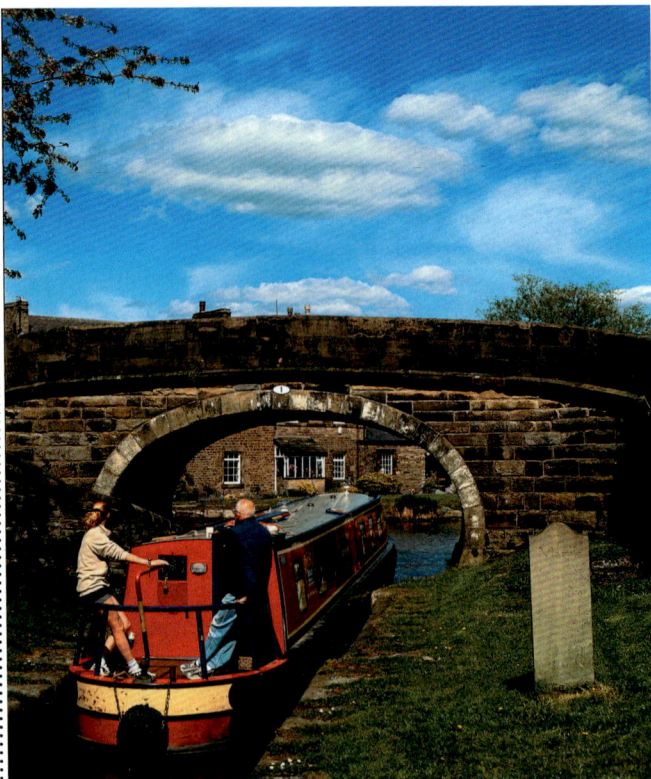

Macclesfield Canal, Marple

flight of 16 locks on the **Peak Forest Canal** and the mighty three-arched aqueduct that carries the canal over the River Goyt. At Marple, the Peak Forest Canal is joined by the **Macclesfield Canal** and there are some attractive towpath walks in both directions.

STALYBRIDGE

6 miles E of Manchester on the A57

Set beside the River Tame and with the North Pennine moors stretching for miles to the east, Stalybridge was one of the earliest cotton towns and its mill workers amongst the most radical and militant during the Chartist troubles of the 1840s. One of their leaders was a former Methodist minister, the Rev. Joseph Rayner Stephens, who had broken away from the Wesleyan ministry and established his own "Stephensite" chapels – one in King Street, Stalybridge, the other in the sister town across the Tame, Ashton under Lyme. He campaigned tirelessly against the long hours worked in the factories and the policy, introduced in 1834, of refusing poor relief outside the workhouse.

When in 1842 the mill-owners tried to impose reductions in pay,

the workers' embryo trade union closed all the mills in north Cheshire and south Lancashire. Stephens was tried and sentenced to 18 months in Chester gaol. On his release, he continued his efforts to improve the workers' pay and conditions for another 38 years. His funeral was attended by thousands and the workers erected a granite obelisk to his memory in Stalybridge's attractive Stamford Park. On it is inscribed a quotation from the speech he delivered at his trial: "The only true foundation of Society is the safety, the security and the happiness of the poor, from whom all other orders of Society arise".

MOTTRAM

4 miles NE of Hyde on the A628

Mottram village is set on a breezy hillside on the edge of the Pennines. According to the 1930s guide-book writer Arthur Mee, the off-Atlantic gusts that scour the village are known locally as Captain Whitle's Wind. In the 1500s, so the story goes, coffin bearers carrying the late Captain were struggling up the steep hill to the church when gale force winds swept the coffin from their shoulders and back down the hill.

104 THE GLOBE HOTEL

Dukinfield

This expertly run hotel is popular with locals and visitors alike who return again and again for the wholesome food on offer.

🛏 ▮ *see page 233*

105 THE BUSH INN

Hyde

This former morgue has certainly livened up its act! The great food and fine ales are definitely something to look forward to!

▮ *see page 233*

106 THE WOODLEY ARMS

Woodley

This warm and friendly pub is well worth a detour from the nearby M60.

▮ *see page 234*

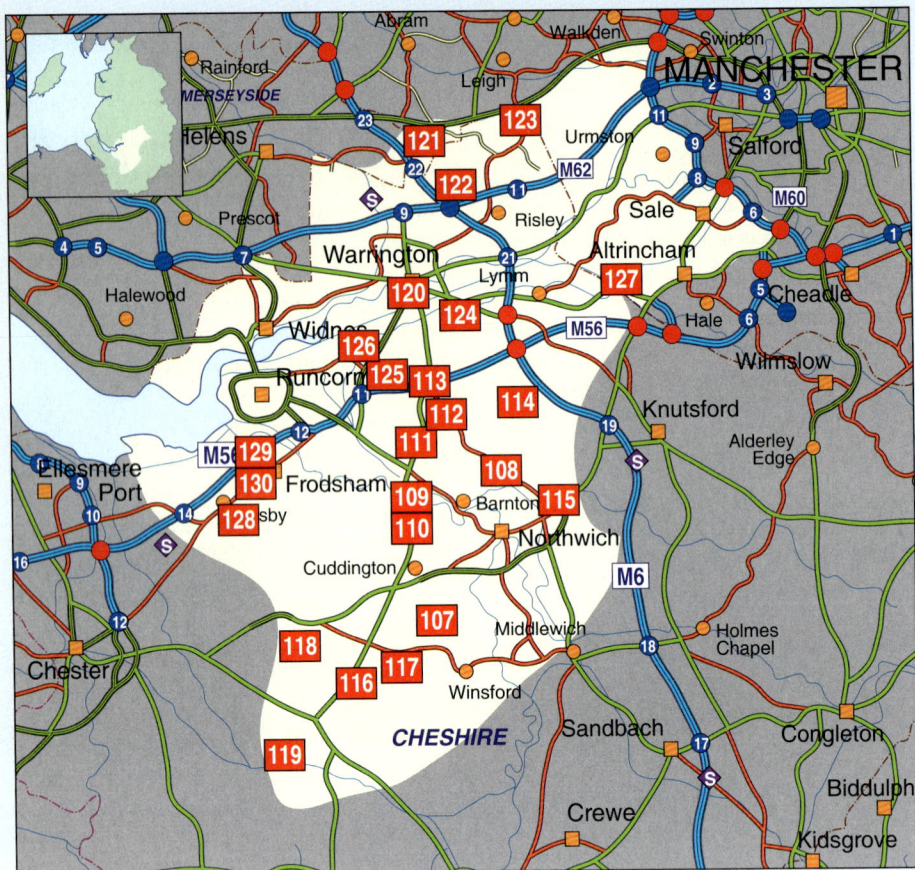

Northwest Cheshire

The north-western part of the county contains the pleasant rural area known as the Vale Royal, and the more industrial environs of Warrington, Widnes and Runcorn. The Vale Royal is a pretty name for a very attractive part of the county. It was Prince Edward, later Edward I, who named it so and who founded the great Abbey of Vale Royal in fulfilment of a solemn vow made in dramatic circumstances. He was returning from the Crusades when his ship was struck by a violent storm. The Prince made a pledge to the Virgin that if his life were spared he would found an abbey for one hundred monks. Lo! the ship was tossed ashore, the Prince and his companions waded through the surf to safety. In 1277, Edward, now King and with his young wife Eleanor of Castile by his side, honoured his vow by placing the first stone of Vale Royal Abbey.

"No monastery" he decreed "shall be more royal than this one in liberties, wealth and honour, throughout the whole world". Vale Royal Abbey, about 3 miles south of Northwich, indeed became the largest and most powerful Cistercian Abbey in England, a building reputedly even more glorious than Tintern or Fountains. Unlike those Abbeys, however, barely a stone of Vale Royal now remains in place. The abuse by the medieval abbots of their vast wealth, and of their unfettered power of life and death over the inhabitants of the Vale, may partly explain why their magnificent building was so quickly and completely destroyed after Henry VIII's closure of the monasteries. Over the centuries, the county has lost many fine buildings unnecessarily but the deliberate destruction of Vale Royal Abbey must take prime place in the litany of crimes against sublime architecture.

see page 234

NORTHWICH

The Vale Royal is now a district borough centred on the old salt town of Northwich. Even before the Romans arrived, Cheshire salt was well known and highly valued. But production on a major scale at Northwich began in 1670 when rock salt was discovered in nearby Marston. Salt may seem an inoffensive sort of product, but its extraction from the Keuper marl of the Cheshire Plain has produced some quite spectacular side-effects. In Elizabethan times, John Leland recorded that a hill at Combermere suddenly disappeared into underground workings, and Northwich later became notorious for the number of its buildings leaning at crazy angles because of subsidence. Even today, the White Lion Inn in Witton Street lies a complete storey lower than its original height.

The arrival in the 19th century of new processes of extraction brought different problems. In 1873, John Brunner and Ludwig Mond set up their salt works at Winnington on the northern edge of the town to manufacture alkali products based on brine. The ammonia process involved cast an appalling stench over the town and devastated vegetation for miles around. On the other hand, Brunner and Mond were model employers. They paid their workforce well, built houses for them and were amongst the first firms in the country to give their employees annual holidays with pay.

The long involvement of Northwich and Cheshire with salt production is vividly recorded at the **Salt Museum**, the only one of its kind in Britain. It stands in London Road and occupies what used to be the Northwich Workhouse which, like so many of those dreaded institutions, is an exceptionally handsome late-Georgian building, designed by George Latham, the architect of Arley Hall. With its unique collection of traditional working tools, and lively displays which include working models and videos, the Salt Museum recounts the fascinating story of the county's oldest industry. Ancient remains such as Roman evaporating pans and medieval salt rakes are on display and there is also much to remind visitors of the vital part that salt plays in the modern chemical industry.

AROUND NORTHWICH

ANDERTON

1 mile N of Northwich on minor road off the A533

One of the most stupendous engineering feats of the canal age was the **Anderton Boat Lift**, built in 1875 and recently restored. This extraordinary construction was designed to transfer boats from the Trent & Mersey Canal to the Weaver Navigation 50ft below. Two barges would enter the upper tank, two the lower, and by pumping water out of the lower tank, the boats would exchange places. Thousands of visitors come every year to marvel at this impressive structure which

Boat Lift, Anderton

108 MARBURY COUNTRY PARK

Comberbach

Marbury Country Park was once part of a large country estate whose history dates back to around AD 1200. Marbury itself means a fortified or stockaded dwelling by the mere or water.

see page 235

was conceived and designed by Edward Leader Williams who later went on to engineer the Manchester Ship Canal.

About a mile north of Anderton, **Marbury Country Park** was formerly part of a large country estate but the area is now managed by Cheshire County Council whose wardens have created a variety of habitats for plants, trees and animals. The Park lies at the edge of Budworth Mere and there are attractive walks and bridleways around the site where you'll also find an arboretum, picnic area and garden centre.

CUDDINGTON

5 miles W of Northwich off the A49

Cuddington is at the western end of the **Whitegate Way**, a pleasant rural walk of about 5 miles which follows the track bed of the old railway that used to carry salt from the Winsford mines. There is a picnic site and car park at the former Whitegate Station.

HATCHMERE

8 miles W of Northwich on the B5152

In medieval times the village of Hatchmere was surrounded by the Forest of Delamere, the largest of Cheshire's three woodlands. It stretched from the Mersey to Nantwich and although there were small areas of pasture and arable land, its status as a royal forest meant that the prime duty of those in charge of it was the preservation of the "beasts of the chase". It was not until 1812 that Delamere was officially "disafforested" and today Delamere Forest covers little more than an area about two miles long and one mile deep. From Hatchmere there are attractive trails through the woods and around Hatch Mere, the sizeable lake that gives the village its name.

ACTON BRIDGE

4 miles W of Northwich off the A49

The bridge here crosses the River Weaver, a waterway whose scenic

109 THE MAYPOLE INN

Acton Bridge

Whether it's a lunchtime snack or evening drink you are looking for, this fine inn will not let you down.

see page 235

110 THE HAZEL PEAR INN

Acton Bridge

A homely and comfortable real ale pub with restaurant, B&B letting rooms and camp site for all the family.

see page 236

111 CHETWODE ARMS

Lower Whitley

This is a super hidden place, tucked into the beautiful Cheshire countryside and set amongst the picturesque village of Lower Whitley.

see page 237

112 THE BIRCH & BOTTLE

Higher Whitley

This popular pub enjoys a well deserved reputation for fine food.

see page 236

113 THE RING O' BELLS

Lower Stretton

A true old fashioned pub with welcoming hosts, serving 3 real ales

see page 238

merits have been largely unsung. The Vale Royal Council has developed the **Weaver Valley Way** which allows walkers to enjoy some lovely stretches, particularly those between Weaver Bridge and Saltersford Locks, and the 6-mile route from Northwich to Winsford Marina.

During World War I, Acton Bridge made an unusual contribution to the war effort. Near the village was a plantation of hazel pear trees whose fruit is quite inedible but whose juice provided the khaki dye for soldiers' uniforms.

MARSTON

1 mile NE of Northwich on a minor road

In Victorian times, the Old Salt Mine at Marston was a huge tourist attraction. About 360ft deep and covering 35 acres, it even brought the Tsar of Russia here in 1844. Ten thousand lamps illuminated the huge cavern as the Emperor sat down to dinner here with eminent members of the Royal Society. By the end of the century, however, subsidence caused by the mine had made some 40 houses in the village uninhabitable, and one day in 1933 a hole 50ft wide and 300ft deep suddenly appeared close to the Trent & Mersey Canal. Happily, the village has now stabilised itself, and at the **Lion Salt Works Museum** on most afternoons you will find volunteer workers keeping alive the only surviving open pan salt works in Britain.

ANTROBUS

5 miles N of Northwich off the A559

Just a couple of miles from the magnificent Arley Hall and its world-famous gardens, is the pleasing little village of Antrobus, the only place in Britain to bear this name. Even the *Oxford Dictionary of English Place Names* is baffled by Antrobus: "Unexplained" it says curtly, adding as its excuse, "Hardly English". But what could be more English than The Antrobus Arms? Set in one and a half acres of land and surrounded by scenic countryside, this impressive building was first licensed in 1760 and ever since has been providing good food and fine ales for both locals and for travellers along the main A559 between Warrington and Northwich.

GREAT BUDWORTH

3 miles NE of Northwich off the A559

A charming small village nowadays, "Great" Budworth was accorded that designation at a time when it was the largest ecclesiastical parish in all Cheshire, the administrative centre for some 35 individual communities. The imposing church on the hill, built in the 14th and 15th centuries, reflects the village's importance during those years. **St Mary & All Saints** attracts many visitors to its host of quaint carvings and odd faces that peer out at unexpected corners: some with staring eyes, others with their tongues poking out. There's a man near the pulpit who appears to be drowsing through some interminable sermon. Under the roof of the nave you'll find a man with a serpent, another in mid-somersault, and a minstrel playing bagpipes. The distinguished 17th century historian, Sir Peter Leycester, is buried in the Lady Chapel, and in the Warburton Chapel there is a finely carved Tudor ceiling and 13th century oak stalls – the oldest in Cheshire. During the 1800s, Great Budworth was part of the Arley Hall estate and it is largely due to the energetic Squire Egerton-Warburton, a "conservationist" well ahead of his time, that so many of the attractive old cottages in the village are still in place.

PICKMERE

4 miles NE of Northwich on the B5391

The delightful village of Pickmere commands superb views of the Cheshire Plain, extending from the Dee estuary to the Pennine hills. The nearby **Pick Mere**, from which the village takes its name, is popular with wind surfers and yachtsmen, and boats are available for hire.

ARLEY

6miles NE of Northwich off the A559

From Junction 19 of the M6, take the A556 towards Northwich, then follow the signs for Arley Hall. There are many grand houses in Cheshire, and many fine gardens, but at **Arley Hall and Gardens** you will find one of the grandest houses and one of the finest gardens in perfect harmony. The present Hall was completed in 1845, a few years after Rowland Egerton-Warburton arrived at Arley with his new bride, Mary Brooke. The newly-married

couple took possession of a dilapidated old mansion, infested with rats and with antiquated drains from which an unbearable stench drifted through the house. Understandably, Rowland and Mary soon demolished the old hall and in its place rose a sumptuous early-Victorian stately home complete with (bearing in mind those drains) such state-of-the-art innovations as "Howden's Patent Atmospheric Air Dispensers". Rowland and Mary were both ardent gardeners and it was they who master-minded the magnificent panoramas of today's Arley Gardens. Rowland is credited with creating what is believed to be the first herbaceous border in England; his descendant, the present Viscount Ashbrook, has continued that tradition by cultivating "The Grove", an informal woodland garden planted with spring bulbs, flowering shrubs and exotic trees, a pleasing contrast to the more formal design of the main gardens.

Other attractions at Arley include a tea room housed in a beautifully converted 16th century barn and a plant nursery offering a wide selection of herbaceous and other plants.

Stockley Farm at Arley, is a 400-acre organic dairy farm that provides a great family day out. A visit begins with a tractor and trailer ride to the farm where there are always baby animals for children to handle and feed. Adult animals include an 18-hand shire horse, Star, a lovely big pig called Olive, and Kate, the Highland cow. There are miniature tractors to ride, pony

114 ARLEY HALL GARDENS

nr Northwich

Amongst the finest in Britain and Europe the gardens have been created over the last 250 years by successive generations of the same family.

see page 238

115 THE SLOW AND EASY

Lostock Gralam

A charming village pub offering superb food and chilled real ales to quench the thirst of passers by.

see page 239

116 THE MILL POOL RESTAURANT

Little Budworth

This restaurant sits in spectacular surroundings and has a well deserved reputation for one of the prime places to dine in Cheshire.

see page 240

117 THE RED LION

Little Budworth

This traditional English country pub features real ales, great food and accommodation.

see page 241

rides, an adventure play area, a souvenir shop and a Country Café.

LOSTOCK GRALAM

2 miles E of Northwich on the A559

What a wonderful name for a relaxing pub: **The Slow and Easy.** It could be referring to the bowls players on the manicured green that lies alongside. If you bowl yourself, you are welcome to use the green, free of charge, unless one of those very English, courteously lethal matches happens to be under way. In fact the inn's name, like that of so many Cheshire pubs, comes from a racehorse who presumably wouldn't have been quite so famous if he had really lived up to his name.

LACH DENNIS

4 miles SE of Northwich on the B5082

The small village of Lach Dennis derives its name from the Old English *laecc*, meaning a bog, and the Dennis family which once had an estate here. A mile or so to the east, **Shakerley Mere Nature Reserve** is host to a diverse range of wildlife with Canada Geese, herons, mute swans and mallards a common sight. Cormorants fly here from their breeding grounds on the coast to feast on the fish and more exotic species arrive at different times of the year. There's a pleasant 1.5 mile walk around the mere.

WINSFORD

6 miles S of Northwich on the A54

Winsford is another of the Cheshire salt towns which expanded greatly during the 19th century, swallowing up the old villages of Over and Wharton on opposite banks of the River Weaver. Two legacies of those boom years should be mentioned. One is Christ Church which was specifically designed so that it could be jacked up in the event of subsidence. The other is Botton Flash, a sizeable lake caused by subsidence but now a popular water recreation area for the town.

LITTLE BUDWORTH

9 miles SW of Northwich on minor road off the A49 or A54

Little Budworth Common Country Park is a pleasant area of heathland and woods, ideal for picnics and walking. The nearby village enjoys splendid views over Budworth Pool but will be better known to motor racing enthusiasts for the Oulton Park racing circuit a mile or so to the south.

UTKINTON

10 miles SW of Northwich off the A49 or A51

During the Middle Ages, the verderers had their own courts in which they meted out rough justice to offenders against the forest laws. One such court was at Utkinton, just north of the town. In an old farmhouse there stands a column formed by an ancient forest tree, its roots still in the ground. When the court was in session, the wardens would place on this tree the symbol of their authority, the Hunting Horn of Delamere. The farmhouse is not open to the public but the horn, dating from around 1120, has survived and can be seen at the Grosvenor Museum in Chester.

TARPORLEY

12 miles SW of Northwich on the A51/A49

In the days when most of this area was part of Delamere Forest, Tarporley was the headquarters of the verderers or forest wardens. It was from Tarporley in the early 1600s that John Done, Chief Forester and Hereditary Bow-bearer of Delamere entertained King James to a hunt. The chase was, he reported, a great success: *"deer, both red and fallow, fish and fowl, abounded in the meres"*. A gratified King rewarded his host with a knighthood.

The village boasts an impressive survivor in the Tarporley Hunt Club which is primarily a dining club for hunting people and still holds an annual banquet in the town. Founded in 1762, it is now the oldest Hunt Club in the country.

TIVERTON

14 miles SW of Northwich on the A49

Set around a delightful village green, Tiverton lies almost in the shadow of Beeston Castle, with the Shropshire Union Canal running nearby. Enjoying an excellent position alongside the bank of the canal, The Shady Oak pub is a popular watering hole for canal travellers.

ASHTON

10 miles SW of Northwich on the B5393

A couple of miles to the northeast of Ashton stretch the 4000 acres of Delamere Forest, a rambler's delight with a wealth of lovely walks and many picnic sites, ideal for a peaceful family day out. In Norman times, a "forest" was a part-wooded, part-open area, reserved as a hunting ground exclusively for royalty or the nobility. There were savage penalties for anyone harming the deer, even if the deer were destroying crops, and household dogs within the forest had to be deliberately lamed to ensure that they could not harass the beasts. James I was the last king to hunt deer here, in August 1617, and enjoyed the day's sport so much that he made his Chief Forester a knight on the spot. Even at that date, many of the great oaks in the forest had already been felled to provide timber for ship-building – as well as for Cheshire's familiar black and white half-timbered houses. Since the early 1900s, Delamere Forest has been maintained by the Forestry Commission which has undertaken an intensive programme of tree planting and woodland management. Delamere is now both an attractive recreational area and a working forest with 90% of the trees eventually destined for the saw mills.

WARRINGTON

Lying on an important bridging point of the River Mersey, Warrington claims to enjoy Britain's most convenient location. It stands midway between the huge

118 THE BOOT INN

Boothsdale, Willington Corner
A fine hostelry offering mouth watering cuisine, unbeatable hospitality and 4 real ales.

see page 240

119 THE SHADY OAK

Tiverton
A delightful inn offering a tempting array of freshly prepared food and two ever rotating real ales.

see page 242

120 THE ALBION FREEHOUSE

Warrington
A popular establishment famous for its wide range of beers and extremely reasonably priced, delicious cuisine.

see page 243

129

121 THE TRAVELLERS REST

Lowton

A friendly inn offering a wide range of beverages, unbeatable hospitality and an organic menu.

see page 242

122 THE HORSESHOE INN

Croft

Good looking inn with a penchant for good food and great service.

see page 244

123 COMFORTABLE GILL INN

Glazebury

This comfortable pub with B & B serves great food with a warm and friendly atmosphere.

see page 244

conurbations and ports of Manchester and Liverpool and on a nodal point of communications close to where the M6, M62 and M56 motorways intersect, and where the electrified West Coast main line links London and Scotland.

Warrington is North Cheshire's largest town – an important industrial centre since Georgian and Victorian times and with substantial buildings of those days to prove it. Its imposing **Town Hall** was formerly Lord Winmarleigh's country residence, built in 1750 with all the appropriate grandeur: windows framed in painfully expensive copper, and elaborately designed entrance gates 25ft high and 54ft wide. Along with its park, it provides a dignified focus for the town centre.

A major Victorian contribution to the town is its excellent **Museum and Art Gallery** in Bold Street, one of the earliest municipal museums dating from 1857. The exhibits are remarkably varied: amongst them are shrunken heads, a unique china teapot collection, a scold's bridle, Egyptian mummies, a Roman actor's mask and other Roman artefacts discovered in nearby Wilderspool. There are some fine paintings as well, most of which are Victorian watercolours and oils, and a rare Vanous still life.

Also worth visiting is **St Elphin's Church** with its 14th century chancel and memorials celebrating the Butler and Patten families.

An interesting curiosity at Bridge Foot nearby is a combined telephone kiosk and letter box. These were quite common in the early 1900s, but Warrington's is one of the few survivors. Also associated with the town are two prominent entertainers: the television presenter Chris Evans was born here, and the durable comedian and ukelele player George Formby is buried in the town's cemetery.

AROUND WARRINGTON

WINWICK

3 miles N of Warrington on the A49

An unusual feature on Winwick's church tower is the carving of a pig with a bell round its neck. Various explanations for its presence here have been mooted. According to one theory, it was the mason's cryptic way of recording the initials of St Oswald's, Winwick (SOW). An old legend asserts that a pig was employed to move stones here during the building, but the most likely reason is that a pig was the mascot of St Anthony whose carved figure stands in a niche next to it.

DARESBURY

5 miles SW of Warrington on the A558

All Saints' Church in Daresbury has an absolutely unique stained glass window. There are panels depicting a Gryphon and a Cheshire Cat, others show a Mock Turtle, a March Hare and a Mad Hatter. This is of course the **Lewis**

Carroll Memorial Window, commemorating the author of *Alice in Wonderland*. Carroll himself is shown at one side, dressed in clerical garb and kneeling. His father was Vicar of Daresbury when Carroll was born here in 1832 and baptised as Charles Lutwidge Dodgson. The boy enjoyed an apparently idyllic childhood at Daresbury until his father moved to another parish when Charles/Lewis was eleven years old.

WIDNES

6 miles SW of Warrington on the A557

Described in the 1860s as a "quiet industrial village", Widnes now has a population of around 60,000. It stands on the north shore of the Mersey, linked to Runcorn by a remarkably elegant road bridge. A popular attraction is **Spike Island** which has recently had a makeover by the local council and now provides a landscaped walk from which the superstructures of ships passing along the Manchester Ship Canal can be seen gliding past.

RUNCORN

7 miles SW of Warrington on the A557

Runcorn is one of Britain's best known post-war new towns, developed around a much older town bearing the same name. Here, **Norton Priory** is always a delightful and intriguing place for a family outing, whatever the weather. Despite being situated close to Junction 11 of the M56, it lies in a peaceful oasis with 16 acres of beautiful woodland gardens running down to the Bridgewater Canal. The Augustinian priory was built in 1134 as a retreat for just 12 "black canons", so named because they wore a cape of black woollen cloth over a white linen surplice. Recent work by the Norton Priory Museum Trust has uncovered the remains of the church, chapter house, cloisters and dormitory, and these finds are informatively explained in an audio-visual

Norton Priory, Runcorn

124 THE RAMS HEAD

Grappenhall

Delicious dishes, super en-suite rooms and thirst quenching real ales all a stones throw from Bridgewater Canal.

🍽 🛏 *see page 245*

125 THE HATTON ARMS & RESTAURANT

Hatton

The ideal venue for a delicious dinner, a perfect pint or a comfortable room for the night.

🍽 🛏 *see page 246*

126 THE RED LION

Moore

This 300 year old pub is in a wonderfully rustic location and the warm & welcoming atmosphere will make you feel right at home.

🍽 *see page 247*

127 DUNHAM MASSEY

Altrincham

Dunham Massey is a country estate including mansion with important collections and 'below stairs' areas, impressive garden and deer park.

see page 250

128 ROBIN HOOD HOTEL

Helsby

This charming hotel offers great food and comfortable beds at reasonable prices, worthy of Robin Hood and his Merry Men.

see page 248

presentation. The Museum is open every afternoon, all year; the Gardens, which include a charming walled garden, are open from March to October.

LYMM

During the stage coach era, Eagle Brow was notorious, a dangerously steep road that dropped precipitously down the hillside into the village of Lymm. To bypass this hazard, a turnpike was built (now the A56), so preserving the heart of this ancient village with its half-timbered houses and well preserved village stocks. The Bridgewater Canal flows past nearby and the church is reflected in the waters of Lymm Dam. Popular with anglers and bird-watchers, the dam is a large man-made lake, part of a lovely woodland centre which is linked to the surrounding countryside and

Market Cross, Lymm

the canal towpath by a network of footpaths and bridleways. The village became an important centre for the fustian cloth (corduroy) trade in the 1800s but is now best known simply as a delightful place to visit.

Lymm stands on the sides of a ravine and its streets have actually been carved out of the sandstone rock. The same rock was used to construct Lymm's best-known landmark, the ancient cross crowned with a huge cupola that stands at the top of the High Street.

DUNHAM MASSEY

4 miles E of Lymm on B5160

Dunham Massey Hall and Park (National Trust) has 250 acres of parkland where fallow deer roam freely and noble trees planted in the late 1700s still flourish. There's a restored water mill which is usually in operation every Wednesday, and there are splendid walks in every direction. The Hall, once the home of the Earls of Stamford and Warrington, is a grand Georgian mansion of 1732 which boasts an outstanding collection of furniture, paintings and Huguenot silver.

HELSBY

8 miles NE of Chester on the A56

There are seven Iron Age forts scattered across Cheshire, but only the one at Helsby, maintained by the National Trust, is open to the public. The climb out of the village along pretty woodland paths to the red sandstone summit is quite steep but the views across the marshes to the Mersey Estuary and Liverpool repay the effort.

FRODSHAM

10 miles NE of Chester on the A56

This is an attractive town with a broad High Street lined with thatched cottages and spacious Georgian and Victorian houses. During the 18th and early 19th centuries, Frodsham was an important coaching town and there are several fine coaching inns here. Built in 1632, The Bear's Paw with its three stone gables recalls the bear-baiting that once took place nearby. Of the Earl of Chester's Norman castle only fragments

remain, but the **Church of St Laurence** (an earlier church here was recorded in the *Domesday Book*) is noted for the fine 17th century panelling in its exquisite north chapel. The Vicar here from 1740 to 1756 was Francis Gastrell, a name that is anathema to all lovers of Shakespeare. Gastrell bought the poet's house, New Place, at Stratford and first incensed the townspeople by cutting down the famous mulberry tree. Then, in order to avoid paying the Corporation poor rate, he pulled the house itself down. The outraged citizens of Stratford hounded him from the town and he returned to the parish at Frodsham that he had neglected for years.

129 THE OLD HALL HOTEL

Frodsham

This beautiful 16th century building provides a wonderful experience; traditionally decorated and very well catered, not to be missed.

see page 249

130 RING O BELLS

Overton

This quaint Tudor pub is packed full of character and must not be missed.

see page 250

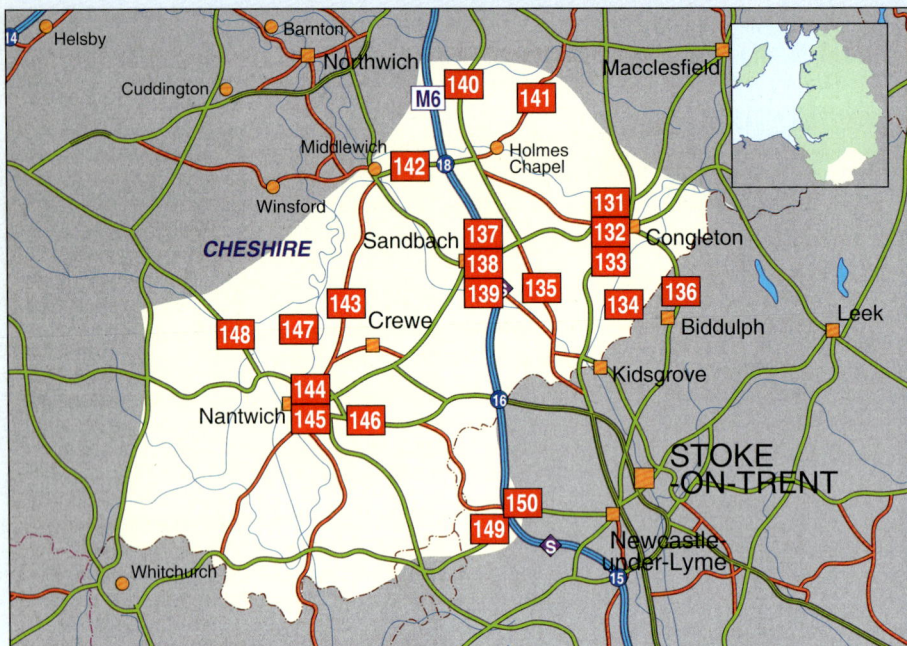

Cheshire Peaks & Plains

To the east rise the Peak District hills, westwards gently undulating pastures and woods drop down to the Cheshire Plain. This is an area of sudden and striking contrasts. Within half a mile you can find yourself travelling out of lowland Cheshire into some of the highest and wildest countryside - acres of lonely uplands with rugged gritstone crags, steep valleys watered by moorland streams. Here too is the old salt town of Middlewich, and Sandbach with its famous Saxon crosses, along with a host of quiet, attractive villages. The busy M6 cuts through the area, north to south, but you have only to drive a few miles off the motorway to find yourself wandering along winding country lanes between fertile fields. The two major towns of South Cheshire are Nantwich, with a history stretching back beyond Roman times, and Crewe, with no history at all until 1837. That was when the Grand Junction Railway arrived and five years later moved all its construction and repair workshops to what had been a green field site. We begin our survey of this varied region at Congleton, set amongst the foothills of the Pennines.

Congleton

A popular village pub offering delicious homemade food and real ales.

see page 251

CONGLETON

In a recent survey carried out by Barclays Bank, Congleton was placed thirty first in the "real wealthiest" places to live in England. The survey looked at the average salary in each area and then took into account the local cost of living to work out the real disposable income. The research found that the top ten places in the survey were all in the North-West.

Some residents have dubbed this thriving old market town the "Venice of the North" because of the number of nearby man-made lakes such as Astbury Mere and in Brereton Country Park which both offer a wide range of recreational activities. Set in the foothills of the Pennines, Congleton was an inhabited place as long ago as the Stone Age. The remains of a 5000-year-old chambered tomb known as **The Bridestones** can be seen beside the hill road running eastwards from the town to the A523 road to Leek.

In Elizabethan times, the townspeople of Congleton seem to have had a passion for bear baiting. On one occasion, when the town bear died they handed 16 shillings (80p) to the Bear Warden to acquire another beast. The money had originally been collected to buy a town bible: the disgraceful misappropriation of funds gave rise to the ditty: *"Congleton rare, Congleton rare, sold the bible to buy a bear"*. Known locally as the "Bear Town", Congleton was the very last town in England to outlaw the cruel practice of bear baiting but the town's emblem is still an upright chained bear. A more attractive distinction is the fact that it is also one of only four towns in Cheshire where the medieval street pattern has remained intact and the only town where the curfew bell is still rung each night at 8pm.

One of the oldest buildings in Congleton is **The Lion & Swan Hotel**, a 16th century coaching inn on the old Manchester to London route. This grand old building with its superb black and white half-timbered frontage has been fully

The Bridestones, Congleton

restored to its Tudor glory, with a wealth of exposed, dark oak beams and elaborately carved fireplaces, as well as the oldest window in town, dating from 1596. Another ancient hostelry is Ye Olde Kings Arms whose pink-washed half-timbered frontage leans picturesquely to the left as if exhausted with the weight of years.

Congleton's impressive Venetian Gothic style **Town Hall**, built in 1864, contains some interesting exhibits recalling the town's long history, including some fine civic regalia. There are displays recording the work of such ancient officials as the swine-catcher, the chimney-looker and the ale-taster. Also on show are such aids to domestic harmony as the "brank" – a bridle for nagging wives which used to be fastened to a wall in the market place. Other exhibits include a prehistoric log boat, coin hoards from the Civil War, and more recent acquisitions covering the Industrial Revolution and the Second World War.

During the 1700s Congleton developed as an important textile town with many of its mills involved in silk manufacture, cotton spinning and ribbon weaving. In Mill Green near the River Dane, you can still see part of the very first silk mill to operate here.

AROUND CONGLETON

ASTBURY

2 miles SW of Congleton on the A34

The pretty little village of Astbury, set around a triangular village green, was once more important

Little Moreton Hall, nr Congleton

132 SHAKERLEY ARMS

Congleton

Taste a piece of Scotland, in Cheshire. A very hospitable atmosphere and great, homemade food.

see page 251

133 CHURCH HOUSE INN

Congleton

An outstanding eating place renowned throughout the country for it's homemade food and unique ambience.

see page 252

134 HORSESHOE INN

Astbury

An old coaching inn offering homemade cooking, friendly hosts and 3 real ales. Well worth a visit.

see page 253

135 THE BULLS HEAD

Smallwood

Charming pub & restaurant offering homemade dishes, real ales, a large rear garden and welcoming hosts.

see page 254

136 BIDDULPH GRANGE GARDENS

Biddulph

Rare and exotic planting and architecture: from and Egyptian court, to elegant Italian terraces.

see page 253

than neighbouring Congleton which is why it has a much older church, built between 1350 and 1540. Arguably the finest parish church in the county, **St Mary's** is famous for its lofty recessed spire (which rises from a tower almost detached from the nave), and the superb timber work inside: a richly carved ceiling, intricate tracery on the rood screen, and a lovely Jacobean font cover.

But just three miles down the A34 is an even more remarkable building. Black and white half-timbered houses have almost become a symbol for the county of Cheshire and the most stunning example is undoubtedly **Little Moreton Hall** (National Trust), a "wibbly wobbly" house which provided a memorable location for Granada TV's adaptation of *The Adventures of Moll Flanders*. The hall's huge overhanging gables, slanting walls, and great stretches of leaded windows, create wonderfully complex patterns, all magically reflected in the still flooded moat. Ralph Moreton began construction in 1480 and the fabric of this magnificent house has changed little since the 16th century. A richly panelled Great Hall, parlour and chapel show off superb Elizabethan plaster and wood work. Free guided tours give visitors a fascinating insight into Tudor life, and there's also a beautifully reconstructed Elizabethan knot garden with clipped box hedges, a period herb garden and a Yew Tunnel.

About a mile south of Little

Moreton Hall is the Rode Hall estate. It was an 18th century owner of the estate, Randle Wilbraham, who built the famous folly of **Mow Cop** (National Trust) to enhance the view from his mansion. This mock ruin stands atop a rocky hill 1100 feet above sea level, just yards from the Staffordshire border. On a clear day, the views are fantastic: Alderley Edge to the north, the Pennines to the north-east, south to Cannock Chase and Shropshire, and westwards across Cheshire. **Rode Hall** itself, home of the Wilbraham family since 1669, is a fine early 18th century mansion standing within a park landscaped by Humphry Repton. The extensive gardens include a formal rose garden of 1860, a large walled kitchen garden, a terraced rock garden with a grotto, and an ice house.

BIDDULPH

5 miles SE of Congleton on the A527

The 10-year restoration of **Biddulph Grange Gardens** (National Trust) has recently been completed and visitors can now enjoy the full beauty of this unique project. The gardens are imaginatively divided into a series of enclosed areas bounded by massive rock structures, hedges, stumps, roots and moulded banks. A trail leads through a superb Chinese garden to an enchanting Scottish glen while other areas reproduce the magic of Egypt or the tranquillity of rural America. The shop is packed with gardening books, Victorian plants, cards and quality souvenirs, and there's also a pleasant tearoom offering local specialities and home-made cakes.

SANDBACH

1 mile SW from Junction 17 of the M6

Sandbach's former importance as a stopping place for coaches (both stage and motor) is evident in the attractive old half-timbered inns and houses, some of them thatched, which line the main street. Sandbach's handsome market square is dominated by its two famous stone crosses, 16 and 11 feet tall. These superbly carved crosses (actually only the shafts have survived) were created some time in the 9th century, and the striking scenes are believed to represent the conversion of Mercia to Christianity during the reign of King Penda. A plaque at their base notes that they were restored in 1816 "after destruction by iconoclasts" – i.e. the Puritans. The restorers had to recover fragments from here and there: some had been used as street paving, cottage steps or in the walls of a well. Somehow they fitted the broken stones together, like pieces of a jigsaw, and the result is immensely impressive.

Old Black Bear Inn, Sandbach

137 THE MARKET TAVERN

Sandbach

A fine hostelry offering fine food, well kept ales and a superb venue for wedding parties.

see page 255

138 SALLY'S CAFÉ

Sandbach

A marvellous café offering a tasty menu at affordable prices, including an unbeatable BIG breakfast.

see page 255

139 FLAVOUR

Sandbach

A bright and airy continental-style café bar perfect for anyone with a love for fine food, freshly made.

see page 256

139

140 THE COTTAGE RESTAURANT & LODGE

Allostock

Fantastic homemade food, a wide range of beverages and comfortable accommodation can all be found at this homely hotel.

see page 257

141 JODRELL BANK SCIENCE CENTRE & ARBORETUM

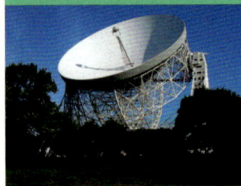

Lower Withington

Jodrell Bank Visitor Centre, home of the third largest radio telescope in the world, the Lovell Radio Telescope.

see page 256

HOLMES CHAPEL

5 miles N of Sandbach on the A50/A54

In the mid-1700s, the little village of Holmes Chapel was stirred by two important events. In 1738, John Wesley came and preached outside St Luke's Church. Fifteen years later, on July 10th 1753, a disastrous fire swept through the village. When the flames were finally quenched, only two buildings had survived the blaze: St Luke's Church and The Old Red Lion alongside. Both still stand.

About 3 miles southeast of Holmes Chapel, **Brereton Heath Country Park** is a popular beauty spot where the heathland and flower meadows are criss-crossed by a network of many footpaths. The former sand quarry provides a congenial habitat for a range of species, details of which can be obtained from the park ranger at the Visitor Centre. The lake here is used for angling, canoeing and windsurfing.

GOOSTREY

6 miles NE of Middlewich on minor road off A50

The village of Goostrey is a quiet little place on a minor road just north of Holmes Chapel but famous for its annual gooseberry shows where competitors vie to produce the plumpest berries. The name of the village has nothing to do with gooseberries but derives from a personal name, Godhere, and the Saxon word for tree. It's not known if there is any connection with the 1200-year-old yew tree in the graveyard of St Luke's Church.

LOWER WITHINGTON

7 miles NE of Middlewich on the B5392

Visible from miles around, the huge white dish of the world famous **Jodrell Bank** radio telescope has a good claim to being the most distinctive building in the county. The Observatory came into service in 1957 and was used by both Americans and the Soviets in their exploration of space. In November 2002, following an upgrading, the radio telescope re-entered service with a capacity 30 times that of the original. Jodrell Bank's Science Centre offers visitors a wonderful array of hands-on exhibits, including a 25ft telescope, while its Planetarium travels through the heavens, explaining the secrets of Rocky Dwarfs and Gassy Giants along the way. The dynamic duo of Albert Einstein and Isaac Newton are at hand to guide visitors on this fascinating exploration of the Universe. Outside, there's the superb 35-acre Granada Arboretum planted with 2000 species of trees and shrubs, each one helpfully labelled, and an Environment Discovery Centre which explains the importance of trees to the natural environment. The site also contains a picnic area, play area, café and shop.

In the nearby village of Lower Withington, old farm buildings have been sympathetically converted to provide an attractive setting for **Welltrough Dried**

Flowers (free) which boasts one of the largest selections of dried and silk flowers in the North. There are literally hundreds of different kinds and shapes, and the eight separate showrooms include a permanent Christmas Room, a Dickensian Street and a demonstration room where Day Workshops are held.

MIDDLEWICH

2 miles W of Junction 18 of the M6

The Romans called their settlement here Salinae, meaning saltworks. Excavations have revealed outlines of their long, narrow, timber workshops, brine pits and even a jar with the word AMYRCA scratched on it - Amurca was the Latin name for brine waste which was used throughout the Empire as a cleansing agent. Middlewich Town Council publishes an informative leaflet detailing the **Roman Middlewich Trail**, a one mile circular walk that reveals the history and layout of the Roman town and shows how Middlewich would have looked in those days.

In modern times, it was the need for Cheshire's salt manufacturers to get their cumbersome product to markets in the Midlands and the south which gave a great impetus to the building of canals in the county. Middlewich was particularly well-provided for with its own Middlewich Branch Canal linking the town to both the Shropshire Union and the Trent & Mersey canals. Today, most of the canal traffic comprises traditional narrow boats which can also be hired for holiday trips.

During the Civil War, Middlewich witnessed two of the bloodiest battles fought in the county. In March 1644, Royalists trapped Cromwell's men in the narrow lanes and alleys of the town and slaughtered 200 of them. A few managed to find refuge in **St Michael's Church**. The church has changed greatly since those days but still has some notable old carvings and a curiosity in the form of a carved coat of arms of the Kinderton family of nearby Kinderton Hall. Their crest shows a dragon eating a child, a reference to the occasion on which Baron Kinderton killed a local dragon as it was devouring a child. The incident apparently took place at Moston, near Sandbach, and a lane there is still called Dragon Lane.

SOUTH CHESHIRE

CREWE

5 miles NE of Nantwich on the A534

The two major towns of South Cheshire are Nantwich, with a history stretching back beyond Roman times, and Crewe, with no history at all until 1837. That was when the Grand Junction Railway arrived and five years later moved all its construction and repair workshops to this green field site. A workforce of nine hundred had to be housed so the company rapidly built cottages, each one shared by four of the lowest paid workers, and detached "mansions" which accommodated four families of the more highly skilled. At one time, seven out of every ten men in

142 THE FOX & HOUNDS INN

Middlewich

A cosy, easily accessible inn serving good wholesome food and fine ales along with a family friendly atmosphere.

see page 258

143 THE COACH AND HORSES

Bradfield Green

A fantastic family run business, suitable for all. A great experience by the family, for the family.

see page 259

144 LIBBY'S LUNCHES

Nantwich

This charming café is loved locally and with good reason, great food and a warm welcome.

🍴 *see page 259*

145 WICKSTEAD ARMS

Nantwich

This historic pub offers good food at great value in a warm and welcoming atmosphere.

🍴 *see page 261*

Crewe worked on the railways.

Later, in 1887, the railway company also provided the town with one of the most splendid parks in the north of England, **Queens Park**, some 40 acres of lawns and flowerbeds together with an ornamental lake. Rolls Royce's engineering works brought further prosperity to the town, but it is as a railway centre that Crewe is best known. Even today, the station offers a choice of six different routes to all points of the compass. Located in the former railway yard of Crewe station, **Crewe Heritage Centre**, (formerly Crewe Railway Age) offers a fascinating insight into Crewe's place in railway history with hands-on exhibits, steam locomotive rides, model railway displays and a children's playground. Also worth a visit is the **Lyceum Theatre**, built in 1902 and with its glorious Edwardian opulence undimmed.

A couple of miles north of Crewe, **Lakemore Country Park Animal Kingdom** is home to a wide variety of animals – llamas, miniature donkeys, owls and many other unusual and rare breeds. Children can feed the farm animals, visit the pets corner and enjoy both the indoor and outdoor play areas. Within the 36 acre site are five fishing lakes and there's also a log cabin coffee shop.

NANTWICH

4 miles SW of Crewe on the A51

Set beside the River Weaver, Nantwich is an attractive market town with some striking half-timbered Tudor buildings, winding medieval streets, specialty food shops and a number of high profile events including the Jazz and Blues Festival.

The most disastrous event in the long history of the town was the Great Fire of 1583 which consumed some 600 of its thatched and timber-framed buildings. The blaze raged for 20 days and the townspeople's terror was compounded when some bears kept behind the Crown Hotel escaped. (Four bears from Nantwich are mentioned in Shakespeare's comedy *The Merry Wives of Windsor*). Queen Elizabeth contributed the huge sum of £2000 and also donated quantities of timber from Delamere Forest to assist in the town's rebuilding. A grateful citizen, Thomas Cleese, commemorated this royal largesse with a plaque on his new house at No. 41, High Street. The plaque is still in place and reads:

*"God grant our ryal Queen in England longe to raign
For she hath put her helping hand to bild this towne again".*

The most striking of the buildings to survive the conflagration, probably because it was surrounded by a moat, is the lovely black and white house in Hospital Street known as **Churche's Mansion** after the merchant Richard Churche who built it in 1577. Astonishingly, when the house was up for sale in 1930, no buyer showed any interest and the building was on the point of being transported brick by brick to

America when a public-spirited local doctor stepped in and rescued it. The ground floor is now a restaurant, but the upper floor has been furnished in Elizabethan style and is open to the public during the summer.

The Great Fire also spared the stone-built 14th century church. This fine building, with an unusual octagonal tower, is sometimes called the **"Cathedral of South Cheshire"** and dates from the period of the town's greatest prosperity as a salt town and trading centre. Of exceptional interest is the magnificent chancel and the wonderful carvings in the choir. On the misericords (tip-up seats) are mermaids, foxes (some dressed as monks in a sharp dig at priests), pigs, and the legendary Wyvern, half-dragon, half-bird, whose name is linked with the River Weaver, 'wyvern' being an old pronunciation of Weaver. An old tale about the building of the church tells of an elderly woman who brought ale and food each day from a local inn to the masons working on the site. The masons discovered that the woman was cheating them by keeping back some of the money they put "in the pot" for their refreshment. They dismissed her and took revenge by making a stone carving showing the old woman being carried away by Old Nick himself, her hand still stuck in a pot.

During the Civil War, Nantwich was the only town in Cheshire to support Cromwell's Parliamentary army. After several weeks of fighting, the Royalist forces were finally defeated on 25th January, 1644 and the people of Nantwich celebrated by wearing sprigs of holly in their hair. As a result, the day became known as "Holly Holy Day" and every year, on the Saturday closest to January 25th, the town welcomes Cromwellian pikemen and battle scenes are re-enacted by members of the Sealed Knot. There are records of the Civil War in the **Nantwich Museum** (free) in Pillory Street which also has exhibitions about the town and its dairy and cheese-making industries.

But it was salt that had once made Nantwich second only in importance to Chester in the county. The Romans had mined salt here for their garrisons at Chester and Stoke where the soldiers received part of their wages in "sal", or salt. The payment was called a "salarium", hence the modern word "salary". Nantwich remained a salt producing town right up to the 1700s but then it was overtaken by towns like Northwich which enjoyed better communications on the canal system. But a brine spring still supplies Nantwich's outdoor swimming pool.

Within a few miles of the town are two notable gardens. A

About 6 miles south of Nantwich along the A51 and straddling the Staffordshire border, Bridgemere Garden World provided the location for BBC-TV's Gardeners' Diary. This is just one of 22 different gardens, amongst them a French rose garden, a woodland setting, a cottage garden and a rock and water area. The extensive glasshouses contain houseplants of every description and the garden centre is stocked with everything a gardener could possibly need. There's also an aquatics house with some splendid fish, a specialist food hall, a flower arrangers' centre, a bookshop, restaurant and coffee shop.

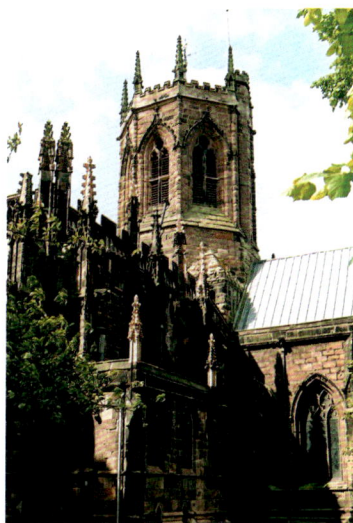

St Mary's Parish Church, Nantwich

Stapeley Water Gardens, nr Nantwich

146 THE HORSESHOE INN

Willaston

A homely old inn where you will find mouth watering homemade fare and a variety of well-kept ales

🍴 see page 261

147 ROYAL OAK

Worleston

This pub offers more than good beer, quality, homemade food, a warm atmosphere and an amazing beer garden.

🍴 see page 260

major attraction, a mile south of the town off the A51, is **Stapeley Water Gardens** which attracts nearly 1.5 million visitors each year. The 64-acre site includes the National Collection of Nymphaea – more than 350 varieties of water lilies - a Tropical Oasis with exotic flowers and pools stocked with piranhas and huge catfish, and a comprehensively equipped garden centre. Other attractions within the attractively landscaped grounds include a restaurant, two cafes and a gift shop.

WILLASTON

2 miles E of Nantwich between the A534 and A500

It was in the village of Willaston that one of the most unusual world records was established in 1994. Some 200 competitors had gathered in the playing field of the local Primary School here for the annual **World Worm Charming Championships**. The prize goes to whoever induces the greatest

number of worms to poke their heads above a 9-square metre patch of playing field aided only by a garden fork. Each contestant is allowed half an hour and the current world champion charmed 511 out of the ground – a rate of more than 17 wrigglies a minute. The secret of his wonderful way with worms has not been revealed. The contest takes place in late June each year.

BEESTON

8 miles NW of Nantwich on minor road off the A49

A craggy cliff suddenly rising 500ft from the Cheshire Plain, its summit crowned by the ruins of **Beeston Castle** (English Heritage), Beeston Hill is one of the most dramatic sights in the county. The castle was built around 1220 but didn't see any military action until the Civil War. On one rather ignominious occasion during that conflict, a Royalist captain and just eight musketeers managed to capture the mighty fortress and its garrison of 60 soldiers without firing a shot. A few years later, Cromwell ordered that the castle be "slighted", or partially destroyed, but this "Castle in the Air" is still very imposing with walls 30ft high and a well 366ft deep. An old legend asserts that Richard II tipped a hoard of coins, gold and jewels down the well, but no treasure has yet been discovered. The castle hill is a popular place for picnics, and it's worth climbing it just to enjoy the spectacular views which extend across seven counties and over to a "twin" castle. **Peckforton Castle** looks just as medieval as Beeston but was, in fact, built in 1844 for the first Lord Tollemache who spared no expense in re-creating features such as a vast Great Hall and a keep with towers 60ft tall. The architect Gilbert Scott later praised Peckforton as "the very height of masquerading". Its authentic medieval appearance has made the castle a favourite location for film and television companies, and on Sundays and Bank Holidays during the season the Middle Ages are brought to life here with mock battles and tournaments. The castle also offers guided tours, refreshments and a speciality shop.

CHURCH MINSHULL

7 miles N of Nantwich on the B5074

This picturesque little village is known to a few people as the home of Elizabeth Minshull before she became the third wife of the poet John Milton in 1660. There's a fine old hostelry here, The Badger Inn, which has been designated as a Building of Historic and Architectural Interest and is attractively located close to the River Weaver. Built in 1760, the inn was originally known as the Brookes Arms, named after the family who were great landowners in the Mere and Tatton area. In a play of words on their name, the Brookes coat of arms bears two brocks, the old English name for badgers, (brocks/Brookes), and so led to the inn's present name.

WETTENHALL

8 miles N of Nantwich on minor road off the B5074

Wettenhall is a pretty little village surrounded by open countryside. Records show that it has enjoyed the amenity of a public house since 1651. The hostelry used to be called The Little John and was located on the very spot where The Little Man Inn now stands. The change of name came about in the 1800s when local licensees decided to pay tribute to a real life "little man". Sammy Grice. Sammy, who was less than four feet tall, was much valued for his skill in providing the licensees with vent pegs and the butchers of Chester with skewers.

WYBUNBURY

5 miles S of Crewe on the B5071

South Cheshire's answer to the Leaning Tower of Pisa is the 100ft high tower of **St Chad's Church** in Wybunbury. It was built in 1470 above an unsuspected ancient salt bed. Subsidence has been the reason for the tower's long history of leaning sideways by as much as four feet and then being straightened up, most recently in 1989. It now rests on a reinforced concrete bed and is unlikely to deviate from the vertical again. The tower stands alone: the body of the church, once capable of holding a congregation of 1600, collapsed on no fewer than five occasions. In 1972, the villagers finally decided to abandon it and build a new church on firmer ground.

148 THE OLDE BARBRIDGE INN

Barbridge

Offering light entertainment and tasty old favourites, this inn is perfect to enjoy a meal and drinks with the family or friends.

see page 262

149 OFFLEY ARMS

Madeley

A great eatery in wonderful surroundings, the Offley Arms is a popular place to meet.

see page 261

150 THE OLD SWAN

Madeley Heath

An impressive property offering fabulous fare with welcoming hosts.

see page 263

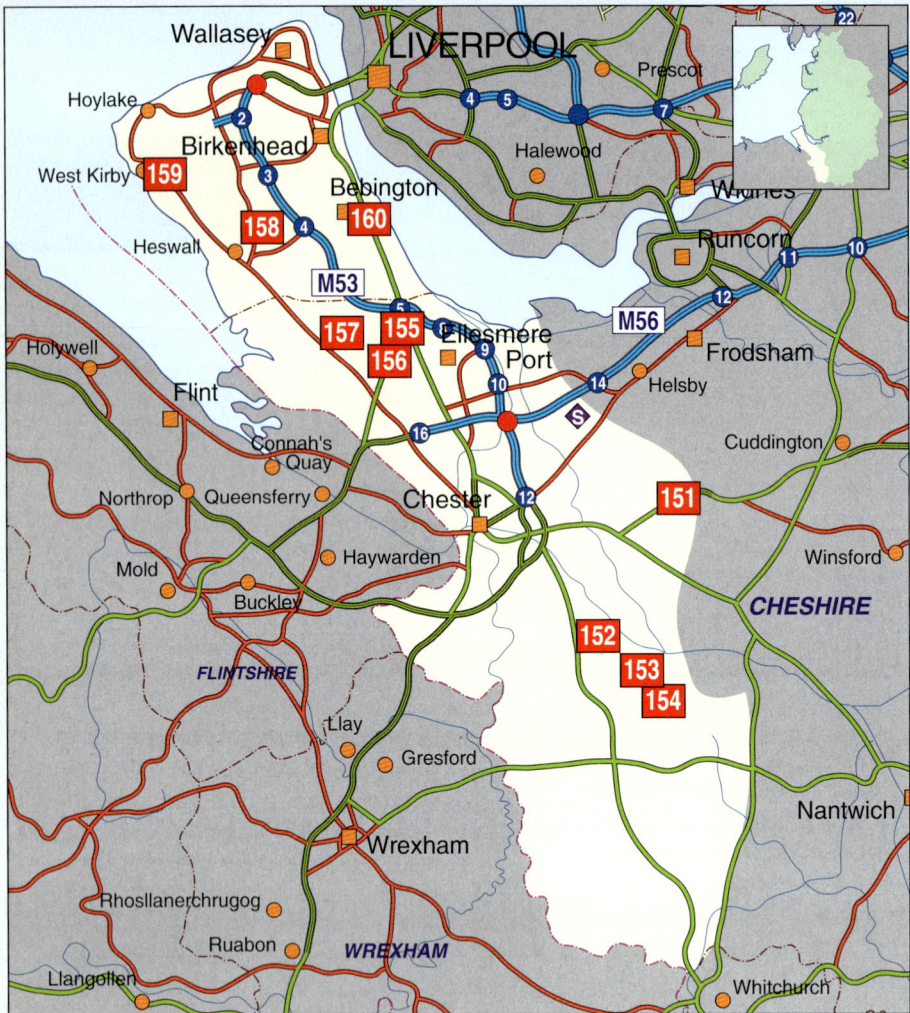

Chester & West Cheshire

Around the 1890s, guide-book writers took a fancy to describing the topography of various counties by comparing their outlines to some appropriate emblem. The hunting county of Leicestershire, for example, clearly resembled a fox's head with its ears pricked up. In Cheshire's county boundaries however they were unable to discern anything more imaginative than the shape of a teapot. Its base is the Staffordshire border, its handle the strip of land running from Stockport up to the Yorkshire border, with the Wirral providing the spout. And, tucked away in the crook of the spout, is the capital of the county, the City of Chester.

The city's actual position, a strategic site on the River Dee close to the Welsh border, was important even before the Romans arrived in AD70. They based a large camp, or *caster*, here and called it Deva after the Celtic name for the river. It was during this period that the splendid city walls were originally built – two miles round, and still the most complete in the country.

In Saxon times "Ceastre" became the administrative centre of a shire, and was the last major town in England to fall to William the Conqueror during his dreadful Harrowing of the North. William pulled down half of Chester's houses and re-inforced the message of Norman domination by building a castle overlooking the Dee.

Subsequent Earls of Chester (the present Prince of Wales is the current one, incidentally) were given a free, and very firm hand, in dealing with the local Saxons and with the still-rebellious Welsh who continued to make a nuisance of themselves right through the Middle Ages. In return for its no-nonsense dealing with these problems Chester received a number of royal privileges: borough status, a licence for a market

and, around 1120, the first commission in England for a Sheriff - long before his more famous colleague in Nottingham received his. And the Mayor of Chester can still claim the medieval title of "Admiral of the Dee".

The problem with the Welsh was finally resolved in 1485 when a Welsh-based family, the Tudors, defeated Richard III at Bosworth Field and Owen Tudor claimed the throne as Henry VII. For more than 150 years Chester enjoyed an unprecedented period of peace and prosperity. Then came the Civil War. Chester supported the King but Charles I had the galling experience of watching from the city walls as his troops were defeated at nearby Rowton Moor. For two long years after that rout, the city was under seige until starvation finally forced its capitulation. **The King Charles Tower** on the wall is now a small museum with displays telling the story of that siege.

Seventy years later, in the course of his *Tour through the Whole Island of Great Britain*, Daniel Defoe came to Chester by the ferry over the River Dee. He liked the city streets, "very broad and fair"; admired the "very pleasant walk round the city, upon the walls", disliked its cathedral, "built of red, sandy, ill looking stone", but was very much taken with its "excellent cheese". Cheshire cheese had been famous for generations. John Speed, the Elizabethan map-maker and a Cheshire man himself, noted: *"The soil is fat, fruitful and rich....the Pastures make the Kine's udders to strout to the pail, from whom the best Cheese of all Europe is made"*. Later, some enthusiasts even promoted the idea that the name Cheshire was actually short for cheese-shire.

The county's other major industry was salt, mined here even before the Romans arrived. By the time of the *Domesday Book*, the salt towns, or "wiches" – Nantwich, Northwich, Middlewich, were firmly established. The process then involved pumping the salt brine to the surface and boiling it to produce granular salt. In 1670, huge deposits of rock salt were discovered and these are still being mined, mostly for use in keeping the country's roads free from ice.

Both these historic industries were overtaken in the 20th century by tourism. Chester, with its long history, varied and fascinating "magpie" architecture, and huge range of shops, restaurants and inns, is now the fourth most visited location in England after the "golden triangle" of London, Stratford and Oxford. One small disappointment, though: visitors don't get to see the county's best known character, the grinning Cheshire Cat. The phrase "To grin like a Cheshire cat" was in use long before Lewis Carroll adopted it in *Alice in Wonderland*. Carroll spent his childhood in the Cheshire village of Daresbury and would have regularly seen the local cheeses moulded into various animal shapes, one of which was a grinning cat.

CHESTER

James Boswell, Dr Johnson's biographer, visited Chester in the 1770s and wrote "I was quite enchanted at Chester, so that I could with difficulty quit it". He was to return again, declaring that "Chester pleases my fancy more than any town I ever saw". Modern visitors will almost certainly share his enthusiasm.

Probably the best introduction to this compact little city is to join one of the frequent sightseeing tours conducted by a Blue Badge guide. These take place every day, even Christmas Day, and leave from the **Chester Visitor Centre**. The Centre can also provide you with a wealth of information about the city, including a full calendar of events that range from the **Chester Regatta**, the oldest rowing races in the world and Chester Races, the oldest in Britain, to the Lord Mayor's Show in May and the Festival of Transport, featuring an amazing parade of vintage cars, in August.

Towering above the city centre is **Chester Cathedral**, a majestic building of weathered pink stone which in 1992 celebrated its 900th birthday. It was originally an abbey and is one of very few to survive Henry VIII's closure of the monasteries in the 1540s. The cloisters are regarded as the finest in England and the monks' refectory is still serving food although nowadays it is refreshments and lunches for visitors. There's a fine 14th century shrine to St Werbergh, the princess/abbess who founded the first church on this site in Saxon times, and some intricately carved Quire stalls almost 800 years old which are reckoned to be the best preserved in Britain. It was at Chester Cathedral, in 1742, that George Frederick Handel personally conducted rehearsals of his oratorio *The Messiah* before its first performance in Dublin: a copy of the score with annotations in his own hand remains on display.

Another curiosity in the cathedral is painting of the

Chester Cathedral, Chester

149

Bear & Billet Inn, Chester

the former parish chuch of St Michael, the **Chester Heritage Centre** tells the city's story from the Civil War siege to the present day. **On The Air** broadcasting museum chronicles the world of radio and television from the pioneering days of BBC radio to satellite and digital TV, while the **Chester Toy Museum** is a nostalgic treasure-house of antique playthings and also boasts the largest collection of Matchbox model cars in the world. Finally, the **Cheshire Military Museum** recounts the story of the county's military history using computers, tableaux and hands-on exhibits to present the soldier's life through the last 300 years.

Quite apart from its historical attractions, Chester is also one of the major shopping centres for the north west and north Wales. All the familiar High Street names are here, often housed in much more appealing buildings than they usually inhabit, along with a great number of specialist and antique shops. For a unique shopping experience you must visit the world-famous, two-tiered galleries of shops under covered walkways known as **The Rows** which line both sides of Bridge Street. The Rows are an architectural one-off: no other medieval town has anything like them. Many of the black and white, half-timbered frontages of The Rows, so typical of Chester and Cheshire, are actually Victorian restorations, but crafted so beautifully and faithfully that even experts can have

Madonna and Child on a moth's web. The ermine moth produces a web whose filaments are rather thicker and tougher than those of other moths. It's known that this extraordinary work of art was produced in the Tyrol in the 1700s when there was something of a vogue for this unusual medium.

The **Grosvenor Museum** (free) has furnished period rooms, a Timeline gallery travelling back through the city's history, a gallery of paintings by local contemporary artists, crafts and other artefacts connected with Chester. Occupying

difficulty distinguishing them from their 13th century originals.

Close by is the **Eastgate Clock**. It was erected in 1897 to celebrate Queen Victoria's Diamond Jubilee and is a beautifully ornate construction which is probably the most photographed timepiece in the world. If *your* timing is right and you arrive hereabouts at 12 noon in the summer, you should see, and certainly hear, the **Town Crier** delivering some stentorian civic message.

A few steps from the Eastgate Clock bring you to Chester's famous City Walls which were originally built by the Romans to protect the fortress of Deva from attacks by pesky Celtic tribes. Nowadays, the two-mile long circuit – an easy, level promenade, provides thousands of visitors with some splendid views of the River Dee, of the city's many glorious buildings and of the distant Welsh mountains. Here, during the summer months, you may come across Caius Julius Quartus, a Roman Legionary Officer in shining armour conducting a patrol around the fortress walls and helping to re-create the life and times of a front-line defender of the Empire. At one point, the wall runs alongside St John Street, which has a curious history. In Roman times it was the main thoroughfare between the fortress and the **Amphitheatre**, the largest ever uncovered in Britain, capable of seating 7000 spectators. During the Middle Ages however this highway was excavated and turned into a defensive ditch. Over the years, the ditch gradually filled up and by Elizabethan times St John Street was a proper street once again.

No visit to Chester would be complete without a trip to **Chester Zoo** on the northern edge of the city. Set in 110 acres of landscaped gardens, it's the largest zoo in Britain, caring for more than 7000 animals from some 400 different species. The Zoo also provides a refuge for many rare and endangered animals which breed freely in near-natural enclosures. What's more, it has the UK's largest elephant facility and is the only successful breeder of Asiatic elephants in this country – to date four youngsters have been born here. The Zoo has more than a mile of overhead railway providing a splendid bird's-eye view of the animals and the Roman Garden. Other attractions include the Rare Penguin Breeding Centre with windows enabling visitors to see the birds "flying" underwater; a Forest Zone with spacious homes for Buffy Headed Capuchin

Chester is famous for its outstanding range of museums. At the Dewa Roman Experience you can re-live the sights, sounds and even the smells of daily life in Roman Chester. A superb display of artefacts from Chester and elsewhere in the Roman Empire are on show and kids love dressing up in replica suits of Roman armour. "Dewa" incidentally is not a mis-spelling of the Roman name for Chester but is how Romans of the time pronounced "Deva".

Roman Garden assembled in 1949, Chester

151

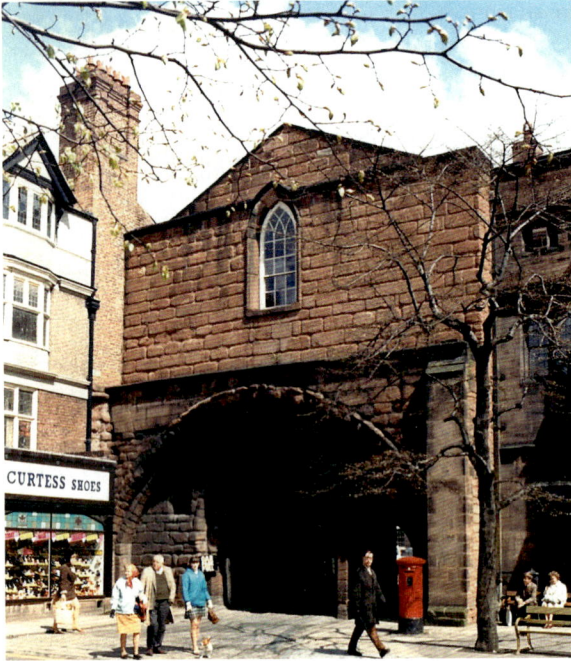

Abbey Gate, Chester

to prominence in the Civil War when Gen. Sir William Brereton made it his headquarters during the siege of Chester. In August 1644 there was fighting near the church and bullet marks can still be seen around its west door. One of them even penetrated a brass by the chancel that had been placed there in memory of a former mayor of Chester. The plaque remained there for many years until a Victorian sightseer prised it out and made off with it. Just over a century after that skirmish, a major fire in 1752 destroyed much of Tarvin but one fortunate result of the conflagration was that the rebuilding of the village left it with an abundance of handsome Georgian buildings.

TATTENHALL

8 miles SE of Chester off the A41

Tattenhall is a fine old village within sight of the twin castles of Beeston and Peckforton perched atop the Peckforton Hills. There are some attractive old houses and a Victorian church with a graveyard which gained notoriety during the 1800s because of the activities of a gang of grave-robbers. They lived in caves in the hills nearby and, once they had disposed of the bodies to medical gentlemen, used the empty coffins to store their booty from more conventional thieving. At that time Tattenhall was a busy little place. The Shropshire Union Canal passes close by and the village was served by two railway stations on different lines. Today, only one railway line

monkeys; and special enclosures for the black rhinos, red pandas and in the Realm of the Red Ape, orang-utans. Offering more than enough interest for a full day out, the Zoo is open every day of the year except Christmas Day.

AROUND CHESTER

TARVIN

5 miles E of Chester off the A54 or A51

In the *Domesday Book* Tarvin is recorded as one of the larger manors in Cheshire and by the 1300s was the centre of an extensive parish. The present church was begun at this time and boasts the oldest surviving timber roof in Cheshire. The village came survives (and no stations), the canal is used solely by pleasure craft, but the village is enjoying a new lease of life as a desirable community for people commuting to Chester, a short drive away.

Small though it is, Tattenhall has entertained some distinguished visitors. No less a personage than King James I once stayed at The Bear & Ragged Staff. This attractive hostelry was then a modest one-storey building with a thatched roof but later became an important coaching inn, (the old mounting steps still stand outside). The pub's unusual name suggests some connection with the Earls of Warwick whose crest it is. (The first Earl supposedly strangled a bear, the second Earl clubbed a giant to death).

BELGRAVE

4 miles S of Chester on the B5445

Belgrave is hardly large enough to qualify as a hamlet but it has given its name to the London area known as Belgravia. Both are owned by the Duke of Westminster, Britain's richest landowner, whose family home, Eaton Hall, stands beside the River Dee a couple of miles west of the village. The Duke's family, the Grosvenors, were well established in Cheshire by the 1300s but it was the acquisition by marriage of a large estate to the west of London that brought them huge riches. As London expanded westwards during the 18th and 19th century, their once rural estate was developed into elegant squares and broad boulevards, many with

names reflecting the Duke's Cheshire connections – Eaton Square, Eccleston Square, Grosvenor Place and Chester Row.

The Grosvenor's monstrous Victorian mansion suffered badly when it was occupied by the military during the Second World War. In the 1970s it was demolished and replaced by a more modest, concrete structure which has divided architectural opinion as to its merits – one writer described it "as modern as a 1970s airline terminal". The house is not open to the public but its gardens occasionally are.

SALTNEY

2 miles SW of Chester off the A5104

For centuries, the ferry boat from Saltney on the south side of the River Dee provided a vital link for travellers from north Wales making their way to the great city of Chester. Modern roads put the ferrymen out of business a long time ago but their memory is honoured at the Saltney Ferry public house.

THE WIRRAL

Two Old English words meaning heath land covered with bog myrtle gave The Wirral its name and well into modern times it was a byword for a desolate place. The 14th century author of *Sir Gawayne and the Green Knight* writes of

"The wilderness of Wirral:
few lived there who loved with a good
heart either God or man".

The Wirral's inhabitants were

---

152 CARRIAGES

Gatesheath, Tattenhall

A homely and comfortable real ale pub with restaurant, B&B letting rooms and camp site for all the family.

see page 265

153 SPORTSMANS ARMS

Tattenhall

This superb village inn offers the best in hospitality, well kept ales and tasty pub grub.

see page 266

154 MICHELLS WINE BAR AND BRASSERIE

Tattenhall

An unbeatable restaurant and wine bar offering unrivalled cuisine and hospitality known throughout Cheshire and beyond.

see page 267

●

The National Waterways Museum in Ellesmere Port, provides the opportunity to explore the former canal port and experience life afloat aboard a collection of canal and river boats. Other exhibits provide interactive displays, film and audio recordings recounting the stories of the people who worked on the waterways. And in the authentic dock workers' cottages visitors can see how people lived from the 1840s to the 1950s.

●

infamous for preying on the shipwrecks tossed on to its marshy coastline by gales sweeping off the Irish Sea. The 19th century development of shipbuilding at Birkenhead brought industry on a large scale to the Mersey shore but also an influx of prosperous Liverpool commuters who colonised the villages of the Caldy and Grange Hills and transformed the former wilderness into a leafy suburbia. The 1974 Local Government changes handed two thirds of The Wirral to Merseyside leaving Cheshire with by far the most attractive third, the southern and western parts alongside the River Dee. Tourism officials now refer to The Wirral as the "Leisure Peninsula", a fair description of this appealing and comparatively little-known area.

ELLESMERE PORT

7 miles N of Chester off the M53

Located on the south shore of the River Mersey, Ellesmere Port developed when commercial trading started along the Shropshire Union Canal and later the Manchester Ship Canal. Today, it is a busy market town with one of Europe's largest designer outlets, Cheshire Oaks, which boasts more than 140 stores full of top brands and leading designer names with discounts of up to 50% off recommended retail prices.

The town also boasts one of the world's largest underwater viewing tunnels at the **Blue Planet Aquarium**. Here, visitors can get right up close to huge sharks, graceful rays and hundreds of other amazing fish. Also, there's a

National Waterways Museum, Ellesmere Port

chance to see the brand new otter enclosure, one of the largest in the UK.

NESTON

11 miles NW of Chester off the A540

Right up until the early 1800s, Neston was the most significant town in The Wirral, one of a string of small ports along the River Dee. In Tudor times, Neston had been one of the main embarkation points for travellers to Ireland but the silting up of the river was so swift and inexorable that by the time the New Quay, begun in 1545, was completed, it had become useless. Visiting Neston in the late 1700s, the poet Anna Seward described the little town set on a hill overlooking the Dee Estuary as "a nest from the storm of the ocean".

One of Wirral's major attractions is **Ness Gardens**, a 64-acre tract of superbly landscaped gardens on the banks of the River Dee. The gardens are run by the University of Liverpool as an Environmental and Horticultural Research Station and are planned to provide magnificent displays all year round. There are children's play and picnic areas, well-marked interest trails, and licensed refreshment rooms.

PARKGATE

12 miles NW of Chester via the A540 and B5134

After Neston port became unusable, maritime traffic moved north along the Dee Estuary to Parkgate which, as the new gateway to Ireland, saw some notable visitors. John Wesley, who made regular trips to Ireland, preached here while waiting for a favourable wind, and George Frederick Handel returned via Parkgate after conducting the very first performance of *The Messiah* in Dublin. JMW Turner came to sketch the lovely view across to the Flintshire hills. A little later, Parkgate enjoyed a brief spell as a fashionable spa. Lord Nelson's mistress, Lady Hamilton took the waters here in an effort to cure an unfortunate skin disease. She was born at nearby Ness where you can still see the family home, Swan Cottage. Another visitor was Mrs Fitzherbert, already secretly married to the Prince Regent, later George IV. When Holyhead developed into the main gateway to Ireland, Parkgate's days as a port and watering-place were numbered. But with fine Georgian houses lining the promenade, this attractive little place still retains the atmosphere of a gracious spa town.

HESWALL

14 miles NW of Chester on the A540

Set on a steep hillside, Heswall was an important port before the silting up of the River Dee. After decades of decline, the town flourished again as a choice retreat for Liverpool commuters following the opening of the railway tunnel under the Mersey in 1888. If you take the road down to the beach from the town centre there are outstanding views across the Dee estuary to the hills of Wales.

156 THE CHESHIRE YEOMAN

Little Sutton

This charming pub manages to combine traditional homemade food with a comfortable and contemporary setting.

see page 269

157 POLLARD'S INN

Willaston

A charming, friendly and accommodating hostelry offering fabulous homemade food and 5 high quality guest bedrooms.

see page 270

158 FOX & HOUNDS

Barnston

This award winning pub is a haven for those seeking a bit of history to accompany their pint.

see page 271

159 HILBRE COURT

West Kirby

Just a short walk from the sea-front, perfect for a good meal.

🍴 see page 272

BRIMSTAGE

14 miles NW of Chester via M53 and A5137

The most striking building in this tiny hamlet is **Brimstage Hall**, a medieval pele, or fortified tower. It's not known why such a tower, more appropriate to the lawless border regions, should have been built in peaceful Cheshire. Another mystery is the date of its construction – estimates range from 1175 to 1350 and a raft of human bones found at the bottom of a long-forgotten well in 1957 failed to resolve any of these questions. There is another puzzle too: could the stone carving of a smirking domestic cat in the old chapel (now a gift shop) be the original of Lewis Carroll's "Cheshire Cat" which had a notorious habit of disappearing leaving only its smile behind? Today, the old courtyard is home to a cluster of craft and speciality shops, together with a tea room and restaurant.

THORNTON HOUGH

14 miles NW of Chester via the A540 and B5136

The huge village green at Thornton Hough, covering some 14 acres and surrounded by half-timbered black and white houses, was one of the most picturesque spots in Cheshire until it was relocated to Merseyside in 1974. Much of the village was built by Lord Leverhulme after he established his soap factory at Port Sunlight a few miles to the north; his grandson lives at Thornton Manor (private). The village boasts two churches, one of which has no fewer than 5 clocks – the fifth was installed by Joseph Hirst, a Yorkshire mill owner who also built houses here and wished to see a church clock from his bedroom window.

WEST KIRBY

20 miles NW of Chester on the A540

Set beside the Dee estuary and looking across to the Welsh mountains, West Kirby was just a small fishing village until the railway link with Liverpool was established in the 1880s. Today, it's a bustling seaside town with some 28,000 inhabitants. A big attraction here is the **West Kirby Marine Lake**, a 52-acre man-made saltwater lake. With a maximum depth of 5 feet it offers a degree of safety unobtainable on the open sea. Courses in sailing, windsurfing and canoeing are available at the

Sunset, West Kirby

Wirral Sailing Centre.

West Kirby is well-known to birdwatchers and naturalists because of the **Hilbre Islands**, part-time islands that can be reached at low tide across Dee Sands. Permits (free) from the Wirral Borough Council are required to visit the main island where there is a resident warden. Two smaller islands, Middle Eye and the tiny Little Eye, do not require permits. The latter is notable for its impressive number of wader roosts.

West Kirby is also the starting point for the **Wirral Way**, a 12-mile long linear nature reserve and country park created mostly from the trackbed of the old West Kirby to Hooton railway. When it was opened in 1973 it was one of the first Country Parks in Britain. The local council has also produced a series of circular walks based around the former stations along the line. One of these, **Hadlow Road Station**, a short distance from the centre of Willaston, is especially interesting. The station hasn't seen a train since 1962 but everything here is spick and span, the signal box and ticket office apparently ready for action, a trolley laden with milk churns waiting on the platform. Restored to appear as it would have been on a typical day in 1952, the station's booking office still has a pile of pre-decimal change at the ready, including silver sixpences, half-crowns and eight-sided threepenny pieces.

BIRKENHEAD

20 miles NW of Chester off the M53

If you were asked "Where is the largest group of Grade I listed buildings in England?", Birkenhead would probably not be your first guess. But you can find these buildings in Hamilton Square where you'll also find the **Old Town Hall**, although that only merits a Grade II rating. It now houses an exhibition telling the story of the famous Cammell Laird shipyard, a model of the Woodside area in 1934 when King George V opened the Queensway road tunnel under

•

Birkenhead Park, to the east of Birkenhead town centre, is a remarkable example of an early Victorian urban park with 2 lakes, rockery, Swiss bridge and formal gardens. This vast parkland was designed in 1842 by Sir Joseph Paxton, architect of London's Crystal Palace. He also designed the spectacular main entrance which is modelled on the Temple of Illysus in Athens.

•

Tranmere Abbey, Birkenhead

157

HIDDEN PLACES OF LANCASHIRE AND CHESHIRE

160 GORGE' US

Bebington

This delightful little café provides satisfaction for those sweet teeth in style.

see page 273

the Mersey, and a collection of delightful Della Robbia pottery. Also within the Town Hall are an art gallery, theatre, cinema and concert hall.

The **Birkenhead Heritage Trail** guides visitors around the town's various attractions and includes trips on a genuine Hong Kong tram and a beautifully restored Birkenhead tram of 1901. The trail takes in the Shore Road Pumping Station with its "Giant Grasshopper" steam pump. It was one of several used to extract water from the Mersey railway tunnel – Europe's very first underwater rail tunnel. Other attractions along the trail include an Edwardian Street scene display, a unique historic transport collection and a visit to the Pacific Road Arts and Exhibition Centre.

Just along from Pacific Road is Egerton Bridge which offers a bird's eye view over the docklands. Moored alongside East Float Dock Road are two historic warships, now museums. Both the frigate *HMS Plymouth* and the submarine *HMS Onyx* served during the Falklands War and are now preserved as they were in the 1980s. Also on display is a German U-boat, U534, whose sinking marked the end of the Battle of the Atlantic in May 1945. The submarine was recovered after lying on the seabed for 50 years.

Just out of town is the purpose-built **Williamson Art Gallery & Museum** which exhibits a wealth of local and maritime history, a permanent display of

Victorian oil paintings, tapestries by Lee and English watercolours, and also hosts a full programme of temporary exhibitions.

BEBINGTON

12 miles NW of Chester off the A41

Much of the Wirral's Merseyside is heavily industrialised but a dramatic exception is **Port Sunlight** near Bebington. This model village was created in 1888 by William Hesketh Lever, later 1st Viscount Leverhulme, to house the workers in his soap factory and was named after his most famous product, Sunlight Soap. Leverhulme wanted to provide "a new Arcadia, ventilated and drained on the most scientific principles". Some thirty architects were employed to create the individually designed rows of rustic cottages and the whole village is now a Conservation Area. The history of the village and its community is explored at the Port Sunlight Heritage Centre where there are scale models of the village, a Victorian port and Sunlight House, original plans for the building and displays of period advertising and soap packaging. A major attraction is the **Lady Lever Art Gallery** which houses a magnificent collection of pre-Raphaelite paintings by Millais and Rosetti, portraits by Gainsborough and Reynolds, dramatic landscapes by Turner and Constable, an impressive Wedgwood collection and some superb pieces of 18th century furniture. The gallery also has a gift shop and a popular tea room, the Lady Lever Café.

EASTHAM

10 miles NW of Chester off the A41

Eastham Woods Country Park
(also now in Merseyside) is a 76-acre oasis of countryside amidst industrial Merseyside and enjoys considerable status amongst bird-watchers as one of few northern woodlands with all three species of native woodpecker in residence. Just a mile or so from the Park is Eastham village, another little oasis with a church and old houses grouped around the village green. The venerable yew tree in the churchyard is reputed to be the oldest in England.

THE WELSH BORDERS

Awake or asleep, the medieval Lords of the Marches made sure their swords were close at hand. At any time, a band of wild-haired Welshmen might rush down from the hills to attack the hated Normans who had dispossessed them of their land. A thousand years earlier their enemies had been the Romans and the centuries-old struggle along the Marches would only end when one of the Welshmen's own people, Henry Tudor, defeated Richard III in 1485 and ascended the throne as Henry VII.

Conflict was to flare up again during the Civil War when the Welsh supported the Royalist forces against mainly Parliamentary Cheshire but nowadays the valley of the Dee is a peaceful and picturesque area, and nowhere more so than around Farndon on the Denbighshire border.

FARNDON

7 miles S of Chester off the B5130

Built on a hillside overlooking the River Dee, Farndon is literally a stone's throw from Wales. Most travellers agree that the best approach to the principality is by way of this little town and its ancient bridge. Records show that building of the bridge began in 1345 and it is one of only two surviving medieval bridges in the county, the other being in Chester. From Farndon's bridge, riverside walks by the Dee extend almost up to its partner in Chester. During the Civil War, Farndon's strategic position between Royalist North Wales and parliamentarian Cheshire led to many skirmishes here. Those stirring events are colourfully depicted in a stained glass window in the church, although only the Royalist heroes are included.

HIGHER KINNERTON

8 miles SW of Chester off the A55/A5104

One of the oldest and most picturesque coaching inns in north Wales, the Royal Oak also boasts a resident ghost and stands where one of the most famous trees in the country once towered. Here in September 1644 King Charles I, fleeing Cromwell's troops after his defeat at Chester, evaded his pursuers by hiding amidst the branches of the Kinnerton Oak. The landlord of the Royal Oak has inscribed this romantic tale around the walls of the old beamed snug.

One Farndon man who deserves a memorial of some kind but doesn't have one is John Speed, the famous cartographer, who was born here in 1542. He followed his father's trade as a tailor, married and had 18 children. He was nearly 50 before he was able to devote himself full time to researching and producing his beautifully drawn maps. Fortunately, he lived to the age of 87 and his fifty-four Maps of England and Wales were the first really accurate ones to be published.

159

It's just one of the many charming features here, along with the inglenook crackling with log fires and the fascinating collection of old pots and water jugs.

MALPAS

14 miles S of Chester on the B5069

With its charming black and white cottages and elegant Georgian houses Malpas is one of the most delightful old villages in Cheshire though its Norman-French name implies that it once lay in difficult terrain – "mal passage". Of the Norman castle that once protected this hill-top border town only a grassy mound behind the red sandstone church survives. Approached through 18th century gates attributed to Vanbrugh, **St Oswald's Church** is lavishly decorated with a striking array of gargoyles but is most notable for the splendour of its interior. The nave roof is brilliant with gilded bosses and winged angels, all created around 1480, and there are two magnificent chapels separated from the nave by delicately carved screens. The Brereton chapel dates from 1522 and contains an alabaster effigy of Sir Randal Brereton, in the armour of a medieval knight, together with his lady. Across the aisle, the Cholmondeley chapel commemorates Sir Hugh Cholmondeley who died in 1605.

The Cholmondeley family owned huge estates around Malpas and it was they who built the town's attractive old almshouses and a school in the 18th century.

They lived at Cholmondeley Castle, a few miles to the north-east. The Gothic-style castle is not open to the public but the 800 acres of **Cholmondeley Castle Garden** are. The gardens are planted with a variety of acid-loving plants including rhododendrons, hydrangeas, magnolias, camellias, dogwoods, mahonias and viburnums. There's a lovely Temple Garden with a rockery, lake and islands, and a Silver Garden planted with distinctive silver-leafed plants as a commemoration of Elizabeth II's Silver Jubilee.

ROSSETT

6 miles S of Chester off the A483

In Rossett, a pleasant village beside the River Alyn, and about a mile across the border into north Wales, is The Golden Grove inn. Here, history strikes as an almost tangible force when you enter the inn's portals for the first time. The entrance and reception area of what is now the bar, (including a tiny snug bar) was the original 13th century inn in its entirety. The low oak beams and ornate carved dark wood bar were additions during the 1600s. There are three dates carved into the intricate workings of the bar, but they are well hidden unless you know where to look. Naturally, such an ancient establishment has its own ghost, one James Clarke who actually expired at the inn on April 21st, 1880. James was generally believed to be the landlady's lover; certainly, she had him buried in the courtyard and erected a headstone to his memory.

Accommodation, Food & Drink and Places of Interest

The establishments featured in this section includes hotels, inns, guest houses, bed & breakfasts, restaurants, cafés, tea and coffee shops, tourist attractions and places to visit. Each establishment has an entry number which can be used to identify its location at the beginning of the relevant chapter or its position in this section.

In addition full details of all these establishments and many others can be found on the Travel Publishing website - **www.travelpublishing.co.uk**. This website has a comprehensive database covering the whole of Britain and Ireland.

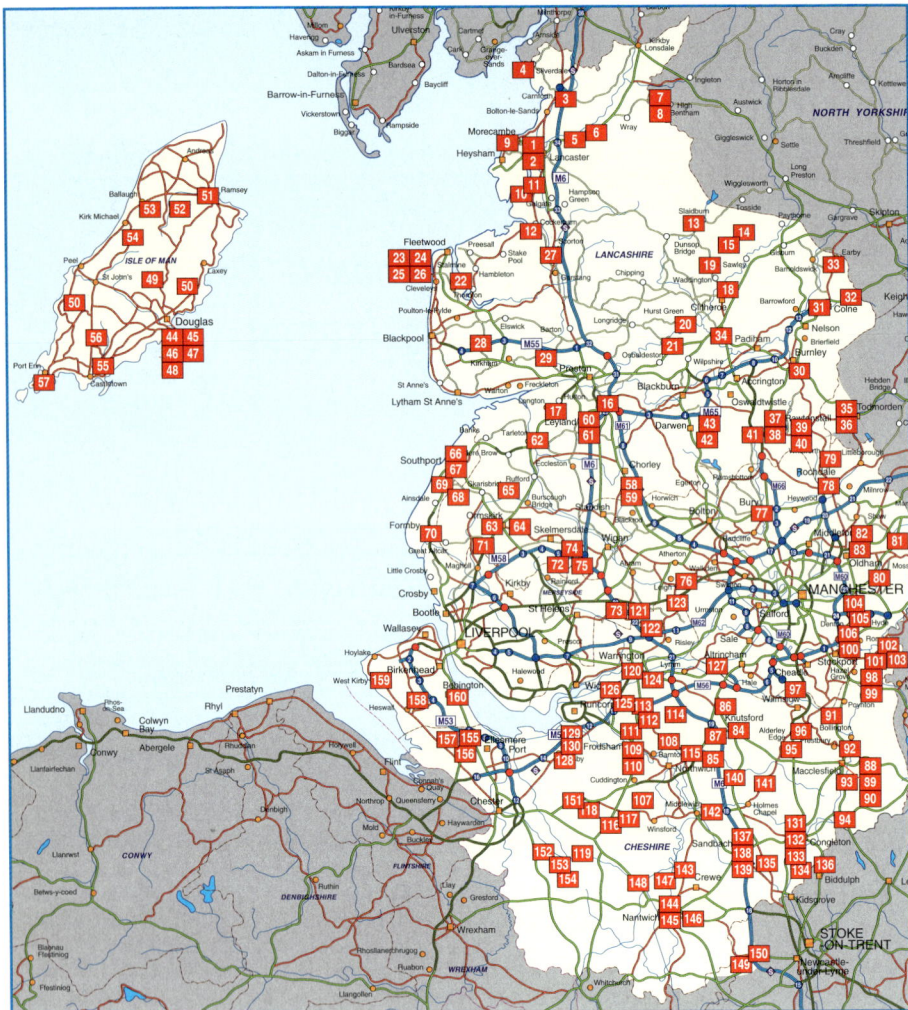

NORTH YORKSHIRE

LANCASHIRE

ISLE OF MAN

Douglas

Peel

Port Erin

Castletown

Ramsey

Kirk Michael

Ballaugh

St John's

Laxey

Fleetwood

Blackpool

Morecambe

Heysham

Lancaster

Preston

Southport

Formby

Crosby

Bootle

Wallasey

LIVERPOOL

Birkenhead

West Kirby

Hoylake

Heswall

Llandudno

Colwyn Bay

Rhyl

Prestatyn

Conwy

Abergele

St Asaph

Denbigh

Ruthin

CONWY

DENBIGHSHIRE

FLINTSHIRE

Mold

Chester

Wrexham

WREXHAM

Llangollen

CHESHIRE

MANCHESTER

Stockport

Macclesfield

Congleton

Crewe

Nantwich

Sandbach

Kidsgrove

STOKE-ON-TRENT

Newcastle-under-Lyme

🛏 ACCOMMODATION

4 The Silverdale Hotel, Silverdale
8 Black Bull Hotel, High Bentham
11 The Stork Inn, Condor Green
13 Hark To Bounty, Slaidburn, Clitheroe
14 Springhead Farm Holiday Cottages, Bolton By Bowland, Clitheroe
15 Copy Nook Hotel, Bolton By Bowland, Clitheroe
19 Moorcock Inn Hotel and Restaurant, Waddington, Clitheroe
20 The Eagle & Child, Hurst Green
21 Rose Cottage, Clayton le Dale
22 The Beachview Hotel, Thornton
26 Briardene Hotel, Cleveleys
27 The Priory Scorton, Scorton, Preston
31 Crown Hotel, Colne
35 The Black Swan, Todmorden
40 Glen Valley Guest House, Waterfoot
43 Rosins Country Hotel & Restaurant, Hoddlesden, Darwen
47 The Sefton, Douglas
52 Ginger Hall Hotel, Sulby
54 The Old Stable, Berk, Kirk Michael
79 Red Lion Inn, Whitworth
85 The Golden Pheasant, Plumley
99 The Red Lion Inn, High Lane
104 The Globe Hotel, Dukinfield
115 The Slow & Easy, Lostock Gralam
117 The Red Lion, Little Budworth
123 Comfortable Gill Inn, Glazebury
124 The Rams Head Inn, Grappenhall
125 The Hatton Arms & Restaurant, Hatton, Warrington
128 Robin Hood Hotel, Helsby, Frodsham
129 The Old Hall Hotel, Frodsham
140 The Cottage Restaurant & Lodge, Allostock, Knutsford
152 Carriages, Gatesheath
155 Woodcote House Hotel & Restaurant, Hooton
157 Pollard's Inn, Willaston

🍴 FOOD & DRINK

3 The Canal Turn, Carnforth
4 The Silverdale Hotel, Silverdale
6 The Black Bull Inn, Brookhouse
7 The Nose Bag, High Bentham
8 Black Bull Hotel, High Bentham
9 Regent Coffee Lounge and Restaurant, Morecambe
10 The Lantern O'er Lune Café, Glasson Docks
11 The Stork Inn, Condor Green
12 The Manor Inn, Cockerham, Lancaster
13 Hark To Bounty, Slaidburn, Clitheroe
15 Copy Nook Hotel, Bolton By Bowland, Clitheroe
16 Ye Olde Hob Inn, Bamber Bridge
17 The Rams Head, Longton, Preston
18 The Black Horse, Pimlico Village
19 Moorcock Inn Hotel and Restaurant, Waddington, Clitheroe
20 The Eagle & Child, Hurst Green
23 Taste Licensed Coffee House, Cleveleys
24 Granny's Coffee Shop and Restaurant, Cleveleys
25 Carousel Diner, Cleveleys
26 Briardene Hotel, Cleveleys
27 The Priory Scorton, Scorton, Preston
28 The Eagle & Child, Weeton
29 The Sitting Goose, Lower Bartle

31 Crown Hotel, Colne
32 The Emmott Arms, Laneshaw Bridge
33 The White Lion, Earby
34 Number 51, Whalley
35 The Black Swan, Todmorden
36 Cherries Tea Room, Todmorden
38 Café Artisan, Rawtenstall
39 The Duke of Buccleugh, Waterfoot
42 The Crown & Thistle, Hoddlesden
43 Rosins Country Hotel & Restaurant, Hoddlesden, Darwen
45 Terminus Tavern, Douglas
46 Copperfields Olde Edwardian Restaurant, Douglas
47 The Sefton, Douglas
48 Spill The Beans Coffee Shop, Douglas
49 The Famous Creg Ny Baa, Onchan
50 Liverpool Arms, Baldrine
50 Niarbyl Café, Dalby
51 Gophers Coffee Shop, Ramsey
52 Ginger Hall Hotel, Sulby
53 The Raven, Ballaugh
55 The Whitestone Inn, Ballasalla
56 Silverdale Glen Restaurant and Tea Rooms, Ballasalla
57 The Shore Hotel, Gansey, Port St Mary
58 The Village Kitchen, Adlington
59 The White Horse, Heath Charnock
60 The Waggon & Horses, Leyland
61 Wyndhams Tea Room, Leyland
62 Pumpkin Seed Café, Tarleton
63 Bramley's Coffee House, Ormskirk
64 The Prince Albert, Westhead, Ormskirk
66 Pippins Coffee House, Southport
67 Cinnamon Bar & Lounge, Southport
69 Satchmo's, Birkdale
70 The Pinewoods, Wicks Green, Formby
71 Stanley Arms, Aughton, Ormskirk
72 Crawford Arms, Skelmersdale
73 The Newmarket, Earlstown
74 The Stanley, Upholland
75 The Holt Arms, Billinge
76 Manchester Road Inn, Astley, Tyldesley
79 Red Lion Inn, Whitworth
81 The Navigation Inn, Dobcross
82 The Farrars Arms, Grasscroft, Oldham
83 Eats & Treats, Lees, Oldham
84 The Courtyard Coffee House, Knutsford
85 The Golden Pheasant, Plumley
89 Mulberry Tree, Macclesfield
92 The Rising Sun, Rainow
93 The Old Kings Head, Gurnett
94 The Harrington Arms, Bosley
96 No 15 Wine Bar, Alderley Edge
98 Blueberries, High Lane
99 The Red Lion Inn, High Lane
100 The Duke of York, Romiley, Stockport
101 Ring O' Bells, Marple
102 The Hare & Hounds, Marple Bridge
103 The Oddfellows Arms, Mellor
104 The Globe Hotel, Dukinfield
105 The Bush Inn, Hyde
106 The Woodley Arms, Woodley
107 The Plough Inn, Whitegate, Northwich
109 The Maypole Inn, Acton Bridge
110 The Hazel Pear Inn, Acton Bridge
111 Chetwode Arms, Lower Whitley
112 The Birch & Bottle, Higher Whitley
113 The Ring O' Bells Inn, Lower Stretton
115 The Slow & Easy, Lostock Gralam
116 The Mill Pool Restaurant, Little Budworth, Tarporley
117 The Red Lion, Little Budworth
118 The Boot Inn, Boothsdale
119 The Shady Oak, Tiverton, Tarporley
120 The Albion Freehouse, Warrington

121 The Travellers Rest, Lowton
122 The Horseshoe Inn, Croft, Warrington
123 Comfortable Gill Inn, Glazebury
124 The Rams Head Inn, Grappenhall
125 The Hatton Arms & Restaurant, Hatton, Warrington
126 The Red Lion, Moore Village
128 Robin Hood Hotel, Helsby, Frodsham
129 The Old Hall Hotel, Frodsham
130 Ring O Bells, Overton, Frodsham
131 Ye Olde White Lion, Congleton
132 The Shakerley Arms, Congleton
133 Church House Inn, Congleton
134 The Horseshoe Inn, Newbald, Astbury
135 The Bulls Head, Smallwood
137 The Market Tavern, Sandbach
138 Sally's Café, Sandbach
139 Flavour, Sandbach
140 The Cottage Restaurant & Lodge, Allostock, Knutsford
142 The Fox & Hounds Inn, Sproston Green, Middlewich
143 The Coach & Horses, Bradfield Green
144 Libby's Lunches, Nantwich
145 The Wickstead Arms, Nantwich
146 The Horseshoe Inn, Willaston
147 The Royal Oak, Worleston, Nantwich
148 The Olde Barbridge Inn, Barbridge
149 Offley Arms, Madeley, Crewe
150 The Old Swan, Madeley Heath
151 The Globe, Kelsall
152 Carriages, Gatesheath
153 Sportsmans Arms, Tattenhall
154 Mitchells Wine Bar & Brasserie, Tattenhall
155 Woodcote House Hotel & Restaurant, Hooton
156 The Cheshire Yeoman, Little Sutton
157 Pollard's Inn, Willaston
158 Fox & Hounds, Barnston Village
159 Hilbre Court, West Kirby
160 Gorge' Us, Bebington

🏛 PLACES OF INTEREST

1 Lancaster Castle, Lancaster
2 Lancaster Maritime Museum, Lancaster
5 River Lune Millenium Park, Caton
27 The Priory Scorton, Scorton, Preston
30 Towneley Hall Art Gallery and Museums, Burnley
37 Rossendale Museum, Rawtenstall
41 Helmshore Mills Textile Museum, Helmshore, Rossendale
44 Manx Electric Railway, Douglas
65 WWT Martin Mere, Burscough
68 British Lawnmower Museum, Southport
77 East Lancashire Railway, Bury
78 Rochdale Pioneers Museum, Rochdale
80 Hollingworth Lake Country Park, Littleborough
86 Tatton Park, Knutsford
87 Tabley House, Knutsford
88 Paradise Mill Museum, Macclesfield
90 West Park Museum, Macclesfield
91 Adlington Hall, Adlington
95 Nether Alderley Mill, Nether Aderley
97 Quarry Bank Mill and Styal Estate, Styal
108 Marbury Country Park, Comberbach
114 Arley Hall Gardens, Arley, Northwich
127 Dunham Massey, Dunham Massey
136 Biddulph Grange Gardens, Biddulph
141 Jodrell Bank Science Centre and Arboretum, Lower Withington

1 LANCASTER CASTLE

Shire Hall, Castle Parade,
Lancaster LA1 1YJ
Tel: 01524 64998 Fax: 01524 847914
website: www.lancashire.gov.uk

Lancaster Castle is owned by Her Majesty the Queen in right of her Duchy of Lancaster. For most of its history the castle has been the centre of law and order for the county, and this magnificent building is still in use as a prison and a crown court.

The castle has dominated the town for almost 1000 years, ever since it was first established in 1093. But the hill on which it stands has a history which goes back a thousand years further, almost to the birth of Christ. The Romans built the first of at least three military forts on the site in AD79. Little is known about Lancaster until 1093 when the Norman Baron, Roger of Poitou, built a small motte and bailey castle which was replaced 50 years later by a large stone Keep which still stands today as the oldest part of the Castle. Throughout its long history it has witnessed many trials, including that of the Lancashire Witches of 1612, which resulted in the execution of ten people.

Although still a working building, guided tours of the castle include where the witches were condemned to die; the beautiful Gillow furniture in the Grand Jury Room; the dungeons and 'Drop Room' from where the condemned went to their deaths; the Crown Court from where thousands were transported to Australia; 'Hanging Corner' the site of public hangings and the magnificent Shire Hall with its display of heraldic shields.

2 LANCASTER MARITIME MUSEUM

Custom House, St George's Quay,
Lancaster LA1 1RB
Tel: 01524 64637 Fax: 01524 841692

The **Lancaster Maritime Museum** was opened in 1985 and occupies the former Custom House of 1764 by Richard Gillow and an adjacent warehouse.

Using sound, smells, reconstructions and audio visuals it tells the story of the port of Lancaster, the Lancaster Canal, fishing and the ecology of Morecambe Bay. A number of exhibitions can be seen and there is an education programme for children. Facilities include a shop, café, car parking and disabled access.

3 THE CANAL TURN

Lancaster Road, Carnforth,
Lancashire LA5 9EA
Tel: 01524 734750 Fax: 01524 734561
e-mail: beverleyboak@btconnect.com
website: www.thecanalturn.co.uk

The Canal Turn boasts a wonderful location in the scenic countryside of Carnforth, with the Lancaster canal being directly to the rear of this charming inn. Beverley and Kevin having years of experience between them, extend a warm welcome to all at their quality premises. Speckled Hen, Black Sheep and Abbot Ale are just a few of the real ales on draught here. Food is served every day between 12- 8pm and until 9pm Easter – September. Expert chefs create a wide variety of excellent, wholesome meals using local produce. Children are welcome and all major credit cards accepted.

4   THE SILVERDALE HOTEL

Shore Road, Silverdale, Carnforth,
Lancashire LA5 0TP
Tel: 01524 701206 Fax: 01524 702258

Little imagination is required to understand why this corner of Lancashire has long been designated an Area of Outstanding Natural Beauty. **The Silverdale Hotel** has a superb location in the charming village of Silverdale, North West of Carnforth, off the A6, overlooking Warton Sands and further to Morecombe bay.

A former coaching Inn dating back to 1836, father and son team, Peter and Stewart Smillie, have been welcoming guests here since November 2008. Being an ideal base for touring this beautiful part of the country, it is a popular hotel both with locals and visitors and welcomes walkers and children. The impressive gardens are spectacular and make visiting this delightful hotel a must. Open all day, every day for ale, with a choice of 2-3 real rotating ales to enjoy and quench that thirst.

Food is served Mon/Sat 12 – 2.30pm and 6 – 9pm and on Sundays 12 – 3pm and 5.30 – 8pm. Stewart has been a chef for three years and will satisfy all appetites with his hearty home cooking. On Sundays, scrumptious roast dinners are added to the menu leaving diners spoiled for choice. As much as possible of the produce used here is sourced locally making the dishes even more appealing.

Accommodation is available here all year round with seven comfortable en-suite rooms upstairs and breakfast being included in the tariff. For guests with children, family rooms are available if needed. With such excellent food, refreshing drink, and cosy accommodation surrounded by the most magnificent countryside there is not much more one could ask for thus making this an ideal choice for a holiday or a short break. All major credit cards are taken for guests convenience.

There are many places of interest to visit in and around Carnforth, whose claim to fame is that its old railway station was used in the film 'Brief Encounter' in 1945. These include Warton Old Rectory, a 14th century ruined manorhouse, Leighton Hall, a gothic mansion owned by the Gillow family with furnished rooms, nature trails, gardens etc and Leighton Moss nature reserve with hides overlooking the marshlands.

5 RIVER LUNE MILLENIUM PARK

Lancaster, Lancashire LA1 5JS
Tel: 01524 32878 Fax: 01524 382849
e-mail:
enquiries.northwest@britishwaterways.co.uk
website: www.citycoastcountryside.co.uk

The **River Lune Millenium Park** stretches some 15 kilometres along the banks of the Lune from Bull Beck near Caton to Salt Ayre in Lancaster. The Park offers leisure and everyday transport opportunities with linked footpaths and cycleways, artworks to discover and stations for information. At its heart is the Millenium Bridge providing a river crossing for pedestrians and cyclists.

A vast array of wildlife and birds can be seen in the park from gulls, ducks and waders at Salt Ayre where the river is tidal, to fishing birds such as cormorants and kingfishers further upstream. The Environment Agency is trying to encourage fish to spawn here to reverse the decline of fish populations Dragonflies can be seen skimming the water and, in the evening, bats are on the wing hunting for insects.

Artworks in various forms can be seen along the route such as Colin Reid's River Rocks - rocks sculpted from glass and nestling by the riverside, and Marjan Wouda's Heron's Head, created from wrought iron and perched above a cycleway. A set of 16 stations, at points of interest along the river, gives detailed descriptions of what can be seen from each.

7 THE NOSE BAG

37 Main Street, Higher Bentham,
Lancashire LA2 7HQ
Tel: 01524 263150

Situated in the popular village of Higher Bentham is **The Nose Bag** - a quaint brick building with a vibrant and light interior and two spaces for 30 in which to dine. A warm welcome awaits you here, along with a powerful aroma of homemade cooking. The owner is Phillippa Brown, who has been here since July 2007 and is a superb cook. Open Monday-Saturday from 9.30-4pm, there is fabulous food served, including a daily rotating homemade soup and Phillippa's homemade quiches' and scones are also very popular with all who visit.

Brookhouse Road, Brookhouse, nr Caton,
Lancashire LA2 9JP
Tel: 01524 770329
e-mail: theblack-bull@btconnect.com
website: www.black-bull-inn.co.uk

Built in the 16th Century, **The Black Bull** stands on Brookhouse Bridge where Bull Beck flows on its way to join the River Lune. This super inn can be found by taking the minor road, sign posted Brookhouse, off the A683 at Caton, north east of Lancaster. In the early 19th century, the inn was used as a courthouse where the Lord of the Manor would summon his tenants to appear for trial.

Experienced licensees and caterers, Tony and Lynne Williams, took over this charming hostelry 2½ years ago but have been in the trade for over twenty years. With their wealth of experience and marvellous hospitality it has become the centre of the community, a pub as it used to be and always should be. Tony is a top class, professional chef and his reputation for his excellent culinary skills is known far and wide, attracting visitors from all over to this quality dining establishment. Lynne is the brains and organiser of the business, forever looking for new and improved ideas to keep the customer happy.

The cosy interior is extremely pleasant and along with the warm welcome from all the dedicated staff here customers are guaranteed to feel relaxed and valued. The well stocked bar offers a choice of three real ales to enjoy, Thwaites Original, Bombardier and Wainwrights, as well as a superb range of wines from all over the world and the original Kingston Press Cider, there is something for everyone. Tony's menu is extensive and contains over 100 tempting dishes including flavoursome meals such as Steak Diane- fillet steak with shallots, mushrooms and tomato in a wine, cream and brandy sauce, grilled fillet of sea bass - covered in a lemon parsley sauce served with mini jacket potatoes, fresh vegetables and a crisp mixed salad, or for the largest of all appetites, the mega mixed grill is sure to satisfy; 10oz gammon, 10oz rump, lamb chop, two sausages, black pudding, egg, onion rings, mushrooms and grilled tomato! As well as numerous other specialities, the menu has a wide range of tasty snacks and lighter bites, which are equally as appetizing. Most of the produce used here is sourced locally and all meals are freshly cooked to order. The 2-4-1 Monday deals have proved very popular and the early bird menu is available between 11am-12.30am and 4.30pm-6pm. Food is available Mon-Sat 11am-10pm & Sunday 12-9pm

13 Main Street, High Bentham,
Lancashire LA2 7HF
Tel: 01524 261213
e-mail: mandy@theblackbullbentham.co.uk
website: www.theblackbullbentham.co.uk

Located between the Lancashire and
Yorkshire border, close to the Yorkshire
Dales, in Higher Bentham lays a former
coaching Inn named the **Black Bull Hotel.**
Dating back to the 18th century, the
handsome black and white painted building is
a charming public house and hotel, featuring a
double, twin and family room. The bedrooms
are recently refurbished and are light and airy,
all with en-suite bathrooms, tea and coffee
facilities, and colour televisions as standard. The prices are competitive, costing just £25 per
person, per night, with a great selection of breakfasts included.

The tenants Amanda and James have been at the Black Bull for 3 years, with Amanda working
here 6 years previously as the cook and manager. Her food is delicious and the menu features a
large array of light and main meals such as filled paninis with sausage and cheese, chicken and sour

cream wraps and tomato and basil pasta on the
lighter menu and goats cheese and red onion
tart, pie of the day and BBQ pork ribs on the
main meal menu. Most of the food prepared at
the Black Bull is home cooked and uses as
many locally sourced ingredients as possible,
making the dishes taste fantastic. Food is
served daily at varying times, Monday 12-2pm,
Tuesday/Wednesday 12-2pm and 5pm-8pm,
Thursday 12-2PM, Friday 12-2PM and 5-8pm,
Saturday 8.30am-8pm (open for breakfast) and
last but not least, Sunday from 12-3pm when
an all you can eat hot lunch buffet is served.

The bar here is traditionally decorated,
with low beams travelling the length of it,
keeping in with the original features of the old coaching inn. There is a pool table for socialising
and also a fourteen seated dining area and cosy chairs for comfortable lounging. The bar sports two
real ales, Thwaites original and rotating
Thwaites Brewery ale. There is weekly
entertainment, which is a great way to meet
new people. On wednesday nights there is a
food themed evening, friday nights see
homemade pizzas added to the menu, perfect
for the whole family and once a month there
is live entertainment, usually on a friday from
9pm. Children are more than welcome at the
property until 8pm and for the adults there is
Sky TV to watch here, an outdoor smoking
area and off road car parking. The Black Bull
also has a small function room with a bar, for
parties of up to 40 people.

9 REGENT COFFEE LOUNGE AND RESTAURANT

40a Regent Road, Morecambe,
Lancashire LA3 1QN
Tel: 01524 833145

Located in the heart of Morecambe, famous for its five-mile stretch of golden coast, is the delightful **Regent Coffee Lounge and Restaurant**. Situated along Regent Road, this fine looking coffee house is owned and run devotedly by Julie and Mark Wilson. It has been in the family for the past twenty years but Julie and Mark took over in August 2008.

The tasteful decor creates a warm, cosy environment where customers can relax and chat over a coffee and slice of cake, or enjoy a little peace while tucking in to their favourite homemade dish available on the extensive menu. There is comfortable seating for thirty and all tables are waitress serviced leaving customers to relax completely. Mark is head of the kitchen and uses his culinary skills and expertise to create a large choice of hearty meals using local produce. Whatever the appetite, there is something here to please all, ranging from cakes, homemade fruit pies and desserts to the more substantial snacks, sandwiches, breakfasts and lunches. Homemade pies are a popular speciality here and all are available with a choice of chips and peas, or roast or boiled potatoes with three vegetables. The large variety of fillings in the 'Super Spuds' caters for all tastes and the refreshing salads will delight those wanting something not too heavy but just as tasty! The delicious array of mouth-watering cakes and desserts on display will tempt those with a sweeter tooth and are all so alluring that customers will be spoiled for choice! Beverages on the menu include tea, coffee, hot chocolate, Bovril, Horlicks and a variety of milkshakes made with fresh milk and ice cream. This rather appealing, upmarket Coffee House is open seven days a week Mon-Fri 9.30-4pm, Sat 9.30-2.30pm and Sun 9.30-2pm.

Morecambe is in the middle of a 5 mile sandy stretch of coast known as Morecambe Bay, with the mountains of the Lake District in the background. It is a popular holiday resort and has all the normal seaside attractions and shops and an all year round market. There is an arts venue in the old railway station, a cinema and a Tourist Information Centre in the town.

169

10 THE LANTERN O'ER LUNE CAFÉ

**West Quay, Glasson Docks,
Lancashire LA2 0BY
Tel: 01524 752323
e-mail: doreen-harry@tiscali.co.uk**

Harry and Doreen Stevenson have owned **The Lantern O'er Lune Café** for the past five years. Situated in a superb location, overlooking Glasson Docks, it is a well-known oasis for locals and visitors alike. Harry is a professional chef and has over 40 years experience in the catering trade.

Open seven days a week; between 9am-4pm in the winter months and 9am-5pm in the summer, everyone is made to feel welcome here. Inside, there is comfortable seating for 42, with seating outside for an additional 20 on warmer days. Everything served here is home cooked with speciality dishes including delicious, homemade pies and fresh fish and chips. The specials board as well as the printed menu gives plenty of choice for customers. The menu includes a wide range of baguettes and jacket potatoes, all served with freshly prepared salad garnish, as well as main meals such as meat and onion pie served with chips, mushy peas & gravy or deep fried whole tail scampi served with chips, peas and salad garnish. Breakfasts range from the typical full English to lighter choices and snacks. Children are welcome and only cash is accepted.

12 THE MANOR INN

**1 Main Street, Cockerham, Lancaster,
Lancashire LA2 0EF
Tel: 01524 791252**

Situated in the pleasant village of Cockerham, found at the junction of the A588 and B5272 is **The Manor Inn**. With plenty of experience behind them, Doreen and Stuart have made this Inn the hub of the village. Impressive bygone pictures of the village and surrounding areas create an interesting ambience.

Four real ales are served including Black Sheep and Tiger along with two rotating guest ales. Charlene, the professional chef here, produces first class homemade food at reasonable prices. Traditional Favourites are served such as lasagne served with garlic bread & fresh salad alongside a good selection of vegetarian options. Lighter meals include, fluffy jacket potatoes or freshly made sandwiches and baguettes with a choice of delicious fillings. Delicious roasts are added to the menu on Sundays and the daily specials board brings further options. Open Lunchtimes and evenings Mon - Fri with food being served 12 – 2.30pm & 5 -8pm, open all day Sat & Sun with food available 12 – 2.30pm & 5 – 8.30/9pm. Children are welcome and booking is advisable in the summer. Entertainment is provided on Saturday evenings between March-October. There is ample parking and a large beer garden.

Carricks Lane, Conder Green, Lancaster,
Lancashire LA2 0AN
Tel: 01524 751234 Fax: 01524 752660
e-mail: tracy@thestorkinn.co.uk
website: www.thestorkinn.co.uk

The Stork Inn, dating back to 1660, is a delightful old English Country Inn situated in the picturesque hamlet of Conder Green. This former coaching inn is just a short distance from Lancaster with its castles & museums, and is located on the estuary of the River Lune where it meets the River Conder.

During the winter months guests are welcomed in from the cold by the roaring log fires and a warm friendly greeting from the hosts. Visitors in the summer however, will enjoy the beautiful gardens, the large children's play area and the BBQ's with a South African influence.

Friendly host Tracy Fairbrother, has been running The Stork Inn over the past two years and her wealth of experience in the hotelier trade combined with her South African influence makes this inn quite unique. Touches of her South African heritage are dotted around The Stork, either on the menu, behind the bar, part of the décor or simply by the large choice of tasty but healthy children's meals available. As a superb team, Tracy, Ian, daughter Megan Lois and "Granny" Jean, extend a warm welcome to all visitors which is complemented by their exceptional customer service.

The bar offers traditional hand pulled real ales including Black Sheep and Timothy Taylor Landlord as well as quality wine & excellent coffee from J. Atkinson & Co of Lancaster. All food is homemade, freshly cooked to order and the super South African specialities include the delicious Boerewors (lightly spiced coarse beef sausage) on a bed of mixed sweet potato & maris piper mash, topped with rich tomato and onion gravy, served with fresh vegetables and the luscious Kassler rib chops (smoked pork), served with fruity apple chutney, choice of potatoes and fresh vegetables.

This traditional coaching inn is open daily from 10am serving morning & afternoon tea, coffee & cakes, lunch from 12pm to 2.30pm & dinner from 5.30pm to 9pm (winter until 8.30pm). Breakfast is available to non-residents on Saturday & Sunday from 08.30 to 10.30am. The charming restaurant seats 60 and booking is advisable on Sundays and Bank Holidays.

A private function area, ideally suited to smaller weddings, christenings, birthday celebrations or funerals, is available catering for up to 50 guests with flexible menu planning to maximise all budgets. The Stork also offers comfortable accommodation, consisting of nine tastefully furnished en-suite rooms of varying sizes.

13 HARK TO BOUNTY

Slaidburn, Clitheroe, Lancashire BB7 3EP
Tel: 01200 446246 Fax: 01200 446361
e-mail: manager@harktobounty.co.uk
website: www.harktobounty.co.uk

The **Hark To Bounty** is a splendid inn located in the scenic village of Slaidburn. This historic inn dates back to the 13th century and has been run for the past five years jointly by Victoria and Nick. The family were first here between 1967 until 1979, then returned to this area of outstanding beauty 15 years ago. A warm greeting awaits for familiar and new faces alike, to this charming, friendly inn. Being a Free House, but owned by the Squirevillage, it is extremely popular with the locals as well as an ideal place for walkers and visitors exploring this picturesque countryside. Open all day, every day with four real ales to choose from you will find it difficult to leave! On offer in the oak-beamed lounge bar you are able to choose between Theakstons Best, Old Peculiar, a local Moorhouses Brew and a Guest Ale, all guaranteed to tantalize your tastebuds!

The superb restaurant serves a traditional home cooked menu alongside an additional range of special dishes which are changed daily. With a vegetarian option always available there is something to please every visitor. Typical traditional Bounty favourites include home made steak and kidney plate pie made with Theakstons Ale and shortcrust pastry, grilled fillet of haddock topped with a tomato and creamy cheese rarebit, or rump steak, chargrilled to your liking, garnished with mushrooms, onion rings and tomatoes. For the vegetarian option, why not try asparagus and stilton wellington made with lentils and mung beans encased in puff Ppastry served with a tomato and basil sauce or Lancashire lattice pie - shortcrust pastry

filled with potato, leeks and tangy Lancashire cheese served with a salad garnish. For the lighter appetite, there is a wide range of appetizing sandwiches and freshly baked baguettes available all served with garnish, crisps and chef's salad as well as fresh salads and jacket potatoes with tasty fillings. Local produce is used whenever possible, and all ingredients are fresh. Fish dishes are a speciality of the chef here. Food is served Mon-Sat 12-2pm then 6-9pm (until 8pm in winter) and Sundays 12-8pm. At weekends booking is advisable.

Accommodation is offered all year round with family-sized rooms as well as en-suite rooms available. Children are welcome and all major credit cards accepted.

15 THE COPY NOOK HOTEL

**Bolton by Bowland, Clitheroe,
Lancashire BB7 4NL
Tel: 01200 447205 Fax: 01200 447004
e-mail: copynookhotel@btconnect.com
website: www.copynookhotel.co.uk**

Overlooking the Ribble Valley in its own small oasis is the delightful **Copy Nook Hotel**. This charming country hotel nestles just outside Bolton by Bowland just off the A59. Surrounded by the picturesque Forest of Bowland National Park, it is ideally situated to explore the Yorkshire Dales, the Lake District and the Trough of Bowland. A former coaching inn dating back 200 years, it is full of character with a wealth of traditional oak beams and a wonderful open log fire that creates the perfect ambience.

The Copy Nook is a family run hotel, extremely well known and famous for its local home-cooked food, which includes roasts, game and fresh fish. Owner, Brendan, who has been in the licensing trade for 34 years, snapped up this little gem fifteen years ago and runs it passionately with his partner Clare. Their love of nature and the countryside is reflected in the cosy interior, which oozes tranquillity and warmth. A wide selection of bar meals are available and the 'specials' board offers extra dishes that complement the main menu. The two tastefully decorated restaurants are homely and pleasant, seating a total of 90. The four course lunch menu offers varied choices such as local roast duckling with apple sauce & stuffing and poached salmon with hollandaise sauce all served with fresh vegetables of the day. The evening dinner menu consists of five courses and includes delicious cuisine such as halibut fillet, grilled with lemon butter & topped with prawns, and a special mushroom stroganoff for vegetarians. The majority of produce used here is sourced from within the county. With so many tempting dishes to choose from, guests will be spoiled for choice!

The bar offers a choice of three Real Ales including Tetleys and two rotating guest ales. Food is served Tues – Sat, 12-2pm and 7-9.30pm and Sunday 4pm-9pm. Booking is advisable on weekends.

The hotel is closed on Mondays. A choice of comfortable accommodation is available with all six bedrooms having en-suites, televisions and tea/coffee making facilities. Tariff includes a hearty breakfast which is served 8-9am. The hotel will organise activities within your stay such as caving, fishing, pony trekking and clay pigeon shooting. For those wanting something a little more relaxing, the area offers a wide choice of tea shops, museums, craft works and potteries. Children are welcome and all major credit cards are taken.

14 SPRINGHEAD FARM HOLIDAY COTTAGES

Bolton by Bowland, Nr Clitheroe,
Lancashire BB7 4LU
Tel: 01200 447245 Fax: 01200 447245
website: www.springheadcottages.co.uk

Located in the heart of the beautiful Ribble Valley surrounded by unspoilt countryside **Springhead Farm Holiday Cottages** provide first class, comfortable accommodation on a 145 acre working farm. Situated off the A59 between Clitheroe and Skipton, these well equipped, cosy cottages make a wonderful base for visiting the Yorkshire Dales, Lake District and the West Coast. They are tastefully decorated, well equipped and sleep between 4 – 8 people. With so many places to visit in the surrounding areas, these cottages are the perfect choice for a self-catering holiday.

16 YE OLDE HOB INN

8-9 Church Road, Bamber Bridge, Preston,
Lancashire PR5 6EP
Tel: 01772 336863

Standing proudly in Bamber Bridge is where you will find **Ye Olde Hob Inn**. This famous historic property has been resident here for many hundreds of years and is still offering a warm welcome to all. Father and son team Robert and Roger, have made the Inn a real hit with visitors and locals who are looking for freshly cooked food and well-kept rotating ales. Robert cooks up some wonderful treats in the kitchen using only the freshest local produce. You can expect to sample dishes such as Chilli con carne, shepherd's pie and Ultimate Nachos. The super food is available 7 days a week and there is a large off road car park for visitors.

17 THE RAMS HEAD

67 Liverpool Road, Longton, Preston,
Lancashire PR4 5HA
Tel: 01772 615012
Fax no: 01772 615012
e-mail: theramsheadlongton@live.com

Just a few miles south west of Preston, off the A59 in Longton lies **The Rams Head.** The welcoming Leaseholders Rob and Angela Green are experienced caterers, with Rob having been a chef for 14 years. They took over this public house in November 2008 . The couple also extend their talents worldwide and own a popular restaurant in Florida, U.S.A.

Although there is a lot of work to be done on the property, before the couple are happy with both the interior and façade of the building, the Rams Head is already becoming popular with the locals, and has a growing number of loyal visitors who return time and time again.

Rob is the chef here and his culinary skills have created a menu offering delcious dishes, catering for every palette. The food on offer is a broad selection of home cooking, using fresh produce which has been sourced from within the country. Fish dishes are a speciality and are extremely popular with all who visit. Open everyday with food being served from 12-9pm, you can also enjoy between two and four rotating real ales to accompany your meal as well as the usual choice of soft drinks for the children. The Rams Head is very much family orientated and children are made very welcome. Please note that there is a good sized car park at this property and credit cards are accepted. Whether you are looking to enjoy a hearty meal with family or a quiet drink with friends, The Rams Head is the perfect place to visit.

174

**Pimlico Village, Clitheroe,
Lancashire BB7 4PZ
Tel: 01200 420906**

Situated in the pleasant hamlet of Pimlico, a short drive between Clitheroe and Chatburn, stands **The Black Horse.** Devoted licensees of this fine freehouse, Carl and Janet, have been welcoming clientele to their much loved pub for the past eighteen months. Customers travel miles to sample the fine cuisine cooked by Janet who has been in the trade for six years. Here, customers can enjoy excellent quality of food in a warm friendly atmosphere. Being in such a beautiful part of the country, this is an ideal eating place for walkers to stop off and replenish their energy or simply a welcome rest for anyone wanting to spoil themselves and have a day off from the kitchen!

Served at the bar visitors can choose from four real ales with Thwaites original being the regular here. All food is cooked fresh to order and nothing is too much trouble for the hosts, you simply have to ask and they will do their best to please. Only local produce is used and all chips are handcut - a real treat! The extensive menu has many mouth watering delights on offer including fresh beer battered haddock served with hand cut chips and mushy peas, the fantastic Thai pasta – chicken breast with chopped onions pan fried in garlic butter, penne pasta, spices and plenty of double cream and ample more. For those wanting a challenge, the signature dish, aptly named Black Horse Steak Sizzler, is a must, strips of 8oz rump steak pan fried in garlic butter with onions, red peppers and mushrooms finished with a black bean sauce and served with a choice of rice, handcut chips or baby new potatoes and veg - Uummm! In addition to the regular menu , the specials board and the extremely popular fish board have plenty of tasty dishes to get those taste buds tingling! To cater for all appetites, lighter meals are available including homemade soup, a variety of refreshing salad bowls and freshly made sandwiches served with garnish and crisps.

Children are made very welcome at The Black Horse and for your convenience all major credit cards are taken. Opening hours are Mon/Tues 12-2pm 6pm-close Weds/Thurs/Fri/ Sat 12-2pm 5pm-close and open all day Sundays.

8 Whalley Road, Hurst Green, Clitheroe,
Lancashire BB7 9QJ
Tel: 01254 826207 Fax: 01254 826207
e-mail: debbietaylor@live.co.uk

The small village of Hurst Green in the Ribble Valley, close to the River Hodder, is to be found on the B6243 between Clitheroe and Longridge. It is home to the popular **Eagle and Child**, a former 19th century coaching inn named after the Eagle Towers of Stonyhurst College which was founded in 1794. It has become the hub of village life here, extending a warm welcome and incorporating the village post office.

Needing a new lease of life and fresh blood, Debbie and Frank Taylor took over this establishment twelve months ago. With dedication, commitment and heaps of enthusiasm they have rejuvenated the premises, heart and soul, with locals returning to enjoy the new facilities and sample the outstanding hospitality which is second to none. Visitors can relax and chat in the cosy bar with a choice of two rotating guest Ales.

Debbie is head of the kitchen where she cooks up some wonderful dishes for her guests to relish. Traditional, satisfying pub grub is offered on the printed menu with even more succulent choices daily on the specials board. Visitors are able to choose from classic favourites such as: roast of the day – served in a large Yorkshire pudding with roast potatoes or beef and ale pie - lean British beef slowly cooked in Guinness with carrots and onions, topped with shortcrust pastry. Fish lovers can delight in the salmon Newburg – poached and served in a cream, prawn and sherry sauce while vegetarians can savour the flavours of the Nice 'n' Spicy Stir Fry. Smaller portions are available for smaller appetites with a selection of freshly made sandwiches and baguettes on the menu to

satisfy those only wanting a light snack. All meals are cooked fresh to order and Debbie will do her utmost to accommodate any special requirements. Food is served Tues – Sat 12-1.45pm and 6pm-8.45pm and Sundays 12-8.30pm when booking is advisable to avoid disappointment. The pub is closed on Mondays excluding Bank Holidays.

Children are made very welcome. Upstairs there is comfortable accommodation comprising of four en-suite rooms, one being family sized. With the tariff including breakfast, it's no wonder this is a popular place for walkers. There is a large car park on the premises and all major credit cards are taken.

19   MOORCOCK INN HOTEL & RESTAURANT

Slaidburn Road, Waddington, nr Clitheroe,
Lancashire BB7 3AA
Tel: 01200 422333 Fax: 01200 429184
e-mail: info@moorcockinn.co.uk
website: www.moorcockinn.co.uk

Located at the head of the beautiful Ribble Valley, the **Moorcock Inn Hotel and Restaurant** offers a warm and friendly atmosphere combined with excellent food and first-class hospitality. This stunning hotel, over 100 years old, has hosted many famous names in the past, including Churchill, George Formby and even members of the Royal Family. It has a well established reputation as a wedding venue and is licensed for Civil Ceremonies. With three meeting and function rooms seating from 10 up to 140 guests, it makes an ideal venue for conferences, business meetings or private parties.

The thirteen, tastefully furnished bedrooms, all ensuite, are well equipped and have the most outstanding views over the Ribble Valley. The chefs at Moorcock change the menus regularly, offering new dishes and use local produce whenever possible. All the menus are full of interest with delights such as homemade cheese and onion pie, hand-cut chips and mushy peas available at lunchtime while the extensive evening menu offers delectable dishes such as herb crusted Bowland lamb chump, sat on a broad bean mash, served with glazed carrots and red wine sauce.

21   ROSE COTTAGE

2 Rose Cottages, Longsight Road (A59),
Clayton Le Dale, Ribble Valley,
Lancashire, BB1 9EX
Tel: 01254 813223 Fax: 01254 813831
e-mail: bbrose.cott@talk21.com
website: www.rosecottagebandb.com

Terry and Marje Adderly welcome visitors from all over the world to their delightful, two hundred year old B&B, **Rose Cottage**. Situated on the A59 at the gateway to the picturesque Ribble Valley, it is an ideal stopover for tourists, offering excellent facilities, outstanding hospitality and a superb, hearty breakfast! Four comfortable, homely en-suite rooms are available, one being family sized and all are extremely well equipped. Well behaved pets are welcome and the tariff includes the tremendously tasty breakfast.

23   TASTE LICENSED COFFEE HOUSE

1A South Promenade, Cleveleys,
Lancashire FY5 1BZ
Tel: 01253 867222

Taste Licensed Coffee House has an enviable location close to the sea front in Cleveleys. Owners, Susan and Jill, have twenty years in the trade but have been running this hidden gem for almost five years doing their utmost to satisfy all dietary needs and special requests. The extensive menu ranges from snacks such as smoked salmon rosti potato filled with cream cheese and lemon wedge to main choices such as roasted rack of lamb with juniper & lingonberry sauce. All dishes are home made using local produce. Children are welcome and only cash is accepted.

177

22 THE BEACHVIEW HOTEL

67-69 Beach Road, Thornton Cleveleys,
Lancashire FY5 1EG
Tel: 01253 854003

The Beachview Hotel is a very popular licensed hotel, graded three star and situated just a short stroll from the sea front in Cleveleys. This was the first venture into the hotel industry for owner Pete Richards, who over the last ten years has built up a successful business, creating a friendly, personally run hotel with a relaxed atmosphere and pleasant decor. The Beachview is open all year round, ideal for quick winter breaks as well as holidays during the summer months and a great base for exploring the surrounding countryside.

There are ten comfortable rooms available, of which six are en-suite with the remaining four all having private sinks but sharing two bathrooms. Three rooms are family sized with children being made very welcome. Only cash is accepted and there is parking for five cars.

Guests will find plenty of places of interest to visit in the surrounding areas including; the Fleetwood Museum, Morecambe Bay, Marsh Mill Village hosting the famous Marsh Mill (one of the largest mills in Europe), the Wyre Estuary Country Park and Wyre Ecology Centre at Stanah.

24 GRANNY'S COFFEE SHOP AND RESTAURANT

27 Nutter Road, Cleveleys,
Lancashire FY5 1BQ
Tel: 01253 850314

Visitors to **Granny's Coffee Shop and Restaurant** will get exactly what the name suggests-good old fashioned hospitality coupled with decent, wholesome cooking. Situated a short stroll from the sea front at Cleveleys, this quaint, homely coffee shop is owned by delightful hosts Julie and Mick Scadding who have ten years experience in the trade behind them. The delightful aroma of home baking is the first thing visitors will notice on entering, followed closely by the quality decor and furnishings of the cosy interior which has seating for 36.

The appealing printed menu offers a wide range of tasty snacks and hearty dishes with an additional specials board offering further choice. Speciality dishes include; steak & Guinness with potato pie as well as the enticing home made cakes and puddings. A take-away service is available and telephone orders are also taken. These attractive premises together with its first class services are available for party bookings and special functions.

Opening hours are Tues-Sat 9-5pm, Sun 11.30-3pm when a three-course lunch is added to the menu, and closed on Mondays. Children are welcome and booking is advisable during the summer season.

25 CAROUSEL LICENSED DINER

2 Kings Road, Cleveleys,
Lancashire FY5 1BY
Tel: 01253 852695
Mobile: 07966 421127
e-mail: allysonhunns@aol.com

Situated just a stones throw from the seafront in the delightful town of Cleveleys is the eye catching **Carousel Licensed Diner**, a very popular business for dedicated owners Martin and Allyson Hunns who have been welcoming visitors here with their superb hospitality for the past five years. Their twenty years experience in the business has helped them to create this rather striking diner style restaurant that serves a wide range of snacks and dishes that delight children as well as adults. The cheery interior, seating 105, brightens the gloomiest of days and helps to occupy the minds of those little ones, leaving mums and dads to enjoy their well-deserved mealtime in peace! The

vibrant menu offers a huge choice of breakfast specials, homemade pies and meals, assorted toasties, as well as a wide range of tempting homemade sweets, all at the most reasonable prices. Fresh produce sourced from within the County is used whenever possible to create dishes such as braised steak and onions served with chips or creamed potatoes and two vegetables and grilled English lamb chops served with salad garnish, chips or potatoes and peas. The 'Kiddies Corner' menu offers a unique, healthy three course meal for children consisting of soup or fruit juice, choice of roast meat served with chips, roast or creamed potatoes and two vegetables followed by ice cream.

The Carousel is open from 7.30am-5.30pm daily except for Christmas, Boxing and New Year days. Bookings are taken and only cash or cheque is accepted.

Being in such a good location close to the seafront in this delightful town, after dining at the Carousel visitors can enjoy a stroll along the nearby promenade and experience the traditional seaside entertainment with amusement arcades and bingo halls, or take the children to Kiddies Corner where they can have hours of fun on all the mini adventure rides. Shoppers will be kept busy in Cleveleys with market stalls and street stores stretching the length of the town. With plenty of bargains there is something to suit all pockets. Nearby attractions to Cleveleys include the Ecology Centre at Stanah, the Fleetwood Museum overlooking Morecambe Bay and Marsh Mill Village housing one of the largest mills in Europe.

179

26 BRIARDENE HOTEL

56 Kelso Avenue, Cleveleys, Blackpool,
Lancashire FY5 3JG
Tel: 01253 338300 / 852312
Fax: 01253 338301
e-mail: briardenehotel@yahoo.co.uk
website: www.briardenehotel.co.uk

Located in the centre of the Fylde Coast, **Briardene Hotel** provides the perfect location from which to explore the unique surrounding areas of outstanding natural beauty. This highly commended hotel has been in the Heywood family for the past fifty years with current owners Rod, Sandra, Deano and Tracy, together with their team of loyal staff, going the extra mile to ensure guests of an enjoyable stay. First class service is a priority here and all guests can be assured of individual treatment.

The licensed Briardene is open all year round, caters for special events and has 16 well appointed, en-suite rooms of various sizes including family sized rooms. Room only, B&B or dinner, B&B options are available.

The Curbside Brasserie Restaurant, open to non-residents but booking advisable, serves award winning cuisine and provides diners with a memorable gourmet experience. Chef, Deano prepares the most delightful, mouth watering dishes such as civit of wild boar 'haunch', slowly cooked in red wine and root vegetables, mashed potato, cooking juices and apple reduction. Children are welcome and all major credit cards are accepted. Ecology Centre at Stanah.

30 TOWNELEY HALL ART GALLERY & MUSEUMS

Burnley, Lancashire BB11 3RQ
Tel: 01282 424213
website: www.towneleyhall.org.uk

Towneley Hall offers the perfect day out for all the family - a country house, a museum and an art gallery all in one. Towneley Hall was the home of the Towneley family from the 14th century until 1902. Charles (1737-1805) was one of the 18th century's best known collectors of antique sculpture and gems. His portrait can be seen in the gallery. Today visitors can still catch a glimpse of how the family lived. Original period rooms include the Elizabethan long gallery and the Regency rooms. See how they compare with life below stairs in the Victorian kitchen and the servants dining room.

The museum's collections surround you - glass, ceramics and 17th century Lancashire oak furniture. Pictures by many favourite Victorian artists can be seen in the art galleries, including works by Sir Edward Coley Burne-Jones, John William Waterhouse and Sir Edwin Landseer. The Whalley Abbey vestments are another highlight. Embroidered in silk and silver thread on cloth of gold, they were brought to Towneley in the 16th century and are now extremely rare. A programme of temporary exhibitions ensures something new to see on every visit. Open daily except Fridays - check for opening times.

27 THE PRIORY SCORTON

Scorton, nr Preston, Lancashire PR3 1AU
Tel: 01524 791255
e-mail: collinsonjulie@aol.com
website: www.theprioryscorton.co.uk

The Priory Scorton is situated in the picturesque village of Scorton, which has a superb location on the edge of the Forest of Bowland and just a short distance from the A6. Steeped in history, parts of the building date back to the 17th century when it was originally a Catholic Mass centre. Local legend has it that Oliver Cromwell's soldiers stayed here.

This superior hostelry offers everything the local or visitor could ever wish for and more. Having been in the ownership of the Collinson family for the past 40 years, The Priory's welcome is second to none and is open every day of the year except Christmas day. Outstanding facilities include quality accommodation, first-class dining, a super bar, well stocked gift shop and a splendid meeting/conference room seating up to 80 people.

For years Scorton was a dry village but now local residents and visitors can enjoy a drink relaxing by the log fire in the Stouts bar and are able to choose from a range of locally brewed real ales including 'Nicky Nook' brewed specially for The Priory. Walkers and cyclists needing to rest and refresh will find this the perfect stopping place in this area of outstanding beauty.

The charming Restaurant and Tea rooms here offer a tremendous choice of delicious homemade cakes and snacks as well as traditional English dishes such as Lancashire hotpot, roast dinners, quality steaks and tasty fish dishes. The Priory is proud of only using local produce and homemade dishes are a speciality. The main dining room seats 80 and outdoor dining areas are available to enjoy the tranquil atmosphere of village life. Food is served from 7.30am for breakfast, right through until 9pm.

The tasteful accommodation, cosy and inviting, comprises of eight en-suite comfortable rooms, all centrally heated with tea/coffee making facilities, televisions, telephones, free of charge Wifi connection and includes breakfast in the tariff. The unique surroundings and warmth of The Priory make this the perfect venue for wedding receptions and guarantees a wonderful experience for that special day. Specialising in small, intimate functions of up to 80 people for the Wedding Breakfast and up to 200 for the Evening Reception, The Priory has it all.

The Gift shop is open 9am – 9pm daily. Children are welcome and good facilities are offered for disabled guests. Plenty of parking is available and most credit cards are taken.

Singleton Road, Weeton,
Lancashire PR4 3NB
Tel: 01253 836230
e-mail: info@theeagleandchild.co.uk
website: www.theeagleandchild.co.uk

Dating back to 1585 **The Eagle & Child**, full of character and charm, takes its name from the family crest of Lord Derby who once owned most of the surrounding land. It is one of the oldest public houses in the northwest. In its historic past, Oliver Cromwell is reputed to have stayed here during the civil war years and the old cellars are supposed to have bricked up tunnels allowing people to escape capture.

Isla & Michael, the present owners, together with the loyal support of their highly motivated staff have created a hard working team which achieves the highest standards. In the short time they have been here, trade has increased significantly.

Isla is in charge of the food side and her cuisine attracts people from miles around . Using as much locally sourced produce as possible, traditional freshly home cooked food is served with a specials board that changes regularly. Guaranteed to please everyone's taste and pocket, the menu includes a wide selection of vegetarian options. One of the favourites here are the giant filled Yorkshire puddings – not to be missed! Delights from the main menu include fillet stroganoff - fillet steak gently cooked in a cream and brandy sauce, served with rice or chips, spicy lamb curry – lamb marinated in a mild curry , slowly cooked in tomato and coconut served with naan bread and rice or chips or for the larger appetite, dare to order The Eagle mixed grill consisting of sirloin steak, gammon, lamb cutlet, liver, sausage, black pudding and free range fried eggs assured to satisfy any hunger! With roast dinners being added on Sundays it's no wonder this pub was a finalist for *'Best Food in the North West'.*

The bar is Michaels domain, winning *The Gold Award for Beautiful Beer 2008* by the British Beer Pub Association. There are always four different traditional hand-pulled cask ales available including Theakstons Best Bitter and Caledonian Deuchars IPA along with two guest ales changed regularly. There is a wine and a beer garden alongside plenty of car parking.

Children are welcome and have a play area for amusement. Food is served: Winter 12 - 2.30pm & 5 - 8.30pm Sat/Sun 12 – 8.30pm Summer 12 – 8.30/9pm. Booking necessary Fri/Sat/Sun.

Lea Lane, Lower Bartle, Preston,
Lancashire PR4 0RT
Tel: 01772 690344

The Sitting Goose, a hidden gem, can be found in the hamlet of Lower Bartle with a superb picturesque location. Ryan, along with his sister Francesca have been hosts here since October 2008 bringing plenty of past experience in the trade with them. They employ skilled chefs that provide the most excellent meals with an extremely wide choice of menu. All their meat is sourced locally from The Forest of Bowland. A homely atmosphere along with pleasant decor awaits visitors to this welcoming inn.

At the attractive bar three real ales are available for you to enjoy, Thwaites original, Lancaster Bomber and a Brewery guest ale. This delightful place is open all day, every day giving you plenty of time to visit! Delicious food is served seven days a week between 12 – 9pm with such a varied menu you will be spoiled for choice. In addition to dining in the lounge bar, the charming conservatory seats 60 and is extremely bright and airy giving diners that much needed feel good factor and being ideal for large groups or parties to dine in. Guests have the option of choosing from the printed menu where they will find such appetizing dishes as steak and mushroom pudding and breast of Goosnargh chicken or they are able to choose from the specials board. The 2 course daytime specials which are available between 12 – 6pm, Mon – Sat are extremely good value with a choice of starters and mains or mains and dessert. The special evening menu includes starters such as mushrooms stuffed with bacon and stilton, and for main course the intensely satisfying Surf and Turf – a 12oz ribeye steak topped with garlic tiger prawns, served with chips, onion rings, mushrooms, tomato and peas; guaranteed to fill! Lite Bites are exceptionally good value for money and include a variety of sandwiches, baguettes and jacket potatoes. Booking is advisable at weekends in order to avoid disappointment. All are welcome to quiz nights on Wednesdays at 9.30pm. For details of other entertainment please ring. The Sitting Goose welcomes children, accepts all major credit cards and has a large off road car park.

31 THE CROWN HOTEL

94 Albert Road, Colne,
Lancashire BB8 0QD
Tel: 01282 863580 Fax: 01282 863580
e-mail: crownhotel94@aol.com
website: www.crownhotelcolne.co.uk

The Crown Hotel has an enviable location in the ancient market town of Colne, in the heart of Pendle Witch country. The hotel is an ideal base for exploring the Yorkshire Dales, the canals and many more beauty spots and places of interest which have made this area famous. The hotel, on the edge of the town centre, is easily accessible by car or train, being only a short drive from the end of the M65 and only a few hundred yards from Colne railway station. Dating back to the mid 19th century, it was a former coaching inn built in 1852 to service the new railway station.

Noel and Peter have been running this charming hostelry over the past ten years and their combined experience of forty years in the trade has undoubtedly proved itself in this pleasant hotel. They pride themselves on offering cuisine of the highest standards and use their wealth of experience to ensure guests have the most relaxing, memorable stay here.

The comfortable upstairs accommodation, which is available all year round, comprises single, double and family bedrooms, all having colour televisions and hospitality trays with most rooms also having en-suite facilities. Guests are able to stay on room only basis or bed and breakfast.

Four real ales are available with regulars being Tetleys and Worthington plus two rotating guest ales. The extensive menu ranges from light bites to the more substantial grills and main courses. The majority of dishes are homemade with produce being sourced from within the county. Popular dishes on the menu include a tasty homemade steak & onion pie, a mouth-watering mince and onion pie, as well as many other appetizing dishes, and a choice of delectable desserts guaranteed to please! Food is served Mon-Fri 12 - 1.45pm & 5 - 8.30pm, Sat 12 - 8.30pm and Sun 12 noon - 5.45pm when it is advisable to book.

Quiz night starts from 9.30pm on Wednesday evenings and on Saturday evenings there is a live singer in the lounge bar. Children are very welcome and all major credit cards accepted. Colne was at the heart of the Lancashire cotton industry with many signs of this still around. With many shops to visit as well as the lively indoor and outdoor markets, visitors will find a stay here most interesting and enjoyable.

184

28 Keighley Road, Laneshaw Bridge, Colne,
Lancashire BB8 7HX
Tel: 01282 868660

The Emmott Arms is situated in the charming village of Laneshaw Bridge on the A6068, a couple of miles northeast of Colne towards Keighley. Although currently named after a once Lord of the Manor, it was previously called The Plough, being an old coaching inn where teams of horses were changed in its stables. Landlord Eddie Baines, a local man from Colne, with four years experience in the trade, has been here for the past three months and what a turn around he has made in that short space of time. With immense enthusiasm and dedication he has completely refurbished the interior using superb furnishings and tasteful decor. He has created an elegant, comfortable dining room with plenty of character and charm, the perfect place to dine.

Open all day, every day four real ales are available with John Smiths cask the regular, alongside the popular draught keg ales, Carling and Becks. At the side of Eddie are two outstanding chefs, Louise and Jamie who use their culinary skills to delight guests, cooking up traditional meals from Wednesdays through to Sundays when a tasty carvery is available. They use produce sourced from the county, or neighbouring counties whenever possible, to guarantee superb freshness and flavour. The menu has a wide choice of main courses as well as lighter dishes and a variety of vegetarian options. Appealing dishes include Emmott's homemade 8oz beef burgers with salad and a choice of bacon or cheese served with homemade chips; home cooked chicken breast with leek and stilton sauce served with a choice of potatoes and vegetables; meanwhile from the vegetarian options, the homemade cheesy leek and mushroom crumble served with homemade chips and a salad garnish will get your mouth watering! The specials board provides even more choice daily and you wouldn't want to miss out on those homemade puddings! This top quality food is available Weds, Thurs, Fri 3pm – 9pm, Sat 12 – 9pm and Sun 12 – 6pm.

Quiz night is Thursdays from 8.30pm and live bands/acts perform occasionally on weekends – ring for details. Outside there is a smoking area, courtyard, beer garden and plenty of car parking. Children are welcome. Cash or cheque only accepted at present. Three en-suite letting rooms are currently being refurbished and should be available in early 2009.

33   THE WHITE LION

Riley Street, Earby, Lancashire BB18 6NX
Tel: 01282 842377

This hidden gem otherwise known as **The White Lion**, is a delightful inn located just a short drive off the A56 from the centre of Earby. This small town is home to the Lead Mining Museum and is even mentioned in the *Doomsday Book* as Eurebi in the Manor of Thornton. There are numerous places of interest to visit in the surrounding area and stunning countryside to discover. The White Lion has plenty of history and dates back over 300 years when it was a former coaching inn on an old Drovers road between the towns of Skipton and Colne.

Peter Mayers, the host here, is a wonderful character and along with his dedicated team does his very best to ensure everyone has an exceptionally enjoyable visit. This attractive inn is open all day, every day and has a very cosy interior where customers can enjoy a drink and a chat at the well stocked bar and relax in the tranquil atmosphere. There is a choice of three real ales with Tetleys and Black Sheep being the regulars along with one rotating guest ale. Good home cooked food is served Thursday – Saturday 12-2pm and 5-9pm and Sunday 12-6pm. The excellent regular menu offers a wide variety of wonderful dishes ranging from home made steak and black pudding pie to vegetarian options such as fresh tortellini arabiatta with basil and black olives. In addition to this, the specials board offers more tantalising dishes which are changed daily. The salad bar offers a superb choice of fresh, crisp salads including prawn & Marie Rose sauce, tuna with ginger dressing and poached salmon, all served with crusty bread and butter. Booking is advisable on Thursday evenings and on Sundays. The charming restaurant seats 38 while the dining room seats 11. Diners are also very welcome to eat in the bar areas.

The White Lion is available for special events and functions and the team always try to accommodate any special requests. Children are welcome to choose from the children's meal section on the menu or have a childs portion of most of the main meals at half price. In the warmer months customers are welcome to dine on the quality outdoor patio. There is plenty of parking available and all credit cards are taken except American Express and Diners.

34 NUMBER 51

51 King Street, Whalley,
Lancashire BB7 9SP
Tel: 01254 825793

You will find "Heaven on Earth" in this delightful tearoom where homemade cakes are a speciality. Situated in the heart of Whalley and family run by locals, Alan and Susan, along with daughter Amanda, this is a must for visitors to this town. Together with their dedicated staff, Sara, Linda, Marj and Peggy, they offer a very warm welcome to all. The pleasant, homely interior provides the perfect atmosphere to relax and unwind with a good cuppa, while sampling the luscious homemade fare available on the mouth-watering menu.

A wide range of pastries, desserts, paninis, sandwiches, salads and light snacks are available, all guaranteed to delight and tempt! Tasty examples include: tuna and onion panini bound with light mayonnaise topped with melted cheddar cheese, smoked salmon fishcakes with ssparagus hollandaise and the delicious deep fried tempura battered prawns with a sweet chilli dip. It's no surprise that this establishment is extremely popular with locals and visitors alike! All produce used here is sourced from within the County. Bookings are taken but not always necessary. Children are welcome and a car park is situated opposite the shop.

37 ROSSENDALE MUSEUM

Whitaker Park, Haslingden Road,
Rawtenstall, Rossendale,
Lancashire BB4 6RE
Tel: 01706 217777/244682
Fax: 01706 250037

Rossendale Museum is a former 19th century mill owner's house set in Whitaker Park. Displays include a Victorian drawing room, fine and decorative art, local and natural history, and costume. Temporary exhibitions are held throughout the year. There is disabled access to ground floor and audio and large print guides are available. Admission is free and a gift shop and café round off your visit.

31 Burnley Road, Todmorden,
Lancashire OL14 7BU
Tel: 01706 810590

In the centre of the picturesque town of Todmorden lies the very popular public house, **The Black Swan**. This is very much a family run pub, and, having been in the trade for the past fifteen years, the family have been busy here since June 2008 and always look forward to greeting new visitors. The team make a perfect combination with complete dedication - tenants Wally and Marie together with their daughters Samantha and Lisa are at the helm. Open all day, every day, visitors and locals alike enjoy favourite draughts, Fosters and John Smiths Smooth, as they relax in the cosy surroundings of the bar.

The high quality food is prepared by Lisa, a chef by trade and queen of the kitchen! She prepares a variety of tempting snacks and good wholesome meals ranging from a Ranch House steak sandwich, or tuna melt, served on toasted white or brown bread with salad garnish, to a delicious homemade chilli or whole tail breaded scampi. If that's not enough to spoil you, the daily specials board will offer even more choice and every Sunday a traditional roast is added to the menu to complete the variety. The fresh produce is mainly purchased from local markets and the local butcher, making meals even more appealing. Food is served Monday & Tuesday 12-2pm, Wednesday & Thursday 12-7pm and Friday, Saturday & Sunday 12-5pm. Children are made very welcome and are able to choose from the Kid's menu at very reasonable prices. Their menu includes pizza, pork sausage, chicken nuggets, veggie fingers, fish fingers or egg, all served with homemade chips, beans, spaghetti or peas. In addition to the normal coffee and tea served here, hot chocolate is also available and very popular. Phone orders are welcome for your convenience.

Over the weekends there is varied entertainment happening in this much loved inn, including a monthly disco at 8.30pm Friday evenings, karaoke on Saturday evenings and live entertainment from 7pm on Sundays. At the rear there is a hidden courtyard which is heated and lit for your comfort.

Comfortable accommodation is available all year round with a choice of one single, two twin/ doubles and one twin bedroom. Guests are welcome to choose from room only, bed and breakfast, or bed, breakfast and evening meal.

I White Hart Fold, Todmorden,
Lancashire OL14 7BD
Tel: 01706 817828

Located in the centre of Todmorden, is the charming **Cherries Tea Room,** a typically old fashioned, quaint, little tea shop owned and personally run by Michael and Nikki who have been delighting visitors with their delicious fare for the past seven months. Take a step back in time into this peaceful haven and relax in the pleasant surroundings while your hosts spoil you with food just like granny used to make! On entering, the smell of home cooking will assure you that you are in for a real treat! Cherries takes pride in using top quality, fresh ingredients sourced from local suppliers in all of their home cooked meals and cakes. Nikki does all the cooking and baking herself assuring her guests of nothing but the best. You are sure to taste the difference here and return again!

You will be spoiled for choice when choosing from their delicious range of home baked cakes and freshly made snacks, ranging from toasted English muffins to brilliantly baked potatoes with a variety of tasty savoury fillings. These include cheese, baked beans, creamed mushrooms, prawns in Marie Rose sauce, tuna mayonnaise or cottage cheese and all are served with a side salad. The daily main course specials will take some serious thought too! Hearty beef stew and appetising meat and potato pie are just a few of the favourites that have been tempting many visitors here. There is a wide breakfast menu too, including porridge made with full cream milk served with a choice of sugar, honey, golden syrup or maple syrup; pancakes with a variety of toppings; creamed mushrooms on white or wholemeal toast, and of course the traditional full English breakfast.

Plenty of hot and cold beverages are available. Why not indulge yourself with Cherries Winter Hot Chocolate Treat- a large luxury hot chocolate served with cream, chocolate buttons, a chocolate flake, marshmallows and chocolate sprinkles- a must for choccie lovers!

Cherries is open six days a week, Tuesday-Sunday from 9am until the last customer leaves and is available for private bookings any evening of the week. Once a month there is a themed evening held with a set menu.

Children are made very welcome and have their own little corner to occupy equipped with games, jigsaws etc enabling mums and dads to have a bit of peace and enjoy their meal. The premises are licensed for diners.

38 CAFÉ ARTISAN

1 Brook Street, Bury Road, Rawtenstall,
Lancashire BB4 6AA
Tel: 01706 211114
website: www.cafe-artisan.co.uk

Café Artisan stands in the heart of Rawtenstall opposite the fire station and is uniquely a café by day and a bar by night. Owned and personally run by delightful couple Tim and Nicola Whiteley for the past three years, the friendly family café provides a high standard of down to earth, good quality food in a stylish relaxed environment. The contemporary design, along with top quality decor and furnishings, creates the perfect ambience for guests to drink and dine in.

Tim and Nicola have created a very successful business here making it one, if not the, premier over 25's music venue for miles around. Also, adding more interest, the café houses pieces of work from local artists, including impressions of some of the musicians that have performed at the café. With capacity for a total of 150, it is an ideal venue for a private party/function where Tim and Nicola will do their best to tailor specifically to your needs and recommend the perfect entertainment for that special occasion. On warmer days, customers can enjoy a drink in the sunshine on the attractive front courtyard.

Top quality food is served until 8pm in this fine venue. The menu offers a wide choice of tasty, wholesome dishes and snacks with most produce being sourced locally. Examples on the Artisan menu include, homemade burgers, chilli and nachos topped with grated cheddar, delicious mussels in a choice of cream and white wine, spicy tomato or spicy Thai sauce served with crusty bread, as well as lighter options and a choice of vegetarian/vegan dishes. The drinks menu offers a large range of hot and cold drinks, wines, bottled and draught beers including Peroni, Guiness and Amstel. Keeping it local Tim and Nicola also stock a lovely range of bottled ales from a micro brewery just down the road, and not to be missed the wide range of flavoured vodkas produced on the premises. The superb Artisan Shakes, a must to try for all ages, are made by combining your favourite chocolate bar or fresh fruit with ice cold milk and ice cream, the most delicious thick shakes ever tasted!

Opening times are, Mon/Tues closed, Weds 11am-3pm, Thurs 11am-9pm, Fri/Sat 11am-11pm and Sun 12-4pm. Children are extremely welcome until 8pm.

The regular entertainment includes Comedy Nights, Acoustic Nights & some of the best Tribute Bands in the UK (details available on the website). Cash and credit cards are taken.

39 THE DUKE OF BUCCLEUGH

634 Bacup Road, Waterfoot,
Rossendale, Lancashire BB4 7AW
Tel : 01706 222637
e-mail: andrew22robson@sky.com

**The Duke of Buccleugh and The Glen Valley
Guest House** (see below) are both situated in the
village of Waterfoot within the Rossendale Valley. It is
ideally located on the A681 between Rawtenstall and
Bacup, with easy access on the M66 to Manchester city
centre and the surrounding areas. Both of these fine
properties are owned and run by Bryan and Andrew
and are just a short distance apart from each other.

The stylish **Duke of Buccleugh**, which has been
redesigned throughout with tasteful decor and quality
furnishings, dates back to 1848 and is open all day,
every day except Christmas and New Year days. Pride
of Pendle Ale is the regular served here along with
rotating guest ales. Good wholesome food is available
between 12-6pm daily except on Fridays. The menu
has a wide choice of freshly cooked, appetizing dishes
to choose from including homemade cottage pie,
homemade steak and mushroom pie, liver and bacon
casserole and vegetarian choices such as Cajun
vegetable fajitas. Lighter bar snacks include jacket
potatoes and freshly cut sandwiches as well as childrens
meals. Local produce is used whenever possible.

Upstairs in the new, soon to be opened restaurant, food will be served from 8-10pm and the menu
will be extended. Only cash or cheques are accepted at present. There is entertainment on the
weekends for over 21's only.

40 GLEN VALLEY GUESTHOUSE

701 Bacup Road, Waterfoot, Rossendale,
Lancashire BB4 7HB
Tel: 01706 228135
website: www.glenvalleyguesthouse.co.uk

Just a short distance away from The Duke of
Buccleugh (sse above), the superb **Glen Valley
Guest House** was originally a public house and
dates back to the 19th century. Bryan and Andy
take the greatest care to ensure your stay is as
relaxing and as comfortable as possible, providing a flexible service to suit all your needs.

There are seven cosy, well decorated
guest rooms of which six are en-suite.
The tariff includes a selection of delicious
breakfasts, available between 8am-9am
served in the smart dining room which is
also fully licensed. Home cooked evening
meals are available upon request by prior
arrangement. Small functions, such as
christenings etc, can be arranged, catering
for up to 15 people.

Bike hire is available daily as well as a
professional massage service and a
chiropodist service. This delightful
guesthouse has been rated a very well
deserved 4 stars by the ETB.

**37 Roman Road, Hoddlesden, Darwen,
Lancashire, BB3 3PP
Tel: 01254 705518**

In an elevated position, surrounded by moorland and close to the pretty village of Hoddlesden sits **The Crown and Thistle**. This hidden gem is situated a short drive east of Darwen, along the old Roman Road, through the village of Blacksnape towards Edgworth. Formerly a farmhouse and smithy on a drovers road, the inn dates in parts to the late 17th century then later becoming an alehouse with rooms. The isolated, scenic position has made it extremely popular with walkers exploring the beautiful moorland in this region and it has become a well-known destination in the surrounding area.

Friendly hosts, Mo and Julie have 20 years of catering experience behind them and took over the free house a year ago making it their first venture in licensing. They offer a warm welcome to all their guests and will do their utmost to ensure all needs are catered for. The olde-worlde interior is extremely pleasant with beamed ceilings and a roaring fire creating a cosy atmosphere.

Customers have a choice of three real ales including Bombardier, plus rotating guest ales. Delicious food is served Sun – Thurs 12-9pm, Fri/Sat 12-10pm. Although Mo employs a talented head chef to create mouth-watering dishes, he also likes to cook himself using his past knowledge and experience. Together they produce delectable delights such as: Chefs Special Fillet – fillet steak wrapped in bacon, served on a bed of onions and mushrooms, topped with Paté and finished in a rich Marcella wine sauce; scrumptious sea bass, baked in foil with white wine and garlic; and the luscious Crowns Special Salad – individual bites on little gems, prawns, tuna, egg mayonnaise, grated cheese, sweetcorn and smoked salmon. Lighter bites include a tasty Tandoori chicken baguette or a juicy ½ lb beefburger topped with cheese&bacon served with homemade chips. The Monday special steak nights are very popular as are the Sunday roasts with a choice of two or three courses. Julie and Mo pride themselves on total satisfaction of their guests and cater for all dietary needs with gluten free dishes etc. A variety of coffees and hot drinks are on the menu and a choice of tempting sweets make an appearance in the display cabinet daily. With so much variety guests are spoiled for choice! Because of its outstanding reputation, booking is advisable at weekends. Children are welcome and all major credit cards are accepted.

43 ROSINS COUNTRY HOTEL & RESTAURANT

Long Hey lane, Treacle Row, Pickup Bank,
Hoddlesden, Darwen, Lancashire BB3 3QD
Tel: 01254 771264 Fax: 01254 873894
e-mail: info@rosins.co.uk
website: www.rosins.co.uk

Hidden in the heart of the scenic countryside of Lancashire stands the attractive, well known **Rosins Country Hotel & Restaurant.** This appealing beamed hotel is renowned far and wide for all the outstanding facilities available here. Situated a short drive from the M65, Junction 5,

Rosins is a privately owned bar, hotel & restaurant set in the heart of the Lancashire moors oozing with character and charm. The combined experience of the team, together with serious professionalism has created an extremely successful venue. The charming interior, with its stunning views of the surrounding countryside and the smart decor, make this the ideal place to enjoy a relaxing meal or favourite tipple.

With a choice of four rotating ales, guests will find it difficult to pull themselves away from the bar! Gastro style food served on the extensive menu ranges from traditional pub favourites to a large choice of starters, main courses and a great choice of home-made desserts, therefore satisfaction is guaranteed. Fresh and local produce is used at all times, with food prepared and cooked in their extensive kitchens. Open all day, every day, food is served between 12-9pm seven days a week; you can even drop in for a bite of breakfast between 7am - 9am Mon-Fri and 8:30 - 10am at weekends. Booking is advisable Fri/Sat/Sun. Children are made very welcome. There is ample free parking on-site.

Rosins also provide guest accommodation comprising 15 beautifully appointed en-suite rooms, including four suites, two family rooms and a four-poster for that special occasion. With a hearty breakfast included, guests can relax and enjoy the Lancashire countryside. A popular venue for hosting special events, Rosins hold a civil wedding licence and provides various wedding packages or a tailor-made service to suit. All major credit cards taken. They have a user-friendly website which is kept up-to-date with upcoming monthly events and news on developments at the hotel.

41 HELMSHORE MILLS TEXTILE MUSEUM

Holcombe Road, Helmshore, Rossendale,
Lancashire BB4 4NP
Tel: 01706 226459

An 18th century water powered fulling mill and a Victorian cotton spinning mill, both in working order on one site. Newly designated as a museum with a collection of outstanding national importance, this museum has developed an interactive gallery for families on the history of the Lancashire cotton industry. Spinning mules, water wheel, an original Arkwright's Water Frame and other machinery dating from the Industrial Revolution can also be seen. Easily reached from Junction 5 of M65 (Haslingden) or from end of M66. Open from Easter to October every afternoon. Refreshments are available in the café. A gift shop sells a range of souvenirs.

HIDDEN PLACES GUIDES

Explore Britain and Ireland with *Hidden Places* guides - a fascinating series of national and local travel guides.

Packed with easy to read information on hundreds of places of interest as well as places to stay, eat and drink.

Available from both high street and internet booksellers

For more information on the full range of *Hidden Places* guides and other titles published by Travel Publishing visit our website on

www.travelpublishing.co.uk
or ask for our leaflet by phoning
01752 697280 or emailing
info@travelpublishing.co.uk

44 MANX ELECTRIC RAILWAY

Douglas, Isle of Man IM1 5PT
Tel: 01624 663366

An ideal way to discover what the Isle of Man has to offer is by train. Supported by a good bus network, you can be somewhere different each day exploring the sights and the scenery. From Douglas, the **Manx Electric Railway** takes you along the east coast to Laxey. here you can climb to the top of the Great Laxey Wheel and go underground on the Mines Trail. Laxey is also the starting point for the Snaefell Mountain Railway which climbs the Island's highest peak. At the top you're rewarded with breathtaking views and refreshments in the Summit Hotel Café.

Further on from Laxey is the largest town in the north, Ramsey. In the town, there are plenty of shops to see, cafés to enjoy and pubs to visit. Nearby is Mooragh Park and boating lake. A short bus ride away is The Gibbs of the Grove. This Victorian period house was formerly the summer retreat of a Liverpool shipping merchant and his family. Inside the house you will find original furnishings, fittings and costumes. Outside in the spacious grounds and gardens are displays of vintage vehicles and agricultural equipment.

The trains run daily between April and October and there are various themed events during the year.

194

45 TERMINUS TAVERN

Strathallan Crescent, Douglas,
Isle of Man IM2 4NR
Tel: 01624 624312

The **Terminus Tavern** overlooks the sea at one end of Douglas's promenade on the Isle of Man. For the last 2½ years, the Tavern has been run by Stuart and Madeline who have been enticing visitors and locals with their splendid food and hospitality. With 16 years experience in the trade between them, they have a beautiful property. The façade is simply charming and inviting and the décor is great - with lovely lighting and a tastefully decorated bar.

There are pool tables and fruit machines to enjoy here, creating a sociable atmosphere as well as a large dining area. Here you can enjoy mouth-watering dishes of sirloin and gammon steaks, chilli and rice, burgers, or something from the vegetarian menu, veggie lasagne or veggie sausage and mash. This food can be enjoyed with one or more of the 4 real ales served, Okell's Bitter and Mild plus two rotating guest ales. Please note that food is not served on Sunday evenings, however it is available the rest of the week from 12-2.30 and 6-8pm in the winter and 6-9pm during the Summer. It is best to book Sunday and Friday lunch times.

**24 Castle Street, Douglas,
Isle of Man IM1 2EZ
Tel: 01624 613650**

Just a stone's throw away from the promenade in Douglas on the Isle of Man is the ever so popular **Copperfields Olde Edwardian Restaurant.** Possibly the best place to dine during the day, the beautiful Edwardian building is eye catching and a real treat. Known to be visited frequently by showbiz stars and sports personalities, it is also popular with visitors to the island and of course the locals, who love the food served here. The owners Glenda and James De-Yoxall have done an outstanding job here. The décor is quirky and truly Edwardian, with lots of ornaments and pictures adorning the walls, as well as wooden panelling throughout. Even the waitresses here are dressed for the part, wearing old-fashioned attire, which really gives the sense of going back in time. The owners have been here for the last 11 years and it really is outstanding.

Glenda is the superb Chef here and creates a number of dishes, all freshly made to order, using top quality produce. The menu is large and offers huge portions of broths, sandwiches with a large array of fillings, bursting between the bread and main dishes such as giant Yorkshire puddings filled with braised steak and gravy or creamy chicken supreme. There are also huge lasagnes, scampi and lobster tails and a wide selection of traditional Manx delicacies, which include meals such as king scallops sautéed in garlic butter, served with all the trimmings.

Open during the winter months between Tuesday and Friday from 11am-3pm and Saturday from 9.30am-5pm and throughout the summer from 9.30am till close, you can also eat breakfast here. Full English breakfasts, including free-range eggs can be chosen, as well as kippers and omelettes. There really is something for everyone here.

If you have already eaten and are just exploring the Isle of Man, you are more than welcome to come to the premises for a desert, milkshake or pot of tea. After 2pm, drinks alone are served, including Auntie Amy's Parlour high teas, which include a bountiful sandwich, large scone with jam/cream, fruitcake and a pot of tea, or hot chocolate with whipped cream and flake or even just a cold glass of milk. It is clear to see why this establishment is so popular, as the owners have catered for every taste, ensuring every guest is happy.

Harris Promenade, Douglas,
Isle of Man IM1 2RW
Tel: 01624 645500 Fax: 01624 676004
e-mail: info@seftonhotel.co.im
website: www.seftonhotel.co.im

The Sefton is a premier hotel with the most enviable location on the Harris Promenade overlooking The Irish Sea. The four star grading assures guests of the highest quality throughout and combined with the award winning restaurants, guests are guaranteed to have the most enjoyable experience here. Hotel manager, Paul Forrest has been at this luxury hotel for the past ten years helping to create lavish accommodation, full of comfort and elegance. When the current refurbishment is complete the hotel will boast 104 luxurious, en-suite rooms of various sizes with three rooms graded as category 2 disabled. Extravagance can only describe the nine new suites to be added, which will vary in decor, with a choice of Victorian, Contemporary or New York 'loft design'.

The Gallery Restaurant, seating 60, offers the most pleasurable dining experience, with tasteful furnishings and a magnificent view overlooking Douglas Bay. Guests can choose from a large selection of mouth-watering dishes with an optional flambé service available at the table. Samples from the excellent main menu include, Manx beef fillet - served with parsnip and potato rosti, sweet onion marmalade and black pepper sauce; pan roasted Anjou pigeon breasts - served with a beetroot puree, peppered creamed shallots, smoked mash, ruby port jus and dressed watercress; or for fish lovers, Dover sole cooked on the bone - served simply plain grilled or with shallot and caper butter, with warm new potatoes and green leaf salad.

Open for dinner between 6pm-10pm, seven nights a week, booking is advisable and essential in the summer months. The Gallery Private Dining Room provides complete privacy, perfect for those special occasions, seating 8-18 people with private butler service and the opportunity for guests to choose from either the à la carte menu or a unique menu of their choice. On the first floor Sir Norman's dining area seats 60 and offers a further choice of tasty dishes including salads, sandwiches, pastas and desserts. The Garden room, conference and banqueting areas accommodate from 10 people up to banquets for 130 or theatre style conferences for 180. The large doors open on to a beautiful Atrium Water Garden creating an outdoor feeling although indoors.

The premises are licensed and serve a choice of Okells and Bushy Ales. Children are welcome in this first class establishment, which has a large underground car park.

48 SPILL THE BEANS COFFEE SHOP

1 Market Hill, Douglas,
Isle of Man IM1 2BF
Tel: 01624 614167

Spill The Beans Coffee Shop, in the heart of busy Douglas is absolutely tremendous. For the last 10 years, this business has been owned and personally run by Sarah Berry and she really has done a great job. Located on a corner in Market Hill, the property is eye catching. The décor is of a high quality, in warm shades, with wooden furniture and comfy sofas. Set over two floors, the popular coffee shop can seat up to 50, 16 upstairs and 34 downstairs in the large dining area.

The food served here is absolutely lovely and is all made directly on the premesis by Sarah's two senior bakers, Gladys who makes savoury dishes and Kat, the cake and sweet baker. The loyal staff here means that there is a fantastic atmosphere and great hospitality-Gladys has been working at Spill The Beans for 10 years and is still producing great food. The food available here varies and from midday Monday-Saturday savoury food can be purchased on a first come, first serve basis. Sweet dishes such as Chelsea buns, chocolate or blueberry muffins, Rocky Road squares, as well as flapjacks and scones can be bought at any time during opening hours. There are cakes available here also, with whole cakes made to order - the likes of Manx Bonnag, lemon drizzle and banana syrup cake - just a small portion of the menu.

A large array of coffee is available to drink whilst enjoying your brownie or cake; Espresso, Macchiato, Americano and Hot Chocolate are a few of the hot drinks to choose from. Spill The Beans is so popular in Douglas, that Sarah has managed to open another business, with the same name that is located within Douglas's main hospital, Nobles Hospital. Seating 20, and run by the manager Jo, this coffee shop is just as popular as the original. The produce used at the hospital is baked and bought from the Market Hill property.

Opening times at Market Hill are Mon-Friday 7.30-5pm and Saturday 10-5pm. The coffee shop within the hospitals opening hours are Monday- Friday from 9-5pm, Saturday 10-5pm and Sunday 12-4.15pm.

198

Main Road, Baldrine, Isle of Man IM4 6AE
Tel: **01624 674787**
e-mail: mail@liverpoolarms.com
website: www.liverpoolarms.com

Dating back 200 years, this property was previously known to locals as the Halfway House. Now known as the **Liverpool Arms,** the public house can be found on a Manx National Heritage site. Since 2000, tenants Nigel and Marilyn Dobson

have been in charge here and have created a fantastic and friendly environment popular to all visiting and living in the Isle of Man. The Liverpool Arms is huge and surrounded by plenty of greenery, making it the perfect place to spend your time during the summer. However if its cooler ,there is no need to worry as Nigel and his wife have ensured that there is plenty for people to do, whilst visiting. There is a wide screen TV, free internet access and Wifi Hot Spot, which are all complimentary. The bar here is extensive and decked out traditionally, with wooden panelling and comfortable bar stools. Two real ales are served, Okells Bitter and a guest ale, which changes twice a week, meaning there is always a surprise. Great food is also available, and the Dobsons take as much care with their food as they do their beer. The property has a fantastic informal atmosphere, which is what makes this pub so great. Having experience in the hospitality trade, the tenants also own the Niarbyl Café, close to Dalby (see below).

Niarbyl Café- this welcoming café is surrounded by beautiful scenery and is well worth a visit especially for those who enjoy a coastal walk. The Dobsons make sure that the quality of food served at both the café and the pub is of a high standard and the food certainly goes down well. Home made grub is the name on the menu and sees favourites such as beef lasagne, steak and ale pie, 'Today's Curry' and lamb shank, which is very popular. Furthermore there is also a Burger bar serving a variety of toppings and Fish bar, which is the speciality and has great dishes such as Cod wrapped in bacon and Whole Scampi Tails. Open all year round, the Liverpool Arms seats up to 60 and truly has a lot to offer both locals and visitors. During the winter, this property serves food from 12-3 and 5-9pm Monday to Friday and Saturday and Sundays 12-9pm. Between Easter and October, food is available daily from 12-9pm. It is advised that you book to eat at this location and also essential that you book at weekends to avoid disappointment.

49   THE FAMOUS CREG NY BAA

Mountain Road, Onchan, Isle of Man, IM4 5BP
Tel: 01624676948 Fax: 01624 674413
e-mail: creg-ny-baa@hotmail.com
website: www.creg-ny-baa.com

Standing just outside of Onchan is **The Famous Creg Ny Baa**, a famous landmark on the World famous TT course, which attracts thousands of spectators annually. This relaxed, family friendly eating-house has been beautifully refurbished by owner Sandrina Teece and family. Together with their loyal team of staff, they offer superb hospitality along with a diverse choice of top quality, reasonably priced, home cooked food. The appetizing menus include delights such as the chef's spicy chicken and pan-fried barberry duck breast. Children very welcome, open all day Sat/Sun and every session except Tuesday evening (Oct-March).

Looking for:

• *Places to Visit?*

• *Places to Stay?*

• *Places to Eat & Drink?*

• *Places to Shop?*

COUNTRY LIVING MAGAZINE RURAL GUIDES

HIDDEN INNS

HIDDEN PLACES

COUNTRY Pubs & Inns

off the motorway 3rd edition

www.travelpublishing.co.uk

51   GOPHERS COFFEE SHOP

2 West Quay, Ramsey,
Isle of Man, IM8 1DW
Tel: 01624 815562
Mobile: 07624 497103
e-mail: sharpey60@hotmail.com

Gophers Coffee Shop is a superb little coffee house overlooking the West Quay and Swingbridge at Ramsey. Owner, Graham Stowell, has been running this delightful café for the past four years and has a real winner on his hands. Visitors and locals alike, return time and time again to enjoy the tasty fayre on offer in this friendly venue.

Homemade dishes are a speciality, especially the deliciously fresh homemade cakes and Scones, straight out the oven – it's no wonder visitors return frequently! The menu offers plenty of choice for all appetites, ranging from Jacket Potatoes with a choice of tasty toppings to cheese melts served on ciabattas, not forgetting the most tempting Gophers big baguettes, with a choice of different scrumptious fillings and available half size upon request.
Beverages include a wide variety of speciality teas/coffees, milkshakes, juices and canned drinks.

Gophers has seating for 30 people and children are made very welcome. Opening hours are 9am-4.30pm seven days a week between Feb-Nov but Gophers is closed on Sundays during December and January. Only cash or cheque is accepted at present.

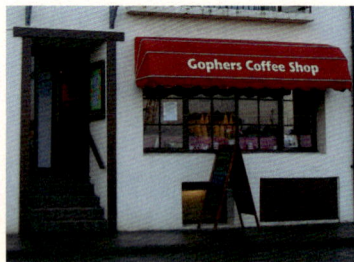

52 GINGER HALL HOTEL

Ballamanaugh Road, Sulby,
Isle of Man, IM7 2HB
Tel: 01624 897231

New Leaseholder Kevin Rogers has only been at the **Ginger Hall Hotel** for a short while however has plenty of previous experience in the trade. This property has 8 quality rooms, all with ensuite, suiting all requirements and can be paid for on a Bed and Breakfast basis or as a room only. The façade of this building is eye catching and attractive, however there is much work to do before Kevin is happy with the overall property. Open everyday for Ale there are 4 Real Ales served here, Okells Bitter and Mild, plus Black Cat Mild and a rotating guest Ale. The food served here; prepared by Kevin who is a Chef by trade includes quality cuisine using local produce. Food is served Lunchtimes and evenings

and features a varied and exciting menu, all of which is served in the superb dining/breakfast room. The dining room is large and bright, with a great view of the beer garden, which has additional seating outdoors perfect for children to play or to relax in the summer months.

53 THE RAVEN

Main Road, Ballaugh, Isle of Man IM7 5ED
Tel: 01624 896128 Fax: 01624 896127
e-mail: alannaveeya@aol.com

Situated in the village of Ballaugh is the top quality premises **The Raven**. Known to many locals and visitors as a great place to eat and drink, with great hospitality, the General Managers Alan and Neveeya Carr have been in the trade together for the last 13 years. This property is truly special and even has its own Real Ale brewed especially for it, Okells Raven Claw, as well as Okells Bitter and a rotating guest Ale - they can be enjoyed 7 days a week.

The food served here is cooked by Chef Neveeya and specialises in traditional Thai cooking, which is a real treat on the Island. A number of different Thai dishes are on the menu, with unusual meals of Thai Masman curry, using chicken or beef, cooked with coconut milk, new potatoes and peanuts, or a simple dish of chicken Pad Thai noodles.

If Thai cooking isn't your thing, you can also try traditional pub meals of sausages and mash, steak and Okells Ale pie or a lasagne verdi. Food is served Mon-Sat 12-2.30 and 6-8.30 and Sunday 12-2.30 only.

201

54 THE OLD STABLE

Berk, Peel Road, Kirk Michael,
Isle of Man IM6 1AP
Tel: 01624 878039 Fax: 01624 878039
e-mail: theoldstable@manx.net
website: www.theoldstable.net

Situated on a quiet farm, with a view over the Irish Sea, **The Old Stable** is a real gem. Anne and Robert Cannell have owned this top quality accommodation for many years and it is renowned for being great - with plenty of repeat visitors and recommendations. The accommodation is an old farm workers house, however now a lovely cottage with 2 ensuite bedrooms, which are available all year round and sleeps 4. Set over two floors, the ground floor has a large dining room and lounge, with widescreen TV and video. The kitchen has all the mod cons needed to make your stay enjoyable and the bedrooms on the first floor are tastefully decorated - light and breezy, one with a king size bed, the other with two singles, perfect for family getaways.

This property is highly rated on the Island and has been given a 5 star rating for the high standard and great service that the Cannells give to their visitors. There are tremendous grounds here and lovely countryside surrounding the property.

55 THE WHITESTONE INN

Station Road, Ballasalla,
Isle of Man IM9 2DD
Tel: 01624 822334 Fax: 01624 822674

The Whitestone Inn located in Ballasalla, southwest of Douglas is a splendid country inn very close to the Islands airport, ideal for visitors just arriving or departing this beautiful Island.

Lawrence, your friendly host, has been running this pleasant inn for over five years offering excellent customer service to all its valued customers.

The cosy interior is surprisingly spacious and has a charming ambience where diners can enjoy good wholesome food, highly recommended by the locals in the area. The varied main menu is complemented by a daily specials board using local produce to create hearty, nourishing dishes such as homemade cauliflower and stilton soup served with crusty bread. This splendid food

is available daily, 12-2pm and 6pm-8.45pm. Booking is advisable on Sundays and is essential during the summer months. Locally brewed Okells Bitter is available here all day, every day, with additional real ales added during the summer.

Children are welcome and will enjoy munching on the special 'Winnie the Pooh' ice cream sundaes. Live entertainment is offered on Friday or Saturday evenings from 9pm. All major credit cards are accepted.

57 THE SHORE HOTEL

Shore Road, Gansey, Port St Mary,
Isle of Man IM9 5LZ
Tel: 01624 832269
e-mail: deboniom@manx.net

The first thing that catches the eye of visitors to **The Shore Hotel** is the stunning location, overlooking the beautiful sea at Gansey, close to Port St Mary. This top quality hotel, which dates back 160 years, has recently undergone a complete refurbishment and its new, outstanding decor has created a pleasant, homely ambience for visitors to enjoy. Owners, Debbie and Andy Lagden, have been here since November 2001 and with their constant drive, enthusiasm and sheer hard work, have turned the place around making it one of the most popular places to visit while on the Island.

Open all day, every day, visitors can enjoy a choice of 2-3 real ales at the stylish bar, Okells and Bushy Tail, both brewed on the Island, plus a guest ale. The food side operation is run by the 'The Two Fat Chefs', Richard and Martin, who have been cooking up culinary delights here since August 2008. Their superb dishes have gained an excellent reputation on the Island leaving diners with plenty to rave about afterwards. The cosy, attractive, dining area seats 40 although guests are welcome to dine throughout or on warmer days can enjoy Al Fresco dining on the terraced bistro area outside. First class food is available Mon-Sat, 12-2.30pm then 6.30pm-9pm and from 12-3pm on Sundays.

All the produce used here is sourced from the Island assuring diners of the highest quality and freshness. Tasty favourites on the main menu include, Manx lamb steak served with mint gravy, traditional steak and ale pie with a puff pastry lid and poached cod served with a cream lemon sauce with a hint of Thai spice. The lunchtime menu offers a variety of appetizing light bites including hot and cold sandwiches served with chips and salad garnish and a choice of main courses such as classic golden scampi, all served with, new potatoes, chips or wild organic rice. The specials board offers further choices daily and on Sundays a traditional roast is top of the menu. Half size meals are available for children and a selection of mouth-watering desserts are available on the chalk board. There is a large off road car park and all major credit cards are taken here.

Silverdale Gen, Ballasalla,
Isle of Man IM9 3DS
Tel: 01624 823474
e-mail: info@silverdaleglen.com
website: www.silverdaleglen.com

In the secret and historic location found via Ballasalla village lies the **Silverdale Glen Restaurant & Tea Rooms.** The surrounding area is jam packed with history and still has its own Victorian Waterwheel within the complex, which is a popular attraction for visitors. Tony and Michelle Waitland, who have been here since October 2008, run the Silverdale Glen and provide great service to all.

Open everyday except Christmas day, the tea rooms serve a great selection of light bites such as jacket potatoes and toasted sandwiches, as well as spaghetti carbonara and burger and chips. Afternoon cream tea is also a favourite, which is served daily between 2.30pm and 5pm and includes a round of sandwiches, scone filled with fresh cream and jam and a pot of tea or a cup of coffee.

At present the restaurant opens only for Sunday lunch between 12 and 2.30 and should be pre-booked to avoid disappointment. The dining here is grand and can seat up to 80. The Silverdale Glen is a fantastic historic building, with tremendous food and great company.

32 Chorley Road, Heath Charnock,
Adlington, Chorley, Lancashire PR6 9JS
Tel: 01257 481776
e-mail: karenfeay@hotmail.com
website: www.whitehorsepublichouse.com

The White Horse, run by Karen and her family since Feb 2008 is a former coaching inn dating back to the early 19th century. Tasty meals are served weekdays until 7.30pm and Sundays until 6.30pm. Chefs, employed to cook the delicious food, use local produce whenever possible and create popular puddings. A new ale is being introduced at the bar for 2009. With entertainment most evenings and pensioners specials on Wednesday lunchtimes, there is something here for everyone. Children are welcome and plenty of parking available. Only cash is accepted.

HIDDEN PLACES GUIDES

Explore Britain and Ireland with *Hidden Places* guides - a fascinating series of national and local travel guides.

Packed with easy to read information on hundreds of places of interest as well as places to stay, eat and drink.

Available from both high street and internet booksellers

For more information on the full range of *Hidden Places* guides and other titles published by Travel Publishing visit our website on

www.travelpublishing.co.uk
or ask for our leaflet by phoning
01752 697280 or emailing
info@travelpublishing.co.uk

104 Chorley road, Adlington,
Lancashire PR6 9LG
Tel: 01257 485600 Fax: 01257 485700
e-mail: orders@thevillagekitchen.co.uk

The Village Kitchen is certainly one for the family by the family. For the last 2½ years, Deborah Hindley has been at the helm of this fabulous place to dine. Open Monday to Friday from 8am to 3pm and Saturday from 8am to 2pm there is a large assortment of food served daily.

Seating 22, there are, in addition, comfortable seats, which provide a more informal setting, enabling visitors to simply enjoy one of their many varieties of coffees and cakes. There is so much food to choose from at The Village Kitchen - this can be eaten in or taken away if in a hurry. Sandwiches of every kind are available here, with white/granary baguettes or white/brown bread/ barms, all served with salad garnishes and homemade coleslaw. There are also plenty of special offers available, so if it is too difficult to decide on one meal, the prices will entice you to take two. Home made soup is served daily, as is a main course special, which sees local produce turned in to a hot meal in the winter and either a hot or cold dish in the summer months. Light meals such as jacket potatoes and toasted sandwiches are also served, as are beef burgers made with 100% beef - one to look out for is the Village burger, which is double the size and overflowing with bacon, cheese, fried onions and more.

Food is served upon opening, so if you are an early riser, you can enjoy a huge full VK breakfast, toast topped with an assortment of toppings, or simply choose to go continental and enjoy a croissant or toasted tea cake with jam.

This premises is truly super. Deborah and her family have created a venue that will appeal to all, whether grabbing something quick on the way to work or lounging in the comfortable settees with a friend and a piece of chocolate fudge cake. If you cannot get enough of the food here at The Village Kitchen, Deborah can organise outside catering for any special occasions you may have. What's more, the venue can also be hired out for private functions. Please note that this establishment is closed on Sundays. Children are more than welcome.

60 THE WAGGON AND HORSES

Bent Lane, Leyland, Lancashire PR25 4HR
Tel: 01772 432297
e-mail: waggonandhorsesleyland@yahoo.co.uk
website: www.thewaggonandhorsesleyland.co.uk

Situated just outside the town centre of Leyland is where you will find the welcoming **Waggon and Horses Inn**. A family friendly pub with traditional values, this fine inn has something for everyone. At the helm is mother and daughter team, Gillian and Beverly, who make sure that your visit is one to repeat! Excellent wholesome food is what you will find here, with tasty favourites such as rump steak, poached chicken breast, mushroom stroganoff and stuffed pepper to name but a few. On Sunday the inn proves even more popular offering the only pub carvery in the area. The meat is sourced locally from the town butcher, T Higham of Leyland. The bar offers many tipples to accompany your meal including a wide range of soft drinks as well as traditional cask ales.

Good honest food is not the only thing that you will enjoy here, amusement is just as important, and Gillian and Beverly have made sure that a wide range of entertainment is available. Tuesday is Jazz night, Friday is Karaoke night and there are live artists that play every Saturday night. Please check the website for information on up-coming events. Open Sunday - Thursday 5pm - 11pm and Friday & Saturday 3pm - 12am.

There is a large off road car park and children are made very welcome.

61 WYNDHAMS TEA ROOM

123 Towngate, Leyland,
Lancashire PR25 2LQ
Tel: 01772 455741

Delightful, welcoming and relaxing are all apt words to describe the **Wyndhams Tea Room**. Situated a short walk from the centre of Leyland, this café is owned and run by friendly host Diane Ezzard. All the food here is homemade and uses local produce as much as possible. Homemade meat and potato pie is a firm favourite from the specials board with jumbo breakfasts, hot sandwiches, soup, salad and jacket potatoes proving close contenders from the takeaway menu. Open Monday – Friday 9am – 4pm and Saturday 9am – 3pm, this quaint café is definitely worth a visit.

62 PUMPKIN SEED CAFÉ

58 Church Road, Tarleton,
Lancashire PR4 6UQ
Tel: 01772 816553

If you are looking for inviting decor, a relaxing atmosphere and friendly staff serving fine food, then a visit to the **Pumpkin Seed Café** is a must. This delightful premises is run by the hospitable Atkinson family and they make sure that every visitor leaves feeling more than satisfied. There is a large selection of home cooked dishes available such as Caramalized Onion & Goats Cheese Tart, Pumpkin & Parsnip Tart and Homemade Minced Beef Pie and the desserts are equally as tempting. Open Tuesday – Saturday 9am – 3.30pm.

63 BRAMLEYS COFFEE HOUSE

6 Church Walks, Ormskirk,
Lancashire L39 3QS
Tel: 01695 578801 Fax: 01695 575647
e-mail: mark@markgore.wanadoo.co.uk

Nestled in the heart of Ormskirk in Church Walks is where you will be glad to find one of the best known and most popular coffee houses/ eating establishments for miles around. Hospitable owner Mark Gore and his staff, make sure that your visit here is one to remember. All the dishes on offer are freshly prepared to order and you can expect to see main courses such as homemade quiche of the day, homemade Chilli con Carne and lasagne verdi as well as lighter options such as toasted sandwiches, jacket potatoes and salad platters. Also, why not finish off a meal with a piece of homemade cake from the dessert menu? Open Mon – Sat, 9am – 5pm.

Looking for:

- *Places to Visit?*
- *Places to Stay?*
- *Places to Eat & Drink?*
- *Places to Shop?*

COUNTRY LIVING RURAL GUIDES

HIDDEN INNS

HIDDEN PLACES

COUNTRY Pubs & Inns

off the motorway 3rd edition

www.travelpublishing.co.uk

64 THE PRINCE ALBERT

109 Wigan Road, Westhead,
nr Ormskirk, Lancashire L40 6HY
Tel: 01695 573656
e-mail: sforshaw982@fsmail.net

In the village of Westhead, a short drive southeast of Ormskirk, is the family owned and run **Prince Albert**. Dating back in parts to the early 18th century, this fine hostelry started off as an old farmhouse welcoming cattlemen as lodgers. The farmer at the time then began to expand his small bed and breakfast business and started to brew his own beer, setting up a smithy on an area which is now thought to be the car park. It is nice to know that this warm, family friendly pub is just as welcoming now as it was back then, and has even been voted CAMRA Community Pub of the Year 2008.

Open all day everyday, visitors can expect to sample up to 5 real ales at any one time with the regulars being Tetley Cask, Tetley Mild and Pendle Witches Brew. The food on offer here is even more varied, with dishes cooked fresh on the premises. Traditional fish and chips, broccoli 3 cheese bake, chicken curry and Chilli con Carne are just a few main courses to get your taste buds going. There is also a 3 course Sunday lunch added to the menu on Sundays for those looking for the traditional Sunday roast.

This pub also boasts 4 quality guest rooms all located upstairs each with private shower. These are available on a room only or B&B basis.

65 WWT MARTIN MERE

Fish Lane, Burscough, Lancashire L40 0TA
Tel: 01704 895181 Fax: 01704 892343
e-mail: info.martinmere@wwt.org.uk
website: www.wwt.org.uk

WWT Martin Mere is one of nine Wildfowl & Wetlands Centres run by the Wildfowl & Wetlands Trust (WWT), a UK registered charity. Visit WWT Martin Mere and come in close contact with wetlands and their wildlife. You can feed some of the birds straight from your hand. Special events and exhibitions help to give an insight into the wonder of wetlands and the vital need for their conservation.

People of all ages and abilities will enjoy exploring the carefully planned pathways. You can go on a journey around the world, from the Australian Riverway, through the South American Lake, to the Oriental Pen with its Japanese gateway, observing a multitude of exotic ducks, geese, swans and flamingos along the way. In winter, WWT Martin Mere plays host to thousands of Pink-footed Geese, Whooper and Bewick's Swans and much more. Visitors can see swans under floodlight most winter evenings. Covering 150 hectares, the reserve (one of Britain's most important wetland sites) is designated a Ramsar Site and SSSI for its wealth of rare wetland plants.

The Wildfowl & Wetlands Trust is the largest international wetland conservation charity in the UK. WWT's mission is to conserve wetlands and their biodiversity. These are vitally important for the quality and maintenance of all life. WWT operates nine visitor centres in the UK, bringing people closer to wildlife and providing a fun day out for all the family.

66 PIPPINS COFFEE HOUSE

30/32 Chapel Street,
Southport, Lancashire PR8 1BH
Tel: 01704 535335

This charming venue situated in the heart of popular Southport greets visitors with a small front door and a staircase then leading to a fine upstairs, coffee house and dining establishment. Althoug the family run coffee house has been in the hands of Dianne and James since 2002 it was handed down to son Oliver in the latter part of 2008. The location is extremely popular with locals and tourists alike and it is not hard to see why.

The food served at **Pippins Coffee House** is homemade on the premises. There is a large range of hot and cold meals, including an outstanding display of sandwiches and cakes, enough to suit any taste, as well as soups and breakfasts which are served at various times throughout the day. You can visit this top quality business without booking as the property seats nearly 140 in its dining area upstairs. Opening times are 9.15am-5.15pm Monday-Saturday with hot food being served from 11.30am onwards.

There will always be a treat on the menu as around 3 or 4 special main courses are added daily to the existing menu. Breakfast is served upon opening and runs until 11.30 am.

13-17 Scarisbrick Avenue,
Southport, LAncashire PR8 1NN
Tel: 01704 536926
e-mail: cinnamonbarandlounge@hotmail.co.uk

Tucked away behind Southports main street, in the centre of Southport, a walkway adjacent to the famous Scarsbrick hotel leads to the **Cinnamon Bar & Lounge.** Previously a small coffee shop and adjoining rock shop, it is now a truly outstanding premises with a lot to offer. Karen and Jess, the owners, have been in charge here since September 2008. They are, however, anything but 'new' to the business. Combined they have 35 years in the industry. The décor here is breathtaking and was entirely designed by Jess, so there is a sense of personality when entering the bar and lounge. This property seats up to 38 on its ground floor, however there is an upstairs function room that can be hired out for special occasions.

The food on offer here is extensive ranging from light bites such as satay chicken skewers and smoked salmon and scrambled egg ciabatta to the more traditional main courses of toad in the hole, hand beer-battered cod and a number of different steaks. Head Chef Paul has provided a menu for a variety of tastes as there are also panini's, soups, pasta and salads with ingredients such as crayfish, lamb, pork meatballs, feta cheese and olives. There is also a menu dedicated to desserts, which is to die for. Paul produces homemade "Cinnamon" doughnuts and homemade sticky toffee pudding to name but a few - the list could go on and on. If that wasn't enough, these can all be washed down with the bar's range of beverages, from tea and coffee, to draught lagers, bottled beers and a fine selection of wines. Food is served daily from 11am-8pm and Friday and Saturday from 11am-9pm.

The Cinnamon Bar and Lounge is suitable for children and there are a selection of child friendly meals available - for example mini pizzas, chicken nuggets and fish fingers, all served with chips or mashed potato and beans or salad. Although the owners have only been here for a short while, the food has already had outstanding reviews and has been recommended by other publicans. To showcase the talents of head chef, Paul, once a month the bar and lounge has a 3 course dinner, which is accompanied by live music. Visitors need to book for this event and can ring for details. Please note that the Cinnamon Bar is closed on Mondays during the winter months.

68 BRITISH LAWNMOWER MUSEUM

106-114 Shakespeare Street, Southport,
Lancashire PR8 4AJ
Tel: 01704 501336 Fax: 01704 500564

The **British Lawnmower Museum** located in the picturesque Victorian seaside holiday resort of Southport, Lancashire houses a private collection of over 200 pristine exhibits of special interest (part of 400) built up over a period of 50 years and is now a tribute to the garden machinery industry which has developed over the past 170 years from the Industrial Revolution, when modern technology was not available, to the present day. Many of the machines have been rescued from the scrap yard and restored to their present very high standard. In addition to early grass cutting and garden machines dating from the 1830's, the exhibition houses the largest collection of vintage toy lawnmowers and games in the world.

The museum has now become one of the world's leading authorities on vintage lawnmowers and is now the largest specialists in antique garden machinery, supplying parts, archive conservation of manuscript materials including 500 original patents from 1799, and valuing machines from all over the world. The museum retains a character not often seen in these modern times.

Included in this unique national collection are manufacturers not normally associated with the garden industry, names such as Rolls Royce, Royal Enfield, Daimler, Hawker Sidley, Perkins Diesel, British Leyland and many more. A lot of the exhibits memorabilia and industrial artifacts are from the Victorian and Edwardian era and have been restored and keep a small part of British engineering heritage alive.

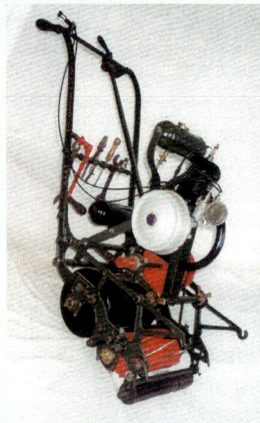

69 SATCHMO'S

31 Liverpool Road, Birkdale,
Lancashire PR8 4AE
Tel: 01704 563430

In 2008 Liverpool Road in Birkdale opened its doors to **Satchmo's**. Created by Alan and Jane, Satchmo's is a superb place to dine and drink 6 days a week. Jane is the chef and produces a number of traditional and international cuisines, including a selection of Tapas, served 12-8pm Tues-Sun, which should ideally be booked in advance. Local produce is used wherever possible to ensure a great dining experience. There is also a decent array of draught keg ales, bottled beers and wines. Visit Tues & Wed from 8pm to take part in a Musical quiz night, inspired and themed by the 60's to 90's.

HIDDEN PLACES GUIDES

Explore Britain and Ireland with *Hidden Places* guides - a fascinating series of national and local travel guides.

Packed with easy to read information on hundreds of places of interest as well as places to stay, eat and drink.

Available from both high street and internet booksellers

For more information on the full range of *Hidden Places* guides and other titles published by Travel Publishing visit our website on

www.travelpublishing.co.uk
or ask for our leaflet by phoning
01752 697280 or emailing
info@travelpublishing.co.uk

St. Michael road, Aughton,
nr Ormskirk, Lancashire L39 6SA
Tel: 01695 423241 Fax: 01695 424824
e-mail: thestanleyarms@yahoo.co.uk

Set in a picturesque location just off the main A59 South of Ormskirk, **The Stanley Arms** is situated across the road from the village church and is extremely popular within the community. The licensees here were featured in the very first edition of Hidden Places, Lancashire and continue to attract a large audience.

Steve and Sandra Williams are no strangers to the business and have been providing their visitors with astounding real ales and traditional, homemade, mouth watering food for many years. Quality cuisine is available 7 days a week between the hours of 12pm and 8pm, with family favourites such as lasagne, steak and kidney pie and breaded scampi to name but a few, as well as more elaborate dishes including slow cooked lamb in a Guinness and rosemary gravy; homemade chicken liver pate and home made leek and potato soup. All of this is served with hand cut and prepared chips, which are simply delicious. If you would prefer a lighter meal, there is also a lunch menu, which provides visitors with salads, sandwiches and a large choice of jacket potatoes with various toppings. There are choices for vegetarians and also a children's menu.

With so much to choose from it may leave you thirsty but that's not a problem as 5 real ales are on offer for all to enjoy. Regulars to The Stanley Arms are the Tetley dark mild, Timothy Taylor Landlord, Marstons pedigree and also a rotating guest ale.

This venue is a great one for the family as there is enough to entertain people of all ages. A children's play area is on site, as is a beer garden, perfect for those warm summer days. There are also plenty of evening activities such as quiz nights, which take place every Tuesday at 9pm, live music showcasing local talents within the area every Friday night and a bowling green, which can be hired at any time. The general atmosphere of the property is hospitable and friendly - there is never a dull moment at The Stanley Arms. This location has off road parking.

70   THE PINEWOODS

Wicks Green, Formby, Lancashire L37 1PR
Tel: 01704 833192
e-mail: ksdowd@btinternet.com

Built in 1968 **The Pinewoods** is an attractive building - inside and out, only a short walk or drive away from the centre of Formby. The owners Kerry and Bev have been in charge of this superb family friendly premises for three years and have certainly put the place on the map, enticing visitors from all over the world with their selection of 3 real ales and fresh, homemade food.

Kerry has many years experience as a chef, wine waiter and restaurant manager so needless to say that when visiting, all customers are in for a treat. The produce here is sourced locally and fresh fish is delivered daily. Just a snap shot of the menu includes a chef's homemade pie of the day and a selection of meats from the grill such as a 10oz gammon steak or an extra-matured prime ribeye steak all served with chips and peas. There is also a Sunday roast menu, which sees everyone's favourites, including beef or turkey served with all the trimmings.

Food is served Tuesday-Thursday and Sunday from 12-8pm and Friday and Saturday 12-9pm (Book for the weekends to avoid disappointment).

73   THE NEWMARKET

47 Market Street, Earlestown,
Newton-Le-Willows, Lancashire WA12 9BS
Tel: 01925 222206
e-mail: jo_mills@live.com

The Newmarket, a large welcoming hostelry, is located in the heart of Earlestown, found via Newton-Le-Willows. It stands overlooking the market square and dates back to the 19th century. Hosts Joanne and Gary have been here since May 2008 using their wealth of experience in the catering and licensing trades to create a delightful hostelry. The current favourites available at the bar are John Smiths Smooth and Carling. The pub is open all day, every day, and on market Days (Mon/Fri/Sat) from 8.30am until midnight.

Joanne is much at home in the kitchen cooks up delightful dishes such as homemade steak and ale pie served with fresh market vegetables and a choice of potatoes, homemade meat and potato pie

simply served with chips and the most hearty All Day breakfast. With most of the produce being sourced from the local butcher and greengrocer, diners can be assured of the highest quality and freshness in their meals.

Food is served from 8.30am – 3pm on Market days (Mon/Fri/Sat) and from 11am – 3pm Tues/Weds/Thurs. Food is not available in the evenings or on Sundays.

Earlestown is named after Hardman Earle who was the Chairman of the London and North Western Railway.

93 Crawford Village, Skelmersdale,
Lancashire WN8 9QS
Tel: 01744 882 421
website: www.crawfordarms.co.uk

The **Crawford Arms** is situated in the tiny village of Crawford, south of the M58 and east of the A570. Purpose built in the late 19th century, this pub guarantees a warm and friendly welcome to all. Run by leaseholders Dominic & Dawn and ably assisted by dedicated staff Jackie, Kieren and chef Sarah, the Crawford Arms has built up a reputation as a place to get great food and drink at reasonable prices. The pub is open from 4pm till close on Monday and Tuesday and from 12pm till close for the rest of the week. The bar is very well stocked and includes two real ales; Old Speckled Hen and Bombardier, and the occasional guest ale.

Quality food is available from 1pm till 8.30pm Wednesday to Sunday and Sarah cooks all the food from locally sourced ingredients, fresh to order. The menu is extensive, catering for all tastes with ease; however, the highlight has to be the selection of steaks from the grill; you can choose from rump, 9oz or 24oz, sirloin, T-bone, rib eye or fillet steaks, all accompanied by salad, vegetables, chips and an optional homemade sauce. For the extra hungry, or insane, there is the Crawford Gut Buster, an enormous 40oz (2 ½ pounds) rump steak with chips and vegetables, there is a twist though; if you clear the plate, Dominic will give you £25 and if you don't then you owe Dominic the £25! Clearly this challenge is not for those with a weak constitution! The rest of the menu is the best of classic pub fayre, for example; liver & onion, homemade pure ground steak burgers, minted lamb, beef & ale stew, fish & chips, local sausages & mash and special char grilled ribs. There is a good kid's menu; kids can eat free if one of the adults is eating a steak, gammon or the mixed grill. The kid's meals come with peas or beans, Cornetto and a drink. For the slightly less hungry there is a fine range of light bites. You can choose from hot or cold baguettes, jacket potatoes and salads or even just skip straight to one of the scrumptious sounding puddings.

The pub is a popular entertainment venue; there is a quiz every Thursday night and on some Saturday evenings there is karaoke.

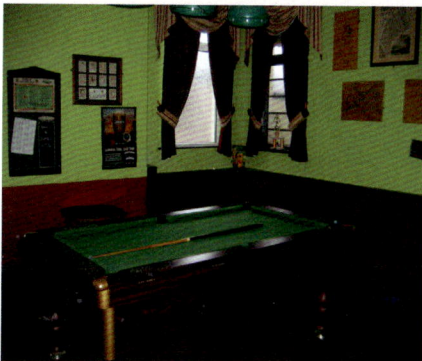

**Crank Road, Billinge,
West Lancashire WN5 7DT
Tel: 01695 622 705**

Locally know as "T' Foot" or "The Foot of the Causeway", **The Holt Arms** is a beautiful 17th century pub in the picturesque village of Billinge. Prior to being named the Holt Arms, the premises were known as The Bowling Green and it still has a magnificent green to the rear of the property, still in use to this day.

The exterior of the pub is extremely well looked after, freshly painted signs and lovely hanging baskets adorn the walls. Inside, the story does not change much, warm and cosy in the winter with roaring log fires, light and cool in the summer with a stylish décor.

The Holt Arms is very much a family run pub; Mother Freda, Father Mike and sons Paul & Andrew have held the lease for 2 ½ years now. Experience is not a problem - Paul alone has been a chef for 20 years. And the expertise in the kitchen shines through; people flock from all over the place to sample the menu in such volume that it is necessary to book tables to avoid disappointment! With the meat sourced locally by the pub's butcher; J. E Cook of Rainford, and local produce used wherever possible, the food is sublime.

The Holts' favourites include the local steaks, fresh battered cod and chips, the homemade steak and stilton pie, homemade Lancashire hotpot and braised local lamb, cooked slowly in mint gravy with mashed potato. There is also a good choice for vegetarians; porcini mushroom ravioli, five bean chilli, enchiladas and a delicious brie & courgette crumble typify the vegetarian options. The quality doesn't falter with the light bites menu either; there is a wide range of choices, including stuffed Murphy's (jacket potatoes), salads and 100% pure beef burgers, cooked to order. Food is available between 12pm – 2.30pm & 5pm – 8.30pm Tuesday to Saturday and between 12pm – 7.30pm on Sundays.

But it is not all about the food, the cosy fires or the well kept beer garden The Holt Arms is also a prime location to enjoy a good pint; there are four real ales on offer at once, two regulars in Banks Bitter and Marstons Pedigree and two rotating guest ales. Despite not serving food on Mondays, the pub opens at 5pm until close, and then all day Tuesday to Sunday. There is a large off road car park and there are disabled facilities.

74 THE STANLEY

122 Ormskirk Road, Upholland,
West Lancashire WN8 0AF
Tel: 01695 625 770
e-mail: gordon.smith@btconnect.com

The Stanley is located in the West Lancashire village of Upholland, close to Downholland, the two taking their name from the former Holland manor of the de Holland family. Just a short drive from the M6 and the M58, long time leaseholders Gordon & Sue ensure a warm and friendly welcome into this 18th century former farm building.

The pub offers sterling food, drink and service and the premises has recently been awarded the 'Taste of Lancashire Award' for 2008-09 by the tourist board. Gordon has 30 years in the trade and over 10 as a chef and his experience shines through both in the running of the pub and in the well thought out menu. Using locally sourced ingredients wherever possible, the menu features classic pub fayre, cooked to perfection. Diners can choose from the extensive menu or from the delicious chef's specials board.

Food is served from Wednesday to Friday between 12pm – 2pm & 5pm – 8pm and between 12pm – 8pm on Saturday and Sunday. The bar features two rotating guest real ales, always well kept and the ever popular Carling and Tetley's Smoothflow.

77 EAST LANCASHIRE RAILWAY

Bolton Street, Bury, Lancashire BL9 0EY
Tel: 0161 764 7790
website: www.east-lancs-rly.co.uk

The **East Lancashire Railway** offers visitors an opportunity to step back in time to the age of steam and travel along this delightful stretch of track. Your journey can be broken at Ramsbottom or Irwell Vale stations where you could enjoy a lineside picnic.

On Platform 2 at Bury Bolton Street Station, the period tearooms offer views of the locomotives arriving or departing from the station, while you enjoy a meal in the pleasant surroundings. Snacks and meals are available and the rooms can be pre-booked for special occasions.

A wide variety of events take place throughout the year, including Santa Specials, a day out with Thomas and Friends, 1940's Wartime weekend and Steam Enthusiasts Weekend - ring for current details.

Adults can actually drive a steam or diesel locomotive on the 'Footplate Experience' or an entire train can be hired for a special occasion or event.

Facilities for the disabled are extremely good with access at all the stations, toilets at the main stations and a specially adapted carriage with wide doors and hydraulic lift.

62 Manchester Road, Astley, Tyldesley,
Lancahire M29 7EJ
Tel: 01942 873803

Ideally located adjacent to the A572 just outside the village of Astley, is the distinguished **Manchester Road Inn**. An old coaching inn dating back to the mid 19th century it has gained a fine reputation in the area for excellent food, well kept ale and most of all, unbeatable hospitality.

Friendly hosts, Vicky and Danny, who have plenty of experience in the trade, have been running this charming inn for the last two years and have turned it around, improving day by day and attracting guests from far and wide as well as locally. They have created a welcoming hostelry with a pleasant atmosphere, giving many reasons for visitors to seek out this friendly establishment.

Open all day, every day; guests have a choice of two real ales to enjoy, Flowers Original plus rotating guest ale. A qualified chef is employed in the kitchen to serve up a wide range of appetizing dishes and Vikki herself also likes to cook adding to the culinary expertise here. Guests can relax in the smart, yet cosy interior while making their choice from the extensive menu. Samples from the grill include a juicy 10oz sirloin steak served with grilled tomato, mushrooms, onion rings and your choice of accompaniment and Hunters chicken – a succulent chicken breast topped with barbecue sauce, grilled bacon and cheese. The main courses include a luscious Lamb Henry, braised in a rich minted gravy and a traditional homemade lasagne as well as many other mouth watering dishes. A wide range of baguettes, sandwiches and jacket potatoes are available Mon-Sat only and include prawn Marie Rose, steak and onion, Cajun chicken and Cumberland sausage with onion. In addition to these choices, the daily specials board adds more delightful bites at very reasonable prices. The tempting desserts

include favourites such as treacle sponge pudding, Knickerbocker Glory, homemade apple pie and chocolate fudge cake - all guaranteed to put a smile on your face! This top class food is served Mon-Thurs 12-2.30pm and 6-8.30pm, Fri 12-2.30pm and 6-9pm, Sat 12-9pm Sun 12-8pm. Local produce is used whenever possible.

Friday evenings, Karaoke starts at 9pm. Children are made very welcome here and all major credit cards are taken. Plenty of car parking is available. There are many places of interest to visit in the surrounding areas including The Astley Green Colliery Museum, housing Lancashire's only remaining colliery.

78 ROCHDALE PIONEERS MUSEUM

31 Toad Lane, Rochdale,
Lancashire OL12 0NU
Tel: 01706 524920
e-mail: museum@co-op.ac.uk
website: www.museum.co-op.ac.uk

The Rochdale Pioneers Museum is regarded as the home of the world wide co-operative movement. It's the perfect place to come and see how your ancestors did their shopping.

In Toad Lane on December 21 1844 the Rochdale Equitable Pioneers Society opened their store selling pure food at fair prices and honest weights and measures, starting a revolution in retailing.

See the recreation of the original shop with its rudimentary furniture and scales. Here the basic needs of daily life such as butter, sugar, flour and oatmeal first went on sale over 150 years ago.

Journey back in time with early advertising, packaging and retailing artifacts, Co-operative postage stamps, commemorative china and rare dividend coins and commodity tokens. See the development of 'dividend' and the Co-op's success.

80 HOLLINGWORTH LAKE COUNTRY PARK

Countryside Ranger Service, Visitor Centre,
Rakewood Road, Littleborough,
Lancashire OL5 0AQ
Tel: 01706 373421 Fax: 01706 378753

Nestling on the edge of the Pennines, just 3 miles from Rochdale town centre, and junction 21 on the M62, **Hollingworth Lake** provides a surprising haven for wildlife and excitement and entertainment for the young and the not so young.

Built to supply water to the recently re-opened Rochdale Canal, the lake has always been a popular destination. In its heyday it boasted dance halls, a skating rink and steamboats. Today there is a nature reserve, visitor centre, and water sports facility.

Easy walking around the lake can be extended by following the trails into the surrounding countryside. The events programmes are packed full of ideas for the pleasure and enjoyment of everyone. Facilities in the area include caravan and camping sites, craft shops, and several pubs, cafés and restaurants.

The Square, Whitworth,
Lancashire OL12 8PY
Tel: 01706 861441
Mobile: 07973 693853
e-mail: redlionwhitworth@hotmail.co.uk
website: www.redlionwhitworth.co.uk

Set in the heart of Whitworth square and dating back to 1674, **The Red Lion Inn** has all the charm and character you would expect from such an historic building. It is the sole survivor of several public houses in The Square which used to serve the needs of the inhabitants in the 1700's. Family run over the past three years by Jane and Steve along with their two sons Tom and Kieran, they have given this place a new lease of life and have made it the hub of the area, with tourists from all over the world enjoying their stay here. With over fifteen years in the trade, this is the third pub they have taken on in the valley, gaining much respect in the local community. This extremely friendly family offer a very warm, sincere welcome to all their guests, locals and visitors alike.

Award winning cuisine is served every day of the week in the tasteful, cosy restaurant. The bar offers a choice of three real ales on tap including Theakstons Best plus ever changing guest ales. Best quality Food is available Mon-Fri 12 – 2pm & 5 – 9pm, Sat 12 – 9pm and Sundays/Bank Holidays 12 – 8pm. The varied menu offers traditional 'pub grub' such as 'minted lamb Henri' and beef lasagne verdi with local produce being used whenever possible. The Red Lion hosts special steak nights on Wednesday evenings and fabulous Thai nights on Thursdays and Saturdays where traditional, tasty Thai meals such as 'Tom Yam chicken with creamy mushroom sauce' and 'south Thai style beef curry' tantalise the tastebuds.

Entertainment on Thursday evenings from 9pm consists of either a live artist or jamming night! Fully refurbished accommodation is available all year round with five bright en-suite rooms to choose from comprising three family rooms which sleep up to four, one twin and one king size room. Cots are available on request and even baby sitting can be arranged. The reasonably priced tariff includes a hearty breakfast, served at your convenience and special dietary needs can be catered for on request. Children are made very welcome and all major credit cards are taken.

The facilities in every part of this establishment are outstanding with excellent reviews in the comments book from past visitors assuring future guests of complete satisfaction.

56 Oldham Road, Grasscroft, Oldham,
Lancashire OL4 0HI
Tel: 01457 872124

The Farrar's Arms is a lovely, historic building situated in Grasscroft, Oldham. The building has been here since the 13th century and has been serving ales to the public since the mid 17th century. Still with all of its charm, the building's façade is traditional and looks inviting, whilst the interior has wood panelled walls, feature beams and a roaring fireplace, which is enticing to all who visit. Tenants Karen and Melanie have been at this premises since October 2008. However Karen had worked here previously for 8 years mainly as the chef, before taking over the tenancy. The public house has accommodation with one family room upstairs and although it is not ensuite, the price includes a hearty breakfast.

The seating in the bar on the ground floor is cosy and has a choice of high backed seating or booths, creating spaces for larger groups.

Melanie is now the chef at The Farrar's Arms and the food is great. The old favourites menu is very popular with locals and visitors alike and includes much-loved dishes such as fish & chips, traditional ham & eggs with chips & garden peas and jam roly-poly, which will take you back to your youth. There are also snack menus which feature pannini's, burgers and sharing platters or if you would prefer some old fashioned homemade cooking, you can dine on a starter of homemade soup of the day, Bury black pudding stack or chicken liver pate and a main meal of Mexican chilli, a cheese and onion pie or a rump steak - that is just the tip of the iceberg. The food here is made with local produce wherever possible and is all homemade and home cooked, ensuring that you enjoy your food and return again and again.

There are also 4 real ales that you can enjoy with your meal. Regulars here are the Timothy Taylor Landlord and the Black Sheep, with two further rotating guest ales. Food is served daily from Monday to Saturday from 12-9pm and Sunday 12-5pm. Upon arrival you will see a pleasant beer garden, which can be enjoyed all year round and is perfect for those with children. There is also a private car park across the road from the premises.

219

81 THE NAVIGATION INN

21/23 Wool Road, Dobcross, Saddleworth,
Lancashire OL3 5NS
Tel: 01457 872418

Dating back to the early 19th century, **The Navigation Inn** is located on the outskirts of the scenic village of Dobcross and is well known for its hospitality, superb cuisine and good range of well kept real ales. This warm and cosy inn, family run for the past five years by Mark, Sue and their daughter Laura, is open Mon-Fri lunchtimes and evenings and all day Sat/Sun. Quality, professional chef, Mark, uses local produce to create outstanding dishes. Food served lunchtimes, 12-2pm Mon - Sat & Sun until 2.30pm, Mon - Thurs evenings 5.30-8pm, Fri 6-8.30pm, Sat 6-9pm, Sun 5.30-7.30pm. Children welcome. Quiz night Sundays from 9.30pm. Ample parking.

83 EATS AND TREATS

93 High Street, Lees, Oldham,
Lancashire OL4 4LY
Tel: 01616 207904

Sitting in the heart of the village of Lees, **Eats and Treats** is a top quality café/takeaway offering a personal service to all its customers. It is family run by Barbara & Michael Brogan and daughter Claire, together with their hard working team of loyal staff, Joanne and Paula. Good quality, homecooked food is served in the modern, attractive interior which is extremely bright and airy. Daily specials such as chilli and curry complement the main menu which has a wide range of appetizing drinks, snacks, sandwiches and jacket potatoes. Children are welcome and only cash is accepted.

85 THE GOLDEN PHEASANT

Plumley Moor Rd, Plumley, Knutsford,
Cheshire WA16 9RX
Tel: 01565 722 261

One of the most well known establishments in Cheshire; **The Golden Pheasant** was taken over by Viscount Christopher Wright and his business partner Tim Hodkinson in March 2008 and with over 60 years experience in the hospitality trade, the pub has gone from strength to strength. A complete refurbishment has helped turn the inn back into one of Cheshire's hidden gems and the new à la carte menu has the regulars singing praises. The interior is superb, beautiful old fireplaces with comfortable armchairs, antiquities and interesting articles are blended with the new décor to create a warming ambience.

Six rooms are available on a room only basis (breakfast is available on request), the rooms are all outstanding with four poster beds in two of them, all the rooms are en-suite and there are named after famous Cheshire estates. Food is served all day, every day and the à la carte menu consists of classic pub fayre cooked with the finest of local produce to ensure the highest quality meals. The bar is well stocked and features three real ales from the J.W. Lees brewery to enjoy next to a roaring wood fire.

84 THE COURTYARD COFFEE HOUSE

Rear and 92 King Street, Knutsford,
Cheshire, WA16 6ED
Tel: 01565 653974

Tucked away behind Knutsfords main street, **The Courtyard Coffee House** has very few equals in its field. Run by Matthew and Sharon Fay this outstanding eating place is renowned throughout the country and far beyond. A warm welcome awaits, hand in hand with a unique ambience for enjoying mouth watering food in the 50 cover main area or outside in the courtyard.

There is plenty for everyone here, morning coffee is served with a selection of scones, toast, tea cakes, tea bread and croissants (9am – 12) and afternoon tea is equally as tempting with dainty sandwiches, home made scones and a large selection of devilish cakes. If it's something more substantial that you are after then The Courtyard Coffee House has a fantastic lunchtime menu offering freshly prepared favourites such as Welsh rarebit, grilled smoked haddock, honey baked ham and many tasty vegetarian options.

Not only does this delightful coffee house offer superb hospitality, great food and a wonderful place to enjoy a piece of cake with friends, but it also have a very unexpected attraction. Inside you will find that the walls and beams are adorned with a historic and treasured collection of Penny Farthings. The Penny Farthing, which in its day was usually known as the Ordinary was in vogue for a 20 years from the early 1870's. It was unrivalled for its speed and elegance. However to mount the bicycle the rider had to first place his left foot on the step above the back wheel and push off with his right foot, after gaining speed he would then stand up on his left leg and slip forward into the saddle.

As well as Penny Farthings, there are also other ancient bicycles in the collection including a rare original Boneshaker. The Boneshaker had an average weight of just 60 pounds and was capable of eight miles per hour but riding this type of bicycle was not easy. They were around $100 to buy so were unaffordable for the working classes.

If it's a morning coffee, a lunchtime meal or a piece of bicycle history you are after, then a visit to The Courtyard Coffee House will not disappoint.

221

86 TATTON PARK

Knutsford, Cheshire WA16 6QN
Tel: 01625 534400
e-mail: tatton@cheshire.gov.uk
website: www.nationaltrust.org.uk

Tatton Park is one of the most complete historic estates open to visitors. The early 19th-century Wyatt house sits amid a landscaped deer park and is opulently decorated, providing a fine setting for the Egerton family's collections of pictures, books, china, glass, silver and specially commissioned Gillow furniture. The theme of Victorian grandeur extends into the garden, with fernery, orangery, tower garden, pinetum and Italian and Japanese gardens. The restored walled garden includes a kitchen garden and magnificent glasshouses, where traditional methods of gardening are used. Other features include the Tudor Old Hall, a working 1930s farm, a children's play area and speciality shops.

87 TABLEY HOUSE

Knutsford, Cheshire WA16 0HB
Tel: 01565 750151
e-mail: inquiries@tableyhouse.co.uk
website: www.tableyhouse.co.uk

Tabley House was designed by John Carr of York for Sir Peter Byrne Leicester and completed in 1767. His son, Sir John Fleming Leicester, later 1st Lord de Tabley, was the first great patron and collector of British paintings. He assembled a splendid collection at Tabley and in his London house during the first decade of the 19th century, ultimately with the intention of establishing a National Gallery of British Art.

JMW Turner, Henry Thompson and James Ward were among the many painters who stayed at Tabley. Today, important works by them can be seen in the rooms for which they were created, together with fine paintings by Dobson, Lely, Reynolds, Cotes, Northcote, Callcott, Fuseli, Lawrence and Martin.

The famous Gallery, created for Sir John before 1809, has been restored (1988-90) to its appearance in the early 1840s when it was remodelled by the second Lord de Tabley with sumptuous, red flock wallpaper. The collection of paintings has been rehung in the restored State Rooms of the main floor, with furniture by Chippendale, Bullock and Gillow of Lancaster and memorabilia acquired by the family.

St Peter's Chapel, originally built on an island in Tabley Moat in 1678, was moved in 1927 and re-erected on its present site adjacent to the house.

Macclesfield Heritage Centre, Roe Street,
Macclesfield, Cheshire SK11 6UT
Tel: 01625 619 909
e-mail: macclesfieldmt@caterleisure.co.uk
website: www.macclesfield.silk.museum.co.uk

The Story of Silk is fascinating. It links Macclesfield with China and the Far East and shaped the development of the town. The development of the silk industry in Macclesfield is told through an award-winning audio-visual programme, exhibitions, models and silk textiles and fashions. The Museum is housed within the Heritage Centre, built in 1813 as a Sunday school to provide education for the children who worked in the silk mills.

In the centre is the Silk shop which has an exciting range of attractive and unusual Macclesfield silk gifts: scarves, ties, textiles, silk cards and woven pictures, plus many inexpensive gifts for children.

Also in the centre is the **Mulberry Tree** Coffee Shop, offering a delicious range of light snacks and a full restaurant service. This bright and well decorated establishment is run by Lesley Carless on behalf of Caterleisure Ltd, a privately owned company who operate similar cafés, notably the Assembly Rooms in Ludlow. Lesley became the manager during the summer of 2008 and has only enhanced the premises already sterling reputation.

The menu can be split into three main areas; morning coffee, where you can enjoy a good quality hot beverage with a homemade scone, or a range of fresh pastries and cakes. Lunch, where the choice is extensive; the Mulberry Tree offers soup, hot meals, hot & cold sandwiches and Panini, jacket potatoes, salads, healthy options, puddings, wine, beer and soft drinks. Finally for the after work crowd, the afternoon tea session offers sandwiches, scones, cakes and biscuits. The Mulberry Tree can also cater for functions, there are four rooms at the Macclesfield heritage Centre available for receptions, dinners, meetings, seminars and luncheons, the rooms are of a good size and will fit between 20 to 50 people.

The café is a good size, they can accommodate 80 people inside and in the summer months there is space outside for al fresco dining! Open between 9am – 5pm Monday to Saturday and from 11am till 4pm on Sunday, the café does a roaring trade from the popular museum and gift shop on site. Also very popular is the senior citizens special, 2 courses for a special price is available between 11.30am – 2.30pm Monday to Friday. Waitress service is there for those who would like it, booking is recommended for larger parties, children are very welcome and there are full disabled facilities on site.

88 PARADISE MILL MUSEUM

The Heritage Centre, Roe Street,
Macclesfield, Cheshire SK11 6UT
Tel: 01625 613210
e mail: info@macclesfield.silk.museum
website: www.silk-macclesfield.org

Paradise Mill Museum was a working silk mill until 1981. Today the top floor is a living museum. Knowledgeable guides demonstrate the silk processes on some of the restored 26 hand jacquard silk looms and ancillary machinery and room sets show what life was like in the 1930s.

HIDDEN PLACES GUIDES

Explore Britain and Ireland with *Hidden Places* guides - a fascinating series of national and local travel guides.

Packed with easy to read information on hundreds of places of interest as well as places to stay, eat and drink.

Available from both high street and internet booksellers

For more information on the full range of *Hidden Places* guides and other titles published by Travel Publishing visit our website on

www.travelpublishing.co.uk
or ask for our leaflet by phoning
01752 697280   or emailing
info@travelpublishing.co.uk

90 WEST PARK MUSEUM

77 Prestbury Road, Macclesfield,
Cheshire SK10 3BJ
Tel: 01625 619831
e-mail: info@macclesfield.silk.museum.co.uk
website: www.macclesfield.silk.museum

West Park Museum was donated by Marianne Brocklehurst and her brother, Peter Pownall Brocklehurst "for the education, refinement and pleasure of the people for all time to come."

In 1894 scandal ensued over the choice of designs for the Museum. Marianne Brocklehurst withdrew her offer after an insulting letter from "a Town Councillor", causing much disappointment among the people of Macclesfield. After four years Miss Brocklehurst relented and the Museum was finally opened on the 3rd of October 1898. The design of the interior was based on a room at the Whitworth Art Gallery.

The Museum is located in one of the earliest public parks, which opened in 1854 and was funded by voluntary subscriptions. The park boasts the largest bowling green in England. Over the years the amenities in the park have developed to match changing leisure activities.

West Park Museum's Collections comprise a wide range of fine and decorative art material and objects relating to local history. This includes the famous Giant Panda. The paintings date from the 19th and early 20th centuries. Local history displays include Law & Order and the life of Charles Roe, an 18th century Macclesfield entrepreneur.

91 ADLINGTON HALL

Mill lane, Adlington, Macclesfield,
Cheshire SK10 4LF
Tel: 01625 827 595 Fax: 01625 820 797
e-mail: enquiries@adlingtonhall.com
website: www.adlingtonhall.com

Adlington Hall, the home of the Leghs of Adlington from 1315 to the present day, was built on the site of a hunting lodge which stood in the Forest of Macclesfield in 1040. The Hall is a manor house, quadrangular in shape, and was at one time surrounded by a moat. Two sides of the courtyard and the east wing were built in 1581 in the typical 'black& white' Cheshire style. The south front and west wing were added between 1749 and 1757 and are built of red brick with a handsome stone portico with four Ionic columns.

Two oak trees, part of the original building, still remain with their roots in the ground and support the east end of the Great Hall, which was built between 1480 and 1505. Between the trees in the Great Hall stands an organ built in the style of 'Father' Bernard Smith (c 1670-80). Handel subsequently played on this instrument and, now fully restored, it is the largest 17th century organ in the country. At the west end of the Great Hall is a very fully developed canopy. This takes the form of a cove or quadrant and is divided into 60 panels containing armorial shields. The windows are on the south side so that the murals which adorn the north and west walls can be seen to advantage. Adlington Hall was a royalist garrison during the Civil War.

Adlington Hall is a great Cheshire garden set in the heart of the Cheshire Plain amidst some of England's finest countryside. The Estate, which is continually evolving, was landscaped in the 'Brownian' style during the 18th century, complete with a ha-ha. Earlier plantings are still in evidence, such as the ancient Lime Avenue dating from 1688 and the Wilderness with its myriad winding paths and open glades, also home to temples, bridges and follies. The large herbaceous border also along the North Drive is packed with interest from spring until late autumn and the woodland border offers exuberant displays of autumn colour. The path through the laburnum arcade leads into the formal Rose Garden which offers a feast of colour and fragrance all summer long. Pillars and rope swags frame the garden with a gazebo centrepiece providing a tranquil seating area. Carry on through the Rose Garden and you will discover a maze created from English yew.

Other features include rockeries, shrub borders and many fine specimen trees. The Father Tiber water garden, created in 2002, goes from strength to strength and offers a peaceful haven amongst ponds, rills, fountains and a water cascade.

The Hunting Lodge is part of the beautifully converted Georgian Mews adjacent to the black and white East Wing of Adlington Hall. The first floor banqueting suite is approached by a beautiful sweeping staircase (a lift is available if required). The hunting Lodge is an ideal venue for wedding receptions, banquets, conferences or indeed any social or business occasion. For more information please contact The Hunting Lodge on 01625 827595.

225

92 THE RISING SUN INN

Hawkins Lane, Rainow nr Macclesfield,
Cheshire SK10 5TI
Tel: 01625 424235
e-mail: risingsunrainow@myway.com

On the edge of the Peak District National Park at Rainow, is where you will find a charming old coaching inn known as **The Rising Sun**. Situated on the B5470, the road was once the haunt of highwaymen, but things are now peaceful and locals and visitors will arrive to enjoy the warm, genuine welcome and friendly hospitality on offer.

Attentive hosts Kathleen and Dickie are joined by Kathleen's sister Linda, who took over the licence in May 2007. You can expect to enjoy 3 real ales in the bar alongside a locally produced beer and a rotating guest ale.

Dickie, who has been a chef for over 40 years, persists on using only the best and freshest ingredients in his cooking and everything is homemade including the bread and all the desserts. Dishes such as scampi and sirloin steak are joined by dishes usually seen on restaurant menus, such as half lobster thermidor and braised oxtail served on a bed of linguine. There is a very affordable 2 course special menu that runs from Mon – Sat, and is well worth a try! Food is served from 12 – 2.30pm and 6pm – 9pm Tuesday – Saturday and 12 – 7pm on Sunday when three succulent roasts are the centrepiece of the popular carvery. And why not enjoy your meal in the newly built conservatory with views over the Cheshire countryside. Friday brings with it Quiz night, offering a bit of fun for everyone.

93 THE OLD KINGS HEAD

30 Bradley Smithy, Byrons Lane, Gurnett,
Macclesfield, Cheshire SK11 0HD
Tel: 01625 423890
e-mail: whothefox@hotmail.com

Set in the Hamlet of Gurnett, **The Old Kings Head** is a historic building dating back to 1695. A mere 12 months ago the property was a pigsty; however thanks to new tenant Marcus Lonyon the décor is now gorgeous. Good food such as leek and potato soup and a famous King's Head pie is served here as well as 3 real ales, which rotate regularly. This property is getting a great reputation for its food and it is worth visiting this beautiful pub close to Macclesfield canal.

94 THE HARRINGTON ARMS

Leek Road, Bosley, Macclesfield,
Cheshire SK11 0PH
Tel: 01260 223224

Situated adjacent to the main A523 at Bosley is **The Harrington Arms**. Customers are assured of a warm welcome by tenants, Jean and Stephen Andrews who have been here for the past five years. This charming inn is open all day Sat/Sun and every other session except Tues lunchtimes. Jean, in charge of the food side, prepares tasty, homecooked meals which are simply the best! The homemade pies are a firm favourite as are the delicious curries available on Monday evenings 5.30-8.30pm. Children are welcome and all major credit cards taken.

London Road, Alderley Edge,
Cheshire SK9 7JT
Tel: 01625 585548 Fax: 01625 585957
e-mail: enquiries@no15winebar.com
website: www.no15winebar.com

No. 15 Wine Bar is located in the heart of affluent Alderley Edge in Cheshire. This establishment is absolutely stunning. There is a small front entrance upon arrival, which leads you into this beautiful, top quality establishment with seating for 40 at ground level and a further 40 downstairs. There is also a rear courtyard surrounded by a walled garden and additional seating areas for another 40 visitors, making this wine bar larger than you would first expect from the façade.

The managers John and Janet have been here for 35 years and have produced a gem in the middle of Cheshire. The interior of the building is quaint and provincial and has a classic look about it, which will suit a number of different tastes. The two dining areas are bright and airy and both feature fireplaces, creating a great atmosphere in cool winter evenings. Head Chef Chris Davies has been here for 12 years and cooks wonderful food, which suits the surroundings.

Dishes such as goats cheese and fig tart, warm chicken and avocado salad, pork fillet with calvados cream, and apple and pheasant casserole grace the menu, as well as desserts of orange and Amaretto parfait and home-made ice cream.

This establishment is very successful and well known in the area and it is not difficult to see why. Located opposite the train station, No. 15 Wine Bar is the perfect place to go after a long day at work. The dishes served here are mouth watering and the wines are from all around the world. There is a choice of ever changing wines by the glass or bottle and these can be red, white or rosé from countries such as France, Italy, Argentina, Australia and South Africa - the list goes on.

Open Monday to Saturday from 10.30am for coffee, lunch is served from 12-2.30pm and evenings are from 6-10.30pm. It is best to book in advance on the weekends, in order to avoid disappointment. Please note that the wine bar is closed on Sundays, except for private parties, which can be arranged.

95 NETHER ALDERLEY MILL

Congleton Road, Nether Alderley,
Macclesfield, Cheshire SK10 4TW
Tel: 01625 584412
website: www.nationaltrust.org.uk or
www.midlandmillsopen.org.uk

With its heavy oak framework, low beams and floors connected by wooden ladders, set beneath an enormous sloping stone roof, this charmingly rustic mill is one of only four virtually complete corn mills in Cheshire. A fascinating and unusual watermill, dating from the 15th century. It has overshot tandem wheels and is powered by water from a lake, beside which the mill is built. The Victorian machinery was restored in the 1960s and is now in full working order, with regular flour-grinding demonstrations.

98 BLUEBERRIES

37 Buxton Road, High Lane,
Cheshire SK6 8DR
Tel: 01663 766900

Owned and run by proud owner Amanda Gilmore, **Blueberries** is a charming sandwich and coffee shop offering a delightful atmosphere and delicious cuisine. Amanda has created the business from scratch and offers only the finest food to keep her customers happy. Food is available to dine in for those wishing to enjoy the excellent décor or take away for those in a hurry. The list of fillings for paninis, jacket potatoes, toasties and sandwiches is endless and you're sure to find more than one favourite! She also does a hot roast carvery sandwich which has proved extremely popular and is well worth a try! Open Mon – Fri 8am – 3pm & Sat/Sun 9am – 3pm.

97 QUARRY BANK MILL & STYAL ESTATE

Styal, Cheshire SK9 4LA
Tel: 01625 527468
e-mail: quarrybankmill@ntrust.org.uk
website: www.quarrybankmill.org.uk

Quarry Bank Mill and Styal Estate once belonged to the wealthy Greg family who founded the Mill and gave the property to the National Trust. The water-powered Georgian mill still produces cotton calico, sold in the Mill Shop.

Hands-on exhibits and demonstrations show how traditional spinning and weaving was transformed through the ingenuity of early textile engineers. The most powerful working waterwheel in Europe and two mill engines help to bring the past to life through sight, sound and smell. At the Apprentice House you can discover what 'home life' was like for the pauper children who worked in the Mill in the 1830s by exploring the dormitories, kitchen, schoolroom, parlour and attic.

The adjoining garden contains traditional varieties of vegetables, fruit and herbs, as well as geese and hens. Visitors should allow at least 1.5 hours to visit the Mill. Guided tours of the House take about 45 minutes.

Styal Village was built by the Gregs to house the mill workers and is still a thriving community. There are two chapels, the school, allotment gardens and cottages. The village and the estate of farmland and woodland walks along the River Bollin provide a delightful contrast to the grandeur of the Mill.

228

99   THE RED LION INN

High Lane, Stockport, Cheshire SK6 8ED
Tel: 01663 765227

Situated adjacent to the main A6 at High Lane in Stockport is a Robinsons Brewery Pub of the highest standard. Offering impeccable service, freshly made food and well-kept ales, **The Red Lion Inn** is open all day everyday and is bound to leave you anticipating your next visit. Welcoming host Patrick Mulqueen used to be the head chef here before stepping into the role of general manager and making the most of his hospitable nature.

The bar offers 3 real ales; Unicorn, Hatters Mild and a seasonal brewery ale to enjoy, as well as a wide range of spirits, mixers, wines and soft drinks. The food here is marvellous and the menu offers something for every taste and budget. homemade soup of the day, Bury black pudding and homemade pâté on toasts with chilli tomato jam are a few of the starter options; bangers and mash, homemade beef lasagne, beef & Unicorn ale pie and rib eye steak propose a few ideas for mains with caramel apple Granny, choc fudge cake and trio of ice cream suggesting a perfect way to round off a meal.

The premises also boasts 6 well decorated en-suite letting rooms, each with the most needed necessities. The tariff includes a succulent breakfast. There is a large off road car park for visitors.

Stockport Rd, Romiley, nr Stockport,
Cheshire SK6 3AN
Tel: 0161 430 2806
e-mail: mail@dukeofyorkromiley.co.uk
website: www.dukeofyorkromiley.co.uk

Dating back to 1786, **The Duke of York** in Romiley is just 2 minutes walk from the Peak Forest Canal and just a few minutes walk away from the beautiful and historic Chadkirk Chapel. The Duke of York is in an ideal location for hungry and thirsty sightseers, and it certainly does a grand job catering for them. The building itself was originally built as a coaching inn, and the archway under which the coaches passed to the stables is still there. The interior is decorated in an 'olde world' style and helps to enhance the welcoming atmosphere offered by Jim and his dedicated staff. Jim certainly takes his beer seriously, on offer are no fewer than six real ales and a very popular real cider; Weston's Old Rosie. The ales consist of John Smiths, Sharp's Doombar, Bombardier, Deuchars IPA, Adnam's Explorer & a regularly changing 'guest' ale.

The pub's unique feature is the Mediterranean inspired restaurant, cunningly called The Mediterranean Restaurant, where the award winning chefs have taken inspiration from English, French, Italian, Spanish, Greek, Turkish and other world cuisines. Examples from the extensive menu include spicy Turkish sausages, stuffed aubergines, calamari, a mezze platter for 2, moussaka, and chilli king prawns. The popular fish menu sees halibut, seabass & swordfish cooked simply and served with lemon sauce and the chef's special chicken dish is cooked in a creamy walnut sauce. There is a whole host of lamb dishes, each cooked with reference to the cuisine style that inspired it; lamb kebabs, Pirzola, which is marinated lamb cutlets grilled to your liking, Orman kebab, which consists of lamb cubes with a selection of fresh vegetables, to name but a few. The variety continues into the starter and sweet menus and provides a unique dining experience that has won the Duke of York the accolade of Stockport's Pub of the Year 2007.

The Duke of York is also a popular entertainment venue, Monday nights sees the weekly quiz, with the winners being able to set the next week's questions and every Tuesday night Dave & Noel play New Orleans Jazz, often accompanied by various guests. The pub is open all day, every day and serves food during these hours; it is advisable to book for the weekends due to the popularity of the restaurant, especially in the summer, when al fresco dining is an option.

101 RING O' BELLS

130 Church Lane, Marple,
Cheshire SK6 7AY
Tel: 01614 272300
e-mail: enquiries@ring-o-bells.com
website: www.ring-o-bells.com

Situated just a short walk from the centre of Marple, alongside the Macclesfield Canal by Bridge No.2, is the welcoming hostelry **Ring o' Bells**. This warm and welcoming establishment has a wealth of history and was here long before the canal, with some parts of the inn dating back to the 1770's. During the late 1800's it was a busy and well patronised beer-house with many flocking to sample the food and drink including; Marple Botanical Society who held their annual 1872 Dinner Dance here for 30 members, a group of villagers who held a grand farewell party here before emigrating to America as well as many wedding parties who enjoyed celebratory meals after services held at All Saints Church.

Over the years The Ring o' Bells has seen many visitors pass over the threshold but it has never lost its appeal, in fact it continues to grow in popularity day by day thanks to friendly tenants Peter and Sue.

A popular venue with boaters, walkers and locals, the Ring o' Bells offers a superb menu and is bound to have you considering seconds! The à la carte menu is prepared fresh daily and has something for everyone. You can expect to see delicious dishes such as; Scottish smoked salmon, king prawns and spicy pork spare ribs to start, steak & kidney pie, pan fried butterfly chicken fillet, traditional cottage pie, boozy beef stew and game & guiness pie for mains with grilled salmon fillet, deep fried scampi, haddock in cripsy batter and Boatmans pie from the fish menu. There is also a succulent roast available everyday offering a choice of 1,2,3 or 4 meats accompanied by a selection of vegetables and potatoes or chips. A tasty large vegetarian selection is also available. For those who are looking to satisfy a smaller appetite, there is a snack and light bite menu offering sandwiches, baguettes, burgers, chips and salads. To help your meal go down why not try one of 3 real ales from the Robinsons Brewery.

Food is served Tuesday – Saturday 12 – 2pm, Tuesday & Thursday 5.30pm – 8pm Friday & Saturday 5.30pm – 8.30pm and Sunday 12 – 7pm.

As well as a sports room to keep the 'Big Kids' entertained, there is also a room decorated with the canal's history and bygone memorabilia for all to admire and reminisce. There is a charity quiz night held every Wednesday and all are welcome to join in the fun from 9pm onwards. There is a large off road carpark and all major credit and debit cards are accepted for transactions over £10.

102 THE HARE & HOUNDS

19 Mill Brow, Marple Bridge, Stockport,
Cheshire SK6 5LW
Tel: 0161 427 4042

Guy Marsh took **The Hare & Hounds** over in 2007 and describes the pub as a 'hidden gem in the beautiful hamlet of Mill Brow, a genuine village community in a great rural setting'. Built on a piece of land bought from Baron Howard of Glossop in 1805, it was known as The Board in the early days, before converting to the modern Hare & Hounds in 1842. The location of the pub makes it very popular amongst walkers and other nature lovers as well as locals and visitors recommended by word of mouth.

The pub has been refurbished recently 'back' to a country pub, the roaring fire adding to the warm and welcoming atmosphere offered to all those who want to enjoy a great pint; Unicorn, Hatters Mild & Dizzy Blonde are the regular real ales. For those who appreciate fine food, the chef has created an excellent menu that is traditional with a twist and which includes the best of local produce from local suppliers. Even though the food is of a very high standard, Guy is keen to stress that the Hare & Hounds is a pub rather than a restaurant and in that vein welcomes well-behaved children and dogs. A hidden gem that is well worth visiting!

103 THE ODDFELLOWS ARMS

73 Moor End Rd, Mellor,
Cheshire SK6 5PT
Tel: 01614 497 826

The Oddfellows Arms' curious name is said to have originated from the Oddfellows Society, the starting point for trade union movements, who used meet here in the 1860's. The exterior sets the mood for the visit; well kept, with hanging baskets providing splashes of colour, and inside, while the atmosphere is warm and welcoming, the décor is smart and modern. The premises were recently taken over by Richard Kitchingman and head chef Adam Stanyer, both of whom worked in the restaurant previously, and while the name may not have changed, the menu, food and style definitely has.

While other restaurants may offer a more extensive menu, The Oddfellows Arms' restaurant now has a carefully chosen menu, utilising the finest of local produce and paying attention what is in season. The Oddfellows Arms is open every day, except Mondays and serves food for every session as well as all day Saturday and Sunday.

The three floors of the property lends itself to catering for functions, and it is possible for a whole host of events to be catered for; including civil partnerships, celebrations, christenings, birthdays and any exclusive event for up to 40 persons.

104 THE GLOBE HOTEL

Globe Square, Dukinfield,
Cheshire SK16 4RF
Tel: 01613 305 561
e-mail: globe-hotel@btconnect.com

This top notch hotel is situated in Globe Square in Dukinfield, close by Bridge no. 2 on the Ashton canal, part of the Cheshire ring. Dating back to the early 18th century, **The Globe Hotel** has been run by Nigel & Jill for 2½ years now and one has only to look at the rave reviews given to the hotel by past guests to realise that it is not a place to be missed.

There are five comfortable, en-suite rooms available on a room only basis and for visitors in the Dukinfield area, this hotel should the first port of call. The Globe Hotel is very popular for its food, two professional chefs use the finest of local produce to create a menu that offers classic pub fayre, cooked with quality ingredients, fresh to order.

The favourite dishes are the Sunday roast dinners, the succulent steaks, homemade pies and liver & onions. Food is served every lunch and evening session, for more information contact the pub.

The weekly Thursday night quiz is very well attended and all are welcome, there are disabled facilities but all the rooms are upstairs.

105 THE BUSH INN

278 Market Street, Hyde,
Cheshire SK14 1HD
Tel: 01613 665 525
e-mail: geordiegran@hotmail.com

The **Bush Inn** is located on Market Street, one of Hyde's major roads and just two minutes from the centre of the town. The premises date in parts to the early 19th century and the property has in the past been a Butcher's, an Abattoir and even a Morgue. The establishment is now more involved with the living and since Sandra & Matt took over in September 2007, the business is flying.

The premises is undergoing a few changes; a new menu is being created, cooked by Sandra using good, local produce and there is a new beer garden, complete with children's play area which only enhances the pub's family feel.

The pub is open every season and all day Saturday & Sundays. Robinson's Unicorn is the ale of choice here but Carling Extra Cold and Robinson's Smooth are equally popular.

The pub is a very good place for entertainment; Friday and Saturday nights host a whole range of live music from acts such as bands, duo's and soloists between 9pm – 1am. The pub has a private car park and there are disabled facilities.

233

106 THE WOODLEY ARMS

85 Woodley Precinct, Hyde Road, Woodley,
Stockport Cheshire SK6 1RJ
Tel: 0161 4 304 143
website: www.woodleyarms.co.uk

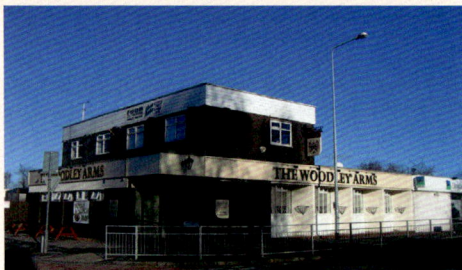

The Woodley Arms at Woodley is only a short drive from Junction 25 of the M60 and it is well worth making the detour. Keith and Liz have been running this charming pub for 2½ years now and have managed to create a warm and welcoming pub that serves decent food and provides a good time with it. The interior looks as though a lot of money has been spent on it. The unusual brass topped bar looks as though it's seen a lot of elbows over the years.

The menu features classic pub fayre, cooked very well by professional chefs. Apart from Tuesdays, when no food is available, food is served between 10am and 4pm every day. Sundays are popular for the fabulous Sunday roasts on offer, and the weekly curry night with a ½ price drink is very well attended.

The pub is a popular venue; Thursday nights see karaoke from 8.30pm, a DJ plays from 8pm – 1am on Friday nights and 3 Saturdays a month there is a DJ playing 60's, 70's and 80's style music, the remaining Saturday features a live band.

107 THE PLOUGH INN

Beauty Bank, Whitegate, Northwich,
Cheshire CW8 2BP
Tel: 01606 889 455
e-mail: info@ploughwhitegate.com
website: www.ploughwhitegate.com

David Hughes, the tenant of **The Plough Inn** since 1996, runs a real gem of a pub - a genuine "Hidden Place" tucked away down in the tiny hamlet of Foxwist Green near Whitegate. The setting, among fields, is serene and attractive, and the inn's two bars are full of charm and character.

There are many reasons for seeking out this delightful place, the main one being the superb food cooked by four chefs (and occasionally David himself) and served in generous helpings at very reasonable prices. The quality and choice are quite outstanding, whether it's a quick snack or a 3 course meal. The regular menu of sandwiches, salads, jacket potatoes and a dozen classic daily courses is supplemented by the longest daily specials list you'll ever see, with inspiration drawn from around the world. The inspiration may be worldwide, but the beef is all British and David is a great supporter of British farming. Real ales and a long list of well chosen wines accompany this splendid fayre.

A particularly nice touch is the regularly produced pub newsletter, which feature local news and gives a real insight into the friendliness of the area.

234

108 MARBURY COUNTRY PARK

Comberbach, Northwich,
Cheshire CW9 6AT
Tel: 01606 77741

Marbury Country Park was once part of a large country estate whose history dates back to around AD1200. Marbury itself means a fortified or stockaded dwelling by the mere or water. The first family took the name Marbury and lived there until 1684. When the last male heir died the estate was bought by Richard Earl Rivers who never lived there. On his death in 1714 it was bought by his son-in-law James, the 4th Earl of Barrymore. It was the Barry family who shaped the park with extensive landscaping and the building of the hall.

A succession of owners and uses then followed, culminating in the hall being demolished in 1968 due to rot. In 1975, 196 acres was leased from the owners, ICI, by Cheshire County Council and restoration work was begun. Further land was later aquired and today it is managed by the Countryside Management Service to benefit wildlife and visitors.

Each habitat is carefully managed to encourage different plants and animals, so there is always plenty to see at all times of the year. In spring the woodland is covered by a spectacular carpet of wildflowers and willow warblers, chiffchaffs and blackcaps herald the arival of summer. Autumn shows the colours of the trees off to their best and in winter, the Mere becomes a focus for many birds including goldeneye and greylag geese.

Guided walks and activities in and around the park are organised throughout the year.

109 THE MAYPOLE INN

Hilltop Road, Acton Bridge, nr Northwich,
Cheshire CW8 3RA
Tel: 01606 853114

Acton Bridge, a small village with old farmsteads and cottages on a picturesque section of the River Weaver, is where you will find an accommodating inn. **The Maypole Inn** has been serving fine ales since the mid 18th century and has been growing in popularity ever since with both the agricultural and local rural communities alike. And it is hardly surprising either, its low beamed ceilings and open log fires make it a wonderfully cosy place to enjoy a meal or a drink.

The comprehensive menu offers something for everyone with starters ranging from homemade soup of the day and black pudding with mustard sauce to Icelandic prawns & mushrooms and homemade pâté with toast. The mains are equally as temping and you can enjoy dishes such as gammon steaks, lamb cutlets, homemade steak pie, lasagne verdi or a traditional roast with chicken, lamb, beef or pork to choose from. And the desserts deserve a mention too but you'll have to pop in to see what treats are on offer as they vary from day to day. For those with a smaller appetite or not much time, there is a snack menu serving jacket potatoes, sandwiches, toasted sandwiches and country platters. Food is served 7 days a week, Monday – Friday 12noon – 2pm & 6pm – 9pm, Saturday 12noon-2pm & 6pm – 9.30pm and Sunday 12noon – 2.30pm & 6pm – 9pm. Whether its a lunchtime snack or evening drink The Maypole will be able to accommodate.

235

110 THE HAZEL PEAR INN

I Hill Top Road, Acton bridge, Northwich,
Cheshire CW8 3RA
Tel: 01606 853195
e-mail: postmaster@hazelpear.plus.com

Quality food, attentive staff and astounding food can all be found at **The Hazel Pear Inn**. Located in the village of Acton Bridge, The Hazel Pear offers something for everyone. The inn, formerly a farmhouse, dates back to the mid 18th century and became a licensed inn some years later when it was called The Station Hotel. The name was then changed to the apt 'Hazel Pear' in the 1970's when there were a large number of pear trees surrounding the inn.

Friendly and experienced hosts Mike and Sue are joined by their sons Jack and Nick, and each pull together to create a hard-working family team. The food here is superb, and with Sue in charge of the cooking you can be assured of some mouth-watering dishes. She persists in using only the freshest produce, the majority being sourced locally. You can expect to see favourites such as chef's homemade soup of the day with crusty bread, shank of lamb wrapped in shortcrust pastry served with minted gravy and the house special Hazel Pear mixed grill with potatoes. The desserts are something to look forward to as well with jam sponge, sorbet and hot chocolate fudge cake to name but a few. Food is served 12 – 2pm & 5.30pm – 9pm (Mon – Sat) & 12 – 8.30pm (Sun & Bank Holidays). If it's something to quench your thirst, then you can sample up to 4 real ales as well as a wide selection of wines and soft drinks.

To the rear there is a small registered animal park including goats, pigs, barn owls, rabbits, ducks and chicken. Children can enjoy feeding them with animal feed provided. Dogs are also welcome and there is a separate dog run for them too.

112 THE BIRCH & BOTTLE

Northwich Rd, Higher Whitley,
Cheshire WA4 4PH
Tel: 01925 730 225

Dorothy and Stephen Rothwell have been running the **Birch & Bottle** for 10 years now and in that time they have raised the pub's reputation to that of a pub known for well kept real ales and fine food. This traditional inn, with just a small conservatory added has managed to retain its warm and welcoming character with the traditional décor inside. The friendly atmosphere, on entry, complements the amply stocked bar and delicious menu. There are two real ales to enjoy; Greene King IPA and Old Speckled Hen and food is available 12pm – 2pm & 6pm – 9pm from Monday to Saturday and between 12pm – 9pm on Sundays.

You can dine throughout the premises; however it is especially popular in the little conservatory. The menu is extensive; including a variety of pub favorites, light bites and vegetarian meals. The pub favourites range from juicy steaks to battered fish and chips, light bites offer salads, jacket potatoes and sandwiches; featuring the famous Birch Butty, a huge baguette filled with hot beef. A popular deal is the senior citizens special which offers 3 courses for just £6.25, available every lunch and evening except Sat eve and Sun lunch.

111 CHETWODE ARMS

Lower Whitley, Warrington,
Cheshire WA4 4EN
Tel: 01925 730 203
e-mail: info@chetwodearms.com
website: www.chetwodearms.com

Originally a small farmhouse built over 400 years ago, then converted to a road-side coaching inn, the **Chetwode Arms** has been a pub for the last century. It certainly has its share of history, there is a friendly ghost and there is rumoured to be a tunnel leading from the pub to the nearby church.

Now the Chetwode Arms is a Grade II listed building situated in the conservation area of Lower Whitley. Claudia & Richard have run the Chetwode Arms for 4 years now and this splendid looking pub has a fine reputation for great food and a warm and friendly atmosphere. This old brick built country inn is full of character inside and out and boasts one of the finest bowls greens in Cheshire.

The defining feature of the Chetwode Arms however is its restaurant, of which Claudia is the head chef and has contributed to its unique style of food service. The 'Hot Rock Grill' involves heating a piece of volcanic granite to 440°C, placing it on a special grill and then leaving it at your table with your choice of meat to cook, and what a choice of meat! The Carnivore medley consists of venison, Goosnargh duck breast and prime English fillet steak. The Safari Rock features prime English fillet steak, ostrich fillet steak and springbok steak. The Crocodile Rock has an English fillet steak and a crocodile steak!

For those special occasions, the caviar menu is a must, featuring a variety of types of caviar, with a handy introduction to each. Equally special, are the daily specials, created using the best of local produce, examples include game pie, which features rabbit, duck, venison and pigeon breast, Hungarian Gulasch with dumplings and Pasta Nonna; pasta in a creamy sauce of pernod, chilli and garlic, this is not for the faint hearted!

As the informative website states: "This spacious Cheshire brick built pub has everything a village pub should have: a charming village location, a garden for al fresco summertime dining, cask marque award winning real ales, good array of wines, warming log fire and the luxury of being able to dine at candle lit tables." It is advised that reservations are made to dine here in order to avoid disappointment. Food is available between 12pm – 2.30pm & 6pm – 9pm all week long, children are welcome during the day and there are full disabled facilities.

237

113 THE RING O' BELLS

Northwich Road, Lower Stretton,
Cheshire WA4 4NZ
Tel: 01925 730556 Fax: 01925 730556

Located in the delightful village of Lower Stretton, is **The Ring O' Bells**, a true old fashioned pub. Welcoming hosts John and Sharlene make sure that every visitor leaves satisfied. The inn serves a selection of beverages including 3 real ales, Tetleys & London Pride the regulars with one ever rotating guest ale. There is a music night once a month on a Tuesday evening from 9pm which is very popular. There is a quiz night the first and third Monday of the month and boules in the summer months for 'Big Kids'. Open Mon 5.30pm-close, Tues & Wed 12-2.30pm & 5.30pm–close, Thurs/Fri 12–3pm & 5.30pm – close, Sat 12–2.30pm & 7pm–close and Sun 12–4pm & 7pm–close.

Looking for:
- *Places to Visit?*
- *Places to Stay?*
- *Places to Eat & Drink?*
- *Places to Shop?*

COUNTRY LIVING MAGAZINE RURAL GUIDES

HIDDEN INNS

HIDDEN PLACES

COUNTRY Pubs & Inns

off the motorway 3rd edition

www.travelpublishing.co.uk

114 ARLEY HALL GARDENS

nr Northwich, Cheshire CW9 6NA
Tel: 01565 777353
website: www.arleyhallandgardens.com

Amongst the finest in Britain and Europe **Arley Hall Gardens** have been created over the last 250 years by successive generations of the same family and thus offer an unusual blend of long history and traditional design with inspired modern ideas and additions. The result is a garden rich in atmosphere, interest and vitality – a wonderful example of the idea that the best gardens are living, changing works of art.

Within its eight acres of formal gardens, southwest of the house, are many different areas, each with its own distinctive character, and on the northeast side of the house, beyond the Chapel is the Grove, a well established arboretum and woodland garden of about 6 or 7 acres. You will see at Arley a huge range of different plants of all kinds, making it a treasure trove both for the keen plantsman and for the less specialised visitor.

115 THE SLOW AND EASY

Manchester Road, Lostock Gralam,
nr Northwich, Cheshire CW9 7PJ
Tel: 01606 42148
e-mail: excelsounds@aol.com
website: www.theslowandeasy.com or
www.theslowandeasyhotel.com

The charming village of Lostock Gralam, two miles east of Northwich where the A559 meets the A556, is where you will find **The Slow & Easy**, a welcoming pub offering impeccable service and mouth-watering fare. Relaxation is the name of the game here, but the wonderful easy-going ambience has been achieved by the hard work of affable leaseholders Tony and Maria Bessant.

Open every lunchtime and evening and all day at weekends, the pub serves two real ales with Greene King IPA being the locals favourite, and a large selection of hearty dishes such as half chicken, minted lamb shank, meat and potato pie, lasagne verdi, mixed grill, gammon steak, breaded plaice, beef madras and a selection of vegetarian options.

The pub is very much at the social heart of the local community and there is plenty to keep the locals entertained with entertainment held on most evenings of the week. Monday is bingo night, poker is on Tuesday, Jamming Session on Thursday, Friday offers the best time to sing your heart out with Karaoke and Saturday keeps your mind ticking over with a weekly quiz. And there's never any shortage of convivial chat at the well themed open plan bar with old wooden beam type décor. For those who enjoy a game of bowls, the pub's superb bowling green can be used by non-members of the bowling club when there is no match.

The Slow and Easy, which takes its name from a racehorse owned in the 19th century by a prominent local landowner, is well placed for both leisure and tourist visitors, the pub has eight excellent bedrooms each with their own en-suite. Available all year round for bed and breakfast guests, the rooms offer a great place to stopover.

If you are looking to enjoy a chilled real ale in a relaxed and friendly atmosphere, then The Slow and Easy will not disappoint you.

239

116 MILL POOL RESTAURANT

Oulton Mill Lane, Little Budworth,
nr Tarporley, Cheshire CW6 9BE
Tel: 01829 760 444
website: www.millpoolrestaurant.co.uk

The **Mill Pool Restaurant** has the distinction of being one of the finest restaurants in Cheshire, situated next to the old mill pool at the edge of the village of Little Budworth and just a short walk from the famous Oulton Park racing circuit.

Partners Tony and Paul have owned the restaurant for 20 years now and have seen the place grow from strength to strength as word got out about this wonderful establishment. The building, finished in white and slate, looks spectacular and the views surrounding the premises are outstanding. Inside it is more of the same, stylish tables and chairs offer space and comfort and the large windows allow amazing views out as well as lots of light in.

The Mill Pool has a remarkably simple pricing structure, on Saturday evenings, two courses cost £13.50 and three courses are just £16.50, some dishes require a small additional cost and during the week the prices drop, offering tremendous value for money. The food is classed as traditional international cuisine, utilising the best of local produce. Highlights include the Indonesian lamb, pan fried lambs liver and a sumptuous fish pie. Food is served all week long, but to avoid disappointment, reservations are required.

118 THE BOOT INN

Boothsdale, Willington,
Cheshire CW6 0NH
Tel: 01829 751375

Situated in the pretty hamlet of Boothsdale, is where you will discover a warm and welcoming hostelry known as **The Boot Inn**. Upon entering, you will be overwhelmed by the outstanding hospitality, relaxed atmosphere and friendly staff. Licensee Mike Gollings has years of experience in the trade and this is clearly visible. He has been improving on the service and food offered on a regular basis, attracting new clientele as well as keeping the loyal visitors happy also.

The menu offers a varied range of starters, mains, salads, sandwiches, baguettes and desserts. Warm smoked salmon and pan fried lambs kidneys are popular choices from the starter selection, plump Cumberland sausage and steak and ale pie are the traditional favourites and the wide selection of desserts and Cheshire Farm dairy ice-cream offers something to satisfy a 'sweet tooth'.

There is also a daily specials board if you can't find what you are looking for on the main menu.

The well stocked bar offers 4 real ales – two of which come from the local Weetwood Brewery and the other two are guest ales which rotate on a regular basis.

The Boot Inn is open Monday – Sunday 10am - late, everyday of the year except Christmas day. A trip to the Boot Inn will not disappoint.

117 THE RED LION

Vicarage Lane, Little Budworth,
Cheshire CW6 9BY
Tel: 01829 760 275

The Red Lion has served the thirsty public since 1797 and even today the pub manages to provide great food and drink under the management of Julie, now at the pub for 4 years. The Red Lion has proved to be a very popular place indeed. Located next to the parish church in the picturesque village of Little Budworth, there is more to this pretty hamlet than meets the eye. Close-by is Oulton Park motor racing circuit, which has seen some of the greats of the motor racing scene and is still the host of the Formula 3 and British Touring Car Championship races.

With the help of a professional chef, the Red Lion enjoys a reputation for its traditional, freshly prepared food with a well-stocked menu that offers all the pub favourites along with the ability to cater for large parties. Typifying the menu are solid favourites such as; battered cod and chips, steak and ale pie and rump steak. Slightly more extravagant offerings include a trio of lamb chops with mint gravy and the fillet of salmon in a cream and white wine sauce. There are also several choices of starter and a delicious roast is added to the menu on Sundays. Locals and visitors alike rave about the food, and with the meat coming from the local butcher and the vegetables coming from just over the border in Wales, it is clear that Julie makes the effort to use fresh and local produce. The bar is well stocked; with well-kept real ales, such as Robinson's Unicorn, and with an open coal fire in the winter or a secluded beer garden during the summer, there is no shortage of places to enjoy a nice pint.

The pub also has three rooms available. The rooms are all en-suite and there is a choice of a double, twin and a family room. With a super breakfast included in the tariff the accommodation is very popular, particularly during race days. This is a very lively pub, which supports no less than three bowls teams and it has its own bowling green as well. There is also a popular quiz night held on the first Tuesday of every month. Children are very welcome and there are facilities for disabled customers, it is advisable to make reservations to eat on Fridays and Sundays to avoid disappointment.

241

119 THE SHADY OAK

Bates Mill Lane, Toverton, Tarporley,
Cheshire CW6 9UE
Tel: 01829 730718
website: www.theshadyoak.co.uk

The scenic village of Tiverton is home to the Shropshire Union Canal and the popular Sandstone trail. Very close to the canal is **The Shady Oak**, a delightful inn offering a tempting array of freshly prepared food and two ever rotating real ales.

Welcoming hosts Alun and David have years of experience in the trade and have given this village pub a new lease of life.

Local chefs prepare a tasty menu, ranging from traditional meals such as beer battered fish and chips with mushy peas and trio of game sausage with Cheddar cheese mash to delicious desserts such as seasonal fruit crumble with custard and chocolate fudge cake with fresh pouring cream. The food is served Monday – Saturday 12 until 9pm and Sunday 12 until 8pm. As the food is a popular choice here, it is advisable to book and is essential on Friday and Saturday evenings and Sunday lunchtimes.

There is entertainment provided on the last Friday of each month with 'Folk Night' from 8.30pm and this is a huge hit with visitors and locals alike. Children and dogs are welcome and all major credits cards are taken.

121 THE TRAVELLERS REST

443 Newton Road, Lowton,
Cheshire WA3 1NZ
Tel: 01925 224391

Dating back to the early 19th century, **The Travellers Rest** is a friendly inn resting peacefully on the outskirts of Lowton, just a short drive from junction 22 of the M6 off the A579.

Welcoming host Chris Pole took over the license in 2008 and was joined by head chef Chris Dougan 2 months later. He wasted no time in putting his stamp on the place, and has brought a lease of new life to the former coaching inn. The bar serves a wide range of beers, spirits, mixers and soft drinks

Chris makes sure that his quality menu offers something for everyone and with dishes such as game terrine, pork and tomato sausages with onion mash & Cheshire tomato chutney, skate wing with citrus mash & local seasonal vegetables and duck breast with grilled potato cake it comes as no surprise that the hostelry has a loyal following. Chris is also introducing a more detailed menu using only organic produce, a lot of which will be sourced from local farms helping to support the local economy. Booking is highly recommended to avoid disappointment.

The restaurant seats up to 65 people and is perfect for family get-togethers. There is a superb rear garden where you can enjoy a drink or meal in the warmer months and a large off-road car park assures a safe spot to leave your vehicle.

242

94 Battersby Lane, Warrington,
Cheshire WA2 7EG
Tel: 01925 231820
e-mail: yates.g@hotmail.com
website: www.albionales.com

The Albion Freehouse is without doubt becoming the best place to enjoy wholesome food, real ales and superb hospitality in the Warrington area. It is located just a short walk from the bustling town centre on Battersby Lane, close to the Cockhedge Centre. This fabulous freehouse has been under the management of Gillian, Mark and Kevin Yates since December 2007 during which time they have been slowly refurbishing this grand place and are now nearing completion.

The newly lit courtyard is perfect for the warmer months and includes a sheltered smokers area.

They offer an ever changing range of beers, sourced mainly from micros and local breweries but with a few well known favourites too. There are usually four to six cask ales and a 'real' cider on draught as well as a wide range of bottled beers and five continental draughts to choose from. In the adjacent Coach House, Mark has installed his own micro-brewery and will be producing his own Albion Ales by Easter 2009.

A wide range of delicious homecooked food is available on the various menus with further choices on the specials board. All the food is freshly prepared and cooked on the premises by experienced chef Debbie. Local butchers supply all the meat and all the vegetables are from farms within the area. Favourites on the regular menu include homemade steak and ale pie made with real ale from the bar, tangy beef and tomato lasagne served with garlic bread or a crusty roll and a juicy 10oz rump steak with onion rings and grilled tomato, served with real chips or jacket potato, peas, carrots and salad garnish. The Albion Almighty Breakfast is available on the Saturday menu. It is fantastic value for money and should satisfy anybody's hunger pains! Lighter choices include homemade pizzas, burgers and a choice of fresh crispy salads, all at reasonable prices. Food is served Mon-Thurs 12-2pm and 5-8pm and Fri 12-8pm. All Day Breakfast menu is served on Saturdays 10am-5pm while Sunday Lunch Menu is served Sundays 12-5pm.

Entertainment is offered on Saturday evenings from 9pm. A special feature of The Albion are the regular Laurel and Hardy nights, held the first Wednesday of each month from 7.30pm where customers can enjoy classic Laurel and Hardy films. Children and pets are welcome until 5pm and all major credit cards are taken.

243

122 THE HORSESHOE INN

Smithy lane, Croft, nr Warrington,
Cheshire WA3 7HQ
Tel: 01925 764 464

Charles & Elizabeth have run the **Horseshoe Inn** for 20 years now and in that time the inn has been transformed into the hub of the quaint village of Croft. The décor inside is 'Olde World', full of

antiques and pieces of interest to create a warm and welcoming atmosphere. The pub is open all day every day and the bar hosts a wide selection, including two rotating guest ales.

Charles is a professional chef and the locals are fond of saying that his culinary skills cannot be bested! The menu is an eclectic mix, featuring the best of traditional pub fayre with some more exotic options; flying the flag for traditional pub grub for

example are the home made steak & ale pie and liver & bacon with mash and onion gravy. The more exotic choices include Moroccan style lamb casserole and tomato, red onion and basil bruscetta on a herb salad. Needless to say, the food, made with the very best of local produce, is massive draw for custom and at the weekends it can be necessary to book in order to avoid disappointment. Food is served every lunchtime and most evenings.

123 COMFORTABLE GILL INN

458 Warrington Rd, Glazebury,
Cheshire WA3 5NX
Tel: 01942 677 742

The **Comfortable Gill Inn** has the distinction of being one of only two pubs in England with the same name, the name originating from it being a comfy place to relax and that a Gill is an old name for a quarter of a pint. The village of Glazebury is a picturesque place near the town of Warrington and it is in the heart of this village that the Comfortable Gill Inn can be found; offering bed & breakfast, good home cooked food and well kept ales.

Victor has been the proprietor for 4½ years now and together with his dedicated staff; this 200 year old inn has developed a very good reputation. The well stocked bar serves two real ales; Timothy Taylor Landlord and the concisely named Copper Dragon Black Gold Mild! Food is available between 12pm – 7pm daily and the best of local produce is used to create wonderful home cooked food, including the very popular curries. B&B is available all year round. There are three comfortable twin rooms, all decorated and furnished to a high standard. The inn is a great venue; every other Friday is a well attended karaoke and there is pub quiz held every Tuesday evening.

124 THE RAMS HEAD

Church Lane, Grappenhall,
Cheshire WA4 3EP
Tel: 01925 262814
e-mail: main@ramshead-inn.co.uk
website: www.ramshead-inn.co.uk

Standing in Grappenhall, one of Cheshires most picturesque villages is **The Rams Head** inn. Dating from 1893, it is listed as being of architectural and historical importance to the village. Surrounded by cobbled streets, a historic church and the Bridgewater canal, the inn is the perfect place to indulge in a meal before exploring what the local area has to offer.

Welcoming host Graham Stewart is the brains behind the business, and has recently gone about refurbishing the inn to an extremely high standard. One of the many unique features that Graham has restored is the original village well, situated near the bar. The well actually pre-dates the existing building at about 150 years old, but is now fitted with walkover glass and is illuminated from the inside.

Graham makes sure that there is a dish & tipple for everyone and the menu is sure to entice you back again and again. Chicken liver parfait with onion marmalade & wholemeal bread and king prawn & roast garlic skewers with leaves & chilli are just a selection from the starters, Slow braised lamb basted with mint sauce served with fondant potato & fresh vegetables and steak & ale pie with fresh market vegetables are just two choices from the main courses. And that's not all; there is a huge selection of side orders, light bites and appetisers for two. With such a mouth-watering menu, it is advisable to book during the week and essential at weekends. Food is served 12 - 9pm Monday to Thursday, 12 - 9.30pm Friday and Saturday and 12 - 8pm on Sundays.

To help your meal go down, why not try one of 6 real ales, with Spitfire, Deuchars IPA, Cumberland Ale and Marstons Pedigree being the regulars as well as two guest ales.

The Rams Head also boasts 3 super en-suite bedrooms located upstairs. Each room has been fitted with the aa essentials and the tariff includes a freshly prepared hearty breakfast.

Every Monday brings with it curry night. This is hugely popular with the locals and is exceptional value for money - you can choose from a selection of freshly prepared curries served with naan bread and chips or rice from just £4.00. Available from 5pm.

The Rams Head Inn has large outdoor areas, and with its unique location, is especially popular with walkers who can enjoy the nearby Bridgewater Canal. Well-behaved dogs are welcome in the bar area.

245

Hatton Lane, Hatton, Warrington,
Cheshire WA4 4DB
Tel: 01925 730 314
e-mail: tables@hatton-arms.co.uk or
rooms@hatton-arms.co.uk
website: www.hatton-arms.co.uk

It is well known that the **Hatton Arms** has always been the heart of the picturesque village of Hatton since the early 18th century when the original building was constructed. The main building has been extended over the years, incorporating the village post office and adjoining cottage but has managed to retain the charm and cosiness befitting a country inn. John & Marusia took over the Hatton Arms in May 2008 and together with the head chef David and bar manager Ian; they have certainly given the place a new lease of life that is gaining wonderful reviews from the locals and visitors alike.

For the traveller, there are three en-suite rooms; all doubles with internet access and digital televisions for entertainment. The rooms are all tastefully decorated and comfortably furnished to give a feeling of a home away from home. The tasteful decoration continues as a theme throughout the inn, the cosy bar boasts traditional beamed walls and ceilings, warming fires feature prominently and there is no shortage of places to sit. As if that wasn't enough, the garden is a big attraction; space for diners, drinkers and even for tethering horses.

John and Marusia are very proud of the food at the Hatton Arms; the newly refurbished restaurant and kitchen produces an interesting menu featuring some unusual dishes. All of the dishes are British but because they have been researched from traditional and often forgotten methods, they may not be familiar to most. For example, the Devilled lambs kidney on toast, pan fried fillet of sea bream with samphire, surf clams, squid & smoked bacon and braised Gloucester Old Spot pork belly with crackling, black pudding & creamed mash. The sweet menu is tantalisingly different as well; Lancashire bomb cheese with eccles cake and iced peanut butter parfait with spiced biscuits and banana. The Hatton Arms' restaurant, known as the Hunter's Restaurant prides itself on a policy of 'if it's produced locally we will buy it locally, if it's not then we will buy the best we can' and the quality of the food really shines through. The restaurant is open from Tuesday to Saturday from midday to 2.30pm and from 6.30pm until 9.30pm and on Sundays between 12pm and 2.30pm, when delicious Sunday roasts are also available.

The community spirit of the inn really shines through in the new 'To the Hatton and back' service whereby diners who live within five miles of the pub can be collected from home and returned afterwards.

Runcorn Rd, Moore, Cheshire WA4 6UD
Tel: **01925 740 205**
e-mail: enquiries@theredlionmoore.co.uk
website: www.theredlionmoore.co.uk

The **Red Lion** at Moore has featured in the annals of Hidden Places, but a lot has changed since their previous entry in 2001; Paul & Kealy took over here 4 years ago and a major internal refurbishment have transformed this lovely pub into a first class dining and entertainment venue. Moore is a village steeped in history, a number of the magnificent old buildings are Grade II listed and the 300 year old Red Lion's exterior certainly fits in, well kept hanging baskets offer a splash of colour and the whole building looks fresh and clean. Inside, the major refurbishment has created an old fashioned style with all the modern comforts necessary, the lovely old fireplaces are packed with old memorabilia and there are lots of candles, which create a warming atmosphere.

The bar is well stocked, hosting a minimum of three rotating guest ales and large selection of wine, champagne and spirits.

The Red Lion has just released a new menu and along with it, some great offers; 2 main meals for £14, two courses for £10 and three courses for £13. The highly experienced chefs have used the finest of local ingredients to create a menu that is packed full of pub favourites cooked to a high standard. The starter menu mixes classics with more exotic fayre; creamy garlic mushrooms, classic prawn cocktail & a farmhouse vegetable soup with lamb croquettes and Thai fishcakes. The main menu offers a great selection, there is a choice of homemade pies and curries offered daily, as well as traditional Toad in the Hole, braised lamb shank & the Red Lion burger to name just a few. And if they weren't enough, there is also the grill to choose from; rump steak, gammon steak, T-bone and for the brave, the mixed grill, featuring gammon, pork, rump steak, sausage, lamb cutlets and fried eggs! The sweets are updated daily depending on whatever is fresh and you are well advised to sample them. Food is available all day long, all week long; however, it is advisable to book at the weekend to avoid disappointment.

The Red Lion is a very popular entertainment venue, in the run up to Christmas 2008; Tina Turner, Tom Jones and Barry Manilow are all performing live! For information about entertainment and themed evenings, see the website.

163 Chester Road, Helsby, Frodsham,
Cheshire WA6 0AU
Tel: 01928 722 639

The **Robin Hood Hotel** is located in a prime position, on the road between Frodsham and Chester, in the village of Helsby. Leaseholder Jason has run the Robin Hood Hotel since September 2008, but he has 12 years experience in the trade and it shines through when you enter the warm and welcoming bar. Wooden floors, nice long, well stocked bar and comfortable stools set the tone for a great visit. This is definitely a good pub for sports fans; the Robin Hood Hotel features a games room with a pool table, dart board and a full size snooker table. Big screen televisions provide Sky and Setanta sports all over the pub.

The hotel consists of 10 fully furnished, en-suite rooms in a mixture of sizes; singles, twins and doubles. The rooms are reasonably priced, including a breakfast and are extremely comfortable.

The bar holds a good selection of beers, including three real ales; Marstons, Burton Bitter and a rotating guest ale.

Food is currently available between 5pm and 9pm every evening, however there are plans afoot to provide food at lunchtime between 12pm and 2pm. The specials menu is written up every day on a blackboard and the main printed menu features references to the pub's name, eg. The Nottingham Shepherds Pie, whatever you choose though, you are guaranteed a superb meal cooked using the best of local produce.

The pub is a very popular venue, offering a whole host of activities on different nights; Monday night is Poker night, people of all levels are more than welcome, Wednesday night is the pub quiz, Friday night brings a disco and karaoke and there is a live band playing on Saturday nights. The pub is also active in the local community; they run their own football team!

There is a large function room available, capable of holding up to 100 people, please contact the pub for more details. The pub has a large off road car park and a sizable beer garden for the summer. Children are very welcome, disabled customers can access the food, drink and entertainment without a problem, however, all the accommodation is upstairs and there is no lift.

129 THE OLD HALL HOTEL

Main Street, Frodsham,
Cheshire WA6 7AB
Tel: 01928 732 053
e-mail: info@theoldhallhotel.net
website: www.theoldhallhotel.net

The Old Hall Hotel is a beautiful 16th century building situated in the heart of Frodsham. Owned and run by the Winfield family for 35 years, the Old Hall Hotel is an extremely popular hotel and restaurant. The family's experience certainly shines through, the rooms are all well kept and comfortable, the dining area is plush and luxurious and quality food is available every day. The hotel is conveniently situated for the commercial centres of Manchester, Liverpool and Runcorn, and for the tourist, the hotel is very close to the historic town of Chester and the beauty of rural North Wales. With 26 en-suite rooms, friendly service and ideal location, the Old Hall Hotel benefits from a large returning customer base. The rooms all provide high speed internet access, tea & coffee making facilities, telephones and colour televisions. The rooms are all comfortably furnished with large beds and ample storage space.

The superb à la carte restaurant is well known throughout the area, professional chefs produce quality food every day between 12pm – 2pm & 7pm – 10pm. Open to non-residents, the restaurant is perfect for those "special occasions"! The food is all cooked fresh to order using the best of local produce and the menu is simply mouth-watering; typifying the tantalising options are roulade of pheasant & guinea fowl served with a wild mushroom and chive stuffing and prime English fillet steak served with a stilton cheese topping & rich bordelaise sauce. With a variety of just as tempting starters and sweets, it is possible to gorge yourself till you burst!

The hotel is full of features, the bar is set in traditional dark wood, both lounges have large fireplaces and there are comfortable chairs galore. The whole place is full of old beams, traditional furniture and decorative plates, which give a wonderful warm atmosphere, it is no accident that the Old Hall Hotel is thought of as one of the best hotels in Cheshire. During the summer, the garden is a joy to explore; there is patio seating for the restaurant, a large, well kept lawn and a wishing well to throw a penny into at the end. There is a large off-road car park and with ground floor accommodation available, there are full disabled facilities.

249

127 DUNHAM MASSEY

Dunham Massey, Altrincham,
Cheshire WA14 4SJ
Tel: 01619411025
e-mail: dunhammassey@nationaltrust.org.uk
website: www.nationaltrust.org.uk

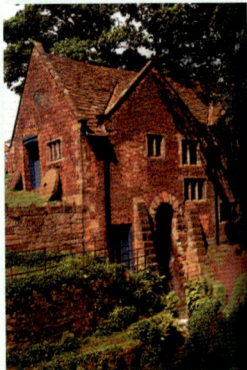

Dunham Massey is a country estate including mansion with important collections and 'below stairs' areas, impressive garden and deer park.

An early Georgian house built around a Tudor core, Dunham Massey was extensively reworked in the early years of the 20th century. The result is one of Britain's most sumptuous Edwardian interiors, housing exceptional collections of 18th century walnut furniture, paintings and Huguenot silver, as well as extensive servants' quarters.

Here is one of the North West's great plantsman's gardens with richly planted borders and majestic trees, as well as an orangery, Victorian bark-house and well-house. The ancient deer park contains a series of beautiful avenues and ponds and a Jacobean mill, originally used for grinding corn but refitted as a sawmill c1860 and now restored to working order.

130 RING O BELLS

2 Bellemonte Road, Overton, Frodsham,
Cheshire WA6 6BS
Tel: 01928 732 068

Situated in the small and picturesque hamlet of Overton, a short walk from the centre of Frodsham lies the Tudor building of the **Ring O Bells**. Though fully modernised now, the full fascinating history of this pub is available at the bar and is well worth a read. Shirley has run the Ring O Bells since 1974 and the pub is renowned

for its hospitality and cuisine. The well stocked bar caters for everybody and the traditional home cooked food is available every lunchtime, 7 days a week. Children are very welcome and there are full disabled facilities.

131 YE OLDE WHITE LION

2 High Street, Congleton,
Cheshire CW12 1BD
Tel: 01260 272702

Congleton is a small market town in the South East of Cheshire. It offers attractive open countryside as well as a popular village pub, **Ye Olde White Lion.** Amanda Thompson, a lovely, lively and friendly lady has made Ye Olde White Lion a huge success since she took over the lease. The much photographed black and white frontage has for centuries been a popular landmark in the town - inside all is olde worlde charm with cosy bars featuring beams, brasses and assorted pictures of the locality. There is a secluded beer garden with a little aviary to the rear or the pub which includes a stunning decked patio, perfect for enjoying the afternoon sunshine.

A minimum of three real ales are always available – Green King Abbot Ale is a regular, a long with a changing local brew. The homemade food here is delicious, with so many to dishes to choose from. Sandwiches, panini and hot baguettes cater for those with less time or a smaller appetites, while for others after something more filling fish & chips, chilli con carne, steak pie, gammon and egg or a giant Yorkshire pudding filled with hot roast beef or chilli fit the bill nicely. The burgers are particularly popular topped with cheese, mayonnaise and crisp lettuce. The premises were once the offices of the solicitors firm for John Bradshaw, the man who was the first – even before Cromwell – to put his signature to the death warrant of King Charles I.

132 SHAKERLEY ARMS

9 Willow Street, Congleton,
Cheshire CW12 1RL
Tel: 01260 270344 Fax: 01260 270344
e-mail: cecileromien@yahoo.fr

The Shakerley Arms is a short walk from the centre of Congleton in Willow Street and is a charming establishment both inside and out. The interior is homely and the leaseholders provide great hospitality to all of their visitors. Having been at the Shakerley Arms for 2½ years, Mike and Cecile have been in the trade for 20 years in total.

Open all day, the premises serves first class cuisine, all made by Mike who is a super chef. In fact he is so good that the local recommendations are unbeatable. A Scot by nationality, Mike only uses Scottish meat for his dishes and his homemade pie of the day is very popular. Other specialities include grilled liver with bacon and onions, penne carbonara and a mixed grill, which is to die for. Currently there are also two real ales served, Directors and Bombardier, which will be increased in the near future. Food is served Tuesday-Saturday at 12-2.30pm and 6-8.30pm. Sunday Lunch is served from 12-3.30pm where there is a roast only, served with all the trimmings. Please note that this property has on street parking only.

133 CHURCH HOUSE INN

Buxton Rd, Congleton,
Cheshire CW12 2DY
Tel: 01260 272 466
website: www.churchhousecongleton.co.uk

The **Church House Inn** is situated about a mile from the centre of Congleton, famous for being the site of the remains of a 5000 year old chambered tomb, known as The Bridestones. Barbara and Graham have run the Church House for 8½ years now and despite it being their first foray into the pub trade, it has been a roaring success. Built to replace close-by premises of the same name in 1941, the Church House suffered two major fires in 1947 and 1950 when the roof was thatched, but has since remained incident free.

The exterior is warm and inviting with large windows and wooden detailing on the second floor. There are also magnificent floral displays in the hanging baskets and planters which are kept by Graham and have won awards for the last four years. The pub features a large off road car park and this is just one of the reasons that the pub is the meeting place for an American car club, a classic car club and motorbike clubs. The pub also has the bonus for being at the start, or end, of many walks and ramblers can choose to order their meal before departing and then enjoy it in the garden during the summer or beside a lovely log fire in the winter.

The food is not to be missed either, Barbara and Graham say that the aim is to provide good quality home-made food, cooked to order and they have certainly succeeded, combining traditional pub grub; burgers, roast dinners, a great selection of steaks and more modern offerings; oatcakes, Quorn fillets and crepes. Along with lighter choices, such as baguettes, sandwiches and salads for lunchtimes, the Church House Inn has a menu that provides food for every occasion. They will even cook most of the same menu using gluten free ingredients, gluten free pasta and breads for example. Food is served between 12pm -2.30pm and 6pm - 8pm on Mondays to Thursdays, and between 12pm – 8pm on Friday, Saturday and Sunday. It is required to make a reservation for tables on Sunday lunches and when the party is greater than four - this is to avoid disappointment. The pub itself is open all day long and the bars hosts 2 regular real ales; Robinson's Unicorn and Hatters Mild along with occasional guest ales.

134 HORSESHOE INN

Fencelane, Newbald, Astbury, Congleton,
Cheshire CW12 3NL
Tel: 01260 272 205
website: www.horseshoeinnastbury.co.uk

Set in the picturesque hamlet of Newbald, the **Horseshoe Inn** is an old coaching inn dating from the 1770's. With old farm buildings still on the eleven acres of land attached to the pub, the pub is certainly aware of its heritage. Charles and Mary, originally farmers, took the Horseshoe Inn over three years ago and it has gone from strength to strength since.

The bar is amply stocked, three real ales available at any one time, mainly from the local Robinsons Brewery, the regular ale is Unicorn. Mary is renowned for her cooking, testament to this is the return again and again of locals and visitors alike; using Cheshire reared meat and Cheshire grown vegetables to create sumptuous daily specials to complement the already tantalising menu. The menu includes delicious offerings such as home-made steak & mushroom pie, home-made cottage pie and locally made Cumberland sausage.

There is also a light meal menu for people looking for a quick snack; the quality doesn't drop at all though, fresh salads, jacket potatoes with a selection of fillings, burgers, sandwiches and toasties. There truly is something for everyone! Food is available all week long, children are very welcome, there is a large car park and the beer garden is huge.

136 BIDDULPH GRANGE GARDEN

Grange Road, Biddulph,
Staffordshire ST8 7SD
Tel: 01782 517999
e-mail: biddulphgrange@nationaltrust.org.uk

Tunnels and pathways lead the visitor on a miniature tour of the world. Rare and exotic planting and architecture: from an Egyptian court to elegant Italian terraces. Unique oriental pagoda garden with its own Great Wall of China. Victorian eccentricities: an upside down tree and strange stone sculptures. New exhibition area and audio-visual room showing short films on the Garden and its history

135 THE BULLS HEAD

Newcastle Road, Smallwood,
Cheshire CW11 2TY
Tel: 01477 500247
website:
www.thebullsheadatsmallwood.co.uk

Located just a short drive from junction 17 of the M6 is **The Bulls Head**, a 300 year old classic English country pub & restaurant offering a genuine warm welcome to all.

The former blacksmiths and coaching inn has a range of charming and original features, and in some parts the inn dates back to 1757. The open oak beams and Cheshire brick fireplaces create a really cosy atmosphere to enjoy a drink or a meal.

Attentive hosts Ian and Sharon Evans have been running this fine inn since 2000 and are always looking to help visitors where possible. Ian makes sure that his menu is created using local produce wherever possible and offers some fantastic dishes. Homemade steak and ale pie is a best seller followed by close contenders such as Somerset pork cooked in olde English cider with chips & salad, chicken curry Madras, roast chicken or beef with all the trimmings, garlic beef with chips and vegetables, Montreal tuna served on a bed of green salad with potatoes and mushroom stroganoff. If it's something for a smaller appetite that you are looking for The Bulls Head also does a range of sandwiches, jacket potatoes and burgers. The menu also includes gluten free options. Due to the popular menu, booking is recommended during the week and is essential at weekends. Food is served seven days a week 12 – 9pm (Saturday 12 – 9.30pm).

The main dining room can hold a maximum of 80 people and further seating is available in the two quality conservatories overlooking the award winning gardens.

Open all day every day, the bar offers a choice of beverages from, wines, spirits, mixers and beers as well as 3 real ales with Tetleys being the regular.

The rear gardens are set within two acres and provide a secluded spot for children to roam and explore and adults to enjoy a drink or a meal in the warming months. All major credit cards are accepted and there is a large off-road car park to leave your vehicle whilst dining.

254

137 THE MARKET TAVERN

The Square, Sandbach,
Cheshire CW11 1AT
Tel: 01270 762099

Standing proudly on the Square in Sandbach, is the fine hostelry **The Market Tavern**. Originally a coaching inn over 200 years ago, a warm welcome awaits everyone who passes through the door.

Helpful hosts Kay and Mike took over the tenancy of this handsome building in September 2006, and have breathed new life into the old place, earning it an ever growing reputation for hospitality, fine food and well-kept ales. The bar is open all day, seven days a week, with plenty of space for enjoying something to drink – the choice includes Unicorn cask ales and a good selection of other keg and bottle beers.

Locals return time and time again to sample the varied menu on offer. Sandwiches, toasties, and jacket potatoes are available for those looking for a snack, whereas homemade steak and ale pie, deep fried scampi and roast beef with Yorkshire pudding cater for those who are looking for something more substantial.

Children are made to feel very welcome and the secluded rear garden has an area where children can play in safety.

The pub is an excellent venue for wedding and christening parties and other celebrations and get-togethers. On the same Market Square as the tavern are the best-known landmarks in Sandbach. Two remarkable stone crosses, one 16 feet high, the other 11 feet, dating from the 9th century, and the scenes depicted are thought to represent the conversion of Mersia to Christianity during the reign of King Penda.

138 SALLY'S CAFÉ

2 Green Street, Sandbach,
Cheshire, CW11 9AX
Tel: 01270 761 985

Sandbach pronounced 'sand-batch' is a pleasant, historic market town located in south east Cheshire. It has marvellous communications being approximately half a mile from junction 17 on the M6 motorway. It is here, just yards away from Sandbach Centre, that you will find the delightful **Sally's Café**. In existence for over 20 years, Sally's has a loyal fan base, who return time and time again to sample the delicious dishes on offer. The light and airy café seats 40 people and has a relaxed atmosphere perfect for enjoying a morning coffee.

Proud owners Mark, and his right hand Caroline, have put their personal touch on the premises to make sure that a visit to Sally's will not be your last.

The menu provides a huge range of dishes, and the majority of the produce is locally sourced. From Sally's BIG breakfast of 2 sausages, 2 rashers of bacon, 2 eggs, hash brown, beans, tomatoes and unlimited coffee and toast to traditional fish and chips with mushy peas there is something to suit everyone all at affordable prices. You can choose to eat in or takeaway and there is also a delivery service offered if you fancy a quiet night in.

The café is open Monday – Saturday 9am – 4pm and children are made very welcome.

139 FLAVOUR

3-4 Georges Walk, Sandbach,
Cheshire CW11 1AR
Tel: 01270 759569
e-mail: flavourbookings@aol.com
website: www.flavourrestaurant.com

Located in the heart of Sandbach is the popular **Flavour**, a bright and airy continental-style café bar. Hospitable owners Graham and David, have over 21 years of experience in the trade, and make sure that this modern, comfortable venue appeals to everyone with a love for freshly prepared fine food.

The restaurant which can seat up to 100 diners is located over two floors and oozes style. The menu on offer is no different with a touch of class added to each dish. The tempting food ranges from smoked salmon & crème fraiche sandwiches and flaked tuna & chive mayonnaise jacket potatoes to braised lamb shank with oyster mushroom & pearl barley risotto and Italian potato dumplings with aubergine & pimento creamy tomato sauce. And if you're looking to satisfy a sweet tooth then the desserts are equally as delicious.

A daytime menu is served from 10am to 7pm offering breakfast, light lunches through to afternoon tea, and during the evening the kitchen steps up a gear with a modern British menu that changes monthly. The wine list offers plenty of choice, including champagnes and organic wines.

Flavour is open every day except Sundays with special deals available Tuesdays through to Fridays. Booking is advisable if you wish to dine on Saturday.

141 JODRELL BANK SCIENCE CENTRE & ARBORETUM

Jodrell Bank, Lower Withington,
Macclesfield, Cheshire SK11 9DL
Tel: 01477 571339
e-mail: linda.bennett@manchester.ac.uk

Jodrell Bank Visitor Centre is home to the third largest radio telescope in the world, the Lovell Radio Telescope. Take a walk around the base of the telescope on the Observation Pathway with exhibition panels about the work of the telescopes. See the changing seasons in the 35 acre Arboretum, with National Collections of Malus and Sorbus. Tour the Solar System or take a Journey to Mars in the 3D Theatre and when you return to Earth why not try some of the delicious home cooked food in the café. The shop is full of unusual gifts and souvenirs. Whispering dishes and picnic areas.

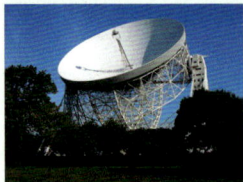

256

London Road, Allostock, nr Knutsford,
Cheshire WA16 9LU
Tel: 01565 72470 Fax: 01565 722749
e-mail: reception@thecottageknutsford.co.uk
website: www.thecottageknutsford.co.uk

Quality, comfort, service and food all excel at the 4 Star **Cottage Restaurant & Lodge**, owned and personally run by the hardworking and hospitable Marr family. Their charming hotel stands in the picturesque Cheshire countryside, in one of the county's most prestigious locations, Allostock. Tatton Park and its many shows are easily accessible just 6 miles away, as is the Lovell Telescope at Jodrell Bank Observatory. The semi-rural hamlet is an ideal location for both leisure and business visitors, whether they've popped in for a quick drink and a snack, sat down to a leisurely meal or booked in for an overnight stay.

The cottage is well known throughout the hamlet and beyond, for serving a fantastic selection of modern British food from both a la carte and fixed price menus. The owners and their staff take great pride and satisfaction in making sure that the freshest seasonal produce is used in their cooking and results on the plate show that preparation, cooking and presentation all get full attention in the kitchen. You can expect to sample mouth-watering starters such as homemade soup with fresh bread; pear, walnut & blue cheese salad with chicory leaf & a nut dressing and homemade chicken liver pâté with Cumberland sauce & hot toast. Typical main courses range from homemade pizza, lamb cutlets served with chips, side salad & red wine sauce and old fashioned recipe sausage and creamy mash, vegetables & onion Gravy. And that's not forgetting the delicious desserts; popular choices such as crème brulee, apple tart and sticky toffee pudding offer a great way to round off a meal. The delightful restaurant can seat up to 60 people and food is served 12-2pm 7 days a week and 6pm-9.30pm Monday – Saturday.

As well as superb food The Cottage Restaurant & Lodge also provides guest accommodation comprising 12 spacious bedrooms, 4 of which have been recently refurbished to a very high standard. Each room has its own bathroom, satellite TV, dial-out phone, radio alarm clock, trouser press, ironing facilities and hot beverage tray. The four doubles and eight twins offer very versatile facilities, and the twins have zip and link beds which can convert them into doubles. The rooms can be booked on a room only or B&B basis, and the basic tariff remains static throughout the year. Discounts are given from longer stays.

The Cottage Restaurant is also an ideal venue for a function and the attentive staff here, have the expertise to ensure that your function, whatever it may be, will be organised with the minimum of fuss and the maximum of efficiency. Individual packages are available for 8hr and 24hr conferences.

257

Holmes Chapel Road, Sproston Green,
Middlewich, Cheshire CW4 7LW
Tel: 01606 832303

'Happiness is a drink and good food'- the rather apt motto of **The Fox & Hounds Inn,** Middlewich. This attractive Olde Worlde Inn, on the A54, is ideal for motorists, North and South on the M6, as it stands less than a mile from junction 18. This super inn ,which is open all day, every day, has a history dating back almost 300 years and has been run for the past twelve by the French family. They have certainly created an inviting, cosy feel to their traditional bar and comfortable restaurant. Along with the usual range of popular brews, you are sure to be tempted by the two real ales, Cumberland Ale and Black Sheep.

Good wholesome dishes await you with local produce being used as much as possible and locally reared meat, along with fresh home grown vegetables always make an appearance. steak & ale pie, lamb Henry and tarragon chicken are just a few of the many specialities on the menu which includes plenty of other mouth-watering delights! This excellent food is served every lunchtime between 12-2.30pm and Tuesday-Saturday evenings 6.30-9pm, Sunday evenings 6-8pm. All are welcome to the Tuesday quiz nights from 8pm.It is such a popular place that from Thursday through to Sunday it is advisable to book to be sure of a table and to avoid disappointment.

Parking will be no problem here as there is a large off-road car park. The popular inn also boasts a pleasant beer garden for those warm summer evenings. Children are made very welcome and can choose from their own menu, and dogs are invited in too! Just to add more ease for customers, all major credit cards are accepted here.

There are plenty of places in the area worth visiting, all within easy reach of The Fox & Hounds Inn. These include the little village of Holmes Chapel, where John Wesley preached outside St Luke's Church; Goostrey, which holds an annual gooseberry fair; Jodrell Bank, home of the landmark Lovell Telescope; the Salt Museum and last but by no means least, the old salt town of Middlewich, where in the centre you will find the 'Bull Ring', an unusual and unique venue where local events are frequently held.

143 THE COACH AND HORSES

Middlewich Road, Bradfield Green,
nr Crewe, Cheshire CW1 4QZ
Tel: 01270 522626
e-mail: mossup@talktalk.net

The Coach and Horses is a family run business located in the hamlet of Bradfield Green. The beautiful grounds and play area surrounding the property make it fabulous for families and the atmosphere is also a terrific reason to visit. Trevor and Sarah Moss are the landlords here and together with their two children Christopher and Helen, the family have treated their visitors to great food and great company. Although having only taken over the Coach and Horses recently, Trevor has over 25 years experience in the trade and his expertise has enabled him to entice new customers daily. The menu here is tantalising and the dining room features a large fireplace, making it homely and comfortable for all.

Dishes that can be found on the menu include Thai fish cakes, chefs homemade chicken madras and a toffee crunch pie, which sounds divine, with smooth toffee, chocolate grenache and mousse. There is also one real ale served, Theakstons Best, which during the summer can be enjoyed in the beer garden. Food is served Tuesday-Friday 12-2pm and 5-9pm and Saturday and Sunday 12-9pm.

144 LIBBY'S LUNCHES

3 The Cocoa Yard, Pillory Street, Nantwich,
Cheshire CW5 5BL
Tel: 01270 625 228

This sweet little café may not have the greatest amount of space; there is only seating for 10 inside and an additional 20 in the courtyard, but what it lacks in size, it more than makes up for in quality and a warm welcome. Using the best of local produce, Libby manages to offer a massive range of choice for very reasonable prices. From all day breakfasts and crumpets to organic soups and burgers made from her own recipe. All the fillings are available on a variety of breads; baguettes, Spanish panini, bloomer bread and wraps, as well as on a jacket potato and salad.

Libby's Lunches also delivers - it is possible to order buffets for all occasions. Featuring a host of different buffet menus, Libby's will provide exactly what you require for the event in question.

With organic gluten free soup and free-trade coffee, Libby's caters for the 21st century with ease and this charming little café is well worth a visit. The place is open between 8am – 4pm from Monday to Friday and between 9am – 4pm on Saturday. There are full disabled facilities available.

147 ROYAL OAK

Main Road, Worleston, nr Nantwich,
Cheshire CW5 6DN
Tel: 01270 624 138

A regular feature in the annals of Hidden Places, **The Royal Oak** is an extremely popular pub, drawing custom from all over Cheshire and the nearby towns of Crewe and Nantwich. The large premises are well kept, the interior decorated with various pub paraphernalia; old pictures, brass plates, etc. The cosy dining area looks out through French doors onto a magnificent beer garden. You could be forgiven for thinking you had visited the gardens of some historic manor. A broad lawn stretches out, with huge trees offering shade in the summer, truly a worthwhile place to sit and enjoy a pint or two. Inside, the wood fronted bar manages to provide a huge range of choice of beverages, including at least 3 real ales, the regular being Tetley's, and guest ales featuring regularly.

Robert and Rachel have now run the Royal Oak for 20 years and their experience shines through, managing to provide a warm welcoming atmosphere, whatever the occasion. Helping to sustain this feeling is their head chef, Andrew Hankey. With five years under his belt, he is not exactly short of experience either. Mostly using local Cheshire produce, and only Aberdeen Angus meat, Andrew has created a menu that manages to cater for everyone. Appetising starters include highlights such as deep fried brie in breadcrumbs and chef's own homemade soup. The pedigree of the meat shines through in the grill section. Four cuts of steak are offered, each sounding more tempting than the last, Rump, Sirloin, Fillet and a mighty 16oz T-bone, clearly not for the faint of heart! The main courses menu features such a variety, from Andrew's home made steak & ale pie to duck a l'orange. There are also options for people looking for a quick bite, a host of salads, jacket potatoes with a lot of filling choice, sandwiches or even a classic ploughman's lunch. On Sundays there is a choice of Sunday lunch and don't forget to check the specials board, updated daily from Andrew's vast repertoire of delicious dishes. Food is served between 11.30am – 3pm & 6pm – 9pm seven days a week. However, to avoid disappointment it is recommended that a booking is made to eat on Saturday and Sunday.

The pub is a popular venue as well, Tuesday nights from 9pm there is music in the 60's and 70's vein and the Royal Oak can also cater for various functions including setting up an outside bar for outdoor events. Pease contact for further details.

145 WICKSTEAD ARMS

Mill Street, Nantwich, Cheshire CW5 5ST
Tel: 01270 625 139

Standing in the heart of historic Nantwich in Mill Street, the **Wickstead Arms** dates back to the early 18th century and is named after wealthy Cheshire land owners of the past. This popular pub has been run by Chris and Mena since 1999, and their experience shines through in the ales, food and general welcome. Three ales include Boddingtons, Bombardier and one rotating guest ale. The dark wood fronted bar is a great place to lean, enjoy your pint and converse with the locals.

The dining area is spacious and comfortable, perfect for sampling Mena's wonderful home cooked style of pub grub. The menu is extensive, reasonably priced and extremely tempting; highlights include a variety of burgers, steaks and fish dishes. On Sunday there is a choice of three roast dinners, each as delicious as the last but you can choose from the main menu as well. The traditional dishes with large portions and reasonable value are extremely popular with locals and visitors alike. Food is served between 10am – 8pm Monday to Saturday and 12pm – 3pm on Sunday.

Children are very welcome, there is lots of car parking available close-by and there are full disabled facilities.

146 THE HORSESHOE INN

Newcastle Road, Willaston, Nantwich,
Cheshire CW5 7EP
Tel: 01270 569404

Two miles east of Nantwich, between the A534 and A500, Willaston put itself on the map as the home of the World Worm Charming Championships. You will also come across the newly refurbished **Horse Shoe Inn,** a homely old inn where you will find mouth watering homemade fare and a variety of well-kept ales including a full range of Robinson's Ales. Tenant Shaun Newall has been a qualified chef for over 25 years, therefore it's hardly surprising that visitors and locals continue to return to sample the popular varied menu. This attractive red brick inn has a large garden and plenty of off road parking.

149 OFFLEY ARMS

Poolside, Madeley, Crewe,
Cheshire CW3 9DX
Tel: 01782 750 242

The **Offley Arms** is situated in the heart of the village of Madeley, a picturesque location overlooking the lake, which is a haven for all kinds of wildlife. The lake, also known as 'the Pool' is a conservation area and attracts a large number of wildlife lovers and photographers from all over the country. Adam and Chris took over at the beginning of the summer in 2008 and with the help of head chef Paul, the Offley Arms has gone from strength to strength. The restaurant is very popular, so popular that it is best to book for a table at the weekends.

261

Old Chester Road, Barbridge, Nantwich,
Cheshire CW5 6AY
Tel: 01270 528443 Fax: 01270 528003
e-mail:
enquiries@the-olde-barbridge-inn.co.uk
website: www.the-olde-barbridge-inn.co.uk

Situated in a delightful location in Barbridge alongside the Shropshire Union Canal, **The Olde Barbridge Inn** presents a mixture of mouth watering food, fine hospitality and a great venue to enjoy a relaxing drink. Landlord David Evans and his wife Kath, who previously managed The Railway pub in Woodley, offer a warm welcome to all and ensure that a visit to the Olde Barbridge Inn will not be your last.

Inside you will find a 40-seat restaurant overlooking the canal side moorings, ideal for enjoying one of many delicious dishes. The menu offers something for everyone with lite bites such as sandwiches, baguettes and jacket potatoes, starters such as crispy Peking duck, chicken liver and Guinness pâté and homemade soup of the day and main meals such as grilled pork chops, home made curry and olde English sausage and mash. On Sunday there is a choice of 3 tasty roasts, each served with seasonal vegetables, new and roast potatoes, Yorkshire pudding and rich gravy. Booking is advisable at the weekends and essential on Thursdays.

After your meal, why not stay a while and enjoy a drink in either the lounge bar, public bar or games room.During the summer months you can enjoy your meal outside in the pretty canal side garden.

Entertainment is offered on a regular basis with a performance from the 'Salt City Jazz Band' every Thursday night, a live artist every Saturday and a Quiz night every Wednesday.

Boaters are made very welcome and are able to stay overnight on one of the customer moorings (max 24 hour stay). Please ask inside for more details. There is an enclosed children's play area and the inn has full disabled access. There is plenty of off road parking.

Open everyday, food is served Monday – Friday 12 -3pm & 5pm – 9pm, Saturday 12 – 9pm and Sunday 12 – 8pm. Summer months Monday - Saturday 12 - 9pm and Sunday 12 - 8pm.

150 THE OLD SWAN

Keele Road, Madeley Heath,
Cheshire CW3 9LD
Tel: 01782 751199

The Old Swan is a cheerful, friendly and delightfully unpretentious pub situated in the village of Madeley Heath. In May 2008, local family the Blairs took over the premises and went about improving and updating the inn with a complete refurbishment. The workmanship is of extremely high standard as is the décor making it a very enjoyable place to dine of a lunchtime or an evening. Husband and wife George and Helen and daughter Mandi always have a warm and genuine welcome to offer to anyone who walks through the door – and that includes families with children.

Since re-opening the establishment the inn has received rave reviews, not just for the outstanding furnishings and hospitality but also for the fine cuisine on offer. Professional chefs prepare a sensational menu using local produce as much as possible. sweet chutney and toasted bread, creamy garlic mushrooms, prawn cocktail and homemade spicy battered king prawns with sweet chilli dip are examples of starters available. Mains range from lamb shank, pan fried salmon with dill sauce and spicy butterfly chicken breast. The delicious desserts vary from day to day. There is a daily specials board to keep the regular visitors satisfied as well as vegetarian options.

If you are looking for something to quench your thirst then there are between 3 & 4 real ales with Marstons Pedigree being the regular plus ever changing guest ales. There are also a wide range of wines, ciders and soft drinks providing something for everyone. The Old Swan is open all day everyday for drinks and food is served between 12 – 2pm & 6pm – 9pm Monday to Saturday and 12 – 7pm on Sundays. Major credit cards are taken and there is a plenty of off road parking available for diners. An impressive property, welcoming hosts and fabulous fare, a visit here is a must.

151 THE GLOBE

Chester Road, Kelsall, Cheshire CW6 0RS
Tel: 01829 751 291

The Globe is newly named, previously the Morris Dancer, since the owners have decided to return to the premises' original name. Dating back to the 17th century in parts, The Globe has been an ale house and coaching inn in its long history. The large establishment has been beautifully decorated and furnished throughout. Linen tablecloths and comfortable chairs provide a touch of class in the ancient surroundings. The new licensees Paul and Rachel took control in February 2008 and have given the place a new lease of life. Locals are frequenting the establishment more and more and visitors are returning once they have discovered it. A big factor is the outstanding food cooked here, thanks to head chef Henry Pimentel.

Henry has cooked around the globe, including prestigious venues in New York and the UK. This includes cooking for world leaders during the G8 Summit at Gleneagles in Scotland; Henry says "I will use only fresh ingredients to produce menus of high quality dishes which are varied, seasonal and uncomplicated. In my short time here I have met with many local suppliers and am very pleased to be able to use local farm suppliers for milk and vegetables, amongst other produce."

The Globe provides two main menus, the bar menu offers traditional pub grub, along with lighter snacks, such as sandwiches, soups and salads. The traditional pub grub consists of dishes such as shepherd's pie, Irish stew and Cumberland sausage and mashed potato. The other menu is from the in-house restaurant; Paul and Rachel say that the newly named seasons restaurant reflects their desire to provide varied and seasonal menus. This menu is loaded with delicious sounding dishes; highlights include a pan roasted Goosnargh duck with cabbage and confit plum tomatoes, grilled Dover sole with mango & papalla salsa and potted confit of rabbit. There is yet more temptation in the pudding menu; real New York cheesecake, chocolate fondant with bourbon ice cream and peach melba, too name but a few. Seasons also offers a sumptuous sounding traditional roast with all the trimmings on Sundays. The Olde World public bar is part of the original building, and it is decorated accordingly; there are three real ales on offer, two from the local Weetwood Brewery and a rotating guest ale.

Food is served all day every day and although the restaurant is quite large, to avoid disappointment, it is advised that a reservation is made to dine on Fridays, Saturdays and Sundays.

New Russia Hall, Chester Road,
Gatesheath, Tattenhall, Cheshire CH3 9AH
Tel: **01829 770958**
website: www.carriages.co.uk

Set in the picturesque countryside of Gateshead roughly a mile from Tattenhall, is where you will find the much-loved **Carriages**. Originally a farm house, it was converted in 2001 into a truly homely and comfortable pub with restaurant, B&B letting rooms and campsite for all the family. At the helm are owners Tracey and Colin, who make sure that your visit to Carriages is one to remember. Tracy cooks up some wonderful homemade treats in the kitchen including prawn cocktail, pork steak, salmon & dill fishcake and filled jacket potato, all incorporating the freshest local produce where possible. Sunday brings with it a traditional roast with all the trimmings plus a fresh fish and vegetarian dish.
You can also enjoy real ales, fine wines and soft drinks to compliment your meal from the well stocked bar.

The well equipped accommodation comprises of four en-suite guest bedrooms finished to a very high standard. Each room comes with central heating, TV, tea and coffee making facilities, hairdryer, complimentary wireless internet and an ironing service. The tariff also includes the speciality super breakfast which shouldn't be missed!

The camp site is open 365 days a year to Camping and Caravan Club members. It offers electric hook-up, showers, toilets and views of the beautiful countryside for a daily rate of just £12.

Open Mon – Sun 12 – 2.30pm for lunch and Mon- Thurs 6pm – 9pm, Fri & Sat 6pm – 9.30pm and Sun 5.30 – 8pm for dinner.

265

Burwardsley Road, Tattenhall,
Cheshire CH3 9NS
Tel: 01829 770 233
e-mail: terry@thesportsmansarms.co.uk
website: www.thesportsmansarms.co.uk

The exterior of the **Sportsmans Arms** is very warm and inviting. A multitude of hanging baskets suggests proprietors who care about the image of their pub and in Terry & Melissa this is certainly true. Having arrived during the summer of '08, Terry and Melissa have wasted no time in putting their 'stamp' on the place. Already the place has been given a new lease of life and their reputation is growing by the day. Terry's 20 years experience in the trade shows in the warm and hospitable nature of the welcome you receive when entering the premises. Inside there is a roaring log fire in the large and spacious dining area which sets off the traditional look of the furniture nicely. The bar is amply stocked, including two real ales; a rotating guest ale and Thwaites Original, as well as a spacious beer garden in which to enjoy them.

A big factor in the improved image of the pub is the food, where the menu, using the best of locally sourced produce, manages to combine the best of traditional pub fayre with good value. Typifying the main meals on offer are the homemade pie of the day, beer battered cod and chips and for the brave; the Sportsman's full mixed grill featuring steak, gammon, pork chop, chips, fried egg, mushrooms, tomatoes, beans and Bury black pudding. There is a tantalising starter menu for the extra hungry and a snack menu for folks looking for a quick bite to eat. The snack menu includes sandwiches, wraps, jacket potatoes, salads and burgers; there really is something for everyone. Food is available every day; between 12pm – 2.30pm on Monday and Tuesday, between 12pm – 7pm on Wednesday and Thursday, 12pm – 2.30pm Friday and Saturday and from 12pm – 5pm on Sunday.

On Wednesday and Thursday it is chef's special nights, there is a choice of 4 or 5 main meals and the customer gets to pay what they think the meal was worth (there is a minimum price in place)! There are other such special offers on for the Early birds and Pensioners during the week, just a sample of the individuality of the Sportsmans Arms which sets it apart from other pubs in the area. Children are very welcome until 9pm and there are full disabled facilities available.

154 MICHELLS WINE BAR AND BRASSERIE

Lynedale House, High Street, Tattenhall,
Cheshire CH3 9PX
Tel: **01829 771477**
e-mail: information@mitchellswinebar.co.uk
website: www.mitchellswinebar.co.uk

The beautiful village of Tattenhall should not only be commended for being the runner up in the best kept village of Cheshire competition, but also for having an outstanding family run restaurant with very few equals in its field. **Mitchells Wine Bar and Brasserie** is an unrivalled restaurant offering superb cuisine and fine wines.

Welcoming owners Martin and Peterene have years of experience in the trade and offer unbeatable hospitality to each visitor. Well known Chef Kevin Morris and his team prepare some tasty homemade treats in the kitchen, and create not only one menu for you to choose from but three! A mid week special menu caters for all, with an example choice being fan of sweet melon to start, pot roast chicken for main and a choice of homemade desserts to finish. The à la carte offers a selection of dishes such as baked flat cap mushroom topped with buttered spinach, brie and basil dressing, pan fried pigeon on beetroot mash with a mustard seed sauce and chef's homemade soup of the day for starters with breast of chicken with linguine pasta, a fresh tomato sauce and local 'Crabtree' cheese, venison steak with a blackcurrant and juniper sauce and baked breast of pheasant on roast vegetables with a spring onion, thyme and cumin sauce for mains. The 'Out Of The Blue' menu is for those who love fresh fish. It presents a range of starters and main courses with a recommended wine to compliment each meal. With such a mouth-watering menu on offer it is advisable to book especially at weekends.

The dining room has a wonderfully relaxed atmosphere with modern, trendy furniture and can hold up to 60 people. The room can also be hired out for parties and special occasions, please call for more details.

Martin and Peterene also provide themed evenings such as a Champagne Boizel Evening which have proved a real hit with locals, and with there only being 4 of these every year it is necessary to book in advance if you wish to be part of the evenings festivities (please visit the website for up-coming evenings).

Open Tuesday – Thursday 12.00 – 3pm & 6.30pm – 10.45pm Friday 12.00 – 3pm & 6.30pm – 12 Saturday 6pm – 12 and Sunday 12.00 – 10.45pm.

155 WOODCOTE HOUSE HOTEL & RESTAURANT

3 Hooton Road, Hooton,
Cheshire CH66 1QU
Tel: 0151 327 1542 Fax: 0151 328 1328
e-mail: enquiries@woodcotehouse.co.uk
website: www.woodcotehouse.co.uk

Woodcote House Hotel and Restaurant enjoys a glorious setting in Hooton on the Wirral and is well worth a visit. Built around 1910, it has provided quality accommodation and mouth-watering cuisine for many years, with diners returning time and again to sample treats on offer. The year 2008 brought a welcomed change to the Woodcote, with friendly mother and daughter team, Ingrid and Katie taking over the premises. Once settled, they wasted no time in completing a total refurbishment, making sure that this beautiful building was given the attention that it deserved.

Open all year round, the 17 well furnished en-suite bedrooms offer a wonderful place to stay overnight, and seven of the bedrooms are located on the ground floor making them easily accessible. Each room varies in size (some suitable for families) and has been decorated individually. The bathrooms come equipped with power showers – no more drizzle!

With a monthly changing menu, it comes as no surprise that the Woodcote has a loyal following not only for it's rooms but also for the diverse menu on offer. Dishes such as smoked chicken with celeriac remoulade & bramley puree, classic beef & suet pie accompanied by whipped potato & split peas and Glamorgan sausage & onion compote with a vierge sauce take over the menu thanks to head chef Alistair Reid. And that's just for starters and main course; hot chocolate fondant with warm berry compote & vanilla ice cream or homemade real treacle sponge with caramel custard are just two options that you could choose to complete your meal. Food is served 11am – 9.30pm Monday – Friday and Sunday lunchtime.

The eye-catching dining room has been finished to a very high standard and seats up to 50 people, perfect if you're looking for somewhere to take the extended family. The Woodcote also holds a number of functions throughout the year, so it's best to keep an eye on their website for details on any up and coming events. Children are made very welcome and all major credit cards are accepted. If you are looking for unrivalled quality, welcoming hosts and delicious, freshly made food then a visit to Woodcote House Hotel and Restaurant will not disappoint.

156 THE CHESHIRE YEOMAN

Ledsham Road, Little Sutton,
Wirral CH66 4QR
Tel: 01513 393 106
e-mail: cheshireyeoman@btconnect.com

Formerly known as the Station Hotel, **The Cheshire Yeoman** dates in parts back to the mid 19th century. The recipient of a thorough refurbishment in September 2007, the Cheshire Yeoman is now a contemporary dining establishment. The interior is well laid out with plenty of space and an attractive bar, which hosts an extensive menu of fine beverages, including a well kept, rotating guest ale. Peter and Sarah took over the Cheshire Yeoman at the end of the summer in 2008 and already there are positive rumours emanating from the area.

Peter's expertise in the kitchen, from 25 years in the trade, has earned him many accolades, including working in a Michelin Star restaurant, as well as with many other fine chefs. Peter and Sarah have worked together for 12 years now and their combined experience really comes to the fore in this classy establishment. The food is clearly the main draw to this stylish pub; the menu is now extensive, catering for every taste with pub favourites, mingling with more exotic fayre. For example, the starter menu features delicious homemade soup and tiger prawns in garlic butter, well known favourites and the slightly more adventurous Italian antipasto meat selection and large Greek platter. The same applies throughout the menu; traditional bangers and mash with an onion gravy and homemade pie of the week are complemented by chicken with a boursin stuffing, served on a bed of spinach and whole roasted sea-bass drizzled in chunky herb butter. Continuing the theme of something for everyone, even the vegetarian meals sound gorgeous, not merely an afterthought; creamy fricassee of crunchy vegetables served with a timbale of rice and Parmigiana di Melanzane. As you would expect from a chef of such standing, Peter ensures that, wherever possible, only the finest of local produce is used and the menus are regularly updated. There is a sumptuous sweet menu for afters of which the warm chocolate fudge cake has to star. Every Sunday is eagerly anticipated by the locals and visitors alike, there is a choice of meats to accompany the fresh vegetables and potatoes roasted in duck fat.

There is plenty of opportunity to sample the menu, food is served between 12pm – 9pm on Monday to Saturday and between 12pm – 6pm on Sundays. The pub also hosts a weekly quiz night every Monday and Thursday to which all are welcome and once a month there is live entertainment. Children are very welcome in all areas of the pub and there are full disabled facilities available.

157 POLLARD'S INN

Off Hadlow Road, Village Sqaure,
Willaston, Wirral CH64 2TU
Tel: 0151 327 4615

Hidden away off the village square is where you will find the superb **Pollard's Inn** at Willaston. Known as 'The Hidden Inn on the Wirral, this charming, friendly and accommodating hostelry was once a 16th century farm house with Medieval features such as mullioned windows, heavy oak beam inglenook fireplaces and sandstone walls. Luckily the premises have been well looked after and there are still many original features still intact from that bygone age.

Business partners Alan Tuohey and Annie Williams took over the inn in 2008 and have given the place a new lease of life with genuine hospitality. The bar offers 6 real ales, fine wines, soft drinks and tea and coffee to quench your thirst.

The menu is equally as varied and tempting, and with so many homemade dishes to choose from you'll be spoilt for choice. A bar menu presents favourites such as homemade steak and ale pie, half rack of baby back ribs, roast fillet of salmon, bangers and mash and jungle style curry (suitable for vegetarians). A deli board allows you to create your own lunch with a choice of charcuterie, cheese, anti pasti, seafood and artisan breads with a choice of homemade dressings.

Sandwiches and baguettes with various fillings cater for those with a smaller appetite or those after a quick snack. There is a 2 course deal Mon - Fri lunchtime priced at £8.95 and the Sunday menu offers a special 3 course deal with starters, mains, pastas, grills (cooked to your liking) and sensational sweets to choose from. Each dish is freshly made to order using ingredients from local suppliers wherever possible. Pollard's Inn offers a great atmosphere, fine food and attentive hosts which makes it a perfect venue for private functions (please call for more details).

As well as the fine food on offer, the property also boasts 5 superb bedrooms available all year round. Each room has its own en-suite and is finished to a high standard. The tariff also includes a hearty breakfast that you can look forward to the following morning.

Pollard's Inn serves food Mon – Fri 12 midday – 2.30pm & 5pm – 8.00pm and Sat – Sun and Bank Holidays midday – 7.30pm. There is ample off road parking and all credit cards are accepted. Full refurbishment starts post Easter 2009. Pollard's is family friendly with a children's menu and play area.

Barnston Village, Wirral CH61 1BW
Tel: 0151 648 7685
e-mail: ralphleech@hotmail.com
website: www.the-fox-hounds.co.uk

Ralph Leech has now run the **Fox & Hounds** in the Wirral village of Barnston for 25 years and it is testament to his hard work that the pub has been voted CAMRA Pub of the Year for 2008. The current premises was built around 1911 on the site of a former ale house and barn and the interior features an amazing array of memorabilia; from brass and ceramic ashtrays to empty whisky cases and even police helmets and other hats! The history of this pub is well documented and the road outside was source of tribulation for both passengers and horses as depicted in this verse from an unknown poet's poem of his train journey between Birkenhead to Heswall:

When we get to Barnston Dale
All the passengers turn quite pale
Conversation flags, no-one can talk
For the driver shouts - get out and walk.

This Edwardian building manages to educate and interest everybody who visits. The exterior of the pub is always presentable, but the summer is special; bringing delightful hanging baskets exploding with colour and well kept climbers around the wooden trellis' that line the garden.

The bar is a nice place to be, quality wood floors and a warm fireplace enhance the well stocked bar; featuring six real ales, Websters, Theakstons Best & Old Peculiar are the regulars and there are 3 rotating guest ales available, normally from the local Brimstage Brewery. With a large choice of lagers and over sixty choices of whisky, this bar can really cater for every taste.

Food is served at the Fox & Hounds every day between 12pm – 2pm and the quality and quantity of the food is proving a real draw. The lunch menu consists of modern favourites along with 'oldies but goodies', you can expect to see toasted ciabattas and baked potatoes featuring a large range of fillings including coronation chicken, Stilton cheese & grape, vegetable medley and cottage cheese & pineapple. There are also popular platters which sound scrumptious; the Barnston platter offers ham, beef & chicken served with chutney and the Neptune platter which brings tuna, salmon and juicy prawns with Marie Rose sauce together. Along with a variety of salads and daily specials which depend on the season, the Fox & Hounds' menu is not to be missed. Especially not the Sunday roasts, a choice of beef, lamb, pork or half a chicken - a superb roast dinner served in the traditional way.

159 HILBRE COURT

Banks Rd, West Kirby, Wirral CH48 3HU
Tel: 01516 254 063

A short walk away from the sea front, **Hilbre Court** is named from the small island just off the coast of West Kirby, a small town on the northwest corner of the Wirral Peninsula. The name West Kirby is of Viking origin, meaning town with a church and indeed the town was centered around St Bridget's church but has evolved to surround the train station, about a 1km away. The town is well known for a Victorian promenade which is flanked by the West Kirby marine lake which permits boats to sail, even at low tide. Popular for all kinds of water-sports, West Kirby marine lake was the venue for the World Windsurfing Speed Record in 1991!

Lee and Rod took over here during the summer of 2008 and have succeeded in putting their stamp on the place, employing a quality chef and injecting a great deal of enthusiasm. The pub has been awarded the Cask Marque for the quality of its ales and with good reason, the regulars; Hobgoblin and Black Sheep are always perfect and the two rotating guest ales present a difficult choice to make.

The new chef has wasted no time in putting his touch on Hilbre Court's menu, traditional food cooked well, what the menu lacks in size, it more than makes up for in substance. The menu changes regularly and you can expect to see traditional pub favourites making an appearance. All meals are cooked fresh to order with fresh ingredients. Fish of the day is a popular choice.

Food is available daily between 12pm – 3pm and 6pm – 8pm Tuesday to Sunday with the exception of Sunday evening, however there is an added bonus of the choice of roasts on Sunday lunch. The pub is a popular venue; Saturday night sees live music from a variety of local bands in various types of music style and from 9pm on Sundays there is a quiz, which everybody is encouraged to join. Children are very welcome and there are full disabled facilities available.

7 Church Road, Bebington,
Wirral CH63 7PG
Tel: 0151 644 8133
website: www.gorge-us.co.uk

Situated in the heart of picturesque Bebington, **Gorge' Us** is a cracking café which provides all manners of refreshments in a relaxed style. What this charming teashop lacks in size, the quality of the food and the friendliness of the hospitality is more than enough to compensate. Ceri Newton created this superb establishment back in late 2007 and together with the dedicated staff of Nicky, Clare and Jo, Gorge' Us has become a well known and popular place to dine throughout the Wirral.

Open between 9.30am – 4pm Monday to Saturday, there is a huge choice of toasties, panini, bagels and sandwiches on offer, or a seemingly endless choice of homemade delicacies. Cakes, scones, brownies and flapjacks are just some of the assortment available to satiate the sweetest of teeth! There is even a takeaway service for those on a flying visit.

All the food is made with local produce wherever possible and there are even gluten free options. Children are made very welcome and there are full disabled facilities available. Just one visit is enough to love this sweet little teashop and convince you to return again.

273

Tourist Information Centres

CHESHIRE

ALTRINCHAM

20 Stamford New Road, Altrincham, Cheshire WA14 1EJ
e-mail: tourist.information@trafford.gov.uk
Tel: 0161 912 5931

CHESTER

Town Hall, Northgate Street, Chester, Cheshire CH1 2HJ
e-mail: tis@chester.gov.uk
Tel: 01244 402111

CONGLETON

Town Hall, High Street, Congleton, Cheshire CW12 1BN
e-mail: tourism@congleton.gov.uk
Tel: 01260 271095

ELLESMERE PORT

Unit 22b, McArthur Glen Outlet Village, Kinsey Road,
Ellesmere Port, Cheshire CH65 9JJ
e-mail: cheshireoaks.cc@visitor-centre.net
Tel: 0151 356 7879

KNUTSFORD

Council Offices, Toft Road, Knutsford,
Cheshire WA16 6TA
e-mail: ktic@macclesfield.gov.uk
Tel: 01565 632611

MACCLESFIELD

Town Hall, Macclesfield, Cheshire SK10 1DX
e-mail: informationcentre@macclesfield.gov.uk
Tel:01625 504114

NANTWICH

Church House, Church Walk, Nantwich,
Cheshire CW5 5RG
e-mail: touristi@crewe-nantwich.gov.uk
Tel: 01270 610983

NORTHWICH

Information Centre, 1 The Arcade,Northwich,
Cheshire CW9 5AS
e-mail: tourism@valeroyal.gov.uk
Tel: 01606 353534

WARRINGTON

Warrington Bus Interchange, Horsemarket Street,
Warrington, Cheshire WA1 1TF
e-mail: informationcentre@warrington.gov.uk
Tel: 01925 428585

WILMSLOW

The Information Centre, Rectory Fields, Wilmslow,
Cheshire SK9 1BU
e-mail: i.hillaby@macclesfield.gov.uk
Tel: 01625 522275

GREATER MANCHESTER

BOLTON

Central Library Foyer, Le Mans Cres, Bolton,
Greater Manchester BL1 1SE
e-mail: tourist.info@bolton.gov.uk
Tel: 01204 334321

BURY

The Met Arts Centre, Market Street, Bury,
Greater Manchester BL9 0BN
e-mail: touristinformation@bury.gov.uk
Tel: 0161 253 5111

MANCHESTER

Manchester Visitor Centre, Town Hall Extension,
Lloyd St, Manchester, Greater Manchester M60 2LA
e-mail: touristinformation@marketing-manchester.co.uk
Tel: 0871 222 8223

OLDHAM

12 Albion Street, Oldham, Greater Manchester OL1 3BD
e-mail: ecs.tourist@oldham.gov.uk
Tel: 0161 627 1024

SADDLEWORTH

Saddleworth Museum, High Street, Uppermill,
Saddleworth, Oldham, Greater Manchester OL3 6HS
e-mail: ecs.saddleworthtic@oldham.gov.uk
Tel: 01457 870336

SALFORD

The Lowry, Pier 8, Salford Quays, Salford,
Greater Manchester M50 3AZ
e-mail: christine.ellis@salford.gov.uk
Tel: 0161 848 8601

STOCKPORT

Staircase House, 30 Market Place Stockport,
Greater Manchester SK1 1ES
e-mail: tourist.information@stockport.gov.uk
Tel: 0161 474 4444

WIGAN

62 Wallgate, Wigan, Greater Manchester WN1 1BA
e-mail: tic@wlct.org
Tel: 01942 825677

LANCASHIRE

ASHTON-UNDER-LYNE

Council Offices, Wellington Road, Ashton-Under-Lyne, Lancashire OL6 6DL
e-mail: tourist.information@mail.tameside.gov.uk
Tel: 0161 343 4343

BARNOLDSWICK

The Council Shop, Fernlea Avenue, Barnoldswick, Lancashire BB18 5DL
e-mail: tourist.info@pendle.gov.uk
Tel: 01282 666704

BLACKBURN

50-54 Church Street, Blackburn, Lancashire BB1 5AL
e-mail: visit@blackburn.gov.uk
Tel: 01254 53277

BLACKPOOL

1 Clifton Street, Blackpool, Lancashire FY1 1LY
e-mail: tic@blackpool.gov.uk
Tel: 01253 478222

BURNLEY

Burnley Bus Station, Croft Street, Burnley, Lancashire B11 2EF
e-mail: tic@burnley.gov.uk
Tel: 01282 664421

CLEVELEYS

Victoria Square Thornton, Cleveleys, Lancashire FY5 1AU
e-mail: cleveleystic@wyrebc.gov.uk
Tel: 01253 853378

CLITHEROE

12-14 Market Place, Clitheroe, Lancashire BB7 2DA
e-mail: tourism@ribblevalley.gov.uk
Tel: 01200 425566

FLEETWOOD

Old Ferry Office, The Esplanade, Fleetwood, Lancashire FY7 6DL
e-mail: ferrytic@wyrebc.gov.uk
Tel: 01253 773953

GARSTANG

Council Offices, Discovery Centre, High Street, Garstang, Lancashire PR3 1FU
e-mail: garstangtic@wyrebc.gov.uk
Tel: 01995 602125

LANCASTER

29 Castle Hill, Lancaster, Lancashire LA1 1YN
e-mail: lancastertic@lancaster.gov.uk
Tel: 01524 32878

LYTHAM ST ANNES

Visitor & Travel Information Centre, 67 St Annes Road West, Lytham St Annes Lancashire FY8 1SL
e-mail: touristinformation@fylde.gov.uk
Tel: 01253 725610

MORECAMBE

Old Station Buildings, Marine Road Central, Morecambe, Lancashire LA4 4DB
e-mail: morecambe_vic@lancaster.gov.uk
Tel: 01524 582808

PENDLE

Pendle Heritage Centre, Park Hill, Barrowford, Nelson, Lancashire BB9 6JQ
e-mail: heritage.centre@pendle.gov.uk
Tel: 01282 661701

PRESTON

The Guildhall, Lancaster Road, Preston, Lancashire PR1 1HT
e-mail: tourism@preston.gov.uk
Tel: 01772 253731

ROCHDALE

Touchstones, The Esplanade, Rochdale, Lancashire OL16 1AQ
e-mail: tic@rochdale.gov.uk
Tel: 01706 864928

MERSEYSIDE

LIVERPOOL '08 PLACE

Whitechapel, Liverpool, Merseyside L1 6DZ
e-mail: contact@liverpool08.com
Tel: 0151 233 2008

LIVERPOOL ALBERT DOCK

Anchor Courtyard, Albert Dock, Liverpool L3 4BS
e-mail: tourism@liverpool08.com
Tel: 0151 233 2008

LIVERPOOL JOHN LENNON AIRPORT

Arrivals Hall, South Terminal, Liverpool John Lennon Airport, Liverpool, Merseyside L24 1YD
e-mail: info@visitliverpool.com

SOUTHPORT

112 Lord Street, Southport, Merseyside PR8 1NY
e-mail: info@visitsouthport.com
Tel: 01704 533333

ST HELENS

The World of Glass, Chalon Way East, St Helens, Merseyside WA10 1BX
e-mail: info@sthelenstic.com
Tel: 01744 755150

Towns, Villages and Places of Interest

TRAVEL PUBLISHING ORDER FORM

To order any of our publications just fill in the payment details below and complete the order form. For orders of less than 4 copies please add £1.00 per book for postage and packing. Orders over 4 copies are P & P free.

Name:

Address:

Tel no:

Please Complete Either:

I enclose a cheque for £ _____ made payable to Travel Publishing Ltd

Or:

Card No: Expiry Date:

Signature:

Please either send, telephone, fax or e-mail your order to:

Travel Publishing Ltd, Airport Business Centre, 10 Thornbury Road, Estover, Plymouth PL6 7PP

Tel: 01752 697280   Fax: 01752 697299   e-mail: info@travelpublishing.co.uk

	Price	Quantity		Price	Quantity
HIDDEN PLACES REGIONAL TITLES			**COUNTRY LIVING RURAL GUIDES**		
Comwall	£8.99	....	East Anglia	£10.99	....
Devon	£8.99	....	Heart of England	£10.99	....
Dorset, Hants & Isle of Wight	£8.99	....	Ireland	£11.99	....
East Anglia	£8.99	....	North East	£10.99	....
Lake District & Cumbria	£8.99	....	North West	£10.99	....
Lancashire & Cheshire	£8.99	....	Scotland	£11.99	....
Northumberland & Durham	£8.99	....	South of England	£10.99	....
Peak District and Derbyshire	£8.99	....	South East of England	£10.99	....
Yorkshire	£8.99	....	Wales	£11.99	....
HIDDEN PLACES NATIONAL TITLES			West Country	£10.99	....
England	£11.99	....			
Ireland	£11.99	....			
Scotland	£11.99	....			
Wales	£11.99	....	**TOTAL QUANTITY:**		
OTHER TITLES					
			POST & PACKING:		
Off the Motorway	£11.99	....			
Garden Centres & Nurseries	£11.99	....	**TOTAL VALUE:**		

READER REACTION FORM

The *Travel Publishing* research team would like to receive reader's comments on any visitor attractions or places reviewed in the book and also recommendations for suitable entries to be included in the next edition. This will help ensure that the *Hidden Places series of Guides* continues to provide its readers with useful information on the more interesting, unusual or unique features of each attraction or place ensuring that their visit to the local area is an enjoyable and stimulating experience. To provide your comments or recommendations would you please complete the forms below and overleaf as indicated and send to:

The Research Department, Travel Publishing Ltd,
Airport Business Centre, 10 Thornbury Road, Estover, Plymouth PL6 7PP

Your Name:

Your Address:

Your Telephone Number:

Please tick as appropriate:

Comments ☐   Recommendation ☐

Name of Establishment:

Address:

Telephone Number:

Name of Contact:

READER REACTION FORM

COMMENT OR REASON FOR RECOMMENDATION:

....
....
....
....
....
....
....
....
....
....
....
....
....
....
....
....
....
....
....

Index of Advertisers

PLACES OF INTEREST

284